Slippery Characters

slippery characters

Ethnic Impersonators

and American Identities

Laura Browder

The University of North Carolina Press   Chapel Hill and London

© 2000 The University of North Carolina Press

All rights reserved

Designed by April Leidig-Higgins

Set in Berthold Bodoni Antiqua by Keystone Typesetting, Inc.

Manufactured in the United States of America

The paper in this book meets the guidelines for permanence
and durability of the Committee on Production Guidelines for
Book Longevity of the Council on Library Resources.

Library of Congress Cataloging-in-Publication Data

Browder, Laura, 1963– Slippery characters : ethnic
impersonators and American identities / by Laura
Browder. p. cm.–(Cultural studies of the United States)
Includes bibliographical references (p.) and index.
ISBN 0-8078-2546-8 (cloth: alk. paper)
ISBN 0-8078-4859-x (paper: alk. paper)
1. American prose literature—History and criticism.
2. Autobiography. 3. Literary forgeries and mystifications—
History. 4. Impostors and imposture in literature.
5. Difference (Psychology) in literature. 6. Identity
(Psychology) in literature. 7. Passing (Identity) in litera-
ture. 8. Group identity in literature. 9. Ethnic groups in
literature. 10. Impersonation in literature. 11. Ethnicity
in literature. 12. Self in literature. I. Title. II. Series.
PS366.A88 B76 2000   810.9′492—dc21   99-053732

04 03 02 01 00 5 4 3 2 1

For Allan

Contents

Illustrations

Acknowledgments

This book has been a real pleasure to write, in large part because so much of this work developed not out of traditional scholarly research but out of conversations. I greatly appreciate the insights on ethnicity that so many people offered me, as well as the many leads I was given that helped me track down impersonators and made the research process lively and fulfilling.

I began working on this project in an NEH seminar on memory and life-writing led by James Olney, who in many ways changed my thinking about the genre of autobiography and who has been unfailingly supportive of this project over the years. My thanks, too, to all the participants in the seminar for their advice, suggestions, and critiques.

I am indebted to Alan Trachtenberg for his years of support and encouragement on this project. His incisive editorial comments helped me see my way through what might have been an overwhelming project. Thanks, too, to Miles Orvell for his helpful critique. At UNC Press, David Perry was a pleasure to work with throughout the process of bringing the book to fruition.

Thanks to John Burt and Joyce Antler for their long-standing support and friendship.

Many early versions of chapters were presented as papers at meetings of the American Studies Association, the New England American Studies Association, Multi-Ethnic Literatures of the United States, the American Jewish History Association, the Southern Popular Culture Association, and the Twentieth Century Literature Conference.

I want to thank, too, the members of my writing groups, past and present, who offered great insights along the way: Georgia Johnston, Toni Oliveiro, Madeleine Sorapure, Kathy Fuller, Carol Summers, and Susan Barstow.

Thanks to the friends and colleagues who pointed me toward their favorite ethnic impersonators and suggested useful resources: Joyce Antler, Marty Brooks, Thea Browder, Michael Campbell, Bill Heath, Jim Mendelsohn, Tim Powell, Joel Schechter, and Ann Woodlief.

I am grateful to Eve Raimon, Lucinda Kaukas, Barbara Burton, and Susan Barstow, who read the entire manuscript. Their advice and generous encouragement were invaluable.

Thanks, too, to Mary Boyes, Nick Frankel, Susan Glasser, Charlotte Morse, Tim Powell, Joel Schechter, and Magdalena Zaborowska, who read parts of the manuscript and offered helpful suggestions and advice.

Thanks to Emily Roderer for her research assistance, to Michael Keller for all of his technical help, and to Sally Browder for her photo assistance.

I am indebted to the staff of the interlibrary loan office at Virginia Commonwealth University, particularly Jeannie Scott; Erin E. Foley at the Circus World Museum in Baraboo, Wisconsin; John M. Cahoon at the Seaver Center for Western History Research, Natural History Museum of Los Angeles; Eleanor M. Gehres at the Western History Department, Denver Public Library; Elizabeth Holmes at the Buffalo Bill Historical Center; Mary Corliss at the Museum of Modern Art Film Stills Archive; and Grace Halsell.

An individual fellowship from the Virginia Foundation for the Humanities and Public Policy provided me with the luxury of time to finish the manuscript and a stimulating work environment in which to do so.

Most of all, Allan Rosenbaum kept me on track with his love, humor, and unflagging support. This book is dedicated to him.

Slippery Characters

Introduction

In October 1991 *The Education of Little Tree*, Forrest Carter's memoir of his Cherokee boyhood, was number one on the *New York Times* best-seller list. *Little Tree* was a true word-of-mouth success.[1] The director of marketing for the University of New Mexico Press recalls purchasers buying a dozen copies at a time to distribute to friends.[2] Sales had reached a half-million copies by 1991. Groups of schoolchildren had formed Little Tree fan clubs. Hollywood planned to bring Carter's gentle, New Age-tinged message of multiculturalism and environmentalism to the big screen.

For thousands of *New York Times* readers, then, October 4, 1991, must have brought an unpleasant surprise. An op-ed piece written by Dan T. Carter, a history professor at Emory University, denounced the critically acclaimed Cherokee memoir as a fake. Its author, Forrest Carter, also known as Asa Carter, was not the Native American he claimed to be. According to Dan T. Carter, "Between 1946 and 1973, the Alabama native carved out a violent career in Southern politics as a Ku Klux Klan terrorist, right-wing radio announcer, home-grown American fascist and anti-Semite, rabble-rousing demagogue and secret author of the famous 1963 speech by Gov. George Wallace of Alabama: 'Segregation now . . . Segregation tomorrow . . . Segregation forever.' "[3] Even Forrest Carter's new first name, Dan Carter revealed, had been taken from Nathan Bedford Forrest, who founded the original Ku Klux Klan (KKK). Articles on Little Tree's identity appeared in *Newsweek*, in *Time*, and in *Publishers Weekly*. Heartbroken readers swamped Dan Carter's office with calls. Equally taken aback were friends of Forrest's in his later Texas years, for whom he would, after a couple of drinks, perform Indian war dances and chant in what he said was the Cherokee language. For editorialists across the country, the exposure of Forrest Carter was an occasion for soul searching. "What does it tell us that we are so easily deceived?" Dan Carter had asked, a question echoed not only by pundits but by the studio heads who had been, until that point, involved in a bidding war over movie rights.

Although Dan Carter's question may have been the one on which the media focused, there are others that may be more to the point. After all, Forrest Carter's story was only one of dozens of what I call ethnic impersonator autobiographies that have been published in the United States—that is, fictions purporting to be autobiographies, authored by writers whose ethnicity is not what they represent it to be.[4] Why was there such a sense of public outrage and betrayal at Asa Carter's ethnic impersonation? And why have so many ethnic impersonator auto-biographies been written, and eagerly read, in the United States over the past 160 years? In the chapters to follow, I explore how, in America, ethnic passage from one identity to another is not an anomaly. Auto-biography, with its valorization of individualism and its emphasis on self-fashioning, is a form peculiarly suited to American national my-thologies. And the ethnic impersonator autobiography, which creatively reconstructs identity using essential racial and ethnic categories, has proved to be particularly enduring in the United States.[5] This study examines the complex interplay between the authors of ethnic imper-sonator autobiographies, the texts they produce, and the readers of these texts.

Over the past 160 years, while rewriting themselves into new eth-nicities, the individual authors of ethnic impersonator autobiographies have escaped the trap of unwanted identities. Paradoxically, by playing into cultural stereotypes of their newly chosen ethnicities, they have mired their readers further in essentialist thinking. Through close read-ings of both famous and obscure impersonator autobiographies and by drawing on a context of social, cultural, and economic history, I trace the development of the ethnic impersonator autobiography from the antebellum South through the expansion of the frontier, and from the dislocations of immigration through the anomie of the postwar period.

American ethnic autobiographies—works that describe the experience of belonging to a minority group in the United States—have traditionally been written and read as a means of helping frame the complex cultural relationships of a multiethnic society. The American tradition of self-fashioning, with its commitment to Emersonian self-reliance, would appear to be distinct from ethnic autobiography, with its tradition of cultural ambassadorship. However, there is a point at which the traditions converge, and that is in what I call the genre of the ethnic impersonator autobiography. These narratives stand as monuments to the tradition of American self-invention as well as testaments to the porousness of ethnic identity.

The dominant strain in American autobiography emphasizes self-construction, as exemplified by Benjamin Franklin, who set out to outline for readers the thirteen steps he considered essential for self-improvement. More than anyone else Franklin introduced Americans to the notion that the self was not a historically determined structure, and that this was what would be distinctive about American life. The self in this model is mutable. The thrill of reading the autobiography is to see how one individual took the raw material of his or her life and formed it into something shapely, unique, and successful.

It may be a commonplace that Franklin's autobiography is paradigmatic of the American tendency toward self-invention. In fact much of the autobiography is a how-to manual for successful performance. In one of the most famous sections of the autobiography, Franklin describes the way that he, as a young printer in Philadelphia, advertised his diligence to the town, not by distributing printed advertisements but by making of himself a walking advertisement: "In order to secure my Credit and Character as a Tradesman, I took care not only to be in *Reality* Industrious & frugal, but to avoid all *Appearances* of the Contrary. I dressed plainly; I was seen at no Places of idle Diversion; I never went out a-fishing or Shooting; a Book, indeed, sometimes debauch'd me from my Work; but that was seldome, snug, & gave me no Scandal: and to show that I was not above my Business, I sometimes brought home the Paper I purchas'd at the Stores, thro' the Streets on a Wheelbarrow."[6]

While the reality of frugality and industry was important to Franklin, the appearance of them was no less crucial. Thus, in his Thirteen Names of Virtues with their corresponding precepts, Franklin placed as much stress on the outward performance of virtue as on the inward reality of it. In Philip Abbott's terms, Franklin is the archetypal American hustler.[7] Yet the plain American costume Franklin wore in his autobiography seems an unassuming disguise for his canniness. While informing his readers that he never remembered what he had eaten two hours after a meal, he in fact loved his food and kept a file of favorite recipes.[8] In telling Americans that it was possible for one to reinvent oneself, Franklin laid the groundwork for not only endless variations on the mythology of success—from Horatio Alger on down through Dale Carnegie—but for the more charged possibility: that even ethnicity need not be a limitation on the re-creation of the self. Franklin, in presenting his life as a performance and in assuming a number of different voices in his prose, foreshadowed the development of the ethnic impersonator autobiography.

Although the voice of the self-created individual may be the loudest in American autobiography, it is certainly not the only one. Autobiography has also been an important vehicle for persons trying to free themselves from the strictures of a subordinate racial or ethnic identity. Even as Benjamin Franklin was publishing his autobiography (1771–90), another form of memoir was emerging: the slave narrative. Through hundreds of eloquent testimonials, slaves could and did persuade white Americans that they, too, were human and that they deserved the rights of American citizens. Nor were slave narratives the only form of nineteenth-century ethnic autobiography. By 1854, when Henry David Thoreau published *Walden*, the American public had been reading Native American autobiographies for twenty years.[9]

Ethnic autobiographies have fulfilled and continue to perform a number of cultural functions, but one purpose has remained the same: to offer the authentic voice of a minority group to a reading audience composed primarily of white, middle-class Americans. Autobiography is a political tool in that it contains an implicit argument for the importance of the self described and for the validity of his or her perspective. In a culture in which minority citizens have often had to struggle for their rights, ethnic autobiography states a case for citizenship and for the value of the ethnic self. As Benedict Anderson has written, a nation "can be imagined as a *community*, because, regardless of the actual inequality and exploitation that may prevail in each, the nation is always conceived as a deep, horizontal comradeship."[10] Ethnic autobiographies have often been constituted as arguments for inclusion by their authors—and by extension the group to whom their authors belong—in the imagined community of the United States. Slave narratives, by providing eloquent testimonials from those enslaved, made a case for emancipation. Immigrant autobiographies, written during the 1910s and 1920s, a period when nativist sentiments were on the rise, offered testimonials for why immigrants should be considered Americans. Sometimes ethnic autobiographies have revised this argument. Following the rise of ethnic awareness and ethnic pride in the 1960s and 1970s, autobiographies appeared that spoke to the need for minorities to maintain distinct identities rather than to be assimilated into the melting pot. The arguments embedded in these autobiographies have often proved politically effective. Through reading ethnic autobiographies, from *The Narrative of the Life of Frederick Douglass* (1845) to *Black Boy* (1937) to *Woman Warrior* (1976), Americans have been outraged, stirred, and sometimes moved to action.

Both the reader and the writer of an ethnic autobiography understand the implied contract: the memoirist is not telling his or her own story as much as the story of a people. In order to be heard, the ethnic autobiographer must often conform to his or her audience's stereotypes about that ethnicity. Frederick Douglass, when touring as a speaker for the Anti-Slavery Society in 1841, was told by abolitionist leader Parker Pillsbury to put a "little more of the plantation" in his speech, and by William Garrison not to sound too "learned," in case his audience not "believe you were ever a slave." Douglass refused both requests.[11]

Ethnic autobiographers, called upon to be representatives, to be the voice of their people, have sometimes even borrowed memories. Although literary critics are accustomed to thinking of fictional texts as being in conversation with one another across time and space, readers generally think of autobiography as the record of an individual's unique past. Yet in his autobiography, *Black Boy*, Richard Wright incorporated stories told to him by friends, including Ralph Ellison, as well as incidents he had observed happening to others.[12] Wright downplayed the middle-class status of his parents; he turned himself into a symbol of the oppressed southern African American. Even the title of his autobiography emphasized the representative nature of Wright's life story.

Not only white readers and ethnic autobiographers have demanded that ethnic autobiographers represent their people. Readers within the ethnic community of the writer have also stated the case for representative authenticity. This is evidenced, for example, by the reception given Maxine Hong Kingston's 1976 *Woman Warrior*, which was attacked by many Chinese American critics for being, as Katheryn M. Fong wrote, "a *very personal* description of growing up in Chinese America." Jeffrey Paul Chan worried that Kingston "may mislead naive white readers."[13] The notion that Kingston was presenting an example of Chinese American life that was misleading or inaccurate implied that the author did not have the right to present her personal experience as such. In the eyes of her critics, she was not telling her own story but (mis)telling the story of her people.

The writers of ethnic autobiographies have historically had to work within what one might call the trope of their given identities—to speak for their people, as a representative of their people. However, not every "people" is what it appears to be, nor is every ethnic autobiography what it purports to be. In a multiethnic society, Americans have always shifted identities. Even before the founding of the United States, colonists moved into new ethnic roles.[14] Yet it was not until the 1830s, with the rise of the abolitionist movement, that the first ethnic impersonator autobiographies, or fictions disguised as memoirs of ethnicity, made their appearance.

The anxiety over racial and ethnic identity and its slipperiness is an issue of autobiography as well as a wider cultural phenomenon. Ethnic impersonator autobiography offers us a range of voices that challenge received ideas about ethnicity, about the autobiographical "I," and about the very notion of self. Through studying these impersonations—as works of literature, as historical documents, and as cultural artifacts—we are forced to confront difficult questions: How much of ethnicity is a construction? Is there such a thing as an authentic ethnic or racial identity? And as Dan Carter asked, What is it about American discourse that makes us accept these impersonators so readily? Ethnic impersonators force us to rethink our easy assumptions about identity; they disrupt the notion of the melting pot and make us question how all identities are constructed. They revise the basis for a national sense of self.

Significantly, ethnic impersonators appear in clusters during critical periods in American history, such as the decades leading up to the Civil War, when slavery was being debated and it was unclear which ethnic groups were to be afforded full human status, and during the 1920s, when laws affecting immigrants and Native Americans were changing and the Ku Klux Klan was on the rise. Later still, during the civil rights era, a new rash of self-conscious ethnic impersonator autobiographies appeared, the work of writers who detailed their passage from whiteness into blackness.

Some impersonators adopt the voice of another group in order to gain political effectiveness, such as the white abolitionists who spoke as slaves in order to present a compelling case for emancipation. Other impersonators seem to have escaped the psychological prison of their own identity by speaking with the voice of an ethnic other. The WASP writer Daniel James broke his thirty-year writer's block, which first manifested itself after his appearance as an unfriendly witness before the House Committee on Un-American Activities (HUAC), by "becoming" the young Chicano activist Danny Santiago, author of *Famous All Over Town* (1983). Elizabeth Stern, a survivor of sexual abuse and the author (Leah Morton) of *I Am a Woman—and a Jew* (1926), took on the ethnic identity and national origins of the foster father who had abused her. However, most ethnic impersonators employ autobiography as only one tool in the larger project of redefining their identity. Typical is the "colored" janitor Sylvester Long, who in the 1920s transformed himself into Chief Buffalo Child Long Lance. He not only authored a best-selling autobiography but became a movie star and had his own line of running shoes. He embraced his "Indian" identity in every aspect of his life.

When ethnic identity is up for grabs in America, ethnic impersonator autobiographies make their claims, and they often find a receptive audience. The reception of these works stands as a reminder of how willing we are to believe. *I Am a Woman—and a Jew* was a success when it was first published and is still taught in college courses on women and Judaism. Danny Santiago's *Famous All Over Town* was the 1982 recipient of the prestigious Richard and Hilda Rosenthal Foundation Award. Thus, rather than being simply curiosities, these ethnic impersonator autobiographies have been influential in shaping American notions of identity.

Ethnic impersonator autobiographies operate at the margins to illuminate a central paradox of American identity. This paradox has changed over the past 150 years and will continue to change, but it has two central features that remain constant: American belief in the fluidity of class identity and the fixity of racial and, to a lesser extent, ethnic identity. This book is about what happens when people apply the logic of class to a construct of race and ethnicity. To borrow Werner Sollors's terms, ethnic impersonators are illustrations of ethnicity by consent rather than descent. According to Sollors, "Descent relations are those defined by anthropologists as relations of 'substance' (by blood or nature); consent relations describe those of 'law' or 'marriage.' Descent language stresses our positions as heirs, our hereditary qualities, liabilities, and entitlements; consent language stresses our abilities as mature free agents and 'architects of our fates' to choose our spouses, our destinies, and our political systems."[15]

Perhaps the clearest example of substituting the structures of class for those of race can be found in impersonator slave narratives. After all, slavery in the United States was a condition in which race and class status were inextricably linked: to be a slave was to be black, and blackness was and is considered a state from which it is impossible to assimilate into another racial or ethnic category. In that sense, impersonator slave narratives are among the most obvious and dramatic examples of the genre of ethnic impersonator autobiography.

Race more than ethnicity can be considered the most essentially recognized category of identity, given that race is commonly understood as having to do with biology, and ethnicity with culture. Of course the terms "race" and "ethnicity" themselves are slippery and change in meaning over time. Jews were once considered a separate race, biologically different from Anglo-Americans, but are now considered ethnics. Scientists and anthropologists have rightly taught us to distrust biological definitions of race.[16] Nowadays "race" usually, though not always, means black or white. Since these are the most clearly drawn racial distinctions that Americans make, it is perhaps unsurprising that most recent books on passing and the construction of identity have focused on the movement between black and white and on the construction of whiteness.[17] Several important recent studies have shown how immigrants have achieved "whiteness" by positing their identities against African Americans' and assimilating into the dominant culture.[18] As Roger Sanjek puts it, they pay "the price of linguistic extinction and cultural loss for the privilege of white racial status," gaining "the prize of race awarded upon the surrender of ethnicity."[19]

However, this is only part of the story. While I agree with Sanjek that "the post-1400s global racial order has always extended beyond black and white in its ranked racial ordering, but these two terms have always defined its poles,"[20] Americans have also escaped the polarities of race by moving along the ethnic spectrum—from white to Chicano, for instance, or from black to Indian.

Ethnicity can provide an escape from whiteness and blackness but cannot be seen as equivalent to race. Werner Sollors, surveying the terrain of American ethnicity in *Beyond Ethnicity*, chose to see race "while sometimes facilitating external identification, [as] merely one aspect of ethnicity."[21] However, ethnicity can be an option in a way that race never can.[22] While blackness and whiteness remain opposite poles in the popular imagination, there are times when these polarities are foregrounded and times when they recede—and when it is more useful to focus on the complex middle ground of ethnicity to avoid getting trapped by binary thinking.[23] As Ishmael Reed writes, "You know, we have these two basketball teams in the United States right now—'White America' and 'Black America.'" These terms, Reed maintains, function as "lazy metonymy," swallowing up ethnicities and providing a monolithic view of America that erases the subtleties of ethnicity.[24]

Scholars from a variety of disciplines have attacked and in fact discarded the notion of race and ethnicity as essential qualities.[25] While I am arguing against an essential view of racial and ethnic identity, I am also aware that much as we may like to think that race and ethnicity are not essential qualities, they are certainly treated as such in the United States. Race may be a construction, but color remains a visual cue; and most Americans use visual, physiological cues to make their judgments about a person's racial identity. The constructions of racial and ethnic identities have the psychological weight of reality.

As Elin Diamond writes in a passage that might apply as easily to race, "Gender, then, is both a doing—a performance that puts conventional gender attributes into possibly disruptive play—and a thing done—a pre-existing oppressive category." That is, gender (or race), while not an essential category, *behaves* as one through its reiteration. Diamond is right to point out that race and gender are not bravura performances but are reified through this repetition. This form of performance is not a one-night stand but might better be compared to, say, a Broadway show that runs for decade after decade. "When being is de-essentialized," writes Diamond, "when gender and even race are understood as fictional ontologies, modes of expression without true substance, the idea of performance comes to the fore. But performance *both affirms and denies this evacuation of identity*." In other words, the performance of gender or race insists on its own reality. It draws its audience into an agreement that what is occurring onstage is in some sense real. "In the sense that the 'I' has no interior secure ego or core identity, 'I' must always enunciate itself: there is only performance of a self, not an external representation of an interior truth."[26] However, the illusion of an exterior truth is created through the repetition of the performance, as well as through the reality that there is no moment that performers let down their guard and become other than what they represent themselves to be.

What better place to study that performance than in the self-conscious, rather than naturalized, performances of race and ethnicity—that is, with those who have consciously shifted their performance of racial or ethnic identity? Autobiography is a space where it is particularly easy to see this performance taking place. Autobiography foregrounds the process of self-fashioning. The memoirist is informing his or her readers how he or she came to be the person he or she is. In contrast to the ephemeral nature of other forms of performance, autobiography is fixed. The autobiographer presents a permanent self-definition to his or her readers. However, these autobiographical performers succeed, paradoxically, by presenting identity as an essential quality. In order to succeed, these performers need to know all of the stereotypes of the racial categories they have entered. So rather than expanding their readers' notions of identity, they restrict them.

In the introduction to her edited collection *Passing and the Fictions of Identity*, Elaine K. Ginsberg points to "the positive potential of passing as a way of challenging those categories and boundaries. In its interrogation of the essentialism that is the foundation of identity politics, passing has the potential to create a space for creative self-determination and agency: the opportunity to create multiple identities, to experiment with multiple subject positions, and to cross social and economic boundaries that exclude or oppress."[27] What would she make, one wonders, of Asa Carter, the former Klansman who experimented with multiple subject positions by reinventing himself as a Cherokee orphan?

While ethnic impersonators may free themselves from the historical trap of an unwanted identity by passing into a new one, their success rests on their ability to manipulate stereotypes, thus further miring their audience in essentialist racial and ethnic categories. Asa Carter, as a professional racist, was expert in manipulating stereotypes. He chanted in "Cherokee" to fit his audience's expectations. Re-creating himself as a Native American seems to have come easily to him. He understood the racial and ethnic categories in which his audience thought and apparently had had little trouble in working with a new set of symbols. The success of ethnic impersonators depends in large part on their manipulation of others' essentialist beliefs about race and ethnicity. It is possible to celebrate creativity, as does Ginsberg, but we should do so without ignoring its costs.

For a Klansman to speak as a Cherokee orphan or for an American-born gentile to speak as a Jew is certainly not seen in late twentieth-century America as a natural state of affairs. In a context where such categories exist, we need to take ethnic impersonators' transgression of these categories as a serious issue, one worthy of examination for what it tells us not only about the individuals whose stories are related but also about American identities in general. While it is serious, it is also humorous. There is a playfulness inherent in the ethnic impersonator, a creativity that comes from having a deep knowledge of the valences of ethnicity and race and a willingness to manipulate those for the sake of his or her own liberation. Some of these impersonators are reprehensible. In the mid-1950s Asa Carter was among the men who incorporated a shadowy paramilitary group called the Original Ku Klux Klan of the Confederacy, six alleged members of which kidnapped and tortured a black handyman. Carter only switched identities after the statewide paramilitary force he set up in 1971 failed, as had his attempt the previous year to establish a string of all-white private schools. While we may not want to hold up these impersonators as exemplars, there is an audacity inherent in their choices, a refusal to accept essentialist rules of race for themselves that has the transgressive quality of an outrageous joke.

Ethnic impersonator autobiographers use a Franklinian model of self-fashioning, but they turn the meaning of self-fashioning on its head. They write themselves out of the margins, to which they have been banished because of their ethnic or racial definition or their political beliefs, and into Americanness. In doing so, they change the definition of what "American" means. When they are successful, impersonators may trap their readers further in essentialist thinking about race and ethnicity. It is their exposure as impersonators that offers readers the possibility of being liberated from their fixed ideas about the meaning of racial and ethnic identity. Reading these texts with the full knowledge that they are impersonator autobiographies and analyzing them as ethnic performances can help us to rethink the construction of American identities by making us reconsider both why the writer wanted so much to escape his or her assigned ethnic identity and why the reader feels so unsettled at the idea of ethnicity as performance.

chapter one

Slave Narratives and the Problem of Authenticity

In the history of the United States, slavery most clearly illustrated the clash between the American precept that all men are born free and equal and the reality that race determined class status. Southern apologists for slavery in the antebellum period employed a variety of pseudo-scientific and religious theories to point to Africans' suitability as slaves and their inability to hold equal status with whites. On the other hand, many of the horror stories published in abolitionist newspapers centered around cases when the link between blackness and slave status was threatened—when white people were enslaved. I have chosen to start with slave narratives because slavery was, after all, a condition in which race and class status were inextricably linked. In the United States, as Werner Sollors points out, from Puritan times to the present the notion of consent rather than descent has been instrumental in defining Americanness. And yet "the concepts of the self-made man and of Jim Crow had their origins in the same culture at about the same time, whereas aristocratic societies had no need for either.... It was not the hereditary privilege of blue blood but the culturally constructed cultural liability of black blood that mattered most in the United States."[1]

Slave narratives were among the first American ethnic autobiographies to be widely produced and widely read. They, more than any group of such texts, illustrate the problems and pitfalls of the autobiographer who must employ a representative rather than an individual voice for what is a fairly pointed political goal: to alter the dominant culture's perception of his or her people. Slave narratives were produced within the context of the abolitionist movement and were elicited and edited by white editors. They were texts marked by the collusion and, sometimes, the struggle between the purposes of the writer and his or her amanuensis. In slave narratives some of the difficulties that subsequent ethnic autobiographers have faced in telling their stories are highlighted: former slaves, for their narratives to have potency, needed to appear authentic. Yet in doing so they had to squeeze their stories into the tightest of narrative fits in order to adhere scrupulously to their audience's idea of what the authentic slave experience entailed. Authenticity required predictability. There was little room for individual experience that fell outside the expected rubric of what everyone—that is, an abolitionist audience—knew to be true about slavery. Yet within the straitjacket of authenticity, former slaves struggled to write themselves into existence, to show that, after all, being African American was no guarantee of object status and that the former slave narrator had just as much claim to humanity as his or her white reader.

In their collaborations with former slaves, abolitionists struggled to create what they saw as a believable version of the slave experience. They worked in their publications to deracialize slavery by insisting that enslavement could happen as easily to a white person as to a black one, and that white skin was no protection against commodification. Ironically, however, in doing so they made it possible for just about any spokesperson to learn what an ex-slave was supposed to have experienced, and they witnessed a rash of fugitive slave impostors, con artists who preyed on credulous abolitionist sympathizers. Finally, despite the lip service abolitionists paid to the power of the stories told by former slaves, some of the literature most highly touted in abolitionist journals was created by white abolitionists speaking in the voice of slaves. In a world where anyone could learn the language of authenticity, the obvious fake was better than the spurious authentic document.

For a brief history of the slave narrative and its reception in nineteenth-century America, there is no better place to start than with the new introduction to the 1855 reissue of *Archy Moore, the White Slave; or, Memoirs of a Fugitive* (1836), in which its author, Richard Hildreth, traced the history of his work's publication and reception. A novel written in the form of a slave narrative, *Archy Moore* centers around a slave, the product of two generations of miscegenation and to all appearances white, as he marries his half-sister and then tries to rescue her from the sexual advances of their father and master.

In his introduction Hildreth explained that when he first sought a publisher in 1836, "neither in New York nor Boston was it very easy to find one. No bookseller dared to publish anything of the sort, and so complete was the reign of terror, that printers were almost afraid to set up the types" (ix). The publication of *Appeal to the Coloured Citizens of the World* (1829), by David Walker, a free black man in Boston, had sparked an angry debate over abolition. Walker's urging of his named audience of all African Americans, including southern slaves, to recognize white slaveholders as their enemy led to a crackdown on persons suspected of abolitionist tendencies as well as slaves. Within a year of publishing his pamphlet Walker himself was found dead under mysterious circumstances. The following year, 1831, Nat Turner's rebellion, the most extensive slave revolt in America until this point, provoked further reprisals by white southerners. In 1835, the year before *Archy Moore* was published, a mob in South Carolina broke into a post office in Charleston and, in a move later applauded by President Andrew Jackson, confiscated and burned abolitionist materials sent from the North. In 1836 proslavery forces successfully passed a gag order preventing Congress from considering antislavery petitions. Antiabolition riots broke out in several cities between 1834 and 1838.

Thus it was not surprising that Hildreth had problems getting his book published. Until 1831 the abolition movement had been quiescent in the North, even as slavery grew stronger in the South. However, Turner's insurrection changed the cry of antislavery activists from a plea for colonization to a call for immediate emancipation. These abolitionists were so successful in mobilizing support in the post-Turner years that they managed to gather more than 400,000 signatures on a petition they sent to Congress in 1838 demanding the end of slavery. By that year the American Anti-Slavery Society claimed a quarter of a million members.[2] Hildreth entered the fray as the debate over slavery was dramatically heating up. Indeed, the few reviews that appeared discussed the book's inflammatory nature, and the editor of the *Boston Daily Advocate*, one of the few pro-abolitionist newspapers in Boston, predicted that "the booksellers won't dare sell it, and a copy will never get into a southern latitude" (xii).

As a sales tactic, the editor of the 1836 edition presented the text as a slave narrative, writing in the advertising copy, "As to the conduct of the author, as he has himself described it, there are several occasions on which it is impossible to approve it. But he has written memoirs—not an apology nor a vindication. No man who writes his own life, will gain much credit by painting himself as faultless, and few have better claims to indulgence than Archy Moore" (x). Although this advertisement linked the value of the text to its supposed veracity as a slave autobiography, reviews of the book referred to it as a pseudonymous novel, albeit a "fiction woven apparently out of terrible truths."

It was unclear in 1836 that authenticity was much of a draw. In one of only two Boston reviews, in the abolitionist *Liberator*, Lydia Maria Child, herself a novelist (and, many thought, the true author of *The White Slave*), compared the book to the recently published memoirs of Charles Ball, a former slave:

> It is said in your paper that some think Charles Ball equal to Archy Moore. The extracts I have seen from Charles Ball are certainly highly interesting; and they have a peculiar interest, because an actual living man tells us what he has seen and experienced; while Archy Moore is a skillful grouping of incidents which, we all know, are constantly happening in the lives of slaves. But it cannot be equal to Archy Moore! Why, it does not belong to the same year, scarcely to the same age, to produce two such books. If I were a man, I would rather be the author of that work, than of anything ever published in America. (xiv)

The "peculiar interest" occasioned by the authenticity of Ball's narrative could not match the skillful fictionality of Hildreth's. In 1861 Child acted as the editor for Harriet Jacobs's *Incidents in the Life of a Slave Girl*. In doing so she brought one of the most powerful examples of the genre to the attention of the reading public.[3] She came to value the slave narrative's authenticity as much as did other abolitionists. But in 1836 authenticity was not yet at a premium. Nor did abolitionist fiction or slave autobiography have the power in the marketplace that it would soon attain. Although the first edition of *Archy Moore* sold out and a new one appeared in 1839, the advertisement for the second edition complained, "No review, or magazine, or hardly a newspaper, took any notice of [the first edition]—a silence caused quite as much by not knowing what to say, as by any indifference to the subject or contents of the book, both of which were certainly in some respect, well calculated to elicit criticism" (xvi). There was as yet no real place for the voice of the slave in the debate over slavery, and as Hildreth complained, even the second edition did not attract much attention.

Some of what notice the book did garner was negative, as evidenced by this paragraph from the (Boston) *Christian Examiner*, which criticized the language of the first-person narrator: "In its present form it is in this respect a constant violation of probability. We read, in what professes to be the language of a slave, that which we feel a slave could not have written" (xvii). At this review Hildreth took umbrage in his introduction to the 1855 edition: "To have been bred a slave, was in the estimation of this critic, (and he no doubt expressed to the sentiment current about him,) to have grown up destitute of intellect and feeling. When the book and the criticism were written, there were yet no Fred Douglasses. The author foresaw them; the critic did not" (xx). Douglass's 1845 autobiography, which sold five thousand copies in its first four months of publication, brought slave narratives to a much wider audience. *Narrative of the Life of Frederick Douglass* was a tale of self-fashioning in the tradition of Ben Franklin—the story of how a man was made a slave, "a man transformed into a brute."[4] Created by a master rhetorician, it was also compelling evidence of the slave's humanity.

Finally, however, it was Harriet Beecher Stowe as much as Frederick Douglass who helped ensure success for Archy Moore. "So matters stood, when the publication and great success of Uncle Tom's Cabin gave a new impulse to anti-slavery literature" (Hildreth, xxi). Within a year of its publication in 1852, *Uncle Tom's Cabin* had sold 305,000 copies in America and 2.5 million copies in translation and in English all over the world. Not only did Stowe find it possible to capture a wide and relatively heterogeneous readership with *Uncle Tom's Cabin* (subsequent dramatic productions of the novel would extend the work's audience even further, in terms of both class and political sympathies). Her work also had a widely acknowledged effect on public policy, as witnessed by Abraham Lincoln's comment upon her visit to the White House: "So this is the little lady who made this big war."[5]

The story of Archy Moore had a happy ending for Hildreth. A new American edition soon appeared, and it was republished in England and translated into French, Italian, and German. Hildreth closed his 1856 introduction by claiming as his invention the antislavery novel. While lauding the writers who came after him, he refused to relinquish his own position within the field. Writing of himself in the third person, he noted that "their achievements are, in a certain sense, his; he has in them the natural pride of paternity; but while fully admitting their merits, he claims, at the same time, the respect and honor due to the father of them all" (xxii).

Between Frederick Douglass and Harriet Beecher Stowe lies the uneasy territory in which slaves wrote themselves into public consciousness. While Lydia Maria Child may have preferred the fictional version of the slave narrative in 1836, by the 1850s authenticity had become a sought-after commodity in the slave narrative.

As Hildreth attested in his somewhat backhanded compliment to Douglass, slave narratives were an emotionally powerful, politically effective, and extremely popular form of literature. Slave narratives provide perhaps the best example of ethnic autobiographies that mattered, that could "speak truth to power" and effect social change. Through the act of writing, former slaves could present themselves to white readers as recognizably human rather than as human chattel. As an anonymous review in the *Anti-Slavery Bugle* put it in 1849, "This fugitive slave literature is destined to be a powerful lever. We have the most profound conviction of its potency. We see in it the easy and infallible means of abolitionizing the free States."[6] As Philip Abbott notes, slave narratives provided the most vivid and compelling illustration of the abolitionist tracts on natural rights.[7]

The authenticity of the narrative gave weight to the claim it made on the reader's moral attention. These narratives, suffused with moral purpose, implicitly or explicitly demanded activism of their readers. They were weapons to be used in the struggle for freedom. For that reason some editors enjoined against reading the narratives as literature, even as they introduced texts that were rife with torture, sexual bondage, and thrilling escape. As Charles Stearns wrote in the preface to *Narrative of Henry Box Brown, Who Escaped from Slavery Enclosed in a Box 3 Feet Long and 2 Wide*, "Not for the purpose of administering to a prurient desire to 'hear and see some new thing,' nor to gratify any inclination on the part of the hero of the following story to be honored by man, is this simple and touching narrative of the perils of a seeker after the 'boon of liberty,' introduced to the public eye; but that the people of this country may be made acquainted with the horrid sufferings endured by [Henry Box Brown]" (v). Even as Stearns cautioned against titillation and prurient interest on the part of the reader, he offered a preview of the wonders that lay in the pages to come: "horrid sufferings" on a "fearful journey." Some advertisements were less coy about their purpose. One notice in the *Anti-Slavery Bugle* advertised and excerpted the narrative of Rev. J. W. Loguen, "that our readers may have a foretaste of the entertainment to which they are invited, we copy from the advance sheets the following sketch of infernal violence and murder."[8]

Slave narratives were gripping and often sensational in that they encouraged readers to experience a range of powerfully felt emotions. Yet any emotion aroused by the narrative was meant to be for a higher purpose. As Stearns continued in his preface to *Narrative of Henry Box Brown*, "O reader, as you peruse this heart-rending tale, let the tear of sympathy roll freely from your eyes, and let the deep fountains of human feeling, which God has implanted in the breast of every son and daughter of Adam, burst forth from their enclosure, until a stream shall flow therefrom on to the surrounding world, of so invigorating and purifying a nature, as to arouse from the 'death of the sin' of slavery, and cleanse from the pollutions thereof, all with whom you may be connected" (1). In this construct the mere act of reading the narrative with rapt attention and of being drawn into the story would help to end slavery. Every tear on a reader's part would have a morally cleansing effect on others; private emotion would lead to public change.

Although advertised as titillating, slave narratives had perhaps the most clearly useful function of any category of American ethnic autobiographies. They were written and read with a clear purpose: to end slavery. They are thus the most transparently didactic American ethnic autobiographies. Their contradictions, disguises, and ambiguities existed for a reason. When a slave wrote about his or her disguise, it was always in the context of gaining freedom. Reader and writer colluded for a straightforward purpose, and the compact they made, although designed to lead to change in the public arena, was fashioned within a private context. It was unspectacular.

Slave narratives were read not just in a political but in a literary context. The antebellum slave narrative was seen not only as politically effective but as the great literature of its time. One reviewer, minister Ephraim Peabody, offering a Homeric comparison, suggested that "if the Iliad should be thought not to present a parallel case, we know not where one who wished to write a modern Odyssey could find a better subject than in the adventures of a fugitive slave."[9] Slave narratives were seen to have the strength not merely of epic but of a peculiarly American form of epic. Theodore Parker, a prominent Transcendentalist, spoke of the slave narrative as the only form of literary production unique to America: "All the original romance of Americans is in them, not in the white man's novel."[10] Slaves did not have the legal privileges of Americans born free and equal, but within their narratives they made claims for their Americanness. Stearns, in introducing Henry Box Brown's narrative, lauded Brown's "endurance, worthy of a Spartan" and claimed that "no one can doubt, when they recollect that if the records of all nations, from the time when Adam and Eve first placed their free feet upon the soil of Eden, until the conclusion of the scenes depicted by Hildreth and Macauley, should be diligently searched, a parallel instance of heroism, in behalf of personal liberty, could not be found" (vi). The stress that so many editors and critics laid on the epic quality of the slave narrative was yet another guide for readers. Slave narratives were not treated as other autobiographies by readers. They were prized not for their individuality but for their representative value.

Like other ethnic autobiographers, but more so, the slave autobiographer needed to tell a gripping personal tale from which could be extrapolated the story of his or her people, and he or she had to do so for a polemical reason. The conditions of literacy in antebellum America ensured that black autobiographies of the period, like Native American autobiographies, were written almost exclusively for a white audience and in a form recognizable to and comfortable for readers. The same readers who might circulate in their parlor a *carte de visite* bearing a photograph of a slave's whip-scarred back would be likely to purchase the slave narratives, and African Americans who would write themselves into existence had this to contend with.

Slave narratives remade the idea of slavery. As John Sekora has written, "The narrative is the only moral history of American slavery we have. Outside its pages, slavery for black Americans was a wordless, nameless, timeless time."[11] Yet slave narratives were often full of names, dates, and place names, geographical and temporal markers that situated slaves within the same national landscape as their readers. All autobiographies are survival narratives, but in slave narratives this aspect was foregrounded. Slave narratives insisted that slavery could end for individuals. After all, slave narratives were produced by slaves who refused to remain enslaved and found their way out of the system.

An examination of slave narratives quickly uncovers the following set of contradictions: While the value of a slave narrative rested on its authenticity (for a narrative written by white abolitionists could quickly be dismissed as propaganda by slaveholders and their sympathizers), authenticity depended on strict adherence to a set of generic conventions. Slaves had to write not for themselves but for their people; an individual's story did not have value in its uniqueness but in its representative quality. Each slave had to have the same story, told in the same way. When this stricture was not observed, scholarly and popular suspicions were aroused. James Olney has gone so far as to prepare a master outline for slave narratives. An engraved portrait, signed by the narrator, precedes each narrative. The title page includes the claim "Written by Himself," and a handful of testimonials and a preface written by a white abolitionist friend of the narrator or by the white amanuensis/author/editor actually responsible for the text follows. Next comes the poetic epigraph, then the actual text. The formula was not confined to the front matter. The text, as Olney demonstrates, can be divided into twelve distinct and predictable parts, from the first sentence beginning "I was born . . ." through the final reflections on slavery.[12] When a narrative must so faithfully observe the generic conventions of all slave narratives—when it must be, in Olney's terms, itself enslaved—what does this say about authenticity? The slave wrote himself or herself into existence, but only under very circumscribed terms.

The status of the slave narrative as the great literature of its time led to the generic blurring of the boundary between fact and fiction, and to the slave autobiographer's effort to fit his or her story into a recognizable fictional narrative. To be believed a slave needed to follow a particular form already familiar to readers. Probably the most striking example is the narrative of Josiah Henson, who was promoted and eventually promoted himself as the original Uncle Tom. His publisher's advertisement, which appeared in the *Liberator*, for the first print run of five thousand copies seemed to straddle the fence in its appeal to both authenticity and fictionality: "Reader, would you know what American slavery is, purchase and read this book, more thrilling than a romance, more startling in its details than any work of fiction, and yet a true story of one colored man's experience, and that man THE ONE FROM INCIDENTS IN WHOSE LIFE MRS. STOWE DREW SOME OF THE MOST INTENSELY INTERESTING AND THRILLING SCENES IN HER WORLD-RENOWNED STORY OF 'UNCLE TOM'S CABIN.' "[13] The fact that his story, or a variant of it, was already familiar to his readers in fictional form made him more credible and made his story seem more gripping. Readers of slave narratives read not to discover what was new or unknown to them but, rather, to have their beliefs about slavery confirmed. What does Henson's self-promotion as a fictional character say about the idea of authentic individual experience?

Both abolitionists and proslavery forces took advantage of the blurring of fact and fiction in slave narratives. An August 7, 1858, headline in the *Anti-Slavery Bugle* proclaimed, "A White Slave Reclaimed Owing to Mrs. Stowe's Key to Uncle Tom's Cabin." An item from the *Kentucky News*, reprinted in the September 4, 1858, *Anti-Slavery Bugle* stated that "the Richmond *South* is in great glee because, as it states, an advertisement of one Raglan at Mobile of a runaway slave, copied into Mrs. Stowe's Key to Uncle Tom's Cabin, has been the means of the capture and return of the negro into slavery."

The *Kentucky News* article went on to stress another abolitionist theme: the deracialization of slavery. "The joke seems to be all the more keenly enjoyed by *The South* because the negro is so nearly white as to be mistaken for a white man, and has left a white wife in Pennsylvania. The satisfaction of enslaving a man, according to *The South*, is very much enhanced if white blood predominates in him, and we conclude the enslavement of free white men would give *The South* the most unalloyed gratification."[14]

In severing the link in readers' minds between race and slavery, abolitionists flew in the face of current anthropological theories. By the second half of the nineteenth century, American anthropology was beginning to emerge as a discipline. The great scientific war of the period concerned whether the races were polygenetic or monogenetic in origin—that is, whether different races were actually different species or if they belonged to the same human family. Until the publication of *The Origin of Species* in 1859, the polygeneticists were clearly winning this war of ideas. In 1854 two leading racial scientists, Josiah Clark Nott and George Robin Gliddon, had published their eight-hundred-page study, *Types of Man*, which disseminated the idea of separate species of humans to a broad audience and included chapters by prominent scientists such as those at Harvard, including Louis Agassiz. Even at the high price of $7.50 the first printing sold out immediately, and by the end of the century the book had gone through at least nine editions.[15] Although by the end of the 1850s the spread of Charles Darwin's ideas had effectively discredited polygeneticist theories in scientific circles, it merely shifted the focus of race theory. The "scientific" study of race now had an evolutionary model that held that Africans and Indians were simply less evolved stages of humanity.

In opposition to this popular theory, abolitionists challenged the notion that blacks were inherently suited for slavery due to their childlike or bestial nature. Articles in abolitionist newspapers challenged prevailing assumptions about the knowability of race. Some items were humorous, such as an account from the *Anti-Slavery Record* of December 1835 that narrated the story of "a colored gentleman" whose presence onboard a ship was objectionable to a fellow passenger. Inevitably, when others aboard did not know Mr. Purvis was defined as black, he was well-received. He "was upbraided by fathers and mothers if he neglected to dance with their daughters."[16]

The indeterminacy of race was highlighted not only in abolitionist newspapers but in slave autobiographies that challenged notions of racial essentialism. While insisting on the authenticity of the narrative, the storyteller emphasized his or her ability to disguise his or her identity, to pass as a member of another race or gender. Because escape almost inevitably required disguise, the authors of slave narratives also stressed the mutability of their identity. They told stories of how their many possible white captors were unable to recognize them as who they were, or who their status made them.

For instance, the first pages of one of the most successful narratives of its time, William Craft's *Running a Thousand Miles for Freedom; or, the Escape of William and Ellen Craft from Slavery* (1860), are devoted to deracializing slavery. After the obligatory "My wife and myself were born" opening, Craft stressed the fact that "slavery in America is not at all confined to persons of any particular complexion" (271). One of his sympathetic appeals to the reader was that "there are a very large number of slaves as white as anyone; but as the evidence of a slave is not admitted in court against a free white person, it is almost impossible for a white child, after having been kidnapped and sold into or reduced to slavery, in a part of the country where it is not known (as is often the case), ever to recover its freedom" (271–72). The examples he gave included one "white boy who, at the age of seven, was stolen from his home in Ohio, tanned and stained in such a way that he could not be distinguished from a person of color, and then sold as a slave in Virginia" (274). These illustrations spoke to readers' anxieties that it was possible for anyone to become black, to take on the status of a slave.

The idea that skin color was immaterial in the slave economy recurred in article after article in abolitionist newspapers. In severing the link between racial characteristics and slavery, abolitionist papers reinforced the idea that being enslaved was a tragedy that could befall almost anyone. It was not inconceivable, then, that despite the assumed protection of their white skin, even the paper's readers could find themselves enslaved.

Consider these sample articles from the *Liberator* and the *Anti-*

Slavery Bugle. On February 16, 1838, the *Liberator* published an item titled "Astonishing Difference between White and Colored Skin." The piece related the story of a slaveholder who had bought a child and a Negro woman he supposed to be the child's mother, only to find out that the child was, in fact, white and had been either abandoned by his or her mother or stolen. An item in the June 11, 1858, issue of the *Liberator* titled "A Fugitive White Slave" concerned "a woman, quite handsome, and perfectly white" who escaped from slavery. An *Anti-Slavery Bugle* article for March 27, 1858, related the story of "a young woman of rather delicate complexion, and having no appearance of affinity with the colored race," who successfully sued for her freedom in a Cincinnati courtroom.[17] A story that had been updated repeatedly and reprinted in other papers as well appeared in the April 22, 1859, edition of the *Liberator*. Titled "The White Slave Woman Set Free," the piece concerned a woman whose cause had been taken up by Henry Ward Beecher, who collected contributions from his congregation to buy her freedom. "The necessary sum was contributed, and the white slave woman last week passed through the Capital of the land of the free—what a burlesque on the Declaration of Independence!—to buy herself and her white children." On September 16, 1858, the *Liberator* published a piece called "A White Woman Set Free," concerning a "handsome young white woman, about twenty-one years of age, perfectly white, with long, luxuriant and straight hair, graceful and easy in manners, and having all the appearance of an accomplished and well-raised lady. Her features bore the highest marks of European perfection, and there was not the slightest indication of African blood in her veins." Surely this was a woman with whom the *Liberator*'s readers could identify. However, her predicament was hardly one in which readers would have liked to imagine themselves. "She brought suit here for her freedom, alleging that she had been forcibly arrested by the officers and lodged in the negro jail of the late James McMillan, under the claim of the defendant, Mary Goddard, that she was a slave, 'when in truth she was a free white woman.'" These stories sought to close the gulf that apparently existed between their readers and slaves and suggested that white women, in particular, had less legal protection against enslavement than they might have assumed.

Perhaps most frightening in this regard were instances of white women sold as slaves by jilted suitors. A front-page article in the *Anti-Slavery Bugle* related the story of a white woman, Patience Hicks, to whom this happened. The man in question "desired to marry the young lady, and finding that her mother was opposed to their marriage, he stole her away and brought her to the house of the Rev. John Guilford, to whom he sold her as a slave."[18] The would-be fiancé then went back and captured her fifteen-year-old brother, whom he also sold. These incidents pointed up women's vulnerability to the designs of unscrupulous men when denied the protection of white status.

In *Louisa Picquet, the Octoroon; or, Inside Views of Southern Domestic Life* (1861), the narrative's editor, H. Mattison, emphasized Picquet's "every appearance, at first view, of an accomplished white lady." The accompanying woodcut reinforced his statement. "No one, not apprised of the fact, would suspect that she had a drop of African blood in her veins; indeed, few will believe it, at first, even when told of it" (5). The Christian framework of Picquet's narrative elided rather than emphasized differences between black and white, slave and free; reader and narrator alike were part of a larger story. As Mattison wrote in the chapter titled "Conclusion and Moral of the Whole Story," "May the Lord arouse this guilty nation to a sense of its deep and unwashed guilt, and bring us to repentance and reformation before the republic shall crumble beneath the weight of our accumulated crimes, and He who led Israel out of Egypt, by his sore judgments, shall arise for the sighing of millions whom we hold in chains, and shall pour out his fury upon us to our utter confusion and ruin!" (52).

Because the slave narrative was predicated on disguise, on the slave's ability to take on another identity temporarily in order to gain full human status, it highlighted as well the slipperiness of identity. Slaves, in order to gain their freedom, often had to effect a temporary shift in appearance. To escape from slavery, William and Ellen Craft traveled north together—she in the guise of a white gentleman, he posing as her slave.

William Craft's *Running a Thousand Miles for Freedom* is not a narrative that seems authentic in any sense. It is hard to believe that a slave who learned to read only after he escaped from slavery as an adult man could not only compare himself to characters in *Uncle Tom's Cabin* but inform the reader as well that "I, like Bunyan's Christian in the arbor, went to sleep at the wrong time, and took too long a nap" (311). Like Josiah Henson, who claimed to be the original Uncle Tom, Craft took advantage of his readers' familiarity with *Pilgrim's Progress* to represent himself as an allegorical figure. For while the value of slave narratives seemed to lie in their authenticity, in fact the success of these stories rested on their recognizability to readers. Slaves had to become typological for their experiences to be appreciated by white readers.

Fictional Slave Narratives

Given the political and literary power of the slave's voice, it is perhaps not surprising that several abolitionists attempted to assume that voice. After all, slave narratives were so formulaic that their emulation ought to be a simple matter. If slaves could do a good job, was it not possible that abolitionists could do even better? The results of these abolitionists' efforts to adopt the voice of the slave point up the limits of the abolitionist vision. In a fake slave narrative, the fissures between the styles that typically make up a slave narrative—the documentary, the sentimental novel, the account of pornographic violence, and the testimony of Christian redemption—are more apparent. Even more than in the authentic examples, these genres coexist uneasily. Fake slave narratives seem even more polyphonous than the real ones; it is as though the warring elements of the antislavery culture are presented as the voice of one person, the slave. In a fake narrative the slave storyteller usually has an epiphany and discovers that slavery is wrong and that he or she would rather be free. Most slave-authored texts do not feature the shocking discovery that slavery is wrong. The ersatz narratives are notable for elements such as a disgust with the African American body—that is, an emphasis on rather than an erasure of racial difference—and an obsession with physical pain.

Add to this an ignorance of some of the features of the institution of slavery and of American geography, and you have *Narrative of James Williams, an American Slave* (1838). The title alone should have been enough to alert the suspicious reader that this was a volume designed at the very least for readers who were not American; the preface, which invokes "the celebrated John Wesley" (iii), William Wordsworth, and "the celebrated Priestley" (vi), strengthens this suspicion. Given that many slave narratives were published for English audiences and that many former slaves went to England to live and to go on speaking tours, this was not so unusual. However, some of the features of the landscape Williams claims to have inhabited—for example, the wolves said to live in Alabama—give evidence of a certain level of English imagination about the American South. *Narrative of James Williams* is conventional, however, in the injunction contained in the preface: "THE SLAVE HAD SPOKEN FOR HIMSELF" (xix).

Unexceptional as well are items included in the front matter, such as a sampling of newspaper ads for runaway slaves and notices that list the evidence of whippings and other barbarities visited upon slave bodies. Yet the slavery described by Williams is in many respects unlike that experienced by most slaves. For instance, his brother, a slave, preaches occasionally at a Baptist church. At one point he gives

> a sermon from a text, showing that all are of one blood. Some of the whites who heard it said that such preaching would raise an insurrection among the negroes. Two of them told him that if he would prove his doctrine by Scripture, they would let him go, but if he did not, he should have nine and thirty lashes. He accordingly preached another sermon, and spoke with a great deal of boldness. The two men who were in favor of having him whipped left before the sermon was over; those who remained acknowledged that he had proved his doctrine, and preached a good sermon, and many of them came up and shook hands with him. (4)

This particular southern parish seems to have many unusual features. That a slave could preach to slaveholders about equality might strike some readers as remarkable; it is remarkable, too, that slaveholders would shake the minister's hand afterward. Stranger still is the reception accorded this same brother when he preaches a sermon during the cholera epidemic in Richmond: "He compared the pestilence to the plagues which afflicted the Egyptian slave-holders, because they would not let the people go. After the sermon some of the whites threatened to whip him. Mr. Valentine, a merchant on Shocko Hill, prevented them; and a young lawyer named Brooks said it was wrong to threaten a man for preaching the truth" (27). Although the Nat Turner insurrection puts an end to the Richmond preaching career of Williams's brother, it is clear from the narrative that a fairly free and open spirit of debate characterized life in the slaveholding South.

It is possible that some American readers might not have found certain elements of the marriage of seventeen-year-old Williams surprising: "We were married by a white clergyman named Jones; and were allowed two or three weeks to ourselves, which we spent in visiting and other amusements" (33). Yet it is hard to believe that an abolitionist did not know that slave marriages were not legally recognized, that slave women were the sexual property of their masters, and that it was far more common for slaves to be separated from those they considered their spouses than it was for them to be sent on honeymoons by their masters.

Considering these conditions, it is perhaps less surprising that when Williams learns he has been sold by his Virginia master to serve as the slave driver on an Alabama plantation, "I stood silent and horror-struck. Could it be that the man whom I had served faithfully from our mutual boyhood, whose slightest wish had been my law, to serve whom I would have laid down my life, while I had confidence in his integrity—could it be that he had so cruelly and wickedly deceived me?" (41). Given the leisurely honeymoon of the slaves, the interracial congregations in which slavery was debated spiritedly among blacks and whites, and the generally egalitarian atmosphere of the Virginia plantation, who could blame Williams for regretting his "kind and hospitable home" (42)? Indeed, when his Virginia master asks him if he would rather be freed and sent to Liberia or continue living as a slave, "I replied that I had rather be as I was" (31).

Yet his experience as a driver on the Alabama plantation to which he has been sold is hellish. He documents runaway slaves being recaptured and shot, whipped to death, or tortured with cats' claws dragged along their backs; slaves found dead in the stocks where they had been imprisoned; pregnant women flogged until they die; and slaves shot for insubordination. Given the fate that befalls a slave who dares to run away, it is amazing that any still do. Williams describes the five bloodhounds set loose to run after an escaped slave and in what shape the dogs returned: "Their jaws, feet and head were bloody" (50). He does not spare any detail. The search party for the slave set upon by the hounds, Williams reports, finds his mangled corpse: "Blood, tatters of clothes, and even the entrails of the unfortunate man, were clinging to the stubs of the old and broken cane" (51).

Williams's departure from slavery is finally motivated by his overseer threatening to give him 250 lashes for not whipping a recaptured runaway slave hard enough, although, writes Williams, "when I had finished, the miserable sufferer, from his neck to his heels, was covered in blood and bruises" (82). As he tends a boiling pot of salt and pepper with which to bathe the runaway's wounds, "reflecting upon the dreadful torture to which I was about to be subjected, the thought of *escape* flashed upon my mind" (83). Telling another slave to mind the pot, Williams walks away.

Fortunately for him, the overseer's bloodhounds "were always good-natured and obedient to me" (84). Still, thinking "of the fate of Little John, who had been torn to pieces by the hounds, and of the scarcely less dreadful condition of those who had escaped the dogs only to fall into the hands of the overseer[,] . . . I ran down to the creek with a determination to drown myself." Yet this story has a happy ending. If the Alabama plantation had been a nightmare of a charnel house, the escape narrative has a dreamy quality: "As I rose to the top of the water and caught a glimpse of the sunshine and the trees, the love of life revived in me" (85). Everything would be all right, even when the bloodhounds did catch up to him: "As the old hound came towards me, I called to her as I used to do when out hunting with her. She stopped suddenly, looked up at me, and then came wagging her tail and fawning around me." Not all the dogs were as friendly as Venus, however: "A moment after the other dogs came up hot in the chase, and with their noses to the ground. I called to them, but they did not look up, but came yelling on. I was just about to spring into the tree to avoid them, when Venus, the old hound, met them, and stopped them. They then all came fawning and playing and jumping about me. The very creatures whom a moment before I had feared would tear me limb to limb, were now leaping and licking my hands, and rolling on the leaves around me" (86).

The rest of his journey to freedom involves a tour through a fantasy of the American Wild West, transposed onto a Deep South landscape. In search of nourishment, Williams comes upon some Indian cabins. "The Indian women received me with a great deal of kindness, and gave me a good supper of venison, corn-bread, and stewed pumpkin" (88)—an unlikely meal for the Indians of southern Alabama. The animal life of the region is equally improbable. As Williams keeps walking, "I heard on all sides the howling of the wolves, and the quick patter of their feet on the leaves and sticks, as they ran through the woods" (88). He encounters bears in Alabama as well and is discomfited to find that he has been traveling in the wrong direction—deeper into the South. However, he soon rectifies his error, in little time strolls through Augusta, Georgia, and then swims over the Savannah River into South Carolina. It takes him only two and a half months on foot to reach Richmond, where he is able to linger a month at the home of friends.

Initially the narrative was embraced by abolitionists. The details that might strike the reader as odd—the slaves preaching freedom to the slave owners without repercussion, the slave enamored of slavery, the friendly bloodhounds, the Alabama wolves, the leisurely walk through the South, the seemingly effortless swims across major bodies of water, the home-owning friends of a man held in slavery all his life—apparently did not bother the reviewer for the abolitionist journal the *Liberator*. The writer claimed that the "narrative of James Williams, therefore, is incontrovertibly true; and is additionally valuable, because it so powerfully corroborates other evidence and facts which have been published." As evidence, the anonymous reviewer cited the scene in which Williams depicts his master's wife: "I maintain that no man could have invented that story; and more, I am convinced that the notion never entered the head of any northern young woman, single or married, to take off her shoe, and smite the head and face of a female domestic with it, until she was tired of her own inhumanity."[19] Thus, the way in which Williams confirms the reviewer's received ideas about southern women is enough to obliterate all the wolves in Alabama.

The *Liberator* gave a fair amount of space to promoting the book. A letter from the narrative's publisher to William Lloyd Garrison, printed in the Communications column of the February 2, 1838, edition of the paper, predicted that the work "will be read with almost unexampled interest." He continued, "No book has been published better calculated to enlighten the minds and melt the hearts of men." Oddest was the single anecdote L. T., the author of this letter, used to illustrate the book's appeal and authenticity: the story of James Williams and the bloodhounds.[20]

Strangely enough, it was the inconsistency of the master's name in the narrative that caused southerners to unmask the work as a fake. The discontinuity between the names and places in Williams's story and those in the territory (Virginia and Alabama) described—that is, the details that had to do with the white world of the text—also alerted southern readers that something was amiss. Since slavery was, despite the descriptions of travelers and of slaves themselves, still a terra incognita, an exotic and hellish world in which anything could and did happen, readers would not question even the most dubious propositions, such as the friendly bloodhounds or the Alabama wolves. If anything written in the first person was to be believed by a white audience, the author had to get the recognizable realities of white life right. The *Liberator* was quick to publish a disavowal of *Narrative of James Williams, an American Slave* when it was exposed as false. The November 3, 1838, issue carried a front-page statement, authorized by the executive committee of the American Anti-Slavery Society, calling for the book to be withdrawn from circulation.

Yet had "James Williams" done a little more research into the names and places of the South, his narrative might never have been exposed as false. The experiences of slaves were not expected to overlap much with those of abolitionists. When knowability on the most basic level remained a problem, impersonation was always a possibility.

Authenticity and the Fear of Imposture

Even as abolitionists hailed the authentic slave voice, their newspapers were full of accounts of impostor slaves. "Beware of an Impostor," warned a September 23, 1859, headline in the Correspondence column of the *Liberator*. This story, like dozens of others that appeared in abolitionist newspapers, detailed the escapades of a man "representing himself to be a runaway slave" and cautioned readers that "he is probably somewhere in this State or near it, trying to defraud the benevolence of the people." As an article three and a half years earlier in the same newspaper had warned, "The increasing anti-slavery feeling in the free States, together with the sympathy extended to those who have escaped from oppression, has induced many unprincipled persons to go through the country soliciting money for the professed purpose of purchasing relatives or friends, or educating the person asking the donation. Several of these impostors have, from time to time, been exposed through the columns of THE LIBERATOR."[21]

Since the form of the slave narrative, complete with a thrilling tale of escape, had become familiar to a wide audience, it is unsurprising that it was easy to duplicate. "Beware of Impostor!" warned a November 17, 1855, headline in the *Anti-Slavery Bugle*. "Beware of Impostors," the paper reiterated on March 22, 1856. In the *Liberator* the exposure of frauds occurred at a fast and furious rate in the late 1850s. "Pretend Fugitive Slave," blared an August 28, 1857, headline. In the same issue "Beware of an Impostor" headed another article. "Bogus Fugitives" announced an October 2 headline the same year. On November 19, 1858, another warning about another pretender appeared. Given that any person of any appearance could plausibly claim to be an escaped slave, how could abolitionists know whom to trust?

In many ways abolitionists had only themselves to blame for this state of affairs. After all, they had worked hard to deracialize slavery in the face of current racial theories that described African Americans as uniquely suited for servitude. They had helped create the formula for slave autobiographies, but by providing a blueprint for the authentic slave story had made it easy for impostors to adopt the voices of the persons they imitated. Abolitionists had used slave narratives as tools to build a political consensus that slavery was wrong and un-American (for were not slave narratives themselves the most American of stories?). However, try as they might, abolitionists could not control the voices of slaves. The only way they could ensure the production of the slave narratives they preferred was to write them themselves.

A Fiction Stranger Than Truth

Perhaps the best example of the slave narrative preferred by abolitionists was Mattie Griffith's *The Autobiography of a Female Slave* (1857). Its appearance occasioned a veritable flurry of critical attention, particularly in the *Liberator*. Appearing on November 28, 1856, the first notice of the anonymously published work was perfunctory but admiring: "Having had not time to give it a critical examination, but only rapidly to turn over its pages, we can now say only that we are impressed to recognize it as the production of an elevated mind and a philanthropic heart, admirable in narrative and powerfully descriptive, characterized by artistic skill, and full of stirring incident, and as worthy to take its place among the first rank of anti-slavery publications. We cannot even surmise the name of its author, nor yet whether it had a masculine or feminine origin."[22]

Two months later the *Liberator* reprinted a review of the book that had appeared in the *Christian Inquirer*. This item, while disclaiming knowledge of the author's name, avowed that "it was written by a lady born, bred and educated at the South, a close and inevitable observer of the institution whose workings she portrays." Thus the reader was offered a different kind of authenticity, not a voice crying from the wilderness but a conversion narrative. "This fact is alone sufficient to stamp the volume with a peculiar character, and to attach to it a peculiar importance and interest. Here is the voice, not of a Northern 'romancer,' but of a Southern witness—a voice articulate, intelligent, as earnest, strong and pathetic as Mrs. Stowe's—a voice that has a right to speak, and a claim to be heard—a voice declaring, not what are the necessary results of certain principles, but what are the actual results of an institution."

Like those critics who hailed the raw, authentic voices of slaves, who were uniquely qualified, after all, to speak of their oppression and who had an undeniable claim on the attention of their readers, this reviewer contrasted the "truth" of *Autobiography of a Female Slave* with the fiction of *Uncle Tom's Cabin*, which the commentator predicted the former would outshine. It was almost as though the supposed authenticity of the narrator's voice obscured the fact that this was, after all, fiction. The reviewer continued, "The tale is terribly sad and painful, and seems more so from the naked distinctness with which it is told, its harsh features wanting the softness which skill and grace of literary execution would give." Given that this was, after all, a novel, it would seem only appropriate that it have some grace of literary execution. However, in a world that valued at least the appearance of authenticity if not authenticity itself, literary skill would remove any illusion for this nameless reviewer that the *Autobiography* had the power of unvarnished truth.

The article in the *Liberator* accompanying the reprinted review from the *Christian Inquirer* included a lengthy excerpt from the book and trumpeted the unsolicited quality of Griffith's conversion. She, "ignorant of the radical abolition movement of the North, out of the depths of her soul brought forth this thrilling testimony against the hideous slave system."[23] Griffith's name soon became a fixture on the masthead of Anti-Slavery Society publications. A convert, she was welcomed into the bosom of the abolitionists' group.

For Griffith a new category of authenticity was created by abolitionist reviewers—what one might term emotional authenticity. As the reviewer for the *Christian Examiner* wrote, "The subject of the book is evidently her own biographer only in the sense—but that is the best sense—of being the narrator of the personal experiences which it presents. We have confidence in the truth of the narrative, and we ask for it its own just share in that fearfully momentous object of teaching and terrifying us all in view of the volcanic fires which are kindled beneath us."[24] The emotional truth of the story was worth more than its lived quality; Griffith was an autobiographer, thus, in the best sense.

Although *Autobiography of a Female Slave*, like other slave narratives, began in the customary way, "I was born," and included some of the usual apparatus, such as the dedication to "All Persons Interested in the Cause of Freedom," it exceeded most narratives in its lurid descriptions of whippings. Sentimental, pornographic, and Christian, *Autobiography of a Female Slave* had something for every reader. It is unsurprising that a number of newspapers, including the *Anti-Slavery Bugle*, the *Liberator*, the *Christian Inquirer*, and the *New York Christian Examiner*, furnished glowing reviews for the book. Moreover, in its narrator, Ann, whose life was changed by her encounters with abolitionists and who conveniently ceded her own wishes to those of her white benefactors, abolitionist readers may have thought they had encountered the ideal former slave.

Slave narratives and published details of slave whippings titillated a nineteenth-century audience with a pronounced sexual interest in flagellation. As Richard von Kraft-Ebbing's Case 57 in his *Psychopathia Sexualis* (1902) recounts, "That one man could possess, sell or whip another, caused me intense excitement; and in reading Uncle Tom's Cabin (which I read at about the beginning of puberty) I had erections."[25] In Louisa Picquet's narrative, for example, her interlocutor showed a high degree of interest in the details of her whippings:

Q.—"Well, how did he whip you?"
A.—"With the cowhide."
Q.—"Around your shoulders, or how?"
A.—"That day he did."
Q.—"How were you dressed—with thin clothes, or how?"
A.—"Oh, very thin; with low-neck'd dress." (Mattison, 13)

Compare, for instance, an incident in Griffith's *Autobiography* with one in Elizabeth Keckley's *Behind the Scenes*. In *Behind the Scenes* the cruel schoolmaster Mr. Bingham asks the slave Lizzie to accompany him to his study.

Wondering what he meant by his strange request, I followed him, and when we had entered the study he closed the door, and in his blunt way remarked: "Lizzie, I am going to flog you." I was thunderstruck, and tried to think if I had been remiss in anything. I could not recollect of doing anything to deserve punishment and with surprise exclaimed: "Whip me, Mr. Bingham! what for!"

"No matter," he replied, "I am going to whip you, so take down your dress this instant."

Recollect, I was eighteen years of age, was a woman fully developed, and this man coolly bade me take down my dress.

Highlighting the sexual aspects of the slave/master relationship, Keckley describes her struggle, her master's overpowering her, and the whipping in great detail: "[He] was the stronger of the two, and after a hard struggle succeeded in binding my hands and tearing my dress from my back. Then he picked up a rawhide, and began to ply it freely over my shoulders. With steady hand and practiced eye he would raise the instrument of torture, nerve himself for a blow, and with fearful force the rawhide descended upon the quivering flesh. It cut the skin, raised great welts, and the warm blood trickled down my back" (32–33). Keckley's emphasis on the physicality of the beating—her references to quivering flesh, warm blood, and her own nudity—all seem to invite the reader to imagine the scene as an intimate observer.

By contrast Mattie Griffith describes her ordeal in terms that are both pornographic and Christian:

> Lindy and Nace tore the last article of clothing from my back. I felt my soul shiver and shudder at this; but what could I do? *I could pray*—thank God, I could pray!
>
> I then submitted to have Nace clasp the iron cuffs around my hands and ankles, and there I stood, a revolting spectacle. With what misery I listened to obscene and ribald jests from my master and his overseer! . . . During this time I had remained motionless. My heart was lifted to God in silent prayer. Oh, shall I, can I, ever forget that scene? There, in the saintly stillness of the summer night, where the deep, o'ershadowing heavens preached a sermon of peace, there I was loaded with contumely, bound hand and foot in irons, with jeering faces around, vulgar eyes glaring on my uncovered body, and two inhuman men about to lash me to the bone. (49)

While Keckley describes a private ordeal, Griffith includes the pornographic element of audience: "vulgar eyes glaring on my uncovered body."

Griffith was expert at playing to a wide array of conceivable audiences: Christians, persons interested in flagellation, lovers of sentimental fiction, and even proslavery and antislavery advocates. However, she deviated from the conventional formula in some important respects.

For one thing, she seemed to assume a slave readership, as when she addressed "You, oh, my tawny brothers, who read these tear-stained pages, ask your own hearts, which, perhaps, now ache almost to bursting, ask, I say, your own vulture-torn hearts, if life is not a hard, hard burden?" (60). Given the laws against teaching slaves to read, it is highly unlikely that many slaves would be perusing her pages. Indeed, Griffith often seemed to have a hard time knowing how to situate herself within the narrative. She, like the editors rather than the authors of other slave narratives, invoked classical examples. "If the African has not heroism, pray where will you find it? Are there, in the high endurance of the heroes of old Sparta, sufferings such as the unchronicled life of many a slave can furnish forth?" (81). Griffith's narrator consistently employed such high-flown language. As a review in the *New York Christian Examiner* asked, "How does it come about that this slave girl has such superfine style, such correct grammar, so well arranged a rhetoric, so many poetic phrases and allusions?" Well might a reader wonder. Yet the reviewer answered the question with confidence: "Withal, there is an aptitude in the negro blood for emotion, and all that expresses it; for music, for poetic sentiment, for expressive language, for the religious, and the ideal."[26] Thus even the improbability of Ann's eloquence could be accounted for using racist theories, now harnessed to the abolitionist cause. For while abolitionists may have elided racial difference in the interests of enabling white Americans to see slaves as just as human as themselves, the success of Griffith's narrative showed only too clearly the limits of this deracialization.

While most slave narratives insisted on minimizing differences between black and white, between slave bodies and free bodies, Griffith demonstrated what can only be called an extraordinary distaste for black bodies. In the passage quoted above, she even referred to her own body as "a revolting spectacle." This was mild compared with what she said about other slave bodies. Of Lindy, another house slave, she wrote, "I always had an aversion to her. There was that about her entire physique which made her odious to me. A certain laxity of the muscles and joints of her frame, which produced a floundering, shuffling sort of gait that was peculiarly disagreeable, a narrow, soulless countenance, an oblique leer of the eye where an ambushed fiend seemed to lurk, full, voluptuous lips, lengthy chin, and expanded nostril, combined to prove her very low in the scale of animals" (65). By the time *Autobiography* was published, evolutionary ideas were beginning to take hold, and Griffiths clearly seemed to have subscribed to the monogeneticist theories about the origin of species. Most of the time, though, she did not bother to couch her racist descriptions in even the flimsiest of scientific trappings. She described Aunt Polly, another slave on the plantation, as having a "decayed and revolting form" (52). The narrator frequently expresses her disgust at African American bodies: "Her face grew ashen pale; it took that peculiar kind of pallor which the negro's face often assumes under the influence of fear or disease, and which is so disagreeable to look upon" (77).

In Griffith's narrative, slaves experience no solidarity among themselves; to the contrary, they are always threatening to inform on one another. When a group of slave children begs Aunt Polly for a piece of hoe cake, she is unsympathetic: "Be off wid you, or I'll tell Massa, or de overseer," she warns them (23). Nor is this an empty threat. As a pair of slaves are dragged away to be whipped, their fellow slaves exhibit no sympathy: "'They be gettin' awful beatin' at the post,' muttered Nace, while a sardonic smile flitted over his hard features" (27).

The slaves, in fact, seem to have completely internalized white racism. *Autobiography of a Female Slave* even features a cross between Little Eva and Jesus Christ, in the guise of John, the master's son. "Fair-haired, with deep blue eyes, a snowy complexion and pensive manners, he glided by us, ever recalling to my mind the thought of seraphs. . . . I always fancied when the boy came near me, that there was about him a religion, which, like the wondrous virtue of the Savior's garment, was manifest only when you approached near enough to touch it" (91–92). In fact, John is barely a male; his father describes him as "pretty enoff to be a gal" (107). When this perfect example of Christianity tells one of his father's slaves that Jesus "values the heart alone; and if your heart is clear, it matters not whether your face be black or your clothes mean," the slave refuses to believe it. "'Laws, now, young Masser,' and the child laughed heartily at the idea, 'you doesn't 'spect a nigger's heart am clean. I tells you 'tis black and dirty as dere faces'" (114).

Oddly enough, it is not the slaves but their owners who understand the injustice of slavery. As Ann tells us, "'Tis well that the negro is of an imaginative cast. Suppose he were by nature strongly practical and matter-of-fact; life could not endure with him. His dreaminess, his fancy, makes him happy in spite of the dreary reality which surrounds him. The poor slave, with not a sixpence in his pocket, dreams of the time when he shall be able to buy himself, and revels in this most delightful Utopia" (121). When her benevolent mistress informs her that "a bad institution is this one of slavery," "I looked surprised, but dared not tell her that often had vague doubts of the justice of slavery crossed my mind" (34). It takes the visit of a handsome abolitionist to persuade her of the worthiness of his cause. As she listens to him talk of Frederick Douglass, she is swept away on a tide of emotion:

"Who," I asked myself, "is this mysterious Fred Douglas?" A black man he evidently was; but how had I heard him spoken of? As one devoted to self-culture in its noblest form, who ornamented society by his imposing and graceful bearing, who electrified audiences with the splendor of his rhetoric, and lured scholars to his presence by the fame of his acquirements; and this man, this oracle of lore, was of my race, of my blood. What he had done, others might achieve. What a high determination then fired my breast! Give, give me but the opportunity, and my chief ambition will be to prove that we, though wronged and despised, are not inferior to the proud Caucasians. (82)

Above all, it is the saintly John who becomes a martyr to the cause of slavery, for he, more than any of the slaves who are beaten to death by his father, sisters, or those they command during the course of the narrative, understands the evils of slavery within the context of Christianity. John, sickly to begin with, contracts a fatal illness while staying up all night to comfort a slave who has been beaten and thrown into the plantation prison, although he knows that doing so will cost him his health: "Go, Ann," he tells the narrator, "leave me to watch and pray beside this forlorn creature, and if the Angel of Death spreads his wings on this midnight blast, I think I should welcome him; for life, with its broken promises and its cold humanity, sickens me—oh, so much" (159). Although John begs his father to free his slaves, Mr. Peterkin will not agree: "I don't know what pity means whar a nigger is consarned." "And 'tis this feeling in you that has cost me my life" (223).

The tragedy of dying slaves is thus dwarfed by the suffering of the blond, blue-eyed young master who must succumb to a martyr's death. Griffith gives him a final scene that outshines Little Eva's. Between long speeches to his captive audience ("This earth is not our home; 'tis but a transient abiding-place, and, to one of my sensitive temperament, it has been none the happiest" [229]), John extracts from his father a promise that he will free all of his slaves.

John's demise is so tragic that any of the slaves who consider their future manumission, guaranteed by that deathbed promise, are said by Ann to be "always intent upon selfishness" (232). However, the sentimentality of John's tear-stained deathbed scene is undercut by his father's utterance a few weeks later: "Set my niggers free, indeed! Catch me doing any such foolish thing. I'd sooner be shot" (239).

Although she gives lip service to the sentiment of African American equality with whites, Ann cannot help but revert to slave owners' stereotypes about blacks: "There is a principle in the slave's nature to reverence, to look upward; hence, he makes the most devout Christian, and were it not for this same spirit, he would be but a poor servant" (122).

Thus, Griffith seemed to affirm that in fact African Americans were well suited for slavery, with their desire to serve and their childlike gift for happiness. It is difficult to imagine that this narrative would persuade any reader of the need for universal emancipation.

Although the other slave characters in the book speak in dialect, the narrator does not. When Aunt Polly asks her, "Law, chile, is dat you stannin' in de dor? What for you git up out en yer warm bed, and go stand in the night-ar?" the narrator replies, "Because I feel so well, and this pleasant air seems to brace my frame, and encourage my mind" (51). Not only is Ann the only slave who speaks standard English, but she can barely restrain herself from pouring forth frothy, sentimental descriptions at every turn, from night, "wrapped in her sombre purple, yet glittering with a cuirass of stars and a helmet of planets" (253), to morning, "when the golden sun had begun to tinge with light the distant treetops, and the young birds to chant their matin hymn" (58).

After Mr. Peterkin finally dies of alcoholism, Ann accompanies his daughter and her new husband to the city of L.—either Louisville or Lexington—where they take up residence in a hotel. If the farm was hell for Ann, the hotel promises riches of every kind, including a handsome mulatto boyfriend, Henry, who is also a slave, as well as the acquaintance of Mr. Trueman, an abolitionist with "deep, fervid blue eyes" and a "magnificent forehead" (255). There is even a library that stocks the leading antislavery journals and where Ann, dispatched on errands by her mistress, is afforded the opportunity to overhear an eighteen-page debate on slavery taking place between the fervid-eyed abolitionist and a Virginia slaveholder. It is Mr. Trueman who protects Ann when yet another of the many lustful whip-wielders of the book threatens Ann's "angel-sealed honor" (282), although he cannot prevent her from being sold to a slave trader.

Ann constantly reaffirms the hierarchy of color. Even when she is sold to a slave trader, she is repelled by the common and apparently contemptible run of slaves who serve only to reinforce racial stereotypes. One girl, Luce, who is ebony colored, is anxious to be sold down the river so that she can eat all the oranges she wants and marry at least four or five men, which her previous master has forbidden her to do. Luce functions as a sort of lascivious, pre-reform Topsy character. By contrast, Henry's friend Charles, who is light-skinned and has Caucasian features, is an attractive companion: "His swarthy cheek glowed with a beautiful crimson, and his rich eye fairly blazed with the fire of a seven-times heated soul, while the thin lip curled and the fine nostril dilated, and the whole form towered supremely in the majesty of erect and perfect manhood!" (323).

Yet apart from Charles's erect manhood, life at the slave trader's has little to offer Ann, and she is more than relieved when she is sold to a gentlewoman who will not require her services until spring. She has, thus, plenty of opportunity to recuperate at the home of a friend, a free woman of color, who brings her such dainties as "a cup of tea and a nice brown slice of toast, and a delicate piece of chicken, on a neat little salver," while Henry, her betrothed, "spent all his spare change in buying oranges and pine-apples for me, and in sending rare bouquets" (340).

True happiness comes, however, when Ann meets her new mistress, a genteel soul who provides her with her own small room, complete with "a cheap little mirror overhanging a tasteful dresser. . . . This room had been prepared for me by my kind mistress. Pointing it out, she said, 'That, Ann, is your *castle*.' I could not restrain my tears. 'Heaven send me grace to prove my gratitude to you, Miss Nancy'" (359). Ann is thrilled with her new life, with the gentility of her home; her breakfasts of "hot coffee, steaming steaks, omelettes, and warm biscuits" (361); the "beautiful, extemporaneous prayers" (361) of her mistress; and even the "friendly tea-urn of bright silver, from which I, even *I*, had often been supplied with the delightful beverage" (362).

Her life as the slave of Miss Nancy is so happy, in fact, that when Henry comes to tell her that he has saved enough money to purchase his own and her freedom, Ann refuses to leave her owner: "Oh, Henry, I cannot leave her, even if I were able to pay down every cent she demands for me. I should dislike to go away from her. She is so kind and good; has been such a friend to me that I could not desert her. Who would nurse her? Who would feel the same interest in her that I do? No, I will stay with her as long as she lives, and do all I can to prove my gratitude" (364). The problem with slavery, as far as Ann is concerned, is not an existential one—that for her to be chattel is an unacceptable condition. Instead, unlike most other slaves, she lacks "the easy indifference as to fate, which many of them wore like a loose glove; but there I was vulnerable at every pore, and wounded at each. What a curse to a slave's life is a sensitive nature!" (326). However, Ann's problem is obviated by the right mistress. If only slavery could be a more refined institution, it seems, it would be preferable to freedom.

Eventually Ann, Henry, and Miss Nancy plan to get the best of both worlds, slavery and freedom. Miss Nancy, who has been eavesdropping on Ann's interchange with Henry, tells Henry to buy himself. She will then fill out Ann's free papers and simply move wherever the two of them decide to settle.

Their happiness is sullied, though. When Henry's master refuses to honor his promise to let Henry buy his freedom on the installment plan and instead sells him down the river, Henry slits his throat. When Miss Nancy dies, she leaves Ann $4,000, with the stipulation that she move to Boston, whereupon Ann "removed to a quiet puritanical little town in Massachusetts" (898).

The Autobiography of a Female Slave may be a terrible novel, but it provides a great illustration of the fundamental problem with the abolitionist-authored slave narrative. Unwilling to trust the slaves, despite their protestations, to tell their own stories adequately, these writers created slave personae who were disgusted by black bodies, revolted by slave characters, and unable to see the truth about slavery without the intercession of wise abolitionists. Their narratives may seem laughable, but they were accepted by contemporary audiences as true, in that they confirmed their readers' notions of what slavery was all about. As the author of a letter to the editor of the *Boston Traveller* wrote, "The assumed autobiographer is by no means an impossible character among slaves." But although the letter writer considered it very important that "there is not one painful incident in the 'Autobiography' which was not a fact," that verisimilitude did not seem the most important feature of the book. Rather, this letter made explicit what was implicit in many reviews; it hailed Mattie Griffith as a survivor of great suffering, not as a slave but as a slaveholder, and a martyr to the abolitionist cause. "Slavery makes greater monsters of women than of men, except in those cases where it makes them sufferers—suffering more than men, also, by reason of this same intensity of temperament. The author of this book was one of those sufferers from childhood; an Eva who has grown up." Just as Griffith conflated fiction with fact in her "autobiography," so this letter writer conflated Griffith's status as a living person with that of a fictional character, further blurring the line between what was authentic and what was fictional. As the letter writer continued, "With no teacher but her own heart and mind, she has developed in her own person an abolitionist out of the bosom of a slaveholding community; one who, single-handed and alone, has not hesitated to begin the great work of emancipation by herself leading the way—and who has impoverished herself entirely, rather than live at the expense of that liberty, which is the life of life to every human being."

The writer highlighted the importance of Griffith to the abolitionist movement for her turncoat status, the propaganda value to the abolitionists of Griffith's conversion. But more than that, he or she extolled Griffith's suffering in terms one would normally use for fugitive slaves rather than their owners. "Here is a testimony," continued the letter writer, "—in spite of self-interest, and from the deepest knowledge,—which cannot be gainsaid."[27] This authoritative testimony seemed to carry more weight with the letter writer than would, necessarily, the words of a former slave.

In fact, a slave narrative that appeared just four years after Mattie Griffith's work, Harriet Jacobs's *Incidents in the Life of a Slave Girl* (1861), was suspected by both contemporary audiences and later scholars to be inauthentic. It simply did not fit readers' expectations of what slave life should be. Although today *Incidents* is frequently anthologized and taught in college classes nearly as often as the most famous slave narrative in its time or ours, *Narrative of the Life of Frederick Douglass*, it was not accepted in its day. According to Rafia Zafar, coeditor of the essay collection *Harriet Jacobs and Incidents in the Life of a Slave Girl*, Jacobs "had to contend with a skeptical readership who said that her work could not be 'genuine' because of her emphasis, her 'melodramatic' style, and her unwillingness to depict herself as an avatar of self-reliance." It is hard, though, to imagine a narrative more domestic and more melodramatic in style and whose narrator is less self-reliant than Griffith's. However, it is true, as Zafar writes, that "Jacobs was either decried as inauthentic or dismissed as atypical."[28] The story Jacobs tells is emotional and dramatic. Offering a devastating picture of the sexual exploitation of slaves by their masters, Jacobs documented her odyssey from slavery to freedom. She described her rebuttal of her owner's advances; her relationship with a local white man, not her owner, with whom she bore two children; and finally the seven years she spent hiding in the attic of her grandmother's house—a space three feet high, nine feet long, and seven feet wide—while beneath her, her children mourned the absence of their mother, who they thought had abandoned them to move north. While dramatic, this story scarcely seems less probable than Griffith's.

Moreover, Jacobs's narrative was edited by Lydia Maria Child, a cohort of Garrison's and one of the most prominent abolitionists. The gripping nature of *Incidents* aside, the normal relationship between the editor of a newspaper and his or her writers, or between members of the same political committee (as were Garrison and Child), would seem to dictate that *Incidents* should receive a fair amount of critical attention—at least as much, one would hope, as Griffith's *Autobiography*.

Sadly enough, Jacobs's autobiography received almost no notice, in the *Liberator* or elsewhere, upon its publication. One letter appeared in the *Liberator* recommending the book to the newspaper's readers because, among other reasons, "in furtherance of the object of its author, Lydia Maria Child has furnished an introduction, and Amy Post a well-written letter; and wherever the names of these two devoted friends of humanity are known, no higher credentials can be required or given." In other words, the authenticating names attached to the manuscript gave it credibility, as much as or more than the voice of the autobiographer. Yet William C. Nell, the author of this letter to Garrison, did include a plea for truth over fiction in his plaudits for *Incidents*: "It presents features more attractive than many of its predecessors purporting to be histories of slave life in America, because, in contrast with their mingling of fiction and fact, this record of complicated experience in the life of a young woman, a doomed victim to America's peculiar institution—her seven years' concealment in slavery—continued persecutions—hopes, often deferred, but which at length culminated in freedom—surely need not the charms that any pen of fiction, however gifted or graceful, could lend."[29]

However, despite this plea for what the abolitionists claimed to value—the power inherent in the unvarnished stories of fugitive slaves—Nell's words fell on deaf ears. In 1845 Lucius Matlock wrote, "From the soil of slavery itself have sprung forth some of the most brilliant productions, whose logical levers will ultimately upheave and overthrow the system." Slave narratives, he predicted, would "become a monument more enduring than marble, in testimony strong as sacred writ against" slavery.[30] Yet the value that abolitionists placed on the power of the slave voice turned out to be more theory than reality. On the whole, abolitionists would, given a choice, turn to fictional productions rather than risk inauthenticity.

Impostor Narratives and the Trap of Authenticity

Because slave realities seemed, to white readers, to exist in another time and place, as something nearly unimaginable, almost any narrative could seem authentic as long as it followed certain well-recognized conventions. That a southern woman would be cruel enough to strike her slave in the face with a shoe was proof of the storyteller's veracity, but the fact that this same narrator spoke of wolves in Alabama was not enough to deauthenticate his story.

Abolitionist authors, not trusting slaves to narrate their personal pasts effectively, felt compelled to imagine their pasts for them. It was a way of controlling narratives as they could not always control the slaves themselves. Fictional characters could be manipulated in ways that real people could not. Because the slaves themselves, in crafting their narratives, fit into recognizable fictional conventions—they became, in other words, characters in their own stories—the abolitionists who sought to tell their tales felt free to take this liberty one step further.

There were former slaves, however, who offered their own version of their pasts and who could break free of the trap of authenticity. Frederick Douglass, after all, refused William Lloyd Garrison's suggestion that he put a little more of the plantation into his voice. Douglass had left that plantation behind him and would not be forced back onto it. However, that did not stop reviewers from finding him less than authentic in his speeches. A review of an 1861 address Douglass delivered in Boston ended, typically, by complimenting the logic of Douglass's presentation but avowing that "it is not in a lecture such as this that Frederick Douglass shows his greatest power—that he is really himself. At the close of the meeting at Tremont Temple, he went directly to Rev. Mr. Grimes's church, on Southae street, which was packed to its utmost capacity to receive him. Here the exuberance of his nature found expression in the glowing imagery of his imaginative race; his wit and drollery were inimitable; and his rollicking good humor, blended with a vein of pathos, took all hearts captive."[31] It was not for his ironclad logic and his rhetorical power that Douglass was most treasured, but as a representative of his "imaginative race." Ironically enough, it was those slaves who dared to offer their own version of their life stories, one that did not so neatly conform to readers' expectations, whose narratives were suspected of being less than authentic.

When abolitionists asked for authenticity, they wanted a specific kind of authenticity that conformed to their stereotypes of slave life, rather than being characteristic of individual experience. It was easier, for example, to value Frederick Douglass for his "drollery," which this abolitionist reviewer could see as an attribute of African Americans (while at the same time being "inimitable"), than it was to understand him as an individual, on his own terms. For their part, many former slaves were willing to render their own experience in terms that conformed to readers' preconceptions—at least enough to make the narrative seem plausible to these readers. It was a way for former slaves to meet readers halfway, involve them in their narratives, and then pull them over the line that separates sympathy from activism. Yet the trope of authenticity of necessity implied its opposite.

Slave narratives were among the first, but by no means would be the last, ethnic autobiographies whose value rested in their credibility but whose authenticating qualities were so fixed as to become easily imitable. Authors of the first slave narratives had to prove their humanity to readers and then argue that the laws of the nation needed changing. However, the ethnic autobiographies that followed contended that their authors could be as American as their readers. Before the next great wave of ethnic autobiographies was published, during the period of extensive immigration, a series of social trends arose in the United States that set up the tension between the desire for authenticity, on one hand, and the performance of ethnicity, on the other.

While slave narratives may have highlighted the disguise and shifting identity of the escaping slave, it was with a purpose: to ensure that the identity "slave" was not contiguous with "person of color." African Americans may have, through disguise, escaped their identities as slaves, but after the escape they would willingly resume a fixed identity, that of free man or woman of color. In this construct, "slave" and "free" were the identities in opposition. After William and Ellen Craft completed their thousand-mile run for freedom, they resumed their identities as husband and wife. In fact, their identities were more firmly fixed afterward because "husband" and "wife" were identities superseded by slavery while slave marriages were not recognized as legal. Slave status was the identity that erased all other considerations—of marital status and even of skin color—as Williams's narrative emphasized.[32] Slave narratives concerned the writer's struggle to free himself or herself from his or her status as commodity, and then to be able to embrace the identities available to white Americans, be they identities of parent or paid worker or spouse.

Slave narratives, after all, concerned the transcending of stereotypes. They deracialized slavery, they were allegorical, and they placed the slave autobiographer into a Christian narrative of redemption familiar to readers. The experience of reading a slave narrative was private and depended on individual religious sentiment operating to wash away slavery with a flood of tears. Slave narratives sought to establish a contract between individual reader and individual author. The ethnic autobiographies to come, however, were tinged with the theatricality of the nineteenth century, inflected by the ethnic and racial spectacles that emphasized outward performance over inner spirituality and that united audience members in their understanding of the stereotypes being enacted onstage.

chapter two

Staged Ethnicities

Laying the Groundwork for Ethnic
Impersonator Autobiographies

It is difficult to understand the ethnic impersonator autobiographies that followed slave narratives without knowing more about the nineteenth-century theatrical performances that made the representation of ethnicity accessible to a wide public and tied the performance of Americanness to ethnic performances. By the 1830s, with the burgeoning of new forms of popular entertainment, ethnicity was being commodified in new ways through the performance of identity. From the 1830s to the 1890s, people developed a new vocabulary of race, embedded in commercial performance. This vocabulary then became established in their consciousness.

Whatever their elements of thrill or playfulness, slave narratives were written for a deadly serious purpose. If anything was being sold in slave narratives it was authenticity itself. Slaves were working for the chance to sell their labor rather than themselves. However, even as slave autobiographies were attaining popular status, American culture was becoming infused with a theatricality that permeated not only the museums and theaters to which big city audiences flocked, but even the middle-class parlor. The new performers were selling performances and fictions rather than themselves. As the relationships between ethnic groups in America changed at a sometimes bewildering rate, and as urban populations swelled, ethnicity and ethnic impersonation began attaining the status of entertainment, of spectacle. The theater at this time became an important site for mediating the sometimes confusing shifts in status between ethnic groups in the United States. In this chapter, by examining five distinct varieties of ethnic or racial performance—blackface minstrelsy, Davy Crockett's political performance of whiteness, P. T. Barnum's display of an "authentic" ex-slave, Wild West shows, and medicine shows, their commercial offspring—I show how, as ethnicity became defined through performance, these systems of packaging made ethnicity itself a commodity.

In the 1830s, congressional candidate and self-fashioned American archetype Davy Crockett represented himself theatrically as American, in contrast to the African Americans and Indians he boasted of killing. Among the places Crockett appeared was P. T. Barnum's American Museum, where immigrants in attendance were able to understand themselves as mainstream Americans in contrast to the "freaks," "savages," and "foreigners" exhibited there. Featured attractions at the museum and throughout New York City were blackface minstrels, what David Roediger has called "the first self-consciously *white* entertainers in the world."[1] These performances helped audiences to understand who would be considered American (the audience) and who would fall into another category (the performers). These three forms of theater defined Americanness and created a white identity in opposition to a range of other identities. Finally, two forms of theater that sprang up in the 1880s supplied a template for the performance of ethnicity. First, the Wild West show provided audiences with a reenactment of the American drama of westward expansion and enabled onlookers to reexperience ritually the conquest of a continent. Second, the more nakedly commercial offshoots of the Wild West show, the Indian and the Oriental medicine shows, which sprang up almost synchronically, tied the profit motive most directly to the performance of ethnicity, as ersatz Oriental princesses and both real and impersonator Native Americans used their exotic identities to peddle nostrums.

The end of the African slave trade in 1808, the rise of abolitionist sentiment in the North and the reaction to it of slaveholders between

1831 and 1861, and finally, emancipation wrought cataclysmic changes in the relationships between white and black Americans. Nor were African Americans the only group whose status changed dramatically during this period. Between 43 and 47 percent of immigrants came from Ireland in the years between 1820 and 1855. The exodus caused by the great famine made 1845–54 the decade of greatest immigration in the antebellum period. With 2 million Irish emigrating as a result of the famine and with three-quarters of the Catholic immigrants landing in the United States, this infusion significantly reconfigured the ethnic makeup of several large cities. In Boston in 1847, one twelve-month period saw 37,000 Irish immigrants pour into a city whose population until that point had been 114,366.[2] Who among these people would be considered American? Who would, in Benedict Anderson's words, be able to participate in the "deep, horizontal comradeship" of the nation? Popular ethnic performances made ethnicity consumable and allowed audiences to unwrap performances and use them in their personal self-definitions of whiteness.

Staged Ethnicities

Any discussion of ethnic impersonator performance during this period must begin with minstrel shows. Indeed, a great deal of recent scholarship has focused on the rise of the minstrel show in antebellum America and on its role in the development of working-class culture.[3] Since the minstrel show is not the focus of this book but, rather, necessary background, I offer here merely a brief discussion of a complex and rich subject. Historians tend to understand the performance of ethnicity through the model of minstrelsy, in which whiteness is defined in opposition to blackness, which becomes performative and ridiculous. The blackface model is useful for understanding ethnic performance, but blackface is also an aberration. Recent scholarship is very helpful in making apparent ethnicity as performance, but it is an incomplete model. For in blackface, inauthenticity is being performed, whereas in other theatrical performances of ethnicity, it is authenticity that is being staged. Blackface minstrelsy is a caricature; it flattens the topography of the racial landscape to black and white. Throughout the second two-thirds of the nineteenth century, performances developed that moved toward brownness as a model and away from the black/white dichotomy.

The antebellum minstrel show was a distinctly working-class, distinctly urban form most popular in large northern cities. Although in the 1820s American actors began "blacking up" and performing, as *entre-acts*, what they claimed were Negro songs, the minstrel show—a full evening's entertainment performed by a minstrel troupe—did not become wildly popular until the 1840s. Although many variations occurred, at the height of their popularity these shows generally consisted of four or more white male performers arrayed in a semicircle, blacked up with shoe polish, costumed in outrageous rags, and playing instruments, usually the tambourine, the banjo, the fiddle, and castanets. The first part of the show featured songs interspersed with "Negro" humor, performed in dialect; the second portion featured comic dialogues, cross-dressed "wench" performances, or pseudo-learned speeches replete with malapropisms. The show concluded with a narrative skit.[4] Sometimes, although not always, minstrel performers claimed to have done extensive research among southern black communities and to be presenting an authentic version of Negro life; contemporary commentators often described performers as black and saw the shows as evidence of legitimate Negro culture.[5]

Working-class whites flocked to minstrel shows, where they could define their whiteness against the drama of performed blackness. Irish immigrants often occupied the same class niche as antebellum free blacks; racial stereotypes conflated the two. "Smoked Irish" was nineteenth-century rural slang for blacks,[6] and comparisons between blacks and Irish were often unfavorable to the latter. Typical was a comment by the Whig patrician diarist George Templeton Strong, who wrote that "Southern Cuffee seems of a higher social grade than Northern Paddy."[7]

Robert Cantwell, David Roediger, and Eric Lott have all written of how mid-nineteenth-century minstrelsy offered white workers—both those who blacked up and those who attended the rowdy shows, often held in mechanics' halls and other working-class arenas—the chance to develop an identity that downplayed their own "foreign" ethnicity and offered them an opportunity for a common, Americanized identity in opposition to blackness.[8] "Minstrelsy," writes Roediger, "made a contribution to a sense of popular whiteness among workers across lines of ethnicity, religion and skill."[9] However, this whiteness, which emerged from performers' ability to become temporarily black, depended on denying blacks the same options for self-transformation. As Roediger points out, "Minstrels claimed the right to turn Black for as long as they desired and to reappear as white. They forcefully denied Blacks that right, parodying fancy dress, 'l'arned' speech, temperance and religion among Blacks as ridiculous attempts to 'act white.' "[10]

On one hand, the passage of whites into blackness was represented as comic. Minstrel shows were played for laughs, not tears, and nineteenth-century melodramas featured a range of comic ethnic characters. On the other hand, the performance of whiteness by those defined as black was deemed tragic. Middle-class whites read sentimental stories by writers such as Lydia Maria Child about the ills that befell light-skinned mulattos attempting to pass as white. The tragic mulatto became a literary trope at the same time that the comic blackface performer became an American theatrical institution.

In the minstrel shows the person performing whiteness was the impresario, someone who packaged and interpreted blackness for a white audience. The impresario made the common link of whiteness between himself, the white audience, and what was occurring onstage.

Performing American Authenticity in the Political Arena

The performance of whiteness could not always be easily separated from the performance of Americanness. In the 1830s the frontiersman Davy Crockett successfully employed a combination of autobiography and melodramatic performance to craft an image of himself as an archetypal American, one whose stature depended in part on his ability to keep blacks and Indians in their places. Crockett's version of Americanness emerged in opposition to the other; his national identity came not from ancestry, blood, or essence but from his ability to conquer the land and its original inhabitants. Davy Crockett rose during the presidency of Andrew Jackson, to whom he was closely allied. Jackson, whose wealth as a self-made man was founded on his ownership of more than one hundred slaves, bought with money gained from speculation on land acquired from Native Americans, built his political reputation on his role as an Indian fighter. As Ronald Takaki has written, "On the dark and bloody ground of the West, General Jackson had developed a justification for violence against the Indians and a metaphysics for genocide. White violence was a necessary partial evil for the realization of a general good—the extension of white civilization and the transformation of the wilderness into an agrarian society and a nursery of the arts."[11]

Perhaps most ironically, the value of Crockett's homespun image was first demonstrated by his Whig opponents, who published a spurious Crockett autobiography, *Sketches and Eccentricities* (1833), designed to discredit Crockett and Jackson. The campaign using the biography, which portrayed Crockett as a man primitive unto bestiality, who offered to "hug a bear too close for comfort, and eat any man opposed to Jackson,"[12] backfired, producing a number of unexpected effects. Instead of discrediting Crockett, it increased his popularity. Paradoxically, however, the very failure of the campaign led to success for the Whigs, as Crockett soon forsook Jackson and allied himself with the Whigs. His rough frontiersman image was an asset to a party friendlier to bankers than to farmers. The first, Whig-authored memoir, however, was only one of four bogus biographies and autobiographies of Crockett that appeared between 1833 and 1836. *Sketches and Eccentricities*, for the most part, played up Crockett's frontier spirit without setting his whiteness against other ethnicities. Its author, whose identity was unknown at the time of the book's publication (it has since been attributed to Matthew St. Clair), mentioned that Crockett had no slaves, noting, "He took me over his little field of corn, which he himself had cleared and grubbed, talked of the quantity he should make, his peas, pumpkins, *etc.* with the same pleasure that a Mississippi planter would have shown me his cotton estate, or a James river Virginia planter have carried me over his wide inheritance."[13]

By the late 1830s, however, the Crockett legend was tinged by racism, whereby his status as a white American was set off against a background of inferior others. The false autobiographical almanacs of the 1830s, 1840s, and 1850s included stories in which Crockett boasted of boiling an Indian to make medicine for his pet bear's stomachache, bragged that he could "swallow a nigger whole without choking if you butter his head and pin his ears back," and described Mexicans and Cubans as "degenerate outlaws," Indians as "red niggers," and African Americans as "ape-like caricatures of humanity."[14] For the Crockett legend in the later years, whiteness—and the frontier American identity—depended on a virulently racist humor to separate him from others of darker skin.

With the help of the Whigs, Crockett developed a crude yet carefully honed self-presentation that propelled him to political success and gained him two terms in the U.S. Congress. While contemporary stereotypes portrayed Indians as barbarians and blacks as savages, Davy Crockett presented himself as a white primitive. He may have boasted of behavior that many would consider savage or barbaric, but he was on the side that was winning. Crockett's performative identity took over his self-image completely. This identity was bolstered not only by the autobiographies and almanacs but by the long-running melodrama *The Lion of the West*, whose hero, Nimrod Wildfire, strongly resembled the mythological Crockett. The play, which ran for two decades, first opened in New York in 1831 and was seen by Congressman Crockett in 1833. In a moment that beautifully illustrates mid-nineteenth-century audiences' level of comfort with the performance of self, Crockett was cheered as he entered the theater to watch a performance based on his legend. James Hackett, playing the Crockett role, was applauded as he bowed toward Crockett, and the audience burst into a storm of appreciative noise as Crockett in turn bowed to the actor playing him.

However, Crockett's second term as congressman is generally considered to be a flop by historians. He was so often touring the north, bolstering his folk image, that he had little time for his duties. As Richard Boyd Hauck writes, "The man's legendary identity had absorbed much of his authentic self."[15] Joel Schechter considers Crockett's celebrity a prime example of poor casting: "He was miscast in a road show that took him to New England dinners and to a Fourth of July celebration in Philadelphia, far from the electorate in Tennessee."[16] It certainly took not only an enormous effort on Crockett's part but a full-time publicity machine to continue polishing the image of the authentic frontiersman. Yet the audiences applauding Crockett applauding his understudy in the theater must have understood that in cheering for Crockett they were hailing not what was authentic but what they understood to be a strenuous performance of American authenticity. Crockett brought the null categories of whiteness and Americanness into existence through performance. Unlike the producers of minstrel shows, he did not need onstage representations of blackness to help his audience feel white. The darker-skinned others who made his performance of whiteness possible existed only as ghosts of people killed by Crockett, specters that hovered unseen but barely acknowledged at the edge of the stage.

P. T. Barnum's American Museum:
A Public Forum for Debating Authenticity

Audiences who applauded Crockett's performance of American authenticity were themselves studying hard to learn how to best present an authentic, sincere appearance in social situations. While not everyone could exemplify the frontier hero, anyone could learn how to perform authenticity. Crockett, after all, exemplified the self-made man, and by the 1840s dozens of self-improvement books were readily available to an eager public. Between 1820 and 1860 Americans poured into the rapidly growing cities. As the U.S. population increased by 226 percent, the proportion of urban dwellers rose by 797 percent. This was the fastest rate of urban growth in U.S. history.[17] As the cities filled with newcomers, Americans experienced a great deal of anxiety about how to judge the many unknown persons with whom they came into contact each day, and equally important, how to control the image they themselves presented to others with whom they had no history—that is, no knowledge based on generations of kinship or commerce. The rise of speculative economies in the Jacksonian age, the industrial revolution, and the resulting shift in population from the countryside to the city led to a widespread feeling of insecurity among middle-class Americans and persons aspiring to middle-class status. A recent urban citizen might not be able to trust his or her neighbor, might not be able to count on making a living in the same way as had his or her parents, and certainly could not rely on a fluctuating economy. The tenuous nature of urban existence contributed to the popularity of the gospel of self-improvement. In a city of strangers, who better to rely on than oneself, and how important it would then be that the self be as effective an agent as possible. In an age of uncertainty the self became an anchor.

As Karen Halttunen has written, "In an open, urban society, the powerful images of the confidence man and the painted woman expressed the deep concern of status-conscious social climbers that they themselves and those around them were 'passing' for something they were not."[18] As Halttunen points out, the sentimental cult of sincerity arose in response to this anxiety. Side by side a preoccupation with self-fashioning and a yearning for sincerity or authenticity shaped mid-century manners. In a culture in which many feared being taken in by confidence men, the performance of authenticity was essential for social success.

Aspiring middle-class Americans performed authenticity at home. For entertainment they flocked to P. T. Barnum's American Museum, where the authenticity of exhibits was a subject for lively debate. The American Museum held a dizzying range of attractions, including, in Barnum's own words, "industrious fleas, automatons, jugglers, ventriloquists, living statuary, tableaux, gypsies, albinos, fat boys, giants, dwarfs, rope-dancers, dioramas, panoramas, models of Niagara, Dublin, Paris and Jerusalem . . . fancy glass-blowing, knitting machines . . . dissolving views, American Indians."[19] Audiences were drawn to the museum by both the desire to see wonders and the desire to see through them. Barnum, in issuing hyperbolic advertisements of his exhibits' authenticity, invited spectators to share the joke of their own credulousness. By the time Barnum opened his American Museum in New York City on New Year's Day 1842, he had perfected the techniques that would make his exhibition of "authentic" curiosities successful: in biographer Neil Harris's words, "The quick discovery, the barrage of rapid and unusual information, the maximum exploitation of the local press, the planted lie, and the indignant denial."[20] Thus Barnum both cast doubt (under an assumed name, of course) on the authenticity of his own exhibits and (under his own name) strenuously vouched for them. Although the audiences who flocked to the American Museum may have feared encountering impostors in their daily lives, where they could be swindled at business or fall prey to confidence games, the Barnum Museum provided them with a safe forum in which to judge authenticity. The only thing audience members had to lose from being rooked by an impostor at the museum, after all, was the relatively low price of admission.

Museums had existed in the United States well before Barnum's time, but they were more placidly educational. The most famous of its time, Peale's Museum, also known as the American Museum, was founded in Philadelphia in 1784 by painter, natural philosopher, and inventor Charles Willson Peale. The exhibits were scholarly in nature—natural history collections were arranged in accordance with Linnaean principles of classification—and the tone was one of quiet dignity. By the time Barnum entered the field, museums had begun focusing more on entertainment than education, exhibiting curiosities to compete with the proliferation of urban entertainments. However, museum directors worked hard to disassociate themselves from the theater, still considered disreputable by many Americans in 1840. To maintain the respectability of their establishments, museum directors rejected obvious fakes. Rubens Peale, who took over his father's museum, would only show curiosities that had been authenticated by the scientific community.[21]

Barnum changed that traditional mode of operation. He offered the performance, not the reality, of authenticity. His reasons for doing so were in part political. As Bluford Adams has convincingly argued, Barnum used the manufacture of authenticity and the exposure of his hoaxes to cast doubts on the narratives published by former slaves. In his serialized pseudoautobiography, *The Adventures of an Adventurer* (1841), written under the name Barnaby Diddledum, Barnum discussed the creation of one of his earliest and most famous hoaxes, the display of Joice Heth, a slave who Barnum claimed was the 161-year-old nurse of George Washington. Barnum and his assistant Levi Lyman had successfully displayed Heth from August 1835 until her death in February of the following year. Their staged dissection of her body after her death revealed her age to be no more than 80 years. As Diddledum explained, the pair of unnamed exhibitors had purchased Heth from her master, extracted her teeth, artificially aged her on a diet of whiskey and eggs, and educated her about the legend of George Washington. The exhibitors had then claimed that the proceeds of Heth's exhibition would go to aid runaway slaves. Heth had, by this account, been a willing and eager partner in the deception and lied to earn her nightly glass of whiskey. As Adams writes, by "depicting Heth as a willing partner to his swindle, Barnum helped launch a literary effort to undermine the ex-slave abolitionists" whose narratives were growing in popularity during this period.[22]

Barnum's museum was insistently democratic, designed to attract a wide range of spectators—what Barnum called "the Universal Yankee Nation."[23] Both Barnum in his American Museum in New York and Moses Kimball at the Boston Museum developed entertainments suitable for ladies as well as for workers. As Bruce A. McConachie notes, these museums drew opera-goers and Bowery theater fans together at a time when almost all urban entertainment was clearly designed with a specific class audience in mind.[24] However, while Barnum welcomed an audience that cut across class lines, and though he and his partner, Moses Kimball, encouraged women and children to come, he did not allow African Americans to enter the building as patrons until the 1860s, although many were featured as freaks and spectacles. Members of the Universal Yankee Nation—which included rich and poor, native-born and immigrants—could gather in discussion and contemplation of spurious freaks marketed as ethnic exotics, including the "Feejee Mermaid," Barnum's most famous fake, made of a monkey's torso and a fish's tail, and a "leopard-spotted slave" (probably an African American suffering from vitiligo). The popular "What Is It?" exhibits purported to be the missing link between man and ape, displayed with a white "keeper." According to Adams, "Barnum used the 'What Is It?' to fortify the racist tradition of a link between blacks and animals."[25] Yet even as he presented category-blurring exhibits, Barnum may not always have intended his claims of authenticity to be taken entirely at face value. In 1850 he exhibited a Negro who claimed to have discovered a weed that would turn black men white, but it is hard to imagine that Barnum wished the experiment to succeed. For if it did, then whom would he exclude from his museum?[26]

Among the first attractions of P. T. Barnum's American Museum were Native Americans who were simply exhibited as themselves. Many immigrants first saw Indians at the museum; it was here that they might affirm themselves as Americans viewing the vanquished subjects of their newly adopted nation. Barnum chose the Native Americans, whom he hired in Iowa, for their authenticity. As he wrote in his autobiography, "The party comprised large and noble specimens of the untutored savage, as well as several very beautiful squaws, with two or three interesting 'papooses.'" However, Barnum was irritated when these exotic "specimens" did not understand the performative nature of their lives: "These wild Indians seemed to consider their dances as realities."[27] Indeed, Barnum's account of the Indians' stay at his museum can be viewed as a complex tug of war between himself and the tribe members. The Indians understood Barnum's need for them to entertain his audiences, yet it is hard to imagine their feelings at reenacting the central rituals of their traditions, such as war dances and wedding rites, day after day for a paying public. Their ceremonies were thus robbed of their traditional cultural meanings, and yet they had to be authentic to be valuable.

The Indians derived what economic power they could from Barnum's twin, and conflicting, needs: that the performance be repeatable, and that it have the appearance of authenticity. Thus, for example, the father of the bride in the Indian Wedding Dance demanded that the bridegroom be given a new woolen blanket to present to him each time the wedding was reenacted; Barnum was forced to give him twelve such blankets each week. In his private correspondence Barnum was less tolerant of the Indians' behavior. He wrote, "D—n Indians *anyhow* they are a lazy shiftless set of brutes—though they will *draw.*"[28]

In 1843 over 24,000 spectators traveled to New Jersey to witness the Barnum-sponsored "Grand Buffalo Hunt," in which a white man dressed as an Indian chased a herd of yearling buffaloes across the Hoboken race course. The crowd "roared with laughter," wrote Barnum, at the weakness and slowness of the buffalo calves. The national drama of westward expansion was reduced to a child-sized joke.[29]

Barnum, while advertising their authenticity, often manufactured crowd-delighting exhibits, such as the baby buffalo herds, that belied his claims. Perhaps, too, audience members who diligently studied conduct manuals to learn how to present a more sincere, unstudied appearance to the world could appreciate the contradiction that Barnum presented in his foregrounding of authentic exhibits of dubious origins.

Barnum, as the white impresario, could help his audiences become the Universal Yankee Nation as they bonded in their difference from—and judgment of—his freakish exhibits.

The Wild West Show

By 1883, when Buffalo Bill Cody opened his first Wild West Show, the display of Indians and buffalo was no longer comic material but, rather, a more solemn exercise in nation building. Cody's display of Native Americans reenacting the battles they had lost softened the brutal history of conquest and made it palatable for audiences. Indians, the most American people of all, became the population against whom audience members could define themselves as American. The authenticity that Barnum used in his promotional materials, but also played for laughs, became deadly serious in the hands of Buffalo Bill. Cody's shows depended for their success on their authenticity, and "Everything Genuine" was a staple of his promotional literature. With the collusion of the government and with the support of reviews that pointed to his shows as a uniquely American kind of education, Cody successfully promoted a theatrical form that used ethnic performance as an overt means of building a national identity. By the 1880s the hostile tribes of the West had largely been subdued by the government. The Indian removal policies in place before the Civil War had given way to government programs, such as Indian boarding schools, designed to assimilate Native Americans into civilization. Most of the spectators at a Wild West show in the 1880s had never seen an Indian; in the public imagination, Indians were passing out of existence. Buffalo Bill's Wild West Shows were events where actual Indians and cowboys reenacted frontier history. They were elegy, education, and entertainment in one package, a combination made possible only because by the time the Wild West shows began, most of the battles between the Indians and the U.S. government were over.

In the early years of the Wild West shows, however, the history reenacted was recent enough, and the line between entertainment and history thin enough, that events in the shows threatened to affect life on the Indian reservations. In 1890, for instance, White Horse, a Native American who traveled with Cody's Wild West Show, left the exhibition in Europe and returned to the United States to tell a *New York Herald* reporter that "all the Indians in Buffalo Bill's show are discontented, ill-treated, and anxious to come home." The charges caused a public out-

Buffalo Bill Cody and his publicity agent meet with government officials and Native Americans in the wake of the Wounded Knee massacre. (Photo courtesy of Denver Public Library, Western History Department; photo by Grabill Portrait and View Company.)

cry, not least because of fears that the report would further inflame reservation Indians caught up in the Ghost Dance movement.[30] Cody quickly replied in another *Herald* article. Damage control was important, since he needed government permission to recruit Indians for the performances each season. The relationship between the Wild West shows and the government was complex. Officials considered participation in the shows a good way of keeping potential troublemakers off the reservations and safely involved in performance. What they did onstage they could not, thus, enact in real life. In fact, about thirty Native Americans captured at Wounded Knee were forced by the army to tour with Buffalo Bill in lieu of prison sentences.[31] In this way, Cody's collusion with the U.S. government in shaping Indian policies through his creation of a theatrical production further blurred the line between theater and history.

Buffalo Bill Cody's Wild West Show, the largest and most elaborate of all the Wild West shows, was an outgrowth of Cody's public persona. Like Davy Crockett, Cody, a former Indian scout, created a publicity machine for himself fueled by dime novels and melodramas in which he himself starred. His reputation was based in large part on his role in destroying the West. Cody was said to be personally responsible for killing 4,280 buffalo, hence his nickname. The novels and stories about the daring exploits of the former army scout and marksman, written by Ned Buntline (Edward Z. C. Judson) and Prentiss Ingraham, created a foundation for Cody's legend and permitted him to transform himself into Buffalo Bill. Beginning in 1872 his appearance in melodramas based on books about his own life added extra resonance to his legend. For four years Cody continued his work as a scout and guide on the plains when he was not representing himself onstage. As time went on, though, he spent more and more energy re-creating western life on-stage, hiring frontiersmen such as Wild Bill Hickok as well as a few Indians to add authenticity to his presentation. By 1883 Cody had opened his first Wild West Show.[32] Nearly from the beginning the shows were extremely popular. In 1885 over a million people attended Buffalo Bill's shows. The early performances featured reenactments of historical events, such as an Indian attack on the Deadwood stagecoach, and exhibitions of western skills, such as roping and riding wild bison and riding wild Texas steers. Within two years of the opening of Cody's presentations, over fifty rival shows had imitated its features.

The theatricalization of the Native American experience was nothing new. After all, the first U.S. playwriting contest, announced by actor Edwin Forrest in 1828, stipulated that the "hero, or principal character" of the five-act tragedy "shall be an aboriginal of this country."[33] The resulting contest winner, John Augustus Stone's *Metamora*, provided Forrest with the role that he was to inhabit for over forty years and that would make his fortune.[34] Naturally a wave of imitations followed. However, what was new about the Wild West show was that Native American experience was not only performed but enacted by the Indians themselves. Moreover, it was offered not, as in the Barnum shows, as part of a mélange of other theatrical events (the display of freaks, the delivery of lectures, or the performance of minstrel shows), but as the show's focus.

The Wild West show, far from being treated by the press as mere entertainment, was accorded the elevated status of a national educational institution. An 1886 *New York Daily News* review lauded the show for having "happily combined instruction and pleasure," while warning that "the scenes enacted here by savages, scouts and cow-boys are pictures of what has occurred and will occur just as long as the Indian is a savage and the great lands on our immense frontier are unsettled."[35] The *St. Louis Globe Democrat* gushed, "Every man, woman and child in the country should see it, not only as a means of an hour or two's amusement, but as a matter of historical education."[36] The show was not only described as educational but was touted by the Rahway, New Jersey, *Censor* as a uniquely American form of pedagogy, said to surpass traditional European means of learning history: "Boys and girls of this Eastern country and old manners learn more of the aborigines of the greater New World in one afternoon at Erastina than they can in a month in the Astor, Oxford, Cambridge or other libraries of modern times."[37]

In this most American of educations, the authenticity—ethnic and otherwise—of the performers was stressed above all. As one review put it, "The performers are genuine cowboys, Mexican vaqueros and wild Indians, and they simply go through in mimic the same performances by which they have been making a livelihood for years."[38] In an age in which scientists ranked ethnic groups on an evolutionary scale, reviewers considered the Wild West show to have not only historical but scientific merit. Other reviewers praised the quality of the human specimens displayed. One wrote, "Ethnologically considered, therefore, the exhibition has merit. Cossacks, Indians, Arabs, cowboys and Mexicans are the very best of their kinds."[39] The Indians, wrote another journalist in 1886, "are perfect specimens of their race and tribe."[40] Many reviews, in fact, presented the show as a lesson in anthropology. The reviewer for the *Philadelphia Evening Bulletin* stated, "No better opportunity was ever offered the people of the East to witness the various features of wild Western life and to study the habits and customs of the Aborigines than is now afforded by" the show.[41] The *Sunday Dispatch* cautioned readers, "It is difficult to disabuse the public of the idea that this entertainment is a 'show.' . . . The work done here is not the result of rehearsal, it is not acting, it is nature itself."[42] Thus the authenticity of the show extended, in this reviewer's mind, beyond the identity of the performers themselves. They were not, he believed, skilled performers enacting well-practiced routines but simply Indians in a state of nature.

Although the government may have valued the Wild West shows for custodial reasons, Indian Bureau officials engaged in civilizing Indians through the boarding school system also recognized the power of the shows to shape public perceptions of Native Americans. The same year that the Wounded Knee massacre occurred, Thomas J. Morgan, the commissioner of Indian affairs, issued a report to the secretary of the interior in which he decried Indian participation in these performances: "The schools elevate, the shows degrade."[43] The struggle over whose version of the Native American the public would see was played out most dramatically at the Columbian Exposition of 1893, where the Indian Bureau opened a model school at which Indian youths were expected to sew, study, recite lessons, and cook meals for the entertainment and edification of visitors. The school was among the least popular of the exposition's attractions. The ethnographic exhibit representing "the ancient people of the New World" was mobbed, and outside the fairgrounds Buffalo Bill's show, banned from the exposition's official activities, was besieged by visitors.[44]

Assimilationists feared that the Wild West performances, in fact, were detrimental to Indians just because the ethnic representations they offered were frozen in time. Chauncey Yellow Robe, a Sioux who costarred with Chief Buffalo Child Long Lance in the 1930 film *Silent Enemy*, inveighed against the shows in a speech he delivered at the Fourth Annual Conference of the Society of American Indians. "How can we save the American Indian," Yellow Robe asked, "if the Indian Bureau is permitting special privileges in favor of the wild-west Indian shows, moving-picture concerns, and fair associations for commercializing the Indian? This is the greatest hindrance, injustice, and detriment to the present progress of the American Indians towards civilization." While the commodification of Indian identity bothered Chauncey Yellow Robe, he was also disturbed by the anachronism of the images being presented by the shows: "We see that the showman is manufacturing the Indian plays intended to amuse and instruct young children, and is teaching them that the Indian is only a savage being."[45]

Ironically enough, however, while audiences and reviewers thrilled to the authenticity of the Indians' performances, the show provided an opportunity for Native Americans to escape the historical roles in which they were trapped. They could leave the reservations for a while, see the world, and gain experience and money. Moreover, as historian L. G. Moses concludes, participating in the Wild West shows was a positive experience for the Native Americans in that it helped them create a pan-tribal identity without weakening tribal ties, and it enabled them to earn a reasonably good living reenacting episodes from their history.[46]

As time went on, reviews began to frame the value of the Wild West show in elegiac terms: "The days of heroic daring, hairbreadth escapes, dire massacres and wild rides across the plains were revived by this wonderfully realistic exhibition. The engine's shriek has taken the place of the red man's war whoop, the shovel and pickaxes have supplanted the scalping knife and tomahawk."[47] While all reviews from this period

Native American participants in the Wild West shows could leave the reservations for a while, earn some money, and see the world. (Photo courtesy of Denver Public Library, Western History Department; photo by Pablo Salviate.)

(or at least the reviews Buffalo Bill clipped and saved in his scrapbook) stressed the cultural importance of this authentic experience, perhaps none went so far as the assessment published in *Brick Pomeroy's Democrat* on July 3, 1886:

> It is not a show. It is a resurrection, or rather an importation of the hotest [*sic*] features of wild Western life and pioneer incidents to the East, that men, women and children may see, realize, understand and forever remember what the Western pioneers met, encountered and overcame. It is in secular life what the representation of Christ and the apostles proposed to be in religious life, except that in this case there are no counterfeits but actual, living, powerful, very much alive and in earnest delegates from the West, all of whom have most effectively participated in what they here re-produce as a most absorbing educational realism.

While the Wild West Show initially focused on the settler/Indian opposition, in time the performances broadened to include other ethnic conflicts, real or invented. By the end of the century the Wild West Show highlighted the competition between ethnic groups. A popular specialty race involved four teams: Filipina Woman versus Indian Squaw, Mexican versus Filipino, Arab Woman versus American Girl, and Cowboy versus Cossack.[48] In an age of imperialism, especially as the United States entered the Philippine-American War in 1899, the Wild West Show provided a playful, amicable version of ethnic conflict. As the Wild West Show expanded its purview to include more and more acts from around the world, newspapers hailed it not only as an education in history but as a lesson in how people of different ethnicities could get along. "This march through the streets of such widely different peoples and military of various countries, is one that marks the progress of man's brotherhood, and is the first exemplification that in time knowledge and acquaintance, will dispel racial prejudices and national hatred, and emphasize the fact of all mankind's kindredness," the *Morning Union* of Bridgeport, Connecticut, reported on the street parade preceding the 1897 show.

> There was seen the fast disappearing race—"the last of the Mohicans"—marching by the side of his erstwhile foe, now friend, the scout and frontiersman. United States cavalry carried "Old Glory," the star-spangled banner, alongside the English-Irish royal lancers and the cross of St. George, the German cuirassier, with the black eagle of Germany, while the noted cowboy band added patriotic impulses to each with the strains of "Wacht am Rhine," "God Save the Queen," "St. Patrick's Day" and "Yankee Doodle." As this assemblage of sons of fighting forefathers marched to the spirit of peace, the Russian Cossack from Caucasus, the gaucho of South America, the Mexican ruralle, the Texas ranger, the Asiatic Tartar, Spanish vaquero, the Bedouin Arab, and that latest addition to historical horsemen, the American cowboy, formed a collection—and all on horseback—that presages the dawn of universal friendship—the millennium.[49]

Nowhere in the review was there an acknowledgment that this parade was, in fact, a performance rather than a spontaneous demonstration of amity. Ethnic theatrics became, in this review, a stand-in for reality.

Buffalo Bill's Wild West Show traded heavily on its authenticity, which it pointedly contrasted with the lack thereof in other forms of ethnic entertainment. Buffalo Bill positioned himself in opposition to the ironized authenticity offered by Barnum and Barnum's imitators, and reviewers cooperated in promoting his vision. A reporter for the *Manchester Chronicle*, in a piece titled "The Red Indian: A Premier Attraction at the Wild West Show," began his article with an anecdote:

A forlorn-looking negro was seen the other day hanging around the entrance to the Wild West Show in Manchester, and when questioned as to his business, declared that he wanted to see Buffalo Bill in order to get a job of some kind. He hailed originally from one of the Southern States of America, but had been some years in England. Asked what kind of work he had been accustomed to, he declared that recently he had been labouring at the Salford Docks, but previously was engaged as "a Zulu chief" in a South African exhibition which was lately before the public.

That the element of the fake enters very largely into the average showman's methods is pretty generally recognized, and so long as the public were entertained, it might be argued that it really didn't matter much whether "the Zulu chief" were a Zulu or a negro. But in regard to Buffalo Bill's exhibition one cannot but be convinced that no such principle is admitted.[50]

As we have seen, this reviewer was merely joining a chorus of commentators who accepted the Indian performances in the Wild West Show not only as authentic but as reality rather than staged entertainment. Cody offered the public an iconic version of the Native American. He recruited only from the Plains tribes, principally the Sioux, and offered the public the same images—over and over again—of Indian clothing, Indian dwellings, and Indian behavior.[51] With his insistence on authenticity, Cody encouraged audiences to take the staged behavior he presented in his show as reality, and he created stereotypes of Indians that persist to this day. These stereotypes, like all stereotypes, locked Indians into a prefabricated image. But they also offered a template for a number of dark-skinned people, who found their options in life limited, a chance to slip into a recognizable role that was more appealing than many of the roles offered people of color.

Even as Native Americans were denigrated by late nineteenth-century scientists as savages who were not yet civilized and, consequently, lower than whites on the evolutionary ladder, other, more flattering (though equally inaccurate) stereotypes persisted. Indians were considered a noble race, albeit one doomed by the progress of civilization, and they were icons of American identity. As historian Philip Deloria writes, "Americans wanted to feel a natural affinity with the continent, and it was Indians who could teach them such aboriginal closeness. Yet, in order to control the landscape they had to destroy the original inhabitants."[52] While Deloria has written extensively about how white men have "played Indian" throughout the history of the United States, Indianness has also been a means for people of color to escape the straitjacket of racial identity. While persons of Mexican, African, or southern European descent have not always been considered fully American, Indians were unquestionably the first inhabitants of the American continent. Playing Indian, thus, for people of color, has been a means of moving beyond racial binaries and into Americanness.

In 1886 the *St. Louis Globe Democrat* noted with interest the addition of the "famous California huntress," Lillian Frances Smith, who went by the title "The California Girl," to Buffalo Bill's Wild West Show. "Miss Lillian Smith, fifteen years old, who is with the Buffalo Bill Wild West, has a most remarkable record for a child of her years. It reads like a romance, and many of her feats with the rifle are marvelous," gushed the reviewer.[53] *Brick Pomeroy's Democrat*, in a section titled "Wild West Celebrities," described Smith as being "as modest and beautiful as she is accomplished with her single-barreled repeating rifle."[54] The accompanying picture depicted Smith, who was given equal billing with Annie Oakley in reviews and public relations material, as a genteel girl wearing a feathered hat and a lace collar, with her hair done up in curls. Some reviews gave her greater importance than Oakley, and when Smith was presented to Queen Victoria in 1887, she charmed the monarch by showing her how to operate her rifle.

However, Lillian Smith did not last with the show. An 1889 letter home from C. L. Daily, one of Cody's cowboys, reported that "Jim Kid, my tent mate, has been having a great time lately. He received a letter a few days ago saying that his wife (Lillian Smith) had gone off with another cowboy, Bill Cook, by name, half white and half Indian. He was with the show last year and was a great friend of Kid's. When Jim got the letter, he almost went crazy. . . . He thinks an awful sight of Smith."[55]

Smith disappeared from Buffalo Bill's show, only to resurface as Wenona in Pawnee Bill's Historic Wild West and Great Far East and Cummins's Indian Congress and Wildest West. By 1902 the heading on her stationary read, "Wenona and Frank, the World's Champion Rifle Shots," and in smaller print, "Formerly Frank and Lillian Smith." The publicity material for Pawnee Bill's show described her as "Winsome Wenona, the Wonder Woman Shot of the World." The accompanying photograph showed Smith with very dark skin and straight hair in braids, dressed in a feathered buckskin costume. "A charming child of nature, reared among the birds, woed [*sic*] to sleep by the lullabies of sparkling streams, awakened of mornings by the call of a thousand tiny songsters, with the wild game ever passing before her sharp, bright eyes, Winsome Wenona grew to be a great shot before she was a grown child," ran the text, which continued by describing "the great Indian Warrior Chiefs" who did homage to her abilities.[56] Wenona appeared as part of Cummins's Indian Congress at the 1901 Pan-American Exposition, and although her known letters end in 1904, she referred to her plans for the upcoming season with the show. A 1907 courier, or free informational program, for Pawnee Bill's exhibition elaborated on Wenona's biography, describing her as "a Sioux Indian girl and the daughter of one of the most prominent chiefs of that nation. 'Wenona,' while a full-blooded Sioux, was adopted by the whites early and educated in their schools. Notwithstanding that she graduated from an Indian school, was raised by the white people and surrounded by our ways, she refuses to renounce the ways of her parents and is still a Sioux and a member of one of her tribes. Her dress is at all times that of the Siouxs and their language she prefers to that of ours."[57] In this interpretation Smith, a voluntary Indian, became an unassimilable Indian. No amount of acculturation into white America could persuade her to renounce her Indian identity or even to speak English except when absolutely necessary. When Wenona died, her *Billboard* obituary dutifully repeated the information provided in her Pawnee Bill show biography.[58]

Smith left no record of the reasons for her shift in identity. However, photographs of Smith reveal her to be dark-skinned (in the lithograph advertisements for the show, she appears pale). Buffalo Bill's show opened possibilities for dark-skinned people to redefine themselves by creating a visual icon of Indianness and an audience for Indian performance. The Wild West show offered a ready-made ethnic identity that an ambiguously dark person could embrace. Buffalo Bill's shows ensured that in the popular imagination, representations of Indian identity were closely tied to depictions of American identity. For Smith and others like her, an identity as a Mexican or an African American could prove a straitjacket. To be a member of a tragically doomed yet noble people like the Indians, however, could be a ticket to freedom.

While Lillian Smith/Wenona may have used her Indian identity as a kind of professional passport, a group of African Americans in New Orleans used the representations of Indian life that they witnessed in Buffalo Bill's Wild West Show to free themselves from racial strictures. In 1875, Jim Crow laws passed in New Orleans forbade blacks from gathering in public squares. The African American groups who had until that point met in the squares to play drums—groups who took

their names from African tribes, such as the Mandingo, the Arada, and the Soso—disappeared. Following the appearance of Buffalo Bill's show in 1885 in New Orleans, they reappeared, but this time as the "Creole Wild West," the "Yellow Pocahontas," and "The White Eagles," among others. Each neighborhood had its own Indian "gang," and on Mardi Gras they would appear in the streets of black neighborhoods masked as Native Americans, a tradition that continues to this day.[59]

By emphasizing the freakishness of ethnic exhibits and foregrounding the dubiousness of their claims to authenticity, Barnum's shows had enabled audiences to unite as a skeptical Universal Yankee Nation.

Lillian Smith, who starred in Buffalo Bill's Wild West Show as "The California Girl" (opposite), transformed herself into Wenona, a Sioux princess (at left). (California Girl photo courtesy of Buffalo Bill Historical Center, Cody, Wyo.; Wenona photo courtesy of Circus World Museum, Baraboo, Wisc.)

Buffalo Bill removed the irony from ethnic authenticity. In doing so he created room for authentic performances of Indianness. Wild West shows may have softened history; after all, the Indians killed in each show got up and repeated their performances in the next act. However, the shows also made it possible for live Indians and would-be Indians to escape history.

Medicine Shows:
Using Ethnicity As a Sales Tool

Kickapoo Indian Sagwa . . . is the only remedy the Indians ever use, and has been known to them for ages. An Indian would as soon be without his horse, gun or blanket as without sagwa.
—Colonel William F. Cody in a Kickapoo testimonial

In endorsing sagwa, the best-known product of the Kickapoo Indian Medicine Company, Buffalo Bill made the natural leap between the Wild West show and its bastard child, the Indian medicine show. Although individual pitchmen had hawked remedies of dubious efficacy on American street corners since the beginning of the nineteenth century, the medicine show—a theatrical form that blended lectures, demonstrations, and sales with entertainment, usually a variety show—only developed around 1870. However, the medicine show in its most distinctive and successful forms, the Indian and the Oriental shows, only emerged with the appearance of the Wild West shows.[60] While Buffalo Bill's Wild West Show enlisted the players in recent historical events to re-create the conflicts and rituals that had changed their lives, Indian medicine shows provided audiences with a funhouse version of Indian life.

Medicine shows depended for their success on audiences familiar with the conventions of the Wild West show. While Wild West shows were vehicles for Indians to escape reservations and experience the wider world, medicine shows were often populated only by Euro-American "Indians." While the more reputable Wild West shows strove for authenticity, medicine shows existed solely as a vehicle for selling a product, by any means necessary. The medicine shows, which by the mid-1880s had evolved into Barnumesque extravaganzas, borrowed from every area of nineteenth-century theater. Just as slave narratives were the nineteenth century's form of ethnic representation most clearly designed to decommodify identity, so the medicine shows offered the most obvious form of ethnic commodification.

The Kickapoo Indian Medicine Company was perhaps the best known of all the Indian medicine shows that flourished from the 1880s until well into the 1930s in rural areas. The Kickapoo company structured itself like a Wild West show, with one crucial difference: its aim was neither entertainment nor edification but selling health products. The Kickapoo company was headed by two white entrepreneurs. "Doc" Healy was a New Haven-based salesman of King of Pain liniment who used his profits from the enterprise to launch Healy's Hibernian Minstrels, a novelty version of a blackface troupe. His partner, Charles "Texas Charlie" Bigelow, was a Texan who had gotten his start touring with a bogus Indian medicine man who billed himself as Dr. Yellowstone. The Kickapoo touring shows claimed to employ up to eight hundred Indians. During the 1880s and 1890s they generally had about a hundred real and impostor Indians on the road to perform shows and peddle the laxative sagwa (a compound of herbs, buffalo tallow, roots, bark, leaves, gum, and alcohol) to small-town audiences. While they sometimes hired Indians from reservations, they also lured away Buffalo Bill's employees or resorted to Indian impersonators. The medicine show functioned as a parody Wild West show. Just as Buffalo Bill worked with U.S. government Indian agents to employ Indians from reservations, so the Kickapoo company hired "Indian agents" devoid of gov-

ernment jobs to recruit performers, and white "Indian fighters" innocent of battle experience to manage the shows.

The Kickapoo building in New Haven was decorated with a hodge-
podge of spears, teepees, shields, and other Native American paraphernalia. Promotional literature for the company invited patrons to "visit
the uncultured sons of the plain and forest, who assist in carrying on
one of the most original enterprises on the continent. . . . The clothing
and food supplies of the band are scattered about with that unstudied
elegance of disorder which, as the initiated are well aware, forms a great
attraction to the free and easy red and pale faces, constituting the grand-
est charm of life away from the trammels of civilization."[61] Of course,
"the initiated" to which the pamphlet referred were individuals who
had attended Wild West shows and understood how Indians *should*
appear. The Wild West show and the medicine show were mutually
reinforcing entities.

Dime novel westerns, too, created a background for audiences to
understand the medicine shows. In fact, Nevada Ned Oliver, one of the
most successful writers of the genre and author of works such as *Mexican Bill, the Cowboy Detective* (1889), also worked as an Indian agent
for the Kickapoo company. Although the literature produced by the
firm implied that the show focused on ethnographic performances by
Native Americans, showcasing authentic rituals, a typical Kickapoo performance might also include Irish and blackface comedy. The exhibitions proved so popular that by the mid-1880s dozens of competing
Indian medicine shows had sprung up, as well as medicine shows that
relied on the commodification of other ethnicities. Of all the ethnic
performances of the nineteenth century, medicine shows were the
arena in which ethnic imposture was paramount, where ethnicity was
most clearly commodified for advertising purposes.

One of the most compelling accounts of medicine show life was left
by medicine woman Violet McNeal, who in 1904, at age sixteen, ran
away from home on the farm to the big city. There she met and
"married"—in a ceremony she later discovered was a sham—an opium-
addicted medicine showman. Quickly addicted herself, she became initiated into life with the medicine show at the St. Louis World's Fair,
where she first learned to ballyhoo a crowd. Although Indian shows
were common, hers was an Orientalist performance, in which the purported wisdom of the East lent authority to nostrums. Working as Princess Lotus Blossom, she read minds and offered healing potions to the
crowds of rubes who were her customers. Because she posed as an

Oriental, her audience presumed she had access to mystical secrets as well as medical knowledge unavailable to white Americans.

The Chinese Exclusion Act of 1882, which banned Chinese immigration for ten years, was passed as a generation of performers embarked on careers as medicine show "Oriental" princesses and mystics, who used their imagined ethnicity to envelop themselves in a cloak of authentic expertise. By definition Asian immigrants of that period could never become Americans. The Naturalization Law of 1790, not repealed until 1952, specified that naturalized citizenship was only available to "whites." Thus Asians who had been living in the United States for decades would always be defined as foreign, as other. Asians, shoved to the margins of American identity, were central in the medicine show as purveyors of exotic wisdom. Except, of course, in the medicine shows there were no real Asians.

In the medicine show world, the fiction of ethnicity did not require strict attention to authentic details. Rather, it required a great deal of collusion between performer and audience. The desire of audience members to buy products from legitimate experts seemed to override any sense of irony or skepticism that might have prevented them from purchasing with confidence. For example, in *Four White Horses and a Brass Band* McNeal described one of her fellow performers, the well-known Arizona Bill: "His story was a mixture of heartbreaking tragedy and peril. He had, he told the audience, been stolen by Indians when he was an infant. The chief of the tribe had adopted him, and thus he had access to their most intimate tribal secrets." Although his invented autobiography conformed to a story-line with which all readers of dime novels were familiar, his accent did not: "Arizona Bill was actually a Welshman and spoke with a cockney accent, but that didn't make any difference to the yokels. They still bought" (36).

In the distorted world of the medicine show, oppression was rewritten as empowerment. Asian immigrants, defined by law as un-American, became in the medicine show powerful exotics. Slavery, which in America was a devastating experience, became in the medicine show narratives an occasion for triumph.

Half-breed Mexican [Prince Nanzetta's] story was a variation of the Indian-abducts-child pitch. As a youngster, so the pitch went, he had accompanied his father on an expedition into the remote fastnesses of the Himalayan Mountains. There the natives had captured the group. With the bloodthirsty callousness historically associated with their race they had put to death, employing intricate tortures, the entire party with the exception of young Nanzetta. Him they had spared for training as a slave. He was taken to the forbidden city of Lhasa, where he was made to wait on the priests. So proficient did he become in the art of medicine as practiced by the priests that they made him a prince. (59)

In the medicine show narrative the line between slave and prince was easy to cross; the prince had slavelike subjects himself: "The prince was the vainest man I have ever met," wrote McNeal. "He was always accompanied by a large Negro who acted as his valet. The Negro's wages depended on how many times he called Prince Nanzetta 'Your Royal Highness' in public" (59).

Not only were these power relationships inverted, but the ethnicities of the performers—and their projected social class—could change at any time. Although most pitches were memorized and performed with little variation, even year after year, "an exception to the single-pitch rule was Curly Thurber, the ex-I.W.W. agitator. There was no telling in what disguise Curly was going to crop up next. One week, dressed in Indian costume, he would be Chief High Eagle. The following week would find him decked out in turban and flowing robes, posing as a swami, and the week after he would be plain Curly Thurber, exhorting his 'fellow workers' to buy" (161). Thus Curly used the disguise of himself—ex-radical organizer—to sell medicines as readily as he employed other costumes. His anticapitalist political identity could be commodified as easily as any other. The rule was, after all, to use whatever ethnic or class identity would sell the most product. For these medicine show workers, many of whom crossed back and forth over the Canadian border with ease and frequency, the ethnic pitches were most useful for their own countrymen and countrywomen. In Vancouver, notes McNeal, "I discarded the Chinese-princess and Americanized my lecture. The Canadians, I had observed, didn't have the touching faith in Chinese medicines that Americans had" (229).

Although medicine shows were hampered by the Pure Food and Drug Act of 1906, they continued until World War II. Generations of small-town Americans gained their impressions of "exotic" ethnicities through these commodified representations. Moreover, they bought products identified with ethnicity to cure their ills. In this way, by the turn of the twentieth century Americans had grown accustomed to the performance of ethnicity but were, paradoxically, basing their essentialized ideas about race and ethnicity on medicine show performances. Audiences were used to seeing African Americans represented by Irish Americans; Native Americans, by themselves; and just about every other nonwhite ethnic group, by medicine show workers. Ethnicity had become a calling card. In an age of theater, from the parlor dramas of everyday life to blackface entertainment and the Wild West show, identity had become something to be performed, rather than an essential quality. The white impresarios who mediated between audience and performers helped to interpret ethnicity to audiences who could then define themselves as white. From the early minstrel shows, in which the line was drawn between black and white and which flattened ethnic differences to create this opposition, modes of entertainment developed that allowed for many shades of brown. Ultimately these productions permitted performers to slip between shades of brownness to find identities that were easier to live with than the ones they had been assigned at birth.

chapter three

Writing American

California Novels of Brown People
and White Nationhood

The 1884 appearance of Lillian Smith, "The California Girl," in Buffalo Bill's Wild West Show was hardly accidental. California figured greatly in the public imagination at that time. Eighteen eighty-four was the year that Helen Hunt Jackson published her best-seller *Ramona*, the novel about shifting ethnic identities that put California on the tourist map and supplied the state with an ethnic mythology that achieved the status of history. As a relatively new state, California seemed unknown and exotic. It provided a perfect site for its residents to work out their ethnic anxieties. Though it once had, like states across the nation, a sizable Indian population, its first settlers were also brown-skinned people, Spaniards and Mexicans of Spanish descent.

California, even before it was granted statehood in 1850, became a locus for people's fantasies about boundless wealth and unlimited possibilities for self-invention. Yet because access to that wealth—and to American identity—was limited by law at the time of the gold rush to persons deemed white, California was also a place where the ability to move from one ethnic identity to another was paramount to successful survival. Thus it is fitting that two of California's foundational texts deployed themes of ethnic impersonation. *The Life and Adventures of Joaquin Murieta* (1854) and *Ramona* (1884) were novels in which the slipperiness of American identity was made evident; they were also sites for working out the problematics of American identities. While these texts concern ethnic identities, they also provide definitions of a singular American identity. They offer a view of Americanness as an operational identity that could be used when needed.

From its beginnings, California had been a place where passage from one national or ethnic identity into another seemed possible. After all, the first permanent American residents had been two sailors, a black man known as Bob and a white man from Boston, Thomas Doak, who in 1816 jumped ship off the California coast. They became Spanish citizens, married Californian women, and changed their names to Felipe Santiago and Juan Cristòbal.[1]

The multicultural nature of Californian society became even more pronounced with the discovery of gold there. As Malcolm J. Rohrbough writes, "California and its Gold Rush brought together the most diverse societies in the nation, and probably in the world."[2] Yet diversity was no guarantee of tolerance. Rhetorically, stereotypes ruled. As *The Annals of San Francisco* (1855), a well-respected account compiled by local newspapermen, described the population of San Francisco,

> All races are represented. There were hordes of long pig-tailed, bleareyed rank smelling Chinese, with their yellow faces and blue garbs; single dandy black fellows, of nearly as bad an odor, who strutted as only a negro can strut in holiday clothes and clean white shirt; a few diminutive Maylays, from the western archipelago, and some handsome Kanakas from the Sandwich Islands; jet-black straight-featured Abyssinians; hideously tatooed New Zealanders; Feejee sailors and even the secluded Japanese, short, thick, clumsy and ever bowing, jacketed fellows.[3]

This crudely racist stereotyping reflected a society increasingly divided by access (or lack thereof) to gold. For among the Mexicans, Hawaiians, Chileans, Welsh, and Chinese miners were the Anglo-Saxon Protestants who traveled from the East to mine gold, bringing with them an ideology of Manifest Destiny. They brought a notion of applied Americanness, a national identity that had little to do with long-term residence in

California, or sometimes even with citizenship, and everything to do with the profit motive.

The Mexican and Spanish residents of the area, called Californios, were pushed aside in the stampede for mineral wealth, and Anglo-American and European prospectors often used an Indian peonage system in mining their gold. One rancher in Calveras County employed six hundred Indians to dig for him in 1848 and 1849. Forty-niners observed that "the Indians on the ranchos . . . are considered as stock and sold with it as cattle and the purchaser has the right to work them on the rancho, or take them into the mines."[4] By 1849 California governor Persifor Smith was declaring that he considered it his duty to stop mining on U.S. land by "persons not citizens of the United States."[5] That year, Fourth of July orations celebrating the triumph of revolutionary patriots over European invaders sparked riots, in which bands of armed Americans attacked Chilean camps; riots spread.

The gold rush further commodified identity in California, literally so through the 1850 Foreign Miners' Tax Law passed by the California legislature. The measure set up a tax system based on ethnicity and effectively confiscated the earnings of all but "native or natural-born citizens of the United States" who wished to mine gold. The definition of foreigner did not exclude Australian convicts, French men and women, Germans, and other non-Mexicans and non-Chileans who were flooding into California at this time. It was expressly designed to encourage persecution of Mexicans, who quite reasonably considered themselves native Californians and who had lived in California for years or even generations before the "Americans" arrived. In this construct, ethnic identity was based on skin color rather than on prior residency. The many U.S. army veterans of the Mexican-American War who became gold miners certainly contributed to the anti-Mexican sentiment.

Into this context, then, a state where ethnic identity was sometimes indeterminate, voluntary, and often explicitly associated with dollar value, two novels entered California history books as foundational myths. The first, *The Life and Adventures of Joaquin Murieta*, is a fictional biography of an ethnic impersonator. The second, *Ramona*, has ethnic impersonation at the heart of its plot. Neither text is an ethnic impersonator autobiography, but both novels foreground questions of ethnic impersonation. Most important, both novels use ethnic impersonation to ask the question that is at each book's heart: What does it mean to be an American? These novels were separated in their publication by thirty years. *Joaquin Murieta* was written and set in the 1850s, a time when the battles over identity were still being fought. *Ramona* is an elegy set during roughly the same period. However, in the solution it proposed for persons not defined as American, it set the pattern for the ethnic impersonators of the next century. Most important, these novels undermined racial thinking by pointing to its economic roots.

Joaquin Murieta

The Life and Adventures of Joaquin Murieta was authored by John Rollin Ridge, a man from a complicated ethnic background tinged with injustice and tragedy. The book bathes the founding of gold rush California in the blood of many cultures and ethnicities. It is a fiction whose central character became accepted as a real and important figure in California history. Most of all, it demonstrates a solution to racial oppression, which is a kind of equal-opportunity death.

John Rollin Ridge was a half-Cherokee, the son and grandson of slaveholding Cherokees who negotiated the Trail of Tears treaty with the U.S. government. Ridge moved to California in 1850, tried mining during the gold rush, and became a hack journalist and poet. As his biographer, James W. Parins, notes, "Ridge's character embraced a series of contradictions. For example, he was very conscious of his Cherokee identity, yet he wrote in favor of assimilationist policies to settle the 'Indian question.' He took great pains to establish a personal image as a firebrand cavalier while he clearly sought middle-class respectability for himself and his family."[6] His politics became more and more extreme as well. He became a Copperhead, or anti-Union Democrat, and recruited for secret antiabolitionist groups.

Indeed, John Rollin Ridge was a Native American who confounded the Indian stereotypes of his day, and of ours. He came from a wealthy and cosmopolitan background. His father, John Ridge, had been educated in an unusually ethnically diverse environment at the American Board of Commissioners for Foreign Missions school in Cornwall, Connecticut. The board wanted southern Native Americans in order to diversify the foreign population of students at the school. John Ridge's classmates included one Bengali, one Abnaki, two Chinese, one Hindu, two Marquesans, a number of Hawaiians, and three white Americans. While at the school, Ridge met his white American wife, whom he married in Cornwall despite the objections, on racial grounds, of many of the townspeople, who threatened to mob the pair after their wedding.

John Ridge owned eighteen slaves and a farm of more than four hundred acres. Both he and his father were among the few Cherokees in favor of President Andrew Jackson's policy of Indian removal to the West, which they saw as an inevitability best bowed to (they were unusual among Cherokees, to say the least, for going so far as to name one of their sons after Andrew Jackson). The wealthy Ridges voluntarily emigrated westward. The rest of the tribe were forced to undergo the march that has come to be known as the Trail of Tears, which began in June 1838 and lasted until the following January. Four thousand Cherokees, a fifth of the nation, died on the journey. To the survivors of this horror, the prosperity of the Ridges, who were widely viewed as collaborators, was an outrage. In 1839, when John Rollin Ridge was twelve, Cherokee execution squads ambushed John Ridge at his house and stabbed him to death in front of his wife and children; later the squad assassinated Major Ridge, John Rollin Ridge's grandfather. The Ridge family fled to Arkansas after the assassinations.

John Rollin Ridge was educated first at Great Barrington Academy in Massachusetts and then at the Dwight Mission School in Arkansas, a school for white children. Thus he was well traveled and well educated from an early age. He married a white woman and continued the family tradition of slaveholding. Ridge nursed fantasies of revenge against the Cherokee faction responsible for killing his father and grandfather, and at one point he unsuccessfully proposed that his cousin, prominent Cherokee leader Stand Watie, raise a company of twenty-five or thirty white men to search for and kill the faction's leader. Ridge's own killing of a neighbor, a man who was a political supporter of the faction that had killed Ridge's father and grandfather, precipitated his flight to the West in 1850. Although Ridge published poetry and journalism in a number of California papers after giving up his attempts at mining, *Joaquin Murieta* was his only novel.

Ridge's publisher capitalized on the author's ethnicity. The preface to the first edition of 1854 hinted that Ridge, or Yellow Bird, his Indian name, had a life not unlike the one he described in his novel:

> The following production, aside from its intrinsic merit, will, no doubt, be read with increased interest when it is known that the author is a "Cherokee Indian," born in the woods—reared with all that is thrilling, fearful, and tragical in a forest-life. His own experiences would seem to have well fitted him to portray in living colors the fearful scenes which are described in this book, connected as he was, from the age of seventeen up to twenty-three, with the tragical

events which occurred so frequently in his own country, the rising of factions, the stormy controversies with the whites, the fall of distinguished chiefs, family feuds, individual retaliation and revenge. (2)

Ridge, with his wealthy background and sophisticated education, was hardly a child of the forest. His publisher, however, evidently felt a need to make Ridge's biography conform to the prevailing model of Indianness. But it was easier to make Ridge's background conform to the plot of his fiction. Since feuds, stormy controversies with whites, and individual retaliation and revenge are among the chief subjects of the novel, it would seem that the publisher was attempting to capitalize on Ridge's own tragic history in order to sell books. One's suspicions increase with the description of Ridge as "intimately concerned for several years in the dangerous contentions which made the Cherokee Nation a place of blood." Finally, the publisher highlighted Ridge's status as an ethnic curiosity, the first Native American to publish a novel: "The perusal of this work will give those who are disposed to be curious an opportunity to estimate the character of Indian talent. The aboriginal race has produced great warriors, and powerful orators, but literary men—only a few" (3). Like ethnic autobiographers before and since, Ridge must not stand for only himself, but for his people.

The conflation of author with subject and the designation of Ridge as an exemplar of Indian talent were supported in some ways by the text itself. As Parins points out, photographs of Ridge reveal a close resemblance between author and subject. As Ridge described his protagonist, his bandit hero clearly resembled himself:

> He was then eighteen years of age, a little over the medium height, slenderly but gracefully built, and active as a young tiger. His complexion was neither very dark or very light, but clear and brilliant, and his countenance is pronounced to have been, at that time, exceedingly handsome and attractive. His large black eyes, kindling with the enthusiasm of his earnest nature, his firm and well-formed mouth, his well-shaped head from which the long, glossy, black hair hung down over his shoulders, his silvery voice full of generous utterance, and the frank and cordial bearing which distinguished him made him beloved by all with whom he came into contact. (9)

This description, in which a few specific traits are swathed in a fluffy blanket of admiring generalities, could easily fit Ridge. Perhaps as interesting is the generic nature of Murieta's ethnicity: he is a medium-dark-skinned everyman.

While Ridge described Murieta in terms of a generic ethnicity, the editor's preface calls attention to the protagonist's Mexican nationality and holds up the text as a racial education: "It is but doing justice to a people who have so far degenerated as to have been called by many, 'A Nation of Cowards,' to hold up a manifest contradiction, or at least an exception to so sweeping an opinion, in the character of a man who, bad though he was, possessed a soul as full of unconquerable courage as ever belonged to a human being. Although the Mexicans may be whipped by every other nation, in a battle of two or five to one, yet no man who speaks the truth can ever deny that there lived one Mexican whose nerves were as iron in the face of danger and death" (3).

Of course, while calling attention to the courageous exception, this editor firmly reinforced the perception of Mexicans as cowardly. Although he claimed that he was "doing justice to a people," he emphasized their degeneration; rather than breaking down stereotypes, he affirmed them. Like the editor of a slave narrative, this editor insisted on the text's educational value as well as its veracity (while dwelling on the "danger and death" limned by Ridge). Yet while stressing the text's plain honesty, the editor highlighted the literary nature of the history it documented: "The author, in presenting this book to the public, is aware that its chief merit consists in the reliability of the ground-work upon which it stands and not in the beauty of its composition. He has aimed to do a service—in his humble way—to those who shall hereafter inquire into the early history of California, by preserving, in however rude a shape, a record of at least a portion of those events which have made the early settlement of this State a living romance through all time" (3).

Slave narratives were commonly compared by their editors to epics; this narrative documents the "living romance" of California history. Mattie Griffith's slave narrative was more greatly acclaimed by reviewers not for its style but for its lack thereof.[7] Similarly, the value of Ridge's novel rested on its wild, unvarnished, primitive quality. As editors of slave narratives did, Ridge's editor authenticated the story he presented to the reader: "In the main, it will be found to be strictly true" (4).

This statement was not in itself strictly true. *The Life and Adventures of Joaquin Murieta, the Celebrated California Bandit*, wrote Joseph

Henry Jackson in his introduction to the 1955 edition, became central to California's invented history: "It is not going too far to say that in this little book Ridge actually created California's most enduring myth" (xi). Although when Ridge wrote his novel there were at least five gangs of bandits operating in California led by men with the first name of Joaquin, according to Jackson, including one with the surname of Murieta, very little was known about any of them. Ridge incorporated a few fragments of recent history. For instance, the name of the American killer of one of the Joaquins, Harry Love, and the nickname of a known thief and murderer, Three-Fingered Jack, both corresponded to the names of characters in the novel. At the end of the novel Joaquin Murieta's head is cut off by his captors, preserved in alcohol, and exhibited. In fact, a small company of rangers headed by Love was delegated by the state legislature to execute any bandit with the first name of Joaquin, and only this group was entitled to collect a reward for the deed. As an 1853 account in the San Francisco *Alta* pointed out shortly after the capture, "It is too well known that Joaquin Murieta was not the person killed by Captain Love's party at the Panoche Pass. The head exhibited in Stockton bears no resemblance to that individual, and this is positively asserted by those who have seen the real Murieta and the spurious head" (xxv). As Jackson exasperatedly concludes,

> The *Alta*'s view, at least, was that the whole business was a swindle; Captain Love and his men had got themselves a head—any head—had arranged for affidavits that it was Murieta's since he was one of those specifically mentioned in the act authorizing the formation of the company, collected the reward and called it a day.
>
> In light of the legislature's subsequent authorization of another five thousand dollars to Captain Love, it looks like the *Alta* may have been right. The so-called "head of Murieta" was shown in museums for many years, though it was never completely accepted. (xxv)

From an incident involving an impostor head, Ridge wrote his fictional biography of Murieta. Within five years his text had been appropriated. It was plagiarized by a writer for the California *Police Gazette* and published there serially. Many other versions followed, including the five-act play *Joaquin Murieta de Castillo*, a Beadle Dime Library edition, and a DeWitt 15-cent Library version. By the 1880s Hubert Howe Bancroft and Theodore Hittell had published their standard histories of California, quoting the third edition of Ridge's novel as a source for their authentication of the possibly apocryphal bandit. Murieta had officially entered California reality. The *Overland Monthly* and the *Argonaut*, which published recollections of pioneers, included "memories" of Murieta. Subsequent accounts, including a serial version in the San Francisco *Call* from December 1923 to February 1924, took pains to provide authenticating materials for their fictions.

The legend that generations accepted as the reality of California history is deeply concerned with ethnicity. It focuses on the ravages produced by racism, and unlike most books written about California during that period, it does not put the experience of whites at the center of the story. While it preserves some racial hierarchies, it also challenges the placement of whites at the top of the racial ladder. It is also a nearly pornographic catalogue of the violence done to members of dozens of different ethnic groups. In this it strips Americanness of its status as a natural, unexamined category and instead foregrounds how many other peoples—the majority of the Californian population, in fact—had to be displaced, oppressed, or killed for California to exist as an American state.

Ridge begins the book by asserting both its historical importance and its hero's status as a sort of psychotic average citizen. The narrator claims to be writing "not for the purpose of ministering to any depraved taste for the dark and horrible in human action, but rather to contribute my mite to those materials out of which the early history of California shall one day be composed. The character of this truly wonderful man was nothing more than a natural production of the social and moral condition in which he lives, acting upon certain peculiar circumstances favorable to such a result, and consequently, his individual history is part of the most valuable history of the State" (7). Although he does not highlight his hero's race or nationality in introducing him, Ridge does, like his own editors as well as the editors of the slave narratives, drop titillating hints (of what those readers with "depraved tastes" can find in his text, which is replete with "the dark and horrible in human action") and then offers a bland disclaimer. His purpose in writing is, after all, just to "contribute my mite to those materials out of which the early history of California shall one day be composed." Moreover, he proposes Murieta as an exemplar of his people; though he is a "man as remarkable in the annals of crimes as any of the renowned robbers of the Old or New World, who have preceded him," his violence is evidence not of his individuality, but of a predictable reaction to his environment: "The character of this truly wonderful man was nothing more than a natural production of the social and moral condition in which he lives."

Like Ridge himself, Murieta begins his career as a miner, a Mexican who has, in the wake of the Mexican-American War, made a conscious decision to live among Americans: "Disgusted with the conduct of his degenerate countrymen and fired with enthusiastic admiration of the American character, the youthful Joaquin left his home with a buoyant heart and full of the exhilarating spirit of adventure" (8).

From the beginning, then, his story is framed in terms of his feelings about Americans and about the attractiveness of an American identity compared with the one Murieta has had. Unfortunately, what Americanness means is not what he has assumed: "The country was full of lawless and desperate men, who bore the name of Americans but failed to support the honor and dignity of that title" (9). There is already a gap between signifier and signified, between what an American is assumed to be and what he actually is. Americanness is a cloak in which any scoundrel can comfortably envelop himself, and race no longer means anything. In nineteenth-century fashion, the narrator conflates race and nationality: Americanness is as much a racial as a national condition. This version of American identity is exclusive rather than inclusive: "A feeling was prevalent among this class of contempt for any and all Mexicans, whom they looked upon as no better than conquered subjects of the United States, having no rights which could stand before a haughtier and superior race" (9). The race of Americans is unspecified. Does it include all white, native-born persons? Must they be of Anglo-Saxon origin? Do those of Scandinavian background count? French? German? In Ridge's construct of race, blood will tell; cultural traits are passed from generation to generation: "If the proud blood of the Castilians mounted to the cheek of a partial descendant of the Mexiques, showing that he had inherited the old chivalrous spirit of his Spanish ancestry, they looked upon it as a saucy presumption in one so inferior to them. The prejudice of color, the antipathy of races, which are always stronger and bitterer with the ignorant and unlettered, they could not overcome, or if they could, would not, for it afforded them a convenient excuse for their unmanly cruelty and oppression" (9). Although it is possible to show "proud blood," to inherit a "chivalrous spirit"—indicating that race is an essential condition—racial thinking is itself a "convenient excuse" for brutality. This, then, is the central paradox of the book. Race may be a reality, but it is also a construction that structures power relations in ways that are not inherently natural. Murieta is more naturally aristocratic than his persecutors, yet this inner nobility can be destroyed by the treatment his outer appearance— his dark skin, that is—attracts from Americans.

This racially motivated brutality drives Murieta to racial madness and transforms him from a successful miner with a "noble and generous nature" (8) into a bandit. American racists break into his house, demand that he leave his mining claim "as they would allow no Mexicans to work in that region" (8), beat him, and gang-rape his mistress, a woman whose identity is also racially determined, for she has followed him "with that devotedness of passion which belongs to the dark-eyed damsels of Mexico" (9). This is but the first blow. The second is an act of dispossession that is also racially motivated: a "company of unprincipled Americans" seizes his fertile land, "with no other excuse than that he was 'an infernal Mexican intruder!' " (9).

Of course, the fact that Mexican settlers preceded "Americans" to California is irrelevant; the end result is that Murieta's essential self is beginning to change. Racial thinking is essential thinking, yet Murieta's essence turns out to be mutable: "Fate was weaving her mysterious web around him, and fitting him to be by the force of circumstances what nature never intended to make him" (12). Thus when an American mob accuses him of stealing a horse lent him by his half-brother, publicly horsewhips him, and then peremptorily hangs his brother, "the character of Joaquin changed, suddenly and irrevocably. Wanton cruelty and the tyranny of prejudice had reached their climax. His soul swelled beyond its former boundaries, and the barriers of honor, rocked into atoms by the strong passion which shook his heart like an earthquake, crumbled around him" (12).

The achievement of this novel is its description of racism as a force as powerful as race in shaping character. While Ridge describes all his characters in racial terms, his text is concerned with the dangers of racism, which can and does destroy racial characteristics. From this point on, the positive traits of his Mexicanness—his honor, for example—disappear, and Murieta becomes a violent bandit. At first his crimes are specifically motivated: "Report after report came into the villages that Americans had been found dead on the highways, having been either shot or stabbed, and it was invariably discovered, for many weeks, that the murdered men belonged to the mob who publicly whipped Joaquin" (13). His criminal activity soon becomes directed not at the individuals who wronged him, but at their race: "He had contracted a hatred to the whole American race, and was determined to shed their blood, whenever and wherever an opportunity occurred" (14). By this, of course, Ridge meant those white Protestant settlers who had laid claim to the land. Americanness in this case is an exclusive category; as becomes apparent throughout the course of the book, white Protestants are the invisible ethnicity cloaked as American, whereas black, Jewish, or other minority citizens of the United States are described as specific groups. Ridge uses the term "American" in a way that makes clear how distinct that identity is from that of persons who might have American citizenship (such as Jews or free blacks) or of long-term residents of California (such as Native Americans or Mexicans). Americanness is an identity to which few have access; Ridge's continual enumeration of Californian ethnicities serves to underscore this point.

Murieta builds his career by using a combination of Mexican skills (the expert use of the lasso in removing travelers from their horses) and a plea to Mexican national pride: "Appealing to the prejudice against the 'Yankees,' which the disastrous results of the Mexican war had not tended to lessen in their minds, he soon assembled around him a powerful band of his countrymen" (16). Among these characters is one who is almost a parody of Don Quixote, a literarily motivated racial nationalist: Reyes Feliz "had read the wild romantic lives of the chivalrous robbers of Spain and Mexico until his enthusiastic spirit had become imbued with the same sentiments which actuated them" (17).

However, in this romantic, racial battle there are bound to be some of history's losers: in the mountains "inhabited only by human savages and savage beasts, did the outlaws hide themselves for many months" (26). Ridge, the Native American author, plays with audience expectations about Indians. He refers to other Indians as "savages" and intimates that the traits of the Indians mirror those of the beasts. In another passage the narrator seems to refer to himself using the same civilized/savage opposition. Expressing his distaste for hanging, he remarks, "Bah! it is a sight that I never like to see, although I have been civilized for a good many years" (138). And speaking of Murieta, Ridge writes that the bandit's success "would almost lead us to adopt the old Cherokee superstition that there were some men who bear charmed lives and whom nothing can kill but a silver bullet" (139). However, the narrator's attitudes toward the Indians of the text turn out to be complex indeed.

Although the Indians operate in solidarity with Murieta's band, helping them in petty crimes such as stealing horses, they suffer the consequences for the bandits' worst crimes of murder and mutilation: "The ignorant Indians suffered for many a deed which had been perpetrated by civilized hands" (27). That the "civilized" bandits are committing these terrible deeds throws into question the narrator's beast/Indian equation of the preceding page.

Joaquin Murieta travels through a complex ethnic landscape. He encounters "impoverished Frenchmen and dilapidated Germans" (32) in the gold fields, and Tejon Indians, whose children resemble "a black species of water-fowl" (36). Murieta and his gang do not discriminate, for the most part. "Robbing a few peddling Jews, two or three Frenchmen, and a Chinaman, as he went along" (50), Joaquin continues his multicultural tour of California. The closest thing to racism displayed by anyone in the gang is the remark of the sadistic, psychopathic Three-Fingered Jack, who tells Murieta that "somehow or other, I love to smell the blood of a Chinaman. Besides, it's such easy work to kill them. It's a kind of luxury to cut their throats" (64).

When he does make ethnic assumptions, Murieta is always mistaken. There is no guarantee of solidarity between ethnic groups who are equally oppressed by the Americans. The "cunning" California Indians, among whom the Murieta gang spends a few days, "feeling perfectly secure amongst so harmless a people as the Tejons" (37), capture and rob them: "The poor, miserable, cowardly Tejons had achieved a greater triumph over them than all the Americans put together!" (38). Ironically, their triumph is vitiated by a Los Angeles judge who, hearing that the Tejons have captured the gang and are trying to decide on a method of execution for them, fails to take the incident seriously: "The judge, supposing that the capture was the result of a little feud between some 'greasers' and the Tejons, advised him to release them" (39). Just as the gang's racial assumptions about the harmlessness of the Indians led them astray, so the judge's racist ideas about Mexicans set the gang loose to perform another 120 pages' worth of shootings, stabbings, throat-slittings, and decapitations, all described in great detail.

The gang learns to manipulate the racial prejudices of Americans to their benefit. When one member of the gang, Vulvia, is in court being tried for murder, a crime of which he will almost certainly be convicted and for which he will be hanged, Joaquin appears in the guise of Samuel Harrington, a San Jose merchant, flourishing a packet of letters addressed to the man from whom he stole them. He tells the judge that Vulvia is one of his employees and that he had heard that "a dark-skinned man, with grey eyes, was in custody on a charge of murder and that, although there was no positive proof against him, yet there was so strong a prejudice against Mexicans that there was great danger of his being hung by the infuriated populace" (94). Appealing to the judge as an American, he is able to free his hired killer: "'Mr. Harrington,' said Squire Brown, 'Your evidence will be taken without a moment's scruple'" (95). Murieta and his men learn to manipulate American theories of race as they cut their bloody swath through the populace of California. As this instance demonstrates, they survive by playing on current theories of racial difference while obliterating racial difference through death.

There are times when Joaquin takes a humorous approach to this business of racial prejudice. While robbing some Germans, he restrains Three-Fingered Jack from killing them, "remarking that it was better to let them live as he might wish to collect taxes off them for 'Foreign Miners' Licenses,' at some other time" (130). Of course, for the purposes of the Foreign Miners' Tax, Germans would not be considered foreign; in part, what Murieta is up to is redefining the categories of entitlement.

At other times, though, the gang cold-bloodedly assesses the racial worth of a person in the eyes of the Americans and behaves accordingly, as when one gang member kills 150 Chinamen: "It was a politic stroke in Reis to kill Chinamen in preference to Americans, for no one cared for so alien a class, and they were left to shift for themselves" (97).

Although many Americans killed by the gang are described by the narrator in highly favorable terms—one is a "generous, noble-hearted, and brave man" (49); another is "honest and hard-working" (33); and a third is "a fine-looking young man with blue eyes and light hair" (57)—their deaths are recounted in gory detail. One such victim of the gang, for example, falls prey to Three-Fingered Jack, who, "drawing a glittering bowie-knife, sheathed it three times in his breast, then, withdrawing the bloody blade, he rudely shoved him back, and the brave but unfortunate man fell dead at his feet. The ignoble wretch, not satisfied with the successful termination of the combat, displayed his brutal disposition by kicking the dead body in the face and discharging two loads from his revolver into the lifeless head" (49). Although the narrator pays lip service to the tragedy of Anglo-Saxon death, he cannot contain his admiration of the violence. "It was perfectly sublime to see such super-human daring and recklessness" (87), he writes of Joaquin's behavior in another context. Finally, everyone will be reduced to carrion. The endless, carefully documented violence flattens moral differences;

all are killed, none is spared. The cloak of dignity in which the narrator wraps these noble Americans can be rudely ripped away in a second by the bandits, and the corpse of one man resembles another, no matter what his race or ethnicity. According to the racial hierarchies of the time, Anglo-Saxon life was considered more valuable than Tejon life or Chinese life. Ridge refused to honor this convention. In his novel he proffered a vision of a democracy of death.

Similarly, although the narrator makes a bow to sentimental convention, he refuses to endorse it. When Murieta's mistress is weeping at the death of her brother, a gang member, the narrator asks, "Why should I describe it? It is well that woman should, like a weeping angel, sanctify our dark and suffering world with her tears. Let them flow. The blood which stains the fair face of our mother Earth may not be washed out with an ocean of tears" (53). Tears cannot accomplish anything. How different this sentiment is from the assumption of the editors of slave narratives, who surmise in their introductions that the ocean of readers' tears will wash away slavery. Tears in the world of Joaquin Murieta can have a more vicious function. When one female criminal dispatches her brutal husband by dropping hot lead into his ear, the narrator quotes Lord Byron: "Woman's tears, produced at will, / Deceive in life, unman in death." "And the truth of this bitter asserveration was partially illustrated when the inconsolable widow wept so long over the husband whom she like a second, nay, the thousandth jezebel, had made a corpse. It is barely possible, however, that her tears were those of remorse" (81). What is Margarita's punishment for this crime? She marries a younger, handsome man "who loved her much more tenderly than did the brutal Guerrara, whom she so skillfully put out of the way" (82), and stays young and beautiful herself.

Under capitalism, where American racism can be used to disenfranchise any group no matter what its moral claims on the land it occupies, sentiment is often pretty but never effective. Thus *Joaquin Murieta* functions as a sarcastic critique of *Uncle Tom's Cabin*. It undermines the moral authority of suffering and exposes the limits of sentimentality. In fact, Christianity in general is ineffectual in this climate. As the handsome Murieta rides through Stockton on a Sunday morning, the admiring eyes of the townspeople are upon him: "They became so much interested in their conjectures about the young man that it is very doubtful if they paid much attention to the very prosy minister who was then acting as the 'bright and shining light' amidst the surrounding darkness" (67).

Finally, when members of the gang are killed, they submit to their fate coolly and bravely. Even Three-Fingered Jack, "the very incarnation of cruelty, was, at the same time, as brave a man as this world ever produced, and so died as those who killed him will testify" (154).

What, then, is the moral of the story—what is the reader left to ponder, after wading through a veritable tide of blood and gore? "The important lesson that there is nothing so dangerous in its consequences as injustice to individuals—whether it arise from prejudice of color or from any other source; that a wrong done to one man is a wrong to society and to the world" (158).

The Life and Adventures of Joaquin Murieta offered readers a multiculturalism of death, a taxonomic description of California's ethnic landscape that nonetheless insists that racial distinctions are misleading and that racism is the root of the worst kind of violence. Most of all, it shows us ethnicity being used as a commodity, with more or less skill, both by the "Americans" who would use race as an excuse for disenfranchisement and by the bandits who would spread their deadly message of equal opportunity throughout the state. Ridge foregrounded the economic roots of racism. Americans create theories about other ethnic groups in order to steal from them, and this racism in turn can create a brutal mirror-world, that of Murieta's color-blind rapacity.

Ramona

While in the world of Joaquin Murieta everyone has an equal opportunity to be killed, in the world of *Ramona* there is no room for even the most skilled ethnic impersonator. Moreover, by presenting the West and California not as blank slates to be inscribed by American settlers but as landscapes populated for thousands of years, *Ramona* foregrounds the loss of history rather than the birth of a new state. It describes a California in which the old and the new cannot coexist, and one in which American identity is unavailable to all but the chosen, avaricious, white few.

In 1914, thirty years after the publication of *Ramona*, journalists Carlyle Channing Davis and William A. Alderson published *The True Story of "Ramona": Its Facts and Fictions, Inspiration and Purpose*. It was a work nearly three hundred pages long, part jeremiad, part love letter to *Ramona*, and part conversion narrative. In it the authors explained that "various considerations, no longer potent, have prompted the suppression of the real facts regarding the story of 'Ramona,' and the principal characters in it, and there have been circulated innumerable fictions" (33). That thirty years after a novel's appearance controversy would still rage about the provenance of its characters—and about the reality of their fictional world—seems extraordinary. Stranger still were the details of that controversy: "Most absurd of the stories with which tourists are regaled is the one that credits the author with having been bribed to write it by interested parties for political effect, and that the $10,000 thus earned were used in setting up her husband in business. An equally absurd yarn that has found believers of a certain class, credited the authorship of the story to an unfrocked priest, whose nearly completed manuscript was appropriated by Helen Hunt Jackson" (33).

That the book's authorship would be in doubt and that lies would spring up about the reasons for its production attested to the novel's power. As strong evidence was the sheer amount of *Ramona* paraphernalia that had appeared since the book's publication, all of which attempted to firmly lodge the novel's characters into the actual history of California. As Alderson and Davis related, "A brochure that has originated in Los Angeles, and which has reached a large sale, contains a half-tone from a photograph of an Indian woman living near San Jacinto, which the author claims is 'the real Ramona.' There is scarcely a settlement south of the Tehachapi that is not pointed out to the traveler as the 'home of Ramona.' She was married at every mission from San Diego to San Luis Obispo, if one but credits local legend. The real facts, until now withheld, are related within these pages" (34).

In 1883 Indian activist Helen Hunt Jackson found herself dissatisfied with the reception of her 1881 work, *A Century of Dishonor*. Jackson, a New England poet and a childhood friend of Emily Dickinson, was described by Ralph Waldo Emerson, who carried one of Jackson's sonnets in his pocket, as the "greatest American woman poet."[8] Jackson had been but recently transplanted to Colorado when, in 1879, she heard Ponca chief Standing Bear speak about the loss of the Ponca homeland, which had been appropriated by Congress. The experience proved transformative for the previously apolitical Jackson, and she became a strong advocate for Indian rights. The journalistic pieces she began publishing at that point eventually took shape as *A Century of Dishonor*, a history that detailed a hundred years of relations between the American government and the Indians, and that sharply criticized the government for repeatedly breaking treaties and for turning a blind eye to frontiersmen practicing depredations against Native Americans. She sent copies of this work at her own expense to every member of

Congress but did not gain much response from them. Although reviews were positive, public reception was lukewarm. Reformers who read the book eventually took up the cause of the Indians, but for the time being, publishing the work seemed to have been a futile exercise.

It is understandable, then, that in 1883 Jackson wrote to a friend, "If I could write a story that would do for the Indian a thousandth part that Uncle Tom's Cabin did for the negro, I would be thankful the rest of my life."[9] Not everyone would agree with Davis's assessment that "it is not an extravagant claim that the humanitarian impulse now giving direction to the conduct of Indian affairs by the Government had its genesis largely in the romantic novel 'Ramona'" (15). It is more true, given that Stowe's novel was produced in a climate in which there was already considerable abolitionist sentiment, that Jackson's work would have a harder time finding an audience of Indian rights activists. *Uncle Tom's Cabin* reached an audience that had been eagerly awaiting the next serialized installment, "but a far different sentiment awaited the coming of 'Ramona.' It was unlooked for and unwanted. It was most indifferently received," wrote Davis (79).

However, *Ramona* became not only a national best-seller but a national institution. Stranger still, its appeal grew over the years. *Ramona* paraphernalia and cultural productions related to the novel continued to appear for decades after its publication. In 1914 Davis and Alderson complained, "It is among the strangest anomalies of histrionic annals in the United States that the great American novel should never have been successfully dramatized.... Fifty-three distinct failures to dramatize the story have been recorded, while 'Uncle Tom's Cabin' holds the record for the largest aggregate box sales of any American play ever staged" (256). However, the first production, in 1923, of the annual Ramona pageant in Hemet, California, rectified that lack, and the event still draws thousands of spectators each year. In 1914, wrote Davis, the public library of Los Angeles stocked 105 copies of the novel, and yet there was a long wait to get even one. To this date the novel has gone through more than three hundred printings.

To Jackson's dismay, however, reviews for the most part focused on what one commentator termed "one of the most tender and touching [love stories] we have read for a considerable period," while another lauded its success as a love story but complained that it was "a little overweighted with misery."[10] While *Ramona* may be, in part, a tender love story, it is a novel that uses this romance as a means of examining home, family, and nation. It depicts America as an amnesiac nation in which citizenship is predicated on race, on greed, and on the ability to forget the past. Most of all, it presents ethnic impersonation as an essential survival tool for navigating the American landscape.

In its beginning, *Ramona* is a text that enforces ethnic and racial distinctions. The novel opens on Señora Moreno's ranch in Southern California, where Ramona lives. Characters are introduced to us in racial terms: Indians are "patient creatures" (19), and Señora Moreno, Ramona's foster mother, is described as looking "amiable and indolent, like her race, but sweeter and more thoughtful than their wont" (2). The Señora, described in racial terms, is full of racialist ideas. She employs only Indians, not Mexicans, to do her sheep-shearing; she believes that "no Catalan has but bad blood in his veins!" (22). She herself, a Mexican émigré to California and the widow of a Mexican general, "simply grew more and more proudly, passionately, a Spaniard and a Moreno" (25). She manipulates her only son, Felipe, by appealing to his class and ethnic pride: "I shall die content, seeing you at the head of the estate, and living as a Mexican gentleman should" (11).

The clear racial distinctions drawn by Señora Moreno were somewhat uncharacteristic of a woman of her time, place, and culture. By the sixteenth century a legal system had been developed to define people throughout the Spanish Americas. Within this system, as Lisbeth Haas writes,

> The categories of "Indian" and "Spaniard" were ethnic and national designations imbued strongly with racial meaning; they undergirded the system centered on the concept of the *casta* that categorized persons by their purported racial heritage. . . . Yet despite a legal codification that entailed fifty-six such categories in Mexico alone and that regulated marriage, work, and other aspects of people's lives, enforcement of the codes, or of *casta* identities generally, was never systematic. A person's or family's racial status could be negotiated over the course of a person's lifetime, and the regional meaning of race identity (indeed, of *casta* terms) was far from constant.[11]

Thus, the world presented by Jackson was not necessarily an accurate representation of Mexican racialist laws or ideology. It was, in fact, much more reflective of current American theories about race and ethnicity. The stark racial distinctions that the Señora draws, however, throw the issue of ethnicity into relief and help to dramatize the book's central debates over the meaning of ethnicity.

Posited against the Mexicans are the Americans, who have fairly recently taken over California and who are defined only in terms of avarice—as the Señora puts it, "running up and down everywhere seeking money, like dogs with their noses to the ground!" (12). Americanness, here as in *Joaquin Murieta*, is presumed to include white settlers of California, emigrants from the eastern United States. However, the landscape of *Ramona* is less crowded with members of different ethnicities than that of *Joaquin Murieta*, and Americans are not so clearly delineated in opposition to blacks, Jews, Tejons, Chinamen, and others. Nonetheless, Americans within *Ramona* are a distinct race with distinct racial attributes: crudeness, brutality, and greed. In short, the Señora has inverted the racial hierarchies common at the time of the novel's publication. Readers accustomed to Darwinist ideas of evolution would find it jarring to think of Americans compared to dogs and other brute beasts. Here as in *Joaquin Murieta*, Americans are described as a race whose primary characteristic is greed. And, as in *Joaquin Murieta*, the linkages between class and race to which most readers were accustomed are inverted. It is the Mexicans who are aristocratic and cultured. They are brown-skinned but do not necessarily occupy a lower place than the white Americans on the class ladder.

The Americans have stripped the Morenos of much of their land, although "it might be asked, perhaps, just how General Moreno owned all this land, and the question might not be easy to answer" (15). The issue of the general's land acquisition provides yet another layer of historical depth to the novel. The Californian land is one step farther, in this depiction, from being a tabula rasa waiting for the arrival of Americans.

The Señora has devoted her life to asserting Mexican Catholicism against the rising tide of Americanism. Setting up a large cross on her land, in full view of travelers, is "a pleasure in which religious devotion and race antagonism were so closely blended that it would have puzzled the subtlest of priests to decide whether her act were a sin or a virtue" (16). "Any race under the sun would have been to the Señora less hateful than the American" (26). For their part, the conquering American troops are contemptuous of a history not their own. Quartered in the church, they "amused themselves by making targets of the eyes and noses of the saints' statues" (20). Besides their avarice and wanton destructiveness, the primary racial characteristic of Americans is their brutality and willingness to shed blood. Although Indians and Mexicans know how to shear sheep without leaving a mark on them, when Americans attempt the task, as one of the Indian sheep-shearers tells his

Mexican employer, "I thought it was a slaughter-pen, and not a shearing. The poor beasts limped off with the blood running" (65). In fact, the Americans themselves are bestial. According to the description of a settler who had commandeered a former Indian dwelling, he "had the countenance of a brute—of a human brute. Why do we malign the so-called brute creation, making their names a unit of comparison for base traits which never one of them possessed?" (252).

As for her foster daughter, the Señora is reluctant to adopt her: "She did not wish any dealings with such alien and mongrel blood. 'If the child were pure Indian, I would like it better,' she said. 'I like not these crosses. It is the worst, and not the best of each, that remains'" (35). Nor is she alone in her opinion. As her head shepherd, Juan Can, says, "A stain on the blood, lad, is a bitter thing in a house" (109). Yet the Señora, with her racialist thinking, may not be expressing a popular opinion: "Ramona was, to the world at large, a far more important person than the Señora herself. The Señora was of the past; Ramona was of the present" (28). The present is a mestizo present.

Thus is the tragedy of Ramona set into motion. She is a girl who does not know her own origins, which make the Señora coldly reject her. Ramona is actually on her second foster mother. The first, the Señora's sister Ramona, was given the baby by the Scotsman to whom she had been promised in marriage, and whom she had thrown over for a mate of her own choice, a brutal officer of the Presidio. Ramona's very birth is an act of revenge. Angus Phail, after squandering his fortune in a state of despair over losing Ramona Gonzaga, disappears. He moves out to the San Gabriel Mission and begins living with the Indians. "Some years later came the still more surprising news that he had married a squaw,—a squaw with several Indian children—had been legally married by the priest in the San Gabriel Mission church" (31). Great stress is placed on the legality of the marriage and the fact that it has been performed by a priest. Yet much else is mysterious. When Angus shows up on Ramona's doorstep twenty-five years after he has been jilted by her, carrying a baby for her, he explains that "you once did me a great wrong. You sinned, and the Lord has punished you. He has denied you children. I have also done a wrong; I have sinned, and the Lord has punished me. He has given me a child." Why the birth of this baby is a punishment is curious, as is his explanation of why he has taken the baby from its natural mother: "That is nothing. She has other children, of her own blood. This is mine, my only one, my daughter" (32).

Out of this mix comes Ramona, as the baby comes to be called, a natural democrat, who "never was seen to pass a human being without a cheerful greeting, to high and low the same" (39). Just as racial classifications are confused in the novel, so are gender conventions. The Señora is powerful and brilliant despite her feminine appearance, whereas her son Felipe, whom she constantly describes as the head of the household, is weak and malleable. Ramona has "straight, massive black eyebrows," which she compares unfavorably with her foster brother Felipe's, "arched and delicately pencilled" (47). Even the way she meets her future husband, the Indian Alessandro, who has come to shear the sheep on the ranch, is a reversal of sentimental conventions. She encounters him as she is repairing a beautiful white lace altar cloth that has been torn and trampled in the mud by animals, rendering whole again this cheap and easy symbol of defilement of purity. Given that white female virginity is rendered in racist thinking as a beautiful garment that can be permanently destroyed by beasts of another race, it is significant that here the opposite occurs, even as Alessandro is described in animal terms: "He halted, as wild creatures of the forest halt at a sound" (55).

Jackson undermines the edifice of racial thinking with one hand and then shores it up with the other. Pablo, Alessandro's father, is, "for one of his race, wise and far-seeing" (61). Yet even as Jackson reinforces racialized thinking, she makes clear that the limitations of Indians are circumstantial: "The Americans would not let an Indian do anything but plough and sow and herd cattle. A man need not read and write, to do that" (61). The knowledge that his people are to be rendered chattel by the Americans desexualizes Alessandro. If he seems, to his fellow villagers, "a cold and distant lad," it is because he is thinking of the future: "And this was the one great reason why Alessandro had not yet thought about women, in way of love" (62). However, Alessandro, while he may have a greater political reason for not falling in love, reverts to his blood when he finally encounters Ramona: "If he had been what the world calls a civilized man, he would have known instantly and would have been capable of weighing, analyzing, and reflecting on his sensations at leisure. But he was not a civilized man; he had to bring to bear on his present situation only simple, primitive, uneducated instincts and impulses" (63).

Just as Jackson undermines racial thinking, so does she critique the notion of civilization. Juan Can, the Señora's head shepherd, can think only in terms of racial categories. To him "an Indian was an Indian, and that was the end of that. The gentle courteousness of Alessandro's manner, his quiet manner, were all set down in Juan's mind to the score of the boy's native amiability and sweetness" (87). Alessandro is guided by "the tireless caution and infinite patience of his Indian blood" (144). Although readers may have been encouraged by the book's narrator to share, at times, Juan's beliefs, they would be wrong to do so. Comparing Alessandro to Felipe, Jackson notes that "when it came to things of the soul, and of honor, Alessandro's plane was the higher of the two. Felipe was a fair-minded, honorable man, as men go; but circumstances and opportunity would have a hold on him they could never get on Alessandro. Alessandro would not lie; Felipe might" (87). (Yet even Felipe considers that Alessandro's wonderful manners are a racial matter: "I've seen other Indians, too, with a good deal the same manner as Alessandro," he tells his mother. "It's born in them" [103].) Only when racial distinctions are set aside is it possible for characters to fully grasp their situations, to fully see one another. After an interchange with Alessandro, "Ramona gazed after him. For the first time, she looked at him with no thought of his being an Indian,—a thought there had surely been no need of her having, since his skin was not a shade darker than Felipe's; but so strong was the race feeling, that never till that moment had she forgotten it" (89).

Skin color, thus, is not a marker of race. In the absence of visual cues, race is indeterminate. This begs the question of what race means, for if there is no visual difference between an Indian and a Mexican, there must be other, inner differences. This view is espoused by the Señora, who can never overcome her own racism. Speaking of the Indians, she asks, "Of what is it that these noble lords of villages are so proud? their ancestors,—naked savages less than a hundred years ago? Naked savages they themselves too, to-day, if we had not come here to teach and civilize them. The race was never meant for anything but servants" (104). Yet Ramona, more sympathetic, deconstructs the notion of race. She had "ceased to think of [Alessandro] as an Indian any more than when she thought of Felipe, she thought of him as a Mexican" (104). "Mexican," in *Ramona*, is the invisible category, much the same way that most novels of the period use whiteness as their invisible racial category.

Although the Señora cannot love Ramona, primarily for racial reasons, she finds herself caught in a bind in regard to the girl's future. Alessandro reasons, "Since she knew that the Señorita was half Indian, why should she think it such a dreadful thing for her to marry an Indian man?" (136). Yet here, in the issue of whether the Señora could approve such a marriage, lies the crux of the novel's debate over ethnicity: Is it genetic or is it environmentally circumstantial? Is Ramona a half-Indian, or is she now a Mexican, by virtue of her position in the Señora's household? The argument is outlined by Alessandro and the Señora. As Alessandro thinks in his moment of despair after the Señora has discovered him embracing Ramona, "What could an Indian do against a Moreno?" (137). As he looks at Ramona, he thinks, "O my loved one, they have made you homeless in your home. They despise you. The blood of my race is in your veins; come to me" (140). As the Señora reflects on Ramona's position now, she thinks, "Base begotten, base born, she has but carried out the instincts of her nature" (147).

However, faced with a choice between a genetic and a positional definition of ethnicity, the Señora opts for the latter. Anxious to prevent Ramona's match with Alessandro, she finds herself faced with opposition for her plans from Felipe, who points out, "You know a great many men would not want to marry her, just because she is half Indian" (167). At this point the Señora pulls out her trump card: "Would you be willing that your own sister should marry Alessandro?" (168). The answer, of course, is no. As for Ramona, "The sudden knowledge of the fact of her Indian descent seemed to her like a revelation, pointing out the path in which destiny called her to walk" (189).

Ramona and Alessandro's destiny is inextricably bound up with the fate of California under the Americans. Their journey to elope from the Moreno ranch begins with Alessandro's return from his village. He had gone there for a few days on Felipe's advice, only to find it had been seized by Americans claiming property rights. Alessandro's father has died of grief, a neighbor has been driven mad by despair, and other Indian families have been destroyed. Even Alessandro's horse has been taken from him. In the moment of crisis, of Alessandro's disclosure to Ramona of the depredations the Americans have wrought and of the life that will be available to her as the wife of a man without land or family, their relationship—and Ramona's ethnic and class identity—changes completely. When Ramona asks him to stop calling her "Señorita," a name that heightens the class difference between them, and points up her Mexican identity, she asks to be called Ramona. Instead, her husband-to-be renames her Majel, an Indian word meaning "wood-dove," and she herself alters it to Majella, a more Spanish-sounding version, telling him, "I am Ramona no longer" (230). However, though she may call herself Majella, the novel's narrator continues to call her Ramona. She has become not only an equal but an Indian as well. When she slips out of her house at night to join him, he does not recognize her at first: "This was surely an Indian woman toiling along under such a heavy load" (226). Ramona herself is delighted with her newfound ethnicity. Pleased with camping out in the canyon, she asks him, "Is it because I am Indian, Alessandro, that it gives me such joy?" (245). She identifies herself to the priest who marries them as Majella Phail, using her father's surname. The priest transcribes it as Majella Fayeel; "The last step was taken in the disappearance of Ramona" (276). Just as Americans eradicated what came before them in order to create their version of California, so Ramona's old self must die if her Indian self is to live. The old Ramona and the new Majella cannot coexist in one person. This both reflects the American tradition of self-fashioning and inverts the cultural logic guiding Indian policy at the time of *Ramona*'s writing. Contemporary Indian policy dictated that Indians must leave behind their "savage" ways, including centuries-old methods of tribal organization and language, in order to become "civilized." As reformer Carl Schurz described it, "The picturesque and proud warrior of the plain or the forest gradually ceases to exist."[12] Ramona is taking the opposite journey.

Ramona and Alessandro's first child is as blue-eyed as Ramona herself and is given the Indian name meaning "Eyes of the Sky." Yet the happy life they have in her first years, living in a small Indian village, soon comes to an end. They are driven out by the Americans who now "own" all the land in the village—driven as far away from the white man as possible. As Alessandro tells Ramona when she suggests moving to Los Angeles, "If they will come to our villages and drive us out a hundred at a time, what would they do to one man alone?" (327).

When they flee, however, the book's first helpful rather than destructive white characters are introduced, defined not as Americans but as residents of southern Tennessee. They are not obsessed by money but are happily poor: "There was hardly to be found in all Southern Tennessee a more contented, shiftless, ill-bestead family than theirs. . . . Good-natured, affectionate, humorous people; after all, they got more comfort out of life than many a family whose surface conditions were incomparably better than theirs" (333). The Hyers are white primitives. In their good nature and backwardness they are the noble savages of the book. They can never be truly American, because Americanness is intimately tied up with greed and bloodshed. Instead, they take the place of Indians; they are characterized as white noble savages. As David Whisnant has suggested, "Like the Indians, mountaineers were ambivalently characterized as noble ('100% Americans of the best stock') or ignoble (inbred degenerates, feudists and moonshiners)."[13] Without carrying any of the racial baggage of Indianness, the Hyers can fulfill one of the traditional functions of Indians in the book: they are the pastoral innocents who can never truly flourish under American capitalism. Here their poverty functions almost as an ethnicity. Although they are, like the other Americans of the novel, white Anglo-Saxon Protestants, they can never truly be identified with the Americanness the Señora deplores. True Americanness is denoted by upward mobility; to be poor, with little ambition for getting ahead at the expense of others, is rendered in this novel as un-American.

Alessandro and Ramona make the Hyers' acquaintance when Jeff Hyer rescues them from a snowstorm and takes them into his home (all the other white characters in the book have been involved in rendering them homeless, rather than sheltering them). Although Hyer's wife, Aunt Ri, is as full of racist ideas as the other Americans they have encountered thus far, she is willing to abandon those ideas. "Well, well, she's fond uv her baby's enny white woman!" (332), she exclaims in wonder when she sees Ramona and her daughter. Although, as she tells her husband, "I've always hed a reel mean feelin' about" Indians (335), she is struck by the respect and affection with which Alessandro treats his wife and compares their relationship favorably to that between white men and white women.

The Hyers function as the reader's cultural ambassadors. Removed as they are from the economic domination of Indians and Mexicans by Americans, they have less of a stake in maintaining racist ideas. They themselves are configured as the folk, the primitive, an essentially good version of whiteness but one that could be lost through civilization.

"Aunt Ri was excited. The experience was, to her, almost incredible. Her ideas of Indians had been drawn from newspapers, and from a book or two of narratives of massacres, and from an occasional sight of vagabond bands or families they had encountered in their journey across the plains. Here she found herself sitting side by side in friendly intercourse with an Indian man and Indian woman, whose appearance and behavior were attractive; towards whom she felt singularly drawn" (335–36). Though she tells her husband that "they're real dark; 's dark's any nigger in Tennessee" (336), she is able to overcome her prejudice. She is surprised that Ramona, with a white father, identifies so strongly with Indian ethnicity, but as the narrator tells us, Ramona "no longer felt any repugnance to the thought of an Indian village; she already felt a sense of kinship and shelter with any Indian people. She had become, as Carmena had said, 'one of them' " (337).

Every encounter between the two families becomes the basis of a comparison between the salt-of-the-earth folk, the Hyers, and Ramona's family. This section of the novel resembles a hands-across-the-water exercise in cultural ambassadorship. Aunt Ri seems surprised by and admiring of every aspect of Ramona's life, such as her skill in interior decorating or her cooking prowess, but she cannot imitate it. Of Ri, her husband, and her tubercular son, Jos, Jackson writes, "Dimly they recognized the existence of a principle here which had never entered into their life. They did not know it by name, and it could not have been either taught, transferred, or explained to the good-hearted wife and mother who had been so many years the affectionate disorderly genius of their home" (338).

Although Aunt Ri, with her folkways and her almost incomprehensible dialect, is not a character with whom any reader of the novel would be likely to identify, she can still express the best, if the most naive, reaction of any Americans in the novel. Told of the Americans' depredations to Alessandro's ancestral village and of the theft of Alessandro's land in San Pasquale, the village where their daughter was born, "Aunt Ri was aghast; she found no words to express her indignation.

" 'I don't bleeve the Guvvermunt knows anything about it!' she said. 'Why, they take folks up, 'n penetentiarize 'em fur life, back 'n Tennessee, fur things thet ain't so bad's thet! Somebody ought ter be sent ter tell 'em 't Washington what's goin' on hyar.'

" 'I think it's the people in Washington that have done it,' said Ramona sadly. 'Is it not in Washington all the laws are made?' " (341). Just as the meaning of Indianness is disputed among the characters in the book, so now is the meaning of Americanness. Ramona treats Americanness as an ethnicity and imputes to Americans racial characteristics. Aunt Ri, on the other hand, sees Americanness as a national identity and herself as an American. However, within the logic of the book, Americanness can only be identified with land-grabbing, and the Hyers, with their folkways, do not see this as right.

" 'It's all cheating!' said Ramona; 'but there isn't any help for it, Aunt Ri. The Americans think it is no shame to cheat for money.'

" 'I'm an Ummeriken!' cried Aunt Ri; 'an' Jeff Hyer, and Jos! We're Ummerikens! 'n' we wouldn't cheat nobody, not ef we knowed it, not out er a doller. We're pore, 'an I allus expect to be, but we're above cheatin'; an' I tell you, naow, the Ummeriken people don't want any o' this cheatin' done, naow!'" (341).

Aunt Ri's idealization of Americanness is portrayed within the text as naive. She represents a lost vision of Americanness, a vision destroyed by capitalism. For not all "Ummerikens" feel as Aunt Ri does, especially not the government officials sent as Indian agents. When Ramona and Alessandro's daughter is sick, the agency doctor initially refuses to treat her because Alessandro is not an "Agency Indian"—is not, as the agent puts it, one of "my Indians." He prescribes medicine without even seeing her. When the medicine causes her to have convulsions, he scoffs incredulously at the idea that he should travel sixty miles to save the dying child.

The death of Eyes of the Sky forces Ramona and Alessandro to flee into the mountains and, finally, drives Alessandro mad. Hounded in their home by the "white dogs" who unfairly accuse the two of stealing cattle and who make sexually suggestive remarks to Ramona, the two cannot get away fast enough. "Take me where I need never see a white face again!" Ramona demands of her husband. "A melancholy joy gleamed in Alessandro's eyes. Ramona, at last, felt as he did" (360). The racial hierarchies embraced by the Americans become quickly enshrined in local custom, even by the Indians themselves. After one white man left the village of his Indian mistress, she "held herself, in consequence of this temporary connection with a white man, much above her Indian relatives and friends. When an Indian man had wished to marry her, she had replied scornfully that she would never marry an Indian; she might marry another white man, but an Indian,— never" (361).

Alessandro, whose "hurts have gone too deep" (366), begins to have episodes of wandering, after which he cannot account for his whereabouts or actions. Even the birth of another daughter, named Majella, is not enough to assuage his pain. This baby, unlike her older sister, has his dark eyes and will, he says, "look ever on woe" (365). During one of his episodes Alessandro wanders off with the horse of a white man. Although everyone in the area knows of and accepts Alessandro's disability, the horse's owner, Jim Farrar, seizes on the opportunity to shoot him for his crime, not once but twice more, in his cheek and his forehead, disfiguring his corpse. Farrar, in a successful attempt to exonerate himself before the law, describes Alessandro as "an Indian, or Mexican, I could not tell which" (374).

The differences that the Señora saw as so important that Ramona had to be banished from her home in order to marry the man she loved have become differences without distinction. Indians and Mexicans have become interchangeable and interchangeably worthless compared with whites. Although everyone in the community knows Farrar to be "a brutal ruffian," the judge will not convict him: "San Jacinto Valley, wild, sparsely settled as it was, had yet as fixed standard and criterions of popularity as the most civilized of communities could show; and to betray sympathy with Indians was more than any man's political head was worth" (376). In a "civilized" world, racism is a tool of imperialism, and only the uncivilized can afford relationships unmotivated by greed.

Felipe, who has finally managed to track down Ramona after a years-long search, has his eyes opened by his quest for her. Struck by the poverty-stricken condition of the Indians he encounters along the way, "Felipe's heart ached, and he was hot with shame, for their condition" (380). He finds that he does not know anything about the world beyond his ranch, nor, as it turns out, does he know much about Ramona. When he comes upon her marriage record, he is sure Alessandro has taken another bride, for "most certainly Ramona would never have been married under any but her own name" (387). He finally comes to San Jacinto as a last resort, and there he meets the Hyers, who bring him to Ramona.

Thus, the Hyers are the only white characters in the book to reverse the racial hierarchies established by the other Americans. As Aunt Ri says, "I take more ter these Mexicans than I do ter these low-down, driven Yankees" (393). Even Merrill, a relatively sympathetic white man who lends his horses and carriage to the Hyers and Felipe in their search for Ramona, although he criticizes Farrar for firing into a corpse, says, "I don't blame him for killin' the cuss, not a bit" (397). When property is paramount, human life becomes secondary.

The ending of *Ramona* fulfills some romantic expectations but leaves niggling doubts in the mind of the reader. Aunt Ri nurses Ramona back to health and even has a moment of transcendence when she overcomes her anti-Catholic prejudices long enough to kneel before the Virgin Mary in prayer with the Indians and Felipe, "a moment and a lesson Aunt Ri never forgot" (400). Ramona returns to the ranch with Felipe. The Señora has died, so there is no one there to remind her of her "tainted" blood. But when she leaves the Indian village, her friends there find that "the gulf between them and the rest of the world seemed defined anew, their sense of isolation deepened, their hopeless poverty emphasized. Ramona, wife of Alessandro, had been as their sister,—one of them; as such, she would have had share in all their life had to offer. But its utmost was nothing, was but hardship and deprivation; and she was being borne away from it, like one rescued, not so much from death, as from a life worse than death" (409).

The traditional consolations of a romantic ending are denied the reader, as the narrator makes it impossible to rejoice in Ramona's individual triumph and forget the fate of her people. As in the ethnic autobiography, Ramona has come to stand not for herself but for an entire people. Ironically, however, Ramona's people are a fluid rather than a fixed category. Paradoxically, Helen Hunt Jackson wrote *Ramona* as an extension of her efforts to increase public awareness of the ill treatment of the Indians by the government. Yet in order to do so, she had to choose not an Indian protagonist, who could be essentialized, but a voluntary Indian. Although Ramona is, in fact, half-Indian, she ultimately chooses to become Mexican instead.

When she returns to the ranch, Ramona becomes the Señorita once again. In fact, she belongs there more than ever: "The friendless, banished Ramona returned now into full honor and peace as the daughter of the house" (417). Not only the daughter of the house and thus Felipe's sister but eventually, too, his wife, she asks "herself fervently now if she would do her brother a wrong, yielding up to him what seemed to her only the broken fragment of a life," although he understands that "part of her was dead" (423). This double bond establishes more firmly than ever her Mexican ethnicity. She renames her daughter Ramona, but this Ramona will not grow up in America. Felipe "was beginning to yearn for Mexico,—for Mexico, which he had never seen, yet yearned for like an exile. There he might yet live among men of his own race and degree, and of congenial beliefs and occupations" (421). Ramona is "the theme of the city" in Mexico City, where they settle down: "It was indeed a new world, a new life. Ramona may well doubt her own identity" (424). Although we have seen Ramona shift from class to class and from one ethnicity to another, it seems that she still cherishes an identity that must now remain secret: "But undying memories stood like sentinels in her breast. When the notes of doves, calling to each other, fell on her ear, her eyes sought the sky, and she heard a voice saying, 'Majella!'" (424). Yet this she keeps a secret from Felipe. In the end, the daughter that both parents love most of the many children Ramona bears is the new Ramona, the Indian child who will grow up as Mexican.

Although Ramona shifts from one ethnicity to another and is the product of a complicated multicultural society, it seems that not only ethnic shifting but the embrace of any ethnicity except whiteness is impossible in America. Ramona can have a happy ending of sorts only when she leaves the country that presents choices too painful for her to make. The lesson of *Ramona* is that it is impossible to have multiple identities, that one identity must be eradicated.

Helen Hunt Jackson's goal—to engage public interest in the oppression of the Indians by the U.S. government—could be most effectively achieved by her choice of a character who was a voluntary Indian, who could move in and out of Indianness, not of an Indian protagonist who could be essentialized as a squaw or an Indian maiden. The Indian part of Ramona's life, however, is associated with traumatic memories of a history that she must suppress in order to live in another ethnicity.

The Real Ramona

Although for Felipe "the ruins of the old Mission buildings were sad to see, but the human ruins were sadder" (380), *Ramona* started not a nationwide movement to save the Indian, but the development of Mission Revival architecture and a thriving tourist trade in Southern California by smitten readers of the novel. As Davis and Alderson wrote in *The True Story of "Ramona,"* "For several years subsequent to the publication of 'Ramona,' 1884, tourist excursions to California were mainly those conducted by a Boston firm, and were composed of New England people. Camulos ranch, the home of Ramona, was one of the places of greatest interest to them; and by special arrangement, the Southern Pacific train stopped at the ranch for a sufficient time to permit the tourists to visit the home of Ramona" (106).

Ramona's story soon became part of California mythology, and some of the people on whom the story was rumored to have been based capitalized on this relationship. Sam Temple, the model for Jim Farrar, Alessandro's killer, "was so elated over his crime and its publication in 'Ramona' that he endeavored to secure financial assistance, that he might place himself on public exhibition, as 'the man who killed Alessandro'" (163). A thriving industry in "Ramona-made" baskets, meant for sale to tourists, sprang up (92). Some of this publicity had unintended consequences. The family upon which, according to legend, the Morenos were based initially welcomed the tourist trade, going so far as to enact scenes from the novel, but soon tired of it. Senator de Valle (the

Helen Hunt Jackson's character Ramona became accepted as part of California mythology. A thriving tourist industry grew up around the history of this fictional character. This postcard depicts Ramona's marriage place. (Photo courtesy of Seaver Center for Western History Research, Los Angeles County Museum of Natural History.)

original, it was rumored, for Felipe) described how the novel affected his mother's family: "They suffered in two ways, he said. The public accepted his mother, Señora de Valle, the widowed owner of the Camulos ranch, as the original of the character of Señora Moreno of the romance, and to her were attributed all the faults, imperfections and eccentricities of Señora Moreno. Public prejudice and criticism were harshly directed toward the noble and saintly Señora de Valle, who was in life the direct opposite of Señora Moreno" (107).

Although Helen Hunt Jackson had intended the novel as a weapon in her struggle for Indian reform, it was generally received as a touching love story. Even readers who loved the novel did not always respond sympathetically to its political message. As Davis, the onetime editor of the *Denver Times* and the *Rocky Mountain News*, wrote of his long acquaintance with Jackson, "Her relation of experiences among the Mission Indians of California was of thrilling interest, albeit comprehension of the import of it all was not easy. Of far greater concern to me was the announced purpose of Mrs. Jackson to tell the story in the form of a romance" (22). Nor was Davis singular in this respect. As he baldly stated, "Mrs. Jackson enjoyed something of a monopoly of her views, and was quite without a genuine sympathizer with her work in the entire State of Colorado. . . . The feeling in Colorado at the time was almost universal that the only good Indian was a dead Indian" (11).

Jackson, in any event, barely lived long enough to appreciate the effects and ironies of *Ramona*. Only months after the book's publication, she died of stomach cancer. Even her grave became a shrine to tourists, and her widower was forced to disinter and relocate her body when he discovered that the owner of the cemetery in which she was buried was charging tourists admission to visit her grave. "The details of her burial on the slopes of Cheyenne Mountain, under the shadow of Pike's Peak, and amidst scenes she loved so much, are familiar topics" (52). Jackson herself had become commodified.

While she did not long survive the publication of her novel, Jackson did hear the first rumblings of debate about the identity of the "real" Ramona. Ironically, her novel about the fluidity of ethnic identity became an excuse for fixing identity all too firmly and of conflating the fictional with the real. Davis and Alderson's book on the subject was by no means the first.

Perhaps the man who did the most to call attention to the "true" identity of the fictional character was George Wharton James. A travel writer and former minister who made Ramona a personal fixation, James did more than any other writer to ensure the commodification of any living person who could be associated with the novel. In his 1908 work, *Through Ramona's Country*, James shared with readers the fruits of his years of research on the subject. "There are those in Ramonaland," he wrote, "who will tell you that *Ramona* is fiction from beginning to end" (22). It is with these critics that he took issue. In fact, James spent nearly a decade researching and writing his book. In 1899 he tracked down Sam Temple, the killer of Juan Diego, the "real" Alessandro. James not only photographed him but in 1900 recorded Temple's version of the killing on an early Edison wax cylinder. And James discovered the woman he called "the Cahuilla Ramona," the widow of Juan Diego.

James found the "real Ramona," a basketmaker in her fifties, on the Cahuilla reservation in the San Jacinto range. It is clear that she did not entirely welcome his attention. "When I first saw Ramona she was at her brother's *ramada* (a small brush shack) at Cahuilla," James explained. "Later, at her own home, she permitted me to photograph her. She promised that on a subsequent visit she would tell all the story of the murder of her husband into my gramophone, I having tried to explain, as fully as I could, the peculiar power of this white man's magical instrument" (156). Ramona Lubo, like her fictional counterpart, had witnessed her husband shot dead by a white rancher during one of Juan Diego's spells, during which he was prone to wander off, sometimes with other people's horses. Like the character Ramona, Lubo had seen her husband's murderer acquitted because she, as an Indian, could not give testimony under U.S. law. However, unlike the Ramona of the novel, she was not able to effect a romantic escape to Mexico in the company of her backup lover. Instead, as James put it, "she herself settled down to the dull and uneventful life of a Cahuilla Indian" (159). It is perhaps not surprising that, as James recounted, "when I arrived at the village a year later she had either forgotten her promise or wished to disregard it, and it took the united persuasions of Mrs. Noble,—the daughter of the much-beloved teacher of the Indian School at Cahuilla, Mrs. N. J. Salisbury,—and myself to prevail upon her to come to the wagon" (156).

James's key to the novel provides a good illustration of how *Ramona* could be read, not as a means of decommodifying identity and inciting readers to work for better treatment of the Indians, as Jackson had intended, but as a means for further commodification. James's attitude toward Ramona Lubo is evident in his description of her as "squat . . . fat and unattractive. With low forehead, prominent cheek bones, wide nostrils, heavy lips, she appears dull, heavy and unimpressionable." Small wonder, then, that her son "refused to show me the grave [of his father], either from the timidity Indians often manifest toward strangers in regard to their intimate personal customs, or because he did not know its location" (160). When James finally pressured Ramona into showing him her husband's gravestone, she was overcome with emotion: "As I put my head under the focussing cloth of my camera, intending to make a picture of her standing there, she suddenly squatted down and, covering her face with her hands, began the soft wailing and sobbing that precedes the louder and more vociferous lamentations of the Indians when they have their *fiesta del Muerto*—feast of the dead. Even after this long lapse of years she could not think of her husband without tears and the deepest emotion" (161). James was touched by the widow's grief and almost, but not quite, unwilling to intrude upon it; in the end he refused to be deflected from his goal. "It seemed like almost a sacrilege to make a photograph of her at this moment, yet I trust she and the recording angel will consider the kindliness of my heart towards her and her people in balancing the amount of my culpability. I did not feel quite so guilty when I asked her to stand by the side of the grave and thus specifically locate it for future visitors" (161). James turned this photograph into a postcard that was widely distributed bearing the legend "The Real Ramona," and which attracted flocks of tourists who visited Ramona Lubo and photographed her for a token amount. The grave of her husband was also a popular tourist destination. His headstone was eventually changed to

Juan Diego
"Alessandro"
Ramona's Martyred Spouse.[14]

Ramona Lubo died in 1922 after she contracted pneumonia while exhibiting herself at the 1922 National Orange Show, at a booth promoting the products of the San Jacinto Valley and the Hemet region. By the time she died, Ramona Lubo was an American. However, the old myths still held sway, and old myths help explain Lubo's poverty. By the end of her life she had gained access to American identity but not to its economic benefits.

In a photograph of Lubo at her booth, she sits surrounded by promotional materials for the fruit industry that had taken over her tribal homelands. She is dwarfed by a smiling beauty queen who, despite her braids and beads, does not look very Indian. It is not difficult to hear the words with which George Wharton James ended his introduction to *Through Ramona's Country*, his apologia for the work: "It is to further contribute to the good work begun and carried on in so masterly a manner and to give to the people at large many facts that nearly thirty years of gleaning have gathered that I have presumed to write the following pages. If they aid in deepening the practical sympathy of the American people for an unfortunate and dying race I shall be gratified" (xvii). In moving away from Jackson's call for radical political change, begun in *A Century of Dishonor*, and shifting to an elegiac stance, James was echoing the mournful, nostalgic view of Indians that had come to dominate public discourse. As representatives of a noble, yet dying race, generations of Native American impersonators escaped their assigned (and frequently problematic) ethnic identities, either in search of personal freedom and power or in order to gain rhetorical power as mouthpieces for causes environmental, racist, or spiritual.

chapter four

One Hundred Percent American

How a Slave, a Janitor, and a Former Klansman Escaped Racial Categories by Becoming Indians

Since the mid-nineteenth century, Americans who have felt trapped within black/white binaries have written themselves into Native American identity and out of whiteness or blackness. Three of these "Indian" autobiographies, the first of which appeared in 1856 and the last in 1976, illustrate both the possibilities and the limitations of such a strategy. The first, *The Life and Adventures of James P. Beckwourth*, was written by a former slave who, rather than joining the forces for abolition, used his autobiography describing his passage into a Native American identity to rewrite himself into whiteness. The second, *Long Lance* (1928), was authored by a former janitor, defined by the racial laws of his time as "colored," who learned how to play Indian while working at a Wild West show—and who enlisted the help of some of the foremost racial theorists of his time to authenticate his Native American identity. Finally, there is *The Education of Little Tree*, the Cherokee orphan's autobiography written by George Wallace's former speechwriter Asa Carter as a means of reinventing and rehabilitating himself from his public past as a white supremacist. Together these three texts demonstrate the many ways in which American autobiographers have employed an Indian identity to negotiate or escape black/white binaries. Most of all, they show how this third identity—Indianness—must be constructed to fit prevailing racist stereotypes in order for these impersonators to succeed.

A Double Passage:
The Curious Case of James P. Beckwourth

The autobiography of James P. Beckwourth was published by Harper and Brothers in 1856, when Beckwourth was fifty-six or perhaps fifty-eight. Dictated by Beckwourth to T. D. Bonner, a con man, temperance advocate, and drunk, *The Life and Adventures of James P. Beckwourth, Mountaineer, Scout and Pioneer, and Chief of the Crow Nation of Indians* fulfills all the expectations its title suggests. Beckwourth's life of western adventure began with his first stint as a fur trapper, work he took on after getting into a fight with the St. Louis blacksmith to whom he was apprenticed as a teenager. Beckwourth's colleagues at the trapping company included William Sublette, discoverer of the geysers at Yellowstone; Jim Bridger, discoverer of the Great Salt Lake; and Jedediah Smith, supposed by many to be the greatest mountain man of all time. Most of Beckwourth's narrative centers on the thirteen years he spent as a war chief with the Crow. But his book also includes accounts of his dozen or so marriages; his later work with trapping companies; his employment as a soldier on the government side of the Seminole wars of 1837; his restless wanderings through Taos and Denver to California, where he discovered the Beckwourth Trail, which became the most commonly used route for pioneers coming from the Great Basin of Nevada to California; and his retirement as an innkeeper at Beckwourth Ranch along the trail.

The autobiography, with its tales of exotic adventure and bloody heroism, was an immediate best-seller and an immediate source of controversy. Typical of the complaints that Beckwourth was no more than a "gaudy liar" was the note Francis Parkman scribbled in his copy of the autobiography. He denounced Beckwourth as "a fellow of bad character—a compound of black and white blood, though he represents otherwise."[1] Parkman, in *The Oregon Trail*, described him as "a mongrel of French, American and Negro blood . . . a ruffian of the worst stamp."[2] In fact, although early historians often acknowledged Beckwourth's status as one of the greatest frontiersmen, they generally linked his veracity (or lack thereof) to his color. Charles Christy, who headed a chapter in his 1908 frontier memoirs "Nigger Jim Beckwith," noted that "Jim was born in that section of the United States where they spell Afro-American with a double g" and went on to call Beckwourth "the biggest liar that ever lived."[3] These historians seemed able only to see Beckwourth in terms of black or white. His autobiography demonstrates both the slipperiness of racial and ethnic identity and the way that Beckwourth himself remained rhetorically imprisoned by the identity trap that he seemed to escape in his life.

Beckwourth, writing when persons of African descent were widely viewed as being either a species separate from—and inferior to—whites, or simply at a lower level on the evolutionary ladder, chose to write himself into whiteness through the deployment of a third identity, Indian. Writing when Native Americans were not yet widely perceived as noble savages doomed to extinction or amenable to civilization but, rather, were considered dangerous threats to the American order, Beckwourth positioned himself in league with the project of white American conquest. Paradoxically, however, he did so by describing his ability to pass as Indian. He lied his way into the tribe by claiming to be a former slave of whites (which he, in fact, was), but a Crow slave, captured at an early age and only recently granted his freedom. Even as Beckwourth insisted, in his memoir, on his own whiteness, he also prided himself on his ability to pass as a member of another race, as Native Americans were defined at the time.

Beckwourth was not white but was born a slave, the son of his master. Although he recounted his childhood relocation to St. Louis, to which "my father removed . . . taking with him all his family and twenty-two negroes,"[4] he was not officially included among the family that he described. Thus the autobiography entails what might be called a double passage, for in it Beckwourth, a man defined by his culture as black, passed as a white man who was passing as Native American.[5]

Even early defenders of the autobiography often centered their discussions around the issue of his race. For instance, the editor of the 1892 British edition of the work (a previous British edition had come out in 1856), while defending Beckwourth's veracity, cited an "authority" as saying that "Beckwourth was the offspring, not of a *negress*, but of a *quadroon* and a planter."[6] A contemporary eyewitness described an

One Hundred Percent American

Although James Beckwourth (opposite) was described by a contemporary as having a "complexion like a Mexican, and eyes like an Indian," he was portrayed in the 1951 movie *Tomahawk* by white actor Jackie Oakie (above). Later works, such as Harold W. Felton's juvenile biography *Jim Beckwourth: Negro Mountain Man* (1966), presented him as African American. (Beckwourth photo courtesy of Colorado Historical Society; Oakie photo courtesy of MOMA Film Stills Collection.)

elderly gentleman with a "complexion like a Mexican, and eyes like an Indian. It is James P. Beckwourth, the half-breed, so long a chief among the Crow tribe, and the most famous Indian fighter of his generation."[7] Even as, in his memoir, Beckwourth described his escape from the strictures of identity, the reception of that work depended on what reviewers saw as the irreducible fact of his race.

That Beckwourth's race as perceived by reviewers determined their response to the autobiography is the second paradox of the work and its reception. While critics writing at the time of the book's publication based their commentaries on Beckwourth's racial identity and attacked him for being black, later generations of critics applauded him as an African American hero, no matter how eager he himself was to escape that racial designation. What one might call this race-based reception of Beckwourth and his work continued for over a century, even as the grounds for it changed. Beckwourth's heritage seemed to shift with the passing decades. In the 1951 Universal Studios western *Tomahawk*, Beckwourth was played by white actor Jackie Oakie. As William Loren Katz wrote in his 1986 study, *Black Indians: A Hidden Heritage*, "Generations of young people never learned that this tough pioneer fur trapper was a black man."[8]

However, Beckwourth's racial identity grew more distinct over the years. The publisher's blurb for Leigh Brackett's 1963 *Follow the Free Wind* described Beckwourth as "a half-breed rebel in search of his identity," but in 1966 Harold W. Felton published *Jim Beckwourth: Negro Mountain Man*.[9] In 1969 the autobiography itself was reprinted in Arno Press's series The American Negro: His History and Literature. Perhaps the greatest sign of Beckwourth's rehabilitation as an African American hero was the 1992 biography for young readers. Complete with an introduction by Coretta Scott King, it was published as part of Chelsea House Publishers' Black Americans of Achievement series, which also includes biographies of Hank Aaron, Paul Robeson, Sojourner Truth, and civil rights leaders James Farmer, Rosa Parks, and Ralph Abernathy. Thus the story would seem to be complete, and the use of the binary restored. As the publisher's blurb describes Lawrence Cortesi's 1971 biography *Jim Beckwourth: Explorer-Patriot of the Rockies*, "Captured by Indians who adopted him as a long-lost brave whose skin had been burned dark by the desert sun, Jim learned to respect and love his tribe." The story of Beckwourth, who escaped the restrictions of life as a black man in St. Louis, seems familiar, a tale of a suppressed history recently unearthed, of oppressed peoples banding together against a common enemy. Yet the truth is much more complicated.

Far from being a tale of the solidarity of people of color in the face of the crushing powers of the government, Beckwourth's autobiography is an apologia for white racism. Rather than expressing unity with the Crow among whom he lived for so long, Beckwourth described them as "savages" and as "wily Indians." His chosen stance is as interpreter to white America of Crow and other Native American culture, "a subject which at the present day is but imperfectly understood by the general reader" (26). His autobiography points up both the fluidity of racial and ethnic identity in the nineteenth century and the dangers of trying to simplify the narrative of race and ethnicity.

Beckwourth's book appeared just a year before the ratification of the Oregon state constitution, which mandated the exclusion from the state of free blacks. This provision was popular among voters. As Oregon's delegate to Congress explained in 1850, the issue of admitting free blacks to the state

> is a question of life and death to us in Oregon. . . . The negroes associate with the Indians and intermarry, and, if their free ingress is encouraged or allowed, there would a relationship spring up between them and the different tribes, and a mixed race would ensue inimical to the whites; and the Indians being led on by the negro who is better acquainted with the customs, language, and manners of the whites, than the Indians, these savages would become much more formidable than they otherwise would, and long and bloody wars would be the fruits of the commingling of the races.[10]

Within the context of this legally encoded fear of racial alliances, Beckwourth's positioning of himself as a white writer makes sense. Mid-nineteenth-century literacy rates among Indians and blacks ensured that he was, after all, addressing a primarily white audience. However, the ambivalence of such a strategy shines through in his comparison of his presumably white self to a slave and in his pride at the success of his racial imposture. Adding another layer of complexity to the story is the fact that Beckwourth, as a black man, had an advantage in trading with Indians, who were more inclined to trust him than his white counterparts. As Colonel James Stevenson of the Bureau of American Ethnology, who had spent thirty years working with and studying Native Americans, wrote in 1888, "The old fur trappers always got a Negro if possible to negotiate for them with the Indians, because of their 'pacifying effect.' They could manage them better than the white men, and with less friction."[11] With his dark skin a commodity whose value was heavily situational, Beckwourth was able to use, deny, and change his racial identity as he saw fit.

While taking care to distinguish his own work from that of other travelers, whose "tales that were related as actual experience now mislead the speaker and the audience" (51), Beckwourth described in detail the way he himself had created a life out of such stories. His life as a Crow began when one of his fellow trappers "invented a fiction, which greatly amused me for its ingenuity" (140). This fiction, that Beckwourth was a small Crow child kidnapped by the Cheyenne during warfare and sold to the whites, is accepted by the Crow. Taking the slavery metaphor further, Beckwourth, who has become a restored favorite son redeemed from captivity, is captured by Crow, who, anxious to verify Beckwourth's false biography, form an examining committee. "I believe," Beckwourth writes, "never was mortal gazed at with such intense and sustained interest as I was on that occasion" (146). In a scene highly reminiscent of a slave market, "arms and legs were critically scrutinized. My face next passed the ordeal; then my neck, back, breast, and all parts of my body, even down to my feet" (146). Beckwourth's false slave narrative becomes an occasion for his ability to move out of a black identity, for this is a story in which the black man whose body is being so minutely examined triumphs. When one of the old women sees a resemblance in him to her lost son, Beckwourth accepts her interpretation without commentary, other than to marvel that "it is but nature, either in the savage breast or civilized, that hails such a return with overwhelming joy" (146).

His impersonation is successful not only with the Crow but with the white settlers. When Beckwourth accompanies the Indians to Fort Clarke to trade pelts, he is not noticed by the white trappers. "Speaking nothing but Crow language, dressed like a Crow, my hair long as a Crow's, and myself black as a crow," Beckwourth explains, "no one at the post doubted my being a Crow" (177).

However proud he might be of his ability to pass as a Crow, or as a man as black as a crow, Beckwourth is anxious to reassure white readers of where his primary loyalties lie. He lives as a Crow, taking eight Indian wives, and most pages of his narrative are replete with accounts of the warfare he engages in and the enemy scalps he takes. Bernard De Voto claimed that Beckwourth "gave our literature our goriest lies" and that in no other book are as many Indians killed.[12] Yet Beckwourth is careful to distance himself from the violence he describes. After recounting in graphic detail how he killed eleven men in a battle in which "it was . . . a work of great difficulty to keep one's feet, as the mingled gore and brains were scattered every where round this fatal place," he extends a caveat: "I trust that the reader does not suppose that I walked through these scenes of carnage and desolation without some serious reflections on the matter. Disgusted at the repeated acts of cruelty I witnessed, I often resolved to leave these wild children of the forest and return to civilized life; but before I could act upon my decision, another scene of strife would occur, and the Enemy of Horses was always the first sought for by the tribe" (198).

His tribe needed him, so the justification goes, and as the Crows' best warrior, he could not let them down. In another logical flip-flop, however, Beckwourth claims that he acted for the best interests of white Americans: "But, in justification, it may be urged that the Crows had never shed the blood of the white man during my stay in their camp, and I did not intend they ever should, if I could raise a voice to prevent it. They were constantly at war with tribes who coveted the scalps of the white man, but the Crows were uniformly faithful in their obligations to my race, and would rather serve than injure their white brethren without any consideration of profit" (198).

Beckwourth describes the "natural ferocity of the savage, who thirsts for the blood of the white man for no other purpose than to gratify the vindictive spirit that animates him. . . . Such is Indian nature." Yet he follows this by noting that "when I fought with the Crow nation, I fought in their behalf against the most relentless enemies of the white man. If I chose to become an Indian while living among them, it concerned no person but myself; and by doing so, I saved more life and property for the white man than a whole regiment of United States regulars could have done in the same time" (233). Beckwourth's use of "white man," rather than "American" is hardly accidental. He constantly draws racial and ethnic distinctions in which others come out unfavorably. He notes that "quelling the Indian problem" will be impossible, "as long as our government continues to enlist the offscouring of European cities into our army" (233). On the other hand, "with five hundred men of my selection I could exterminate any tribe in North America in a very few months" (233). Beckwourth thus insists with patriotic pride on the power of American violence. He compares himself not only to European offscourings, but to blacks. Upon hearing that a mulatto has joined with a number of "my Indians" (249) and a group of white men in robbing a trader, he confronts the man, to whom he assigns primary responsibility for the crime, asking him, "What are you doing here, you black velvet-headed scoundrel? . . . I will have your scalp torn off, you consummate villain!" (250). On another occasion he compares an escaping Indian to "a negro with an alligator at his heels" (339).

Even as he re-creates himself as white in his autobiography, Beckwourth cannot refrain from bragging about his remarkable ability to shift identities. While he takes care to align himself with white men to the point of seeing European features as the touchstone of beauty in the Crow women he marries, he remains insistent on his own apparent Indianness. He cites many examples of his going unrecognized by white traders and of trappers telling him that "I should certainly not have distinguished you from any other Indian" (299). However, his thirteen years among the Crow do not prevent him from offering advice to his readers on how to exterminate the Indians most effectively (sell them liquor) or from taking his own counsel and eventually working for a trading company that does just that. Characteristically, he is as proud of his ability to sell huge amounts of liquor to Indians as he once was of scalping the enemies of the tribe.

If Beckwourth was a hero, he was one singularly unsuited to the needs of contemporary schoolchildren and the biographers who wrote the inspirational narratives designed for them. Rather, he was a hero from a much older mold: a shape-changer, a slaughterer of thousands, a survivor. Beckwourth may have escaped the racial strictures of antebellum America, perhaps even triumphed over them through sheer force of will. However, it is difficult to extract a neat moral from his life.

James Beckwourth passed away in 1866 from an undiagnosed illness while visiting the Crow. Yet a persistent rumor would have it that the Crow, delighted to have Beckwourth back among them, asked him to be their chief again, an honor that he graciously refused on the grounds that he was too old. At the feast to celebrate Beckwourth's return, this story goes, he was fed poisoned dog, because even in death he would be "good medicine." The annals of nineteenth-century medicine being what they are, it is impossible to determine what finally killed James Beckwourth. However, it seems only fitting that his death is as ambiguous as was his life.

As the West was won and as Native Americans were pushed farther west and herded onto steadily shrinking reservations, popular and official attitudes toward the Indians began to change. As the century waned, the "savages" whom Beckwourth had joined were no longer the threat they had once been. By the time the frontier officially closed in 1890, Native Americans' refusal to be quietly relocated to reservations had resulted in a series of Indian wars that swept the prairies and mountains, leaving the tribes devastated and nearly powerless. After the Civil War, Christian concern for the defeated Indians gained momentum, and a group of people who called themselves the friends of the Indian began to dominate the debate over the direction government policy should take. This direction was one of "Americanization" and Christianization. As reformer Carl Schurz rhetorically asked in calling for the establishment of Indian boarding schools such as the one at Carlisle, "Can Indians be civilized?" His answer was a resounding yes.[13]

Chief Buffalo Child Long Lance:
Romantic Racialism and Native American Autobiography

As Carl Schurz and other reformers in charge of many Indian agencies diligently worked for the passage of an Indian citizenship act, for the assimilation into white America of the defeated tribes, a new kind of Indian autobiography began to emerge. Perhaps the most noteworthy was that of Long Lance, whose life is an exemplar of the cult of personality that began to emerge in the 1920s and whose work stressed both his American success and his connection to a tragically vanished past.

In his foreword to *Long Lance*, the 1928 autobiography of Chief Buffalo Child Long Lance, humorist Irvin S. Cobb wrote admiringly of his friend's many accomplishments. Not included in this childhood memoir were Long Lance's mastery of half a dozen tribal languages besides his own; his presidential award of appointment to West Point; his bravery in World War I, from which he came out "as a captain of infantry, his body covered with wounds and his breast glittering with medals bestowed for high conduct and gallantry";[14] and his distinction as a writer for magazines.

Indeed, by the time Long Lance's autobiography appeared, he was well on his way to becoming a celebrity. The international press showered praise on his autobiography. *The Silent Enemy* (1930), an ethnographic film about Indian life in northern Canada in which Long Lance starred, was dubbed by Paramount into German, Swedish, Dutch, Polish, French, Spanish, Italian, and Portuguese. Authenticated at the time by Madison Grant, one of America's leading naturalists, the movie is still acclaimed by film historians. Long Lance became a cultural icon. He appeared in comic strips, attended glittering cocktail parties with movie stars and aristocrats, and lived in New York City at the famed Explorers Club, whose members included Fridtjof Nansen, Theodore Roosevelt, and Ernest Thompson Seton. He authored a best-selling book on Indian sign language and even had his own line of B. F. Goodrich running shoes, endorsed by none other than the great Native American athlete Jim Thorpe.

Long Lance was a self-invented Indian, however. Born in North Carolina in 1890 as Sylvester Long, the son of former slaves who claimed white and Native American rather than black forebears, Long Lance was classified according to the racial laws of Winston-Salem as colored. A binary definition of race allowed him little latitude. His family was part of the black community in Winston-Salem, where Long worked as a janitor, one of the few jobs open to him.

In the world of American mythmaking, it is appropriate that Sylvester Long first learned how to be an Indian when he ran away and joined Robinson's Circus and Wild West Show as a youth of fourteen. He traveled throughout the South with the show then, and again when he was eighteen. It would not have been hard for Long to see how the exoticism of his Indian role could enable him to escape the black/white binary of the world in which he had grown up. However, just as he first glimpsed the possibilities of a new life as an Indian through his work with the Wild West show, he understood clearly that the Indian boarding schools offered him the best shot at a permanent Indian identity.

Long's first act of self-fashioning occurred in 1909 when he lied about his ancestry on his application to the Carlisle Indian Residential School, since he was too white to qualify under the regulations. At Carlisle he was shunned by other students, who suspected him of being black. As his Native American classmates shed their pasts as part of the assimilationist policies mandated by the school, Long took on their stories as his own. By the time he left the school in 1912, he had become Sylvester Long Lance, half-white and half-Cherokee. In 1913, as he continued his education at St. John's, a prestigious military school, official racism was on the rise. While Long Lance was serving in the Canadian army and working to become a journalist, President Woodrow Wilson was arranging for the official segregation of federal employees. As D. W. Griffith's film *Birth of a Nation* (1915) reframed U.S. racial history to audiences of millions, spurring the rebirth of the Ku Klux Klan and its incredible growth during the 1920s, Long Lance moved further from the binary racial definitions of the period. From his experiences in the Wild West show, Long Lance realized that, to the general public, Plains tribes were most easily recognizable and Cherokees were not sufficiently iconographically Indian. By 1921 Sylvester Long Lance, who was working as a journalist in Alberta, had evolved into Chief Buffalo Child Long Lance, a Blackfoot.[15]

By assuming an Indian identity, Sylvester Long escaped the limitations of his "colored" status. As an articulate, handsome, international spokesman for the Native American, he proved appealing to Europeans and Americans alike, furnishing them with a focus for their primitivist fantasies. Long Lance used characteristics that could have been disabilities, such as dark skin, to transform himself into a consumable icon, becoming in Europe the symbol of Native Americanness. Abandoning a racial identity that was indeterminate and, at the time, tragic, he inserted himself into a new ethnic character that fifty years previously would have been immensely problematic. By the time Long began the process of reinventing himself, the reservation uprisings had been quelled. Because the battles between Indians and settlers over territory were long past, his new identity appeared nostalgic rather than fraught. Classified as colored, he took his color and packaged it. By dressing in tribal costume one night and a tuxedo the next, he assumed a variety of postures that called into question the categories under discussion. Were Indians noble savages or assimilated sophisticates? As Long Lance demonstrated, they could embody both roles. His politics, likewise, seemed slippery. Although he began by criticizing the Bureau of Indian Affairs, he ended by consorting with aristocratic Nazi sympathizers in Europe.

Long Lance's career as an Indian depended in large part upon the support of racial theorists determined to prove the superiority of the Anglo-Saxon race by positing Native Americans as a noble but dying breed that had been swept away by the inevitable march of civilization. Irvin S. Cobb's foreword to Long Lance's autobiography served as an endorsement not only of the book's literary quality but of its authenticity: "I claim there is authentic history in these pages and verity and most of all a power to describe in English words the thoughts, the instincts, the events which originally were framed in a native language."[16] These words are clearly similar to those of the abolitionists who authenticated slave narratives. No slave narrative would appear without an endorsement by a white sponsor. However, while most of the authenticators of slave narratives pledged themselves to racial justice or, at the very least, to the end of slavery, Irvin S. Cobb, the son of a Confederate army veteran, was a humorist whose living depended on his vast store of "darkie" jokes. Madison Grant, who authenticated *The Silent Enemy*, was the author of *The Passing of the Great Race* (1916), in which he alerted Americans to the danger of their superior races, the Nordics, being submerged by inferior immigrants. In his 1933 work, *The Conquest of a Continent*, Grant warned of the dangers of racial miscegenation, advocating laws banning intermarriage and stressing the constant vigilance that Nordics must maintain to unmask mulattos passing for whites.

It was no accident that both Long Lance's autobiography and his film were authenticated by men dedicated to racist theories. By the turn of the century, Native American autobiography held a special place in a culture that was concerned both with mourning a people who could never return and with using Indian narratives to maintain racial theories of the time. Indeed, *We Indians: The Passing of a Great Race* (1931), the prominent autobiography of White Horse Eagle, an Osage, was elicited and edited by Edgar von Schmidt-Pauli, a German academic whose chief scholarly interest lay in demonstrating the inevitability of the rise of the German race in general and of Adolf Hitler in particular.

We Indians is among the more bizarre Indian autobiographies of its era. White Horse Eagle claimed to be 107 years old and to have been acquainted with every U.S. president since Abraham Lincoln. He was capable of a number of remarkable feats, including sensing the presence of gold, silver, or water in the earth beneath his feet and reading Egyptian hieroglyphics. His most salient trait, however, was his exemplification of racial purity. According to Schmidt-Pauli, White Horse Eagle was a "thorough gentleman." The only time he became enraged was when he was sorely provoked, as the editor's example illustrates: "I once remember a tipsy and uneducated man shouting out that all colored races, Indians, Hindoos, and niggers were equal. All at once this bowed and aged man seemed to assume gigantic proportions, his countenance became distorted with fury as though he was on the warpath and about to scalp his adversary" (26). White Horse Eagle himself rarely missed an opportunity to proselytize on racial matters. The Osage culture was effective, he claimed, because it "was founded upon a severe disciplinary system which preserved us from thinking that everyone was equal. That is nonsense, as the Great Manitoo has differentiated everything in nature" (84). As H. David Brumble points out, to Schmidt-Pauli, "White Horse Eagle and the Indians in general [were] living—or rather dying—evidence of inborn racial characteristics."[17] For Schmidt-Pauli, the Indians faced such a grim future because "they began to succumb to the seductions of civilization. They began to be attracted to white women. Cross-breeding ruined the ancient stock" (23). According to some reports, "White Horse Eagle found it profitable to travel Europe in the 1920s and 1930s, adopting unsuspecting museum directors and chairmen of anthropology departments into his tribe. Photographs show him sporting a feather bonnet, Navajo silver jewelry, and a button reading *Lions Club Pasadena*. A Viennese museum director found him particularly convincing, because the Big Chief had made it a matter of principle not to shake hands with Jews."[18]

Long Lance's autobiography occupied a curious place within this nexus of Social Darwinist or romantic racialist thought. It appeared just three years after the Indian Citizenship Act of 1924, which made every

Native American an American citizen, and fifteen years after the publication of Joseph K. Dixon's 1913 volume of photographs and text, *The Vanishing Race*, which had come out of what might be termed the Bureau of Indian Affairs' official farewell to the disappearing Indians.[19] With Dixon as prime mover, the bureau had arranged the Last Council, a meeting of chiefs and aging warriors from several western tribes. Long Lance's achievement was the negotiation of the territory between the tragic nostalgia emblematized by Dixon's work and the assimilationist claims of the Citizenship Act. Long Lance became the ultimate American, a Horatio Alger type whose story resonated with the mythology of the frontier, a natural man who was able to adapt to industrial America while preserving his authenticity.

In his autobiography Long Lance described a vanished way of life, including a chapter on hunting the buffalo, which had vanished long before his childhood. He also presented himself as an example of someone who, as witnessed by the title of his 1926 *Cosmopolitan* article, "My Trail Upward," had effected a transformation in the style of Booker T. Washington. Writing, "I'm proud to be as much like a white man as I am—and I'm proud, too, of every drop of Indian blood that runs through my veins," he built a reassuring bridge between the white and the Indian worlds. As he concluded, "I have reached no dizzying heights of material success, but I have succeeded in pulling myself up by my boot straps from a primitive and backward life into this great new world of white civilization.

"Anyone with determination and will can do as much."[20]

Long Lance thus maintained an affectionate distance from his roots and from the reservation he claimed to visit a few times a year, while asserting the superiority of a white way of life. Most important, he offered a reassuring message to individuals who might have qualms about the laws, dating back to the Indian Removal Bill of 1830, which had effectively destroyed the possibility of Native Americans living their traditional lives. It was all right, Long Lance seemed to be saying; although the end of this way of life may have been sad, it was not tragic, since any Indian with determination could succeed in the white world— and, as Irvin Cobb writes of Long Lance in his preface, not only survive but conspicuously flourish. In fact, Long Lance dedicated his autobiography to "the two White Men who have guided and encouraged me most since I have taken a place in civilization." While acknowledging that his grandfather's dire predictions of the end of the traditional Indian way of life had come true, Long Lance ended his autobiography by claiming that these changes were, in fact, not only inevitable but ordained by the deity: "But the new day is here: it is here to stay. And now we must leave it for our old people to sit stolidly and dream of the glories of our past. Our job is to try to fit ourselves into the new scheme of life which the Great Spirit has decreed for North America."[21]

Long Lance, whose autobiography is full of stirring scenes of warfare fit for an audience that craved boys' adventure stories, thus perfectly fulfilled the needs of an audience perhaps not fully comfortable with the conditions that had made Indian autobiography possible. Indian autobiography is a post-contact literary form that has been predicated on defeat and disappearance. Native American memoirs did not exist before the passage of the Indian Removal Act of 1830, which mandated the forced migration of the eastern tribes to locations west of the Mississippi River. The first Indian autobiography, the *Life of Ma-Ka-tai-me-she-kia-kiak or Black Hawk*, by the Sauk leader, appeared in 1833 after his defeat by federal troops in the campaign known as the Black Hawk War. Native American autobiography has always been a solicited form, traditionally elicited and edited by a white person though narrated by its subject. As Arnold Krupat points out, "The production of an Indian's own statement of his inevitable disappearance required that the Indian be represented as speaking in his own voice."[22]

While nineteenth-century Native American autobiographies were the stories of defeated leaders, of heroes in the mold of Kit Carson or Sam Houston, twentieth-century works began to represent the process of Americanization. Many of these tales, like Long Lance's, stress not only the assimilation but the Americanness of their teller. The life history of Crow chief Plenty-Coups, for example, was published in 1930 under the title *American: the Life Story of a Great Indian*. The title of Charles Eastman's 1916 memoir, *From the Deep Woods to Civilization*, emphasized the same kind of progress as did Long Lance's. Long Lance's self-fashioning to fit the needs of his audience was particularly successful, as evidenced by a 1930 *Herald Tribune* article about him by Beverly Smith, "One Hundred Percent American." The piece begins with the claim, "There is romance always in the man who can play the game and live the life of another race." Rather than questioning Long Lance's identity, though, Smith attributes the American success of Long Lance, "a splendid specimen of the American Indian," to his Indian background. His very foreignness, his exotic quality, makes his heroism in the service of the nation possible. For instance, his acts of bravery in

Sylvester Long transformed himself into the internationally famous Chief Buffalo Child Long Lance. Here he appears in *The Silent Enemy* (1930), an ethnographic film about Indian life in northern Canada. (Photo courtesy of MOMA Film Stills Collection.)

World War I, for which he claimed to have been decorated by three governments, came about because "there was war in Europe, and it called to the warrior blood in Long Lance."[23]

The publicity material released by Paramount to promote *The Silent Enemy* reflected this preoccupation with authenticity, as did the movie's reviews. The marquee of the Criterion, a theater in New York, advertised the picture as "a drama of wild life, wild people, wild beasts." *Exhibitors Herald-World*, a trade publication, noted that "the characters are all real Indians, who act in a manner in keeping with the tone of authenticity sustained throughout the entire production."[24]

Although in his other published writings Long Lance emphasized individual accomplishment, his constructed autobiography, ironically enough, exemplified many of the traditions of Indian autobiography, as enumerated by Hertha Wong, in its "lack of rigid chronology [and] incorporation of multiple voices that emphasize tribal identity."[25] Long Lance's chronology, including such iconographic yet historically impossible scenes as hunting buffalo, can hardly be called rigid. Since Long Lance incorporated stories from his Blackfoot friends such as Mike Eagle Speaker, as well as events that he had heard from his classmates at the Carlisle Indian School, into his narrative, he was in a sense creating a new tribal identity. It just was not his own.[26] The fact that his autobiography had been elicited and edited by Ray Long, the editor in chief of *Cosmopolitan*, simply placed him in a long tradition of other Native American speakers.

If, as Arnold Krupat has written, "victory is the ennobling condition of western autobiography, [but] defeat is the ennobling condition of Indian autobiography,"[27] Long Lance managed to have his cake and eat it too, by recording both the tribal defeat and his individual triumph. Thus Long Lance was drawing from two distinct traditions of American autobiography: ethnic autobiography, understood by both teller and audience to be the story of a group as much as of an individual, and self-construction, the triumphant individual struggle upward of Benjamin Franklin or Booker T. Washington.

As a skilled journalist with nearly a decade of newspaper and magazine experience by the time he wrote his autobiography, Long Lance had the professional writer's ease with forms. As someone who had negotiated his way between a number of ethnic and racial identities, Long Lance was well aware of his audience's expectations. One of the best eyewitness accounts of Long Lance's performative skill came from Norwegian journalist Theodor Findahl, who in his travelogue *Manhattan Babylon: En Bok om New York Idag* [A book about New York today] described an evening he spent with Long Lance, whom he characterized as "a full-blooded redskin and a genuine aristocrat," at the Park Avenue home of Irvin S. Cobb. To Findahl's evident surprise, Long Lance

> was by no means on the warpath, wore no paint, nor a feather head-dress, but was dressed in a fashionable New York tuxedo, patent leather shoes, and a white waistcoat. . . . The rouged ladies, glittering with pearls, are thrilled. "Isn't it wonderful," one of them whispers to me, "that colored people can seem so distinguished? All the Indians I've seen before this have seemed just like gypsies, and this one is a gentleman. So confident in his manner, so effortlessly superior. I could almost imagine addressing him as 'your highness,' like him," and she glanced over at the desk, where Mussolini's portrait, with a long handwritten inscription, a souvenir from Irvin Cobb's last visit to Rome, glared menacingly back at us. "And listen to what perfect English he speaks, and what interesting things he talks about."

To Findahl's interlocutor, Indians were just another variety of colored people, more similar to the despised gypsies than to noble savages. Yet Long Lance, dressed in the uniform of high society, managed to escape such classification and define himself as an aristocrat, a leader, albeit of a fast-vanishing people. Although he told his audience that he was the head of a tribe of 1,196 Blackfeet, he also informed them that in all of America there were now only 150,000 Indians remaining, and that in another generation they will have vanished with the Mohicans. In doing so, he clinched his role as a glamorous representative of a dying race. It was a role, moreover, in which he excelled.

Among the interesting things Long Lance talked about that night was Indian sign language: "Though the fifty-eight languages spoken by North American tribes were as different as Turkish and English, Indians had nonetheless developed a sign language so wonderfully colorful and poetic as to be understood by every redskin, so witty and gracious that the sign language white civilization has created for the deaf is clumsy and helpless by comparison." He gave a demonstration. "Just by gesturing with his hands and arms, Long Lance conjured visions before our eyes. . . . *Spring*, his hands fluttered as though to indicate rain, and suddenly he thrust a hand upwards to indicate the spring's regenerative powers. . . . *Winter*—snowflakes which dance in the air, masterful portrayal with his fingers."

Long Lance speculated on why even the Anglo-Saxons with the strongest racial instincts—the individuals most fearful of miscegenation—were still proud to claim even a drop of Indian blood: "Could it be a subconscious acknowledgment of the fact that the country's true heirs and owners are Indians, is it in sympathy with the Indians' tragic destiny, or is it just that Indians are no longer dangerous at all?" As he continued to discourse on topics such as his tribe's marriage customs and prophesied the eventual return of the "only true Americans," "Irvin," said an elderly woman in a stage whisper, "You must help me get the chief to lecture to my women's club. He'd be a sensation. You must, you hear?"[28]

This performance of Long Lance's entailed thus not only an act of literary imposture but one that encompassed his every waking moment. His life was a stage he could never leave, whether inventing Indian sign language at a cocktail party or politely listening to Irvin Cobb's seemingly endless and oft-repeated store of racist jokes. His comments about "true Americans" also reveal how well he understood his audience's expectations. It is no wonder that Long Lance was immensely successful in his disguise, when he so fully understood the ramifications of the role he was playing. However, no matter how skillfully he was able to escape the trap of binary racial definitions, he of necessity remained on the outside looking in. Thus, his impersonation meant that he could never go home to see his parents or siblings, who were firmly ensconced in the black community of Winston-Salem.

Although his stories, which became increasingly grandiose, were generally believed, there were dangerous moments when questions put to him forced him to improvise a past quickly. Chauncey Yellow Robe, the great-nephew of Sitting Bull and Long Lance's costar in *The Silent Enemy*, became suspicious of Long Lance's demeanor—his punctuality, his boisterousness, and his small talk with strangers—on the set. This behavior, though it may have fulfilled white expectations, certainly did not meet those of Yellow Robe, who made discreet inquiries while in New York on a lecture tour following the production of the movie. Although he had his suspicions confirmed by the Bureau of Indian Affairs and went so far as to contact the movie's legal counsel, he eventually came to Long Lance's defense. Although Yellow Robe never explained why he shifted his stance, it is probable that he chose to embrace a more inclusive definition of what it meant to be an Indian. James P. Beckwourth was, after all, readily adopted by the Crow; the Seminoles he fought on behalf of the U.S. government had admitted many African Americans to their tribe.[29] Yellow Robe had, after all, spoken out against government support of "wild-west shows, moving-picture concerns, and fair associations for commercializing the Indian," the very venues by which Long Lance had achieved his fame. Given his call for "equal opportunities, equal responsibilities, equal education" for the American Indian, and given his criticism of depictions of "savage" Indians, it is also possible that Yellow Robe was reluctant to fully condemn an Indian spokesman who had achieved so much.[30]

Long Lance's was at best an ambiguous accomplishment. In the early years of his journalistic career he had rethought the assimilationist goals of the Carlisle Indian School and was using his position to forcefully criticize actions taken by the Canadian Department of Indian Affairs, such as the government decree to ban potlatch ceremonies. However, he eventually retreated from this confrontational stance. When members of the Blood tribe expressed dismay that Long Lance was using his ceremonial adoption by them for his own ends, he grew resentful that they were not sufficiently grateful. One sign of his movement away from activism was the thanks he gave in his autobiography to Duncan Campbell Scott, the deputy superintendent of Indian affairs in Ottawa, a powerful government official who had questioned the sense of expending money and social services on a "dying people" and had lobbied for Indians to conform to what he called "that worldwide tendency towards universal standardization which would appear to be the essential underlying purport of all modern social evolution."[31]

Unfortunately, Long Lance was finally unable to inhabit the narrative he had written for himself. Rumors that he had African ancestry began to circulate toward the end of his life and caused some of his patrons, such as Cobb, to disavow their connection to him. Long Lance committed suicide in 1932, at age forty-two, in the home of Anita Baldwin, one of his wealthy patrons. He left no note, so one can only guess that the strain of living a lie for over twenty years had finally become unbearable.

Back in Winston-Salem, where Long Lance had not visited in twenty years, his brother, Abe Long, spent the 1930s and 1940s directing the flow of traffic up the steps to the colored gallery of the Carolina Theater. In a diary he kept all his life, he commented on progress in civil rights. He opened one such entry by writing, "We the better thinking negroes . . . ."[32] Of course, according to Abe Long's parents, his ancestry was not African American but Indian and white. However, he was defined by the racial laws of his time as black, and he embraced that identity.

In a sense, the article titled "One Hundred Percent American" was not far off the mark in describing Long Lance, though perhaps not for the reasons its author intended. Condemned by the racial definitions of his time to a life devoid of possibilities for advancement, Long Lance used the very racist theories that had imprisoned him to successfully create a new identity. The Indian Citizenship Act finally granted "American" status to Indians. Sylvester Long, condemned by the racial classifications of his time to second-class status, could become truly American only by assuming another ethnicity. His struggle upward, documented by him in the best fashion of success manuals and inspirational literature, offered his audience a vision of the Indian not as aboriginal American, but as American in the best tradition of self-fashioning.

The Education of Little Tree *Reconsidered*

In 1973, little more than forty years after Long Lance's death, Forrest Carter, or Little Tree, was born with the publication of his first novel, *The Rebel Outlaw, Josey Wales*, which became the source for the Clint Eastwood film *The Outlaw Josey Wales*.[33] *The Education of Little Tree* followed three years later. Some Alabamians recognized the Klansman they had known as Asa Carter in Forrest Carter's 1974 interview with Barbara Walters on the *Today* show. One journalist, Wayne Greenhaw, went so far as to publicize the fact in a brief *New York Times* article in August 1976, but news of the imposture seemed not to have registered in the public consciousness.[34] Not until Dan Carter's exposure of Forrest Carter's former identity as a speechwriter for George Wallace and as a Klansman in a 1991 *New York Times* editorial, after the book had already sold more than a half-million copies, did readers across the country became aware of Asa Carter's deception.

What was it about the book that seemed to resonate so strongly with readers? *Little Tree* sold much better than any other Native American autobiography published at the same time. It found adherents in the Washington State court system, where it was used to rehabilitate youthful offenders, and among the cast of the Broadway musical *The Will Rogers Follies*, who received gift copies from their director, Tommy Tune.[35] In fact, as Rennard Strickland, a Cherokee and the director of the Center for Indian Law and Policy at the University of Oklahoma, noted in his foreword to the University of New Mexico Press edition, the book was sold in tribal souvenir shops on Indian reservations. According to Strickland, "Students of Native American life found the book to be as accurate as it was mystical and romantic."[36]

Asa Carter's past, grinding out impassioned speeches in a basement office of George Wallace's statehouse, seems to have served him well in writing *The Education of Little Tree*. The book is, in fact, a hack's dream, a slender volume (216 pages) in which every rhetorical trick known to the speechwriter is used to full advantage. Carter managed to appeal effectively to a number of different constituencies in telling the story of Little Tree's life with the grandparents who adopted him after the death of his parents.

Environmentally oriented audiences can warm to Little Tree's descriptions of "Mon-o-lah, the earth mother, [who] came to me through my moccasins. I could feel her push and swell here, and sway and give there . . . and the roots that veined her body and the life of the water-blood, deep inside her. She was warm and springy and bounced me on her breast, as Granma said she would."[37] Nature is not only a mother, but one whose creatures, especially the hunting dogs belonging to Little Tree and his grandparents, seem incessantly to perform cute, Disneyfied antics. Living in harmony with Mother Earth is a theme endlessly repeated throughout the text. As the narrator notes, "Granpa lived *with* the game, not *at* it" (23).

Little Tree may only be the latest iteration of what the English impostor Archie Belaney, who in the 1930s became Grey Owl, an Apache halfbreed, expressed when he declared that "the Indians were always conservationists. Indians are in tune with their surroundings."[38] Grey Owl's authority as a Native spokesperson enabled him to lecture effectively throughout North America and Britain on conservation, to broadcast his appeals, and to publish a number of books on conservation, specifically on beavers, which he referred to as "little Indians." Whatever his other motivations, Grey Owl used his identity to present his environmental message in the most dramatic way he knew. By the time of his death, in 1938, he had used his position as caretaker of animals for the Canadian Park Service as a platform to advance his environmental cause across the world. Advising his publicity agent that he wished to be packaged as a "modern Hiawatha," Grey Owl posed in his version of full native dress when on tour. During his first British excursion, in 1935, he addressed more than fifty thousand people. He gave a royal performance in 1937 for the king and queen of England and starred in the movies produced by the Canadian Park Service. Although Grey Owl may have anthropomorphized the beavers whose preservation he advocated, he seems to have used his native persona primarily for political purposes. His version of Indianness involved a somewhat romantic but relatively uncomplicated vision of nature.[39] For Little Tree, nature is a much more directive force.

Knowledge of Mother Earth is, of course, integral to understanding The Way, for in *The Education of Little Tree*, nature is not just a mother who must be respected, but also a guide to wisdom. Little Tree's grandparents teach him the secret of living in harmony with nature, so that "I knew now why we only used the logs that the spirit had left for our fireplace" (62). Interestingly, Granpa also preaches a kind of Social Darwinism of the forest, telling Little Tree not to be distressed at the sight of a hawk eating a quail, for "it is The Way. Tal-con caught the slow and so the slow will raise no children who are also slow" (9). In one of the poems that stud the text, Little Tree advises readers to "learn the wisdom of Mon-o-lah," his invented term for the earth, in order to "know The Way of all the Cherokee" (12).

In this mystical amalgam, spiritual knowledge is tied to the Cherokee Way, which is tied to an awareness of nature. That Native Americans have a primordial wisdom is an idea to which many Americans have responded, especially since the 1960s. *Little Tree* goes this notion one better and mixes such New Age concerns as reincarnation into the spiritual stew. "Granma said your spirit mind could get so big and powerful that you would eventually know all about your past body lives and would get to where you could come out with no body death atall" (60).

Little Tree plays into the idea that authenticity is found through a return to cultural primitivism and, not incidentally, anti-intellectualism. Thus Little Tree tells us that "Granma began to hum a tune behind me and I knew it was Indian, and needed no words for its meaning to be clear" (4). And Granpa, who is by turns mystically attuned to the earth and homespun, tells Little Tree that "the meddlesome son of a bitch that invented the dictionary ought to be taken out and shot" (90). The primal wisdom of the Native Americans occurs in a universe outside time, outside politics. Thus, when Granpa hears news of the ravages of the Depression—"fellers was jumping out of winders in New York and shootin' themselves in the head about it"—he explains to Little Tree that "New York was crowded all up with people who didn't have enough land to live on, and likely half of them was run crazy from living that-a-way, which accounted for the shootin's and the winder jumping" (91). It is not economic hardship but cultural impoverishment that leads people to despair during the Great Depression. A post-Watergate readership, disillusioned with the political process, would seem a natural constituency for a narrative in which politicians appear suspect.

The Education of Little Tree is not only a fantasy about Native American primal spirituality; it is also a fantasy perfectly attuned to an American public well versed in the rhetoric of self-actualization and, more specifically, the recovery movement. If previous impersonators have given us Indians as noble savages, romantic racialists, people specially attuned to the environment, and spiritual guides, Little Tree presents us with a new vision of Native American identity for the 1970s and beyond, what I call the inner child Indian, a figure that represents lost innocence and a sense of wonder. If Long Lance and Grey Owl presented themselves in the 1920s and 1930s as Indians whose virility was unquestioned and whose masculinity, in fact, rested on their Native identities, Little Tree offers us a world where sex is not even an issue, an idealized world of childhood.[40] In the era of AIDS, this world appealed to many readers.

In a time of rising divorce rates and fractured families, Little Tree provided a vision of an idyllic family unit.[41] In a period when pop psychology writers such as Jon Bradshaw brought discussions of the inner child and toxic families to talk shows seen by millions, and when works such as M. Scott Peck's *The Road Less Traveled* spent several years on the *New York Times* best-seller list, Little Tree offered readers a vision of a family that healed rather than inflicted pain. In his portrait of his grandparents, especially his grandfather, whose father had survived the Trail of Tears, Little Tree offered a model of successful recovery from trauma. While Dee Brown's best-selling *Bury My Heart at Wounded Knee* (1973) presented a history of unrelieved horror, Little Tree's narrative offered a way out of history.

We first meet Little Tree on the occasion of his mother's death, when he is five, a year after the loss of his father. The bond between the child and his newly discovered grandfather is instantaneous and instinctive. While a crowd of relatives "thrashed it out proper as to where I was to go, while they divided up the painted bedstead and the chairs" (1), Granpa stays aloof from the fray, uninterested both in material possessions and in treating the child as a thing to be disposed of. He is every child's fantasy, the chosen parent. Little Tree literally picks him from the crowd, holds on to his leg, and will not let go—and so the matter is decided. Granma lulls the boy to sleep with an Indian song in which the forest, wind, and various animals welcome him, promising that "Little Tree will never be alone." At that moment, "I knew I was Little Tree, and I was happy that they loved me and wanted me. And so I slept, and did not cry" (5).

Little Tree grows up in a near-Rousseauean idyll. Granpa and Granma do not restrain him; no matter how dirty or wet he gets while playing, his grandmother does not mind, for "Cherokees never scolded their children for having anything to do with the woods" (57). They encourage every aspect of his growth: "Granpa bragged on me a lot to Granma at the supper table and Granma agreed that it looked like I was coming on to being a man" (50). Not once in the book does Little Tree feel anger at either grandparent, nor does either grandparent behave, at any point, in a less than loving way. The world of the family is safe and free from conflict, a nurturing cocoon.

Tellingly, family happiness depends on isolation from the mainstream of American life, in which dysfunction is rampant. Little Tree must venture into the wider world to find brutality (a sharecropper whips his daughter), dishonesty and sanctimony (a man claiming to be a Christian sells him a dying mule), exploitation (big-city bootleggers try to muscle their way into Granpa's bootlegging business), and racism. Whereas James P. Beckwourth claimed to have become an Indian only in order to aid the American government, and while Long Lance prided himself on his trail upward from the enclosed world of his tribe and his family into American civilization, Little Tree can only attain maturity within the sheltered context of his family. Exposure to the outside world is scarring, both literally and figuratively. Whereas citizenship and its responsibility are eagerly embraced by Beckwourth and Long Lance, only the folly of government intervention can endanger Little Tree's idyll.

Government intervention takes many forms, such as Granpa's imprisonment for bootlegging, but perpetrates its worst crimes when the state takes Little Tree from his grandparents and places him in an orphanage of Dickensian horror. Within the orphanage is childhood in its most dysfunctional form, civilization at its most discontented. The minister who runs the orphanage brands Little Tree a bastard and tells him that, as such, he cannot be saved. According to the clergyman, "Granpa was not fittin' to raise a young'un, and . . . I more than likely had not ever had any discipline" (184). This, to Little Tree and his readers, is the beauty of the arrangement. Discipline, in the minister's terms, includes a beating so severe that he breaks a stout stick across Little Tree's back and fills his shoes with blood. The reason for this punishment is the boy's innocent reference in class to mating deer, which causes his teacher to "holler, 'I should have *known*—we *all* should have known . . . filth . . . filth . . . would come out of you . . . you . . . little *bastard!*'" (191).The orphanage is a world in which the disabled, as represented by Little Tree's clubfooted roommate and only friend, are humiliated. It is a world of disconnection from nature, of sexual repression, and of Christian pieties and manufactured sentiment: "The white-headed lady said Christmas was might near on us. She said everybody was to be happy and sing" (193). Politicians visit at Christmas, as do drunken country club members, who distribute broken gifts to the children. To mark the occasion, "a male pine . . . died slow, there in the hall" (194). Only by talking to an oak tree and communicating with his grandparents by watching the Dog Star at night, so that his grandparents can "sen[d] me remembrance" (189), can Little Tree survive and finally tell them that he wants to return home. As conditions in the orphanage worsen, Little Tree relies more and more on Indian ways to survive—whether he is letting his "body mind" sleep in order to endure the pain of the minister's physical abuse, or whether he is listening to the oak tree. "She was supposed to be asleep, but she said she wasn't, on account of me. She talked slow—and low" (193).

Little Tree has no doubts that his grandparents will rescue him, and indeed, Granpa shows up on Christmas to reclaim Little Tree. He is returned to the world of the mountain, where he can live happily, listening to his grandparents' message of harmony with nature, freedom from government intervention, distrust of language, love and respect of one another, and condemnation of racial and ethnic prejudice.

As Granpa tells Little Tree, "Foreigners is people that happens to be someplace where they wasn't born" (37). He also discusses Jews, as personified by the kind old peddler, Mr. Wine. When Little Tree asks, "Granpa, what is a damn Jew?" in response to overhearing a slur, "Granpa stopped and didn't look back at me. His voice sounded tired too. 'I don't know; something is said about 'em in the Bible, somewhere's or other; must go back a long ways.' Granpa turned around. 'Like the Indian . . . I hear tell they ain't got no nation, neither'" (177). Granma and Granpa preach tolerance and remain dignified in the face of prejudice. *Little Tree* is full of touching stories of people reaching across seemingly insurmountable cultural and ideological chasms to help one another—a fragile peace that is, as often as not, shattered by government intervention. Former Union soldiers help former Confederates (and their still-loyal former slave); Grandpa and Mr. Wine find common cause; and brotherhood seems not only possible but the only real choice, if one is to follow The Way.

In 1955 Asa Carter was hired as a spokesman by the anti-integration American States Rights Association. He was fired for his on-air diatribes against National Brotherhood Week, sponsored by the National Conference of Christians and Jews. Caught up in the movement to halt civil rights progress, he ran into trouble with other Alabama Citizens Council leaders because he would not allow Jews into his white supremacist organization. "We believe that this is basically a battle between Christianity and atheistic communism," he told a reporter. As late as 1978, in his guise as Forrest Carter, he delivered a drunken speech to the Wellesley College Club in Dallas, in which he talked, à la Little Tree, about the need for people to love one another. According to reporter Dana Rubin, "In an expansive moment, Carter pointed across the podium at his fellow speaker, historian Barbara Tuchman.

"'Now, she's a good ol' Jew girl,' Carter said. Then he swung his arm toward Stanley Marcus, who was in the audience.

"'Now, Stanley,' he went on, 'there's a good ol' Jew boy.'"[42]

As far as is known, however, Carter confined his anti-Semitism to verbal abuse. This was not true of his feelings toward African Americans. In the mid-1950s he was among the men who incorporated a shadowy paramilitary group called the Original Ku Klux Klan of the Confederacy, six alleged members of which, on Labor Day 1957, kidnapped a black handyman, sliced off his scrotum, and poured turpentine on his wounds. In speeches Asa Carter vowed to put his "blood on the ground" to halt integration. By the time George Wallace hired him as a speechwriter in 1958 after Wallace was trounced by a Klan-backed candidate in his quest for the lieutenant governorship, Carter's reputation as an extremist was such that Wallace's men, nervous about having him linked to their candidate, paid him through back channels and, after Wallace's victory, gave him a rear office in the state capitol. Over time he became disillusioned with Wallace, whom he saw as caving in to integrationist forces. Carter came in fifth in a field of five in his protest bid against Wallace for the 1970 governor's race. The statewide paramilitary force he set up in 1971 failed, as had his venture the preceding year to set up a string of all-white private schools. The following year Carter was arrested three times on alcohol-related charges. The year after that he and his wife sold their home, bought their sons a home in Abilene, Texas, and moved to Florida. That year Asa Carter sold his first book, a Confederate adventure novel called *The Rebel Outlaw, Josey Wales*, under a new name. Forrest Carter was born.

When he visited his sons in Texas, Forrest called them his nephews. He made new friends, for whom he invented an Indian past. He began to speak ungrammatically, to wear jeans and a black cowboy hat, and to talk about his people, the Cherokee, with whom he claimed to live for part of the year. Apparently Carter's new identity was a fantasy in which even his wife, India, participated, in her own way. After Wayne Greenhaw first exposed Asa in his August 1976 article for the *New York Times*, India wrote to him to clear up matters. Forrest was, according to her, not Asa at all, but Asa's sensitive, artistic nephew, with whom she had fallen in love during his visit to her and Asa, for whom she had left her racist husband, and to whom she was now married.[43] Ironically, while James P. Beckwourth and Sylvester Long escaped the historical trap of their racial identity by becoming Indian, Asa Carter took on a Native self as, among other things, a way of leaving his racist reputation behind him.

Little Tree was very much an Indian for the 1990s. As the waif look became popular in fashion in the late 1980s, as lifestyle pages reported that cocooning had become a new trend, as Earth Day was resurrected in 1990, and as New Age and spiritual volumes filled the shelves of bookstores, Asa Carter stepped forward to give Americans the Native American they wanted. In the process he shed, not quite effortlessly, his racist past. As a white supremacist Asa Carter's day had passed. By the early 1970s his following had evaporated. His name surfaced in the newspapers only to report his arrests for drunken driving. His re-creation of himself as a Native American offered Carter a second chance, a way out of the black/white binary in which, ironically, he had trapped himself through his white supremacist politics. While Long Lance and Beckwourth certainly did not choose to be trapped by their blackness the way that Carter, in his first life, chose to capitalize on his whiteness, he, like them, was trapped by racial categories and escaped racial binaries through assuming an Indian identity. However, like Long Lance and James Beckwourth before him, Carter succeeded in his impersonation by trading on his deep knowledge of racial and ethnic stereotypes, a knowledge honed during his years as a professional racist. Sylvester Long's choice of escaping his colored identity by becoming Indian seems fairly understandable. It is easy to see that being a film star and Indian chief would offer more possibilities than being a janitor. However, Asa Carter was never forced into a life as a white supremacist. After a career spent capitalizing on his whiteness, he simply chose to manipulate stereotypes of race and ethnicity in another way. Just as James Beckwourth was challenged by critics who saw his ethnicity at birth as being an impediment to his ability to tell the truth, and just as Long Lance built his career as an Indian through collaboration with white supremacist race theorists, so Asa Carter skillfully employed his knowledge of racialist thinking to create an Indian self who could appeal to the masses.

chapter five

The Immigrant's Answer to Horatio Alger

The story of Chief Buffalo Child Long Lance can be seen not only in the context of Native American autobiography but as very much a narrative of the 1910s and 1920s. By the 1920s ethnicity had become functional. As the dominant culture glorified the business success of the self-made man, debates over the ethnic and racial makeup of the United States raged. In this context individuals shaped new selves in the dramatic exercise of individual social mobility. Immigrants who had seen the open door slam shut and had experienced the increasingly theatricalized nature of the debate over who might be considered American produced autobiographies in which their ethnicity was a strategically employed weapon in the struggle for cultural survival, rather than an essential component of selfhood.

Ethnicity As Theater

As eugenics theories attained academic and popular respectability, as debates over immigration raged in Congress, and as Indians finally became U.S. citizens, the notion of ethnic impersonation took on increasing importance. While it was hard for most African Americans to appear white, eastern European immigrants did, in fact, have the option of shifting from their native culture into American culture, and from one class into another. In the business culture of 1920s America, immigrants could effect the most culturally sanctioned transformation—from poverty to success. But their precarious position within a hostile culture also enabled them to rewrite the story of American success in a way that native-born Americans could not.

The genre of immigrant literature was being created and read in the context of the rapidly changing ethnic composition of the United States. Between 1890 and 1920, 18.2 million newcomers, many from eastern and southern Europe, arrived on U.S. shores; between 1899 and 1924, 17 percent of these immigrants were Italians and 14 percent were Jews. More significantly, while return migration among Italians reached 45.6 percent during this period, and some immigrant groups returned home at rates as high as 87.4 percent (Bulgarians, Serbs, and Montenegrins), Jewish return migration rates, at 4.3 percent, were the lowest recorded for any group. While in 1920 the percentage of foreign-born Americans had fallen to 13 percent from a high of 14.5 percent in 1910, the proportion of second-generation Americans had risen to 21.5 percent. Thus, immigrants and their children comprised a little more than a third of the populace.[1]

Anti-immigrant sentiment, as articulated by eugenicists and expressed through national and state legislation, grew steadily throughout the first twenty-five years of the twentieth century. Eugenics theorists such as Henry Fairchild Osborne and Charles B. Davenport, one of the country's leading biologists, extended theories about animal breeding to cover human heredity. By their reasoning, immigration of the wrong elements—that is, eastern and southern Europeans—could only result in pollution of America's future population with degenerate breeding stock. Although the eugenicists presented their ideas as a positive program of racial improvement and were thus able to attract progressive as well as conservative support, their agenda had dire implications for immigrants. Their legislative influence was first felt in anti-immigration statutes of 1903 and 1907 that barred the mentally deficient and politically suspect from entering the United States. The greatest triumph of the eugenicists, though, was the passage in 1924 of the severely restrictive Johnson-Reed Immigration Act by Congress, which established quotas designed to reduce the influx of immigrants from southern and eastern Europe. However, their influence was by no means limited to the arena of government. Popular magazines and college textbooks spread the message. As a 1916 textbook would have it, "From the rate at which immigrants are increasing, it is obvious that our very life blood is at stake."[2] Members of the Immigration Restriction League, invigorated by the eugenics movement, found their position bolstered by the racial arguments of Davenport and his followers. Soon they joined forces with Charles Davenport's American Breeders Association to fight for the preservation of what they termed the American race.

Because many Americans considered southern and eastern Europeans less worthy by biological definition than the northern European native-born populace, the autobiographies written by these "inferior" immigrants were a means of showing how closely allied their stories could be to those of native-born Americans. Immigrant autobiographies written before the passage of the Johnson-Reed Act had a mission that was in some ways similar to that of slave narratives written before emancipation. Just as slaves had to show that they were more than "dumb beasts" by using eloquent voices to tell biblically tinged stories of oppression, so immigrants had to document their eminent eligibility to be Americans.

In particular, the literature of Jewish immigrants took on increased political importance as institutionalized anti-Semitism grew, and as immigration laws were rewritten to exclude more eastern European Jews. Although anti-Semitism was by no means new to America, the arrival of large numbers of immigrants prompted it to fully blossom. In 1922 the president of Harvard College, Abbot Lawrence Lowell, announced that Harvard had a "Jewish problem" and moved to curb growing enrollments. Two years later President Lowell was among the supporters of the Johnson-Reed Act. Following passage of this law, Jewish immigration fell dramatically.[3]

Immigrant autobiographies such as Mary Antin's *The Promised Land* (1912), which presented a mainstream audience with a nonthreatening view of the influx from abroad, had much with which to contend and to compete. The eugenics movement dominated scientific and popular discourse about race. Another movement enacted, through performance, the nation's rejection of immigrants, particularly Catholics and Jews. The recently resurgent Ku Klux Klan had been reformed in the wake of D. W. Griffith's breakthrough 1915 film, *The Birth of a Nation*. The movie offered a mythic restaging of American slavery from the first bondsmen through Reconstruction, backed by a thirty-piece orchestra.

The Birth of a Nation depicted, as an intertitle put it, "the agony which the South endured that a nation might be born." This nation, thus, was explicitly composed of white, native-born Protestants, united in opposition to the threat posed by immigrants and African Americans. The movie culminated in a noble Klansman saving a white lily of the South, played by Lillian Gish, from a mob of lust-frenzied, Reconstruction-charged African Americans. It is an epic whose "collective hero," as David A. Cook puts it, "is the 'Aryan' race."[4] *The Birth of a Nation* was adapted from Thomas Dixon Jr.'s 1905 novel, *The Clansman: An Historic Romance of the Ku Klux Klan*, which Dixon later successfully adapted as a play. (He even starred in one of its several touring companies.)

Although the play had been successful, the movie was a blockbuster. It made $18 million before its retirement to art theaters and film clubs. It also became a focus for the national debate over race. Jane Addams, Booker T. Washington, and Harvard president Charles W. Elliot protested it; it was almost banned by the Massachusetts legislature; riots ensued when it was shown in Boston; and it was egged in New York. However, it was also shown in the White House to Dixon's Johns Hopkins classmate Woodrow Wilson, his cabinet, and their families.

Nationally syndicated columnist Dorothy Dix urged her readers to "go see it, . . . for it will make a better American of you." To her, *The Birth of a Nation* was "history vitalized."[5] Yet the vitalization to which she referred could take on an ominous tone. Benjamin Mays, president of Morehouse College and mentor of Martin Luther King, recalled in his 1971 autobiography, *Born to Rebel*, watching the movie in Lewiston, Maine. A member of the class of 1920 at Bates College, Mays was one of few African Americans living in the small town in the late 1910s. "Along with other Negro students at Bates, I went to see it," Mays recalled. "It was a vicious, cynical, and completely perverted characterization of Negroes. Even in Maine, the picture aroused violent emotions and threats from the audience. My fellow Negro students and I were not sure we would be able to get back to the campus unmolested. This was my only experience with a prejudiced and hostile audience during my years in Lewiston."[6]

Theater could be effective indeed in crystallizing racism. For his part, Thomas Dixon Jr. was urged by scores of letter writers to take the lead in a Klan revival. Although nervous about the risks of miscegenation, he felt that his correspondents' suggestions were premature. However, the man who did father the new Klan, failed minister William J. Simmons, organized the beginning of his new group around the opening of *The Birth of a Nation*. On the eve of the movie's Atlanta release, Simmons gathered nearly forty men, including the Speaker of the Georgia legislature, and conveyed them to Stone Mountain, an immense, dramatic outcropping of granite. Under his direction they erected and lit a pine cross. The Klan was reborn; white Protestants enacted rituals as exotic as those seen in Wild West shows and as part of minstrel performances.

Of course, counterposing whiteness against blackness was nothing new. The blackface in *Birth of a Nation* followed a long tradition. In the film, blackness was a performance that could be enacted at will. As Michael Rogin points out, not only were blacks in the movie played by white actors in blackface, but there is a scene in which "black" characters appear on screen, identified by a caption as "White spies disguised."[7] From its very origins, blackface performance had been a means of assimilating marginalized groups, such as the Irish, into a white identity that could be contrasted with blackness: "Creating a new sense of whiteness by creating a new sense of blackness," as David Roediger puts it.[8] Blackface performance thrived throughout the 1910s and 1920s, receiving its apotheosis in Al Jolson's *The Jazz Singer* (1927), in which the son of a Jewish cantor becomes a music-hall star by performing in blackface. By demonstrating his ability to move between racial and ethnic identities, Jolson's character identified himself as able to assimilate successfully.[9]

Blackness was not the only background against which to contrast whiteness. Businessmen's lodges evolved elaborate means of "playing Indian."[10] The secret rituals of manhood in Victorian America detailed by Mark C. Carnes—Freemasonry, Odd Fellowship, and Knights of Pythias—were enacted primarily in private. The theater of the 1920s Klan was public. Although the identity of Klan members may have, at least technically, been secret, their whiteness was not. Whereas many of the nineteenth-century lodges, such as the Improved Order of Red Men and the Ancient Order of Foresters, were based on Victorian conceptions of the primitive, the KKK developed a theater of whiteness.[11] For the first time, whiteness could be an achieved ethnic identity. The 1920s KKK found a way to theatricalize whiteness without blackness, which turned whiteness itself into a subject for ethnic performance.

From these theatrical beginnings the Klan continued, at first slowly. By 1920, with the help of hired public relations specialists, it was growing rapidly. At its height in the mid-1920s, approximately 4 million Americans, including about a half-million women, had signed up as members nationwide. The Klan fielded political candidates across the country, in many cases successfully, as in the Klan-backed Oregon legislature. To understand what those numbers mean, consider that in Indiana, 32 percent of native-born white women are estimated to have joined the KKK during the 1920s.[12] The Klan was bolstered by the reemergence, on a wide scale, of anti-Semitism. While President Woodrow Wilson, even as he segregated government employees by race, had hailed a vision of a melting-pot nation in which white citizens of a variety of national origins could unite, the reborn KKK focused its energies on counterposing a Nordic, Protestant version of whiteness against not only African Americans but Jews and Catholics as well. The Klan could draw comfort from the words of President Calvin Coolidge, who declared that "Nordics deteriorate when mixed with other races," and from Herbert Hoover's admonishment that immigrants "would be tolerated only if they behaved."[13] Naturalist Madison Grant authored the best-selling *The Passing of the Great Race* (1916), while Lothrop Stoddard, in *The Rising Tide of Color* (1920), alerted millions to the dangers posed by the flood of immigrants of inferior stock.

The essence of the Klan was its theatricality, the way it packaged xenophobia in a series of costumed rituals, both private and public. Klan weddings, which sometimes involved as many as fifty couples at a time; Klan christenings; and Klan funerals were all means of drawing members together, in small- as well as large-scale events. As Kathleen Blee reports, many klaverns sponsored sing-alongs, for which Klan musicians would alter the lyrics of well-known songs, so that "Yes, We Have No Bananas" became "Yes, the Klan Has No Catholics." Other favorites included "Onward Christian Klansmen" and "Klansmen Keep the Cross A-Burning." Community theatrical groups were another feature of the Klan. One man remembered playing the role of Ima White in a Klan play. The Marion, Indiana, chapter of the Women's Ku Klux Klan even made its own movie, starring local Klanswomen. These events reinforced a sense of klannishness among those who were already members.[14]

Some Klan performances, designed for broader audiences, echoed the historical pageants popular in late nineteenth-century and early twentieth-century America, in an ironic reversal of the civic-minded, melting-pot oriented pageants of the Progressive era. The organizers of the 1914 St. Louis pageant, intended to celebrate the 150th anniversary of the city's founding, were, as one of them later noted, "strong in the faith that if people play together, they will work together, and in the knowledge that a beautiful expression of an ideal increases many-fold the power of the ideal." The committee was composed of "persons, not only of every nationality, profession, trade, religion, and social status, but from every ward and precinct of the city." To that end, citizens desiring to participate in the pageant were offered fifty registration places throughout the city. Casting cards asked individuals to list not only their name, address, occupation, and height but also their national origin and sex. The 1915 pageant produced by the city of Boston, titled *Cave Life to City Life*, for instance, was based on organizers' belief that through working and playing together, different ethnic groups would be able to achieve harmony. Thus immigrants from Hale House played the parts of Flames, alongside middle-class youths from the Curry School of Expression, who represented Dust Clouds and Disease Germs. Russian immigrants from the Peabody House danced alongside students from the Latin Girls School, who embodied "the Greek element in the Athens of America."[15]

The Klan offered a competing version of American identity, a nation cleansed of immigrants and African Americans. By contrast, the Klan pageants were free from notions of plurality. Indianapolis Klanswomen worked with the Colonial Dames to stage a two-day "pageant of Protestantism," in which Klanswomen were cast as Uncle Sam, Columbia, Liberty, and Justice. Atlanta's historical pageant of 1920 featured members of the Klan, playing themselves, chasing carpetbaggers and their African American followers out of town to the music from *The Birth of a Nation* in a triumphal scene from the end of Reconstruction. During a similar scene in a pageant in Morgantown, North Carolina, in 1925, the audience burst into applause when the Klan rode onto the stage.[16]

In fact, many events were geared toward presenting the KKK to outsiders. Klan leaders were well aware of the importance of theatricality in planning these spectaculars. Local Klan leaders received complex instructions from state and national headquarters on staging konklaves, or rallies, including timelines for planning and the appropriate use of fireworks and other props. The results could prove awe inspiring to viewers. One 1924 rally in Marion County in southwestern Indiana involved two thousand KKK members who marched in full regalia through the county. As they neared a town, an airplane would fly overhead discharging paper bombs that opened to become tiny American flags suspended from parachutes. Streetlights were extinguished to make the burning and electrically lit crosses glow brighter. In other rallies, formations of hooded and robed Klanswomen held burning torches aloft to create living fiery crosses. In a sense, this was ethnic theater. In the same way that Yiddish theater helped reinforce group identity among members of immigrant communities in New York City, so the KKK provided the dramatic glue to bind together its coalition of racists. The Klan highlighted whiteness, not just in opposition to blackness, but as an entity unto itself—not as something neutral against which other groups could be measured as alien, but as a positive identity.

The carefully choreographed rituals of the Klan, highlighted by flag waving and other showy expressions of patriotism, were an all-too-effective means of presenting a positive group identity—and declaring it synonymous with Americanism. To counter the Klan's vision of an all-white, all-Protestant America, immigrant groups needed to find an equally powerful form of self-presentation to a not-always-sympathetic audience. In particular, Jewish immigrants, whose culture was already imbued with theatricality, needed to find a way to open up the stage on which Jewish identity was played out and to make it available for public, rather than simply in-group, consumption.

While *yiddishkeit* had found theatrical expression since the great migrations from eastern Europe of the 1880s, it had primarily been for an immigrant audience. By the early 1880s, immigrants were packing theaters in the Lower East Side; by the turn of the century, roughly 2 million audience members per year were attending the Yiddish theater in New York City alone, reveling in dramas of Jewish martyrdom and triumph.[17] They came to see tales of Jewish heroism in productions such as *The Hebrew Medea* or *The Jewish Macbeth* or even *The Rabbinical Student (Hamlet)*, in which Hamlet was a young scholar, Claudius was a lecherous and arrogant rabbi, the ghost of Hamlet's father was a dybbuk, and Ophelia was Queen Esther. A production of *Romeo and Juliet* turned the Capulets and Montagues into feuding religious groups, the rationalist Mithnagdim and the pietist Hasidim. Friar Lawrence became a reform rabbi. In the balcony scene, Raphael (Romeo), told Shaindele (Juliet), "Look yonder! See the Eternal Light! It is a sign that the Jewish light of God is everlasting!"[18] Performances tended to be long, about four hours. Watching plays such as *Dos yidishe harts* [The Jewish heart] or *The Pogrom*, immigrants celebrated *yiddishkeit*. By the 1910s, as the Zionist movement began to develop, it was always possible to garner a wild round of applause by shouting from the stage, "A yid bin ikh, un a yid vel ikh blaybn" [A Jew I am, and a Jew I will remain]. While, by the 1890s, cosmopolitanist playwrights such as Jacob Gordin sought to bring "serious" or modernist theatrical techniques to the Yiddish stage, a strong melodramatic tradition of theater endured throughout the 1920s. Debates over Jewish nationalism were fought not only within the labor movement and in the Yiddish press but also on the stage.

The Yiddish theater reinforced notions of identity within the immigrant community. However, it was inaccessible to the native-born Americans who were, as World War I came to a close, exhibiting more suspicion and distrust of eastern European immigrants. In the battle over who was to be welcomed into the United States, the immigrants needed a strong cultural voice that would be readily available to a non-Yiddish-speaking, native-born audience.

In 1908 Israel Zangwill provided American audiences the first melodrama that addressed these issues, *The Melting-Pot*. Zangwill's drama reached new, non-Yiddish-speaking audiences but was closely linked thematically to the tradition of onstage debates over Jewish nationalism. As Matthew Frye Jacobson rightly points out, the drama was not simply a commentary on immigration but stemmed from Zangwill's long involvement in the Jewish Territorial Organization. It was a play about nationalism as much as internationalism. *The Melting-Pot* added a new phrase to the popular lexicon and a new framework for the debate on immigration. Although a British citizen himself, Zangwill was passionately dedicated to the proposition embraced in the play's title. He dedicated the published edition of the play, "by his kind permission," to Theodore Roosevelt, "in respectful recognition of his strenuous struggle against the forces that threaten to shipwreck the great republic which carries mankind and its fortunes."[19]

Zangwill's play proved tremendously popular, not only with audiences but with public figures such as Roosevelt, Hamlin Garland, Booth Tarkington, and Jane Addams. It opened in Washington, D.C., to an audience that included the president and his family. The play ran for six months in Chicago and for 136 performances in New York and then, for the next decade, played in dozens of cities across America. The script, published a year after the play opened, became widely used as a text in high schools and colleges and was reprinted once a year until 1917, when the United States entered the war.[20] The melodrama features stock ethnic characters and a denouement in which the son of a Russian Jewish immigrant marries the daughter of the man who organized the pogrom that drove his father to America; love conquers all, effectively erasing the past. As Werner Sollors writes, "More than any social or political theory, Zangwill's play shaped American discourse on immigration and ethnicity, including most notably, the language of self-declared opponents of the melting-pot concept."[21] While audiences of Yiddish theater could share the sense that they were part of a nation, it was not an American nation. *The Melting-Pot* made an explicit bid for a more expansive sense of U.S. nationhood.

The Melting-Pot was successful in shaping the early terms of the debate about immigration. However, theater, by its very nature, is accessible only to a limited audience. While the communication that can take place between audience and performers may foster community-building, it is not an intimate experience. Moreover, no matter how effectively theatrical productions are presented, audiences view them as entertainment, as constructed artifacts.

The Ku Klux Klan succeeded in deploying theater as a nation-building exercise in the service of constructing an all-white nation. However, the Klan used theater in its broader sense, to invest every aspect of daily life with theatricality and make audiences feel that they were participants in a grand spectacle. The nation-building effected by earlier theatrical forms such as minstrel shows and Wild West shows had been either implicit (audiences at early minstrel shows did not necessarily see them as political exercises but, rather, as entertainment) or inclusive (Buffalo Bill's vision of nationhood included a wide range of ethnic groups). The Klan, on the other hand, was explicit about its aim of building a nation of only native-born whites.

Immigrants, in order to make an effective bid for inclusion in the American nation, needed to find a means of communication that could reach more people than the traditional theater. To most effectively persuade audiences of the unvarnished truth of their narratives, immigrants produced autobiographies. Autobiographers have truth-claims that are absent from the stage, and autobiographers speak to their readers in the tone of an intimate conversation. Readers of an ethnic autobiography could be afforded the impression that the author of the book was speaking to them alone. A series of popular ethnic autobiographies and fictions posing as autobiographies provided American readers with a means to see the trope of immigration unfolding. However, the authors of these autobiographies had learned well from the theater how to package their ethnicity and display it to maximum effect.

The Melodramatic Autobiography

In literature the first crossover success from a drama of *yiddishkeit* performed for Jewish immigrants to a presentation of ethnicity for an audience of outsiders was Mary Antin's 1912 autobiography, *The Prom-ised Land*. Like Zangwill's play, Antin's autobiography offered an image not of a robust culture but of a dissolving identity. When in 1911 the Dillingham Commission issued to Congress a forty-two-volume report arguing for the limitation of immigration from southern and eastern Europe, the stirrings of what would become a nativist groundswell be-gan. The textile strikes of 1912 in Lawrence, Massachusetts, helped to raise more suspicions against immigrant labor. Antin's memoir, which its editor, Ellery Sedgwick, perceptively compared to *Up from Slavery*, was in the classic tradition of ethnic autobiography. In *The Promised Land* Antin explained that "although I have written a genuine personal memoir, I believe that its chief interest lies in the fact that it is illustra-tive of scores of unwritten lives" (xiii). Antin conscientiously addressed native-born Americans. She provided footnotes to explain Jewish prac-tices and at times even exhorted her readers to better acts of citizenship: " 'The Jew peddler!' you say, and dismiss him from your premises and from your thoughts, never dreaming that the sordid drama of his days might have a moral that concerns you. What if the creature with the untidy beard carries in his bosom his citizenship papers? What if the cross-legged tailor is supporting a boy in college who is one day going to mend your state constitution for you?" (182). Antin earnestly affirmed that the ability to empathize and understand the immigrant or the Jewish experience would be enough to eradicate prejudice. Writing of a gentile tormentor in Russia, she declared that "if he could feel with my heart, if he could be a little Jewish boy for one day, I thought, he would know—he would know" (17). Antin's memoir was, as she intended, read as a citizenship manual of sorts. It quickly sold eighty-five thousand copies and went through thirty-four printings. The editors of a class-room edition, *At School in the Promised Land*, explained "that educa-tion and social influence may triumph over the obstacles of heredity and the circumstances of environment. . . . Besides explaining to Ameri-cans the experiences, the hopes, and the problems of immigrants, the author reminded the native born of their priceless heritage of liberty and opportunity, and stirred new inspiration for its preservation by the present generation."[22]

While Antin pleaded for understanding of what it meant to be an im-migrant Jew, her autobiography was based on her self-transformation, her ability to become like a native-born American. She identified her-self as a typical immigrant, with her "noble dreams and high ideals," but she was the immigrant of melodrama rather than of life. She described no feelings of ambivalence about her transformation. Her memoir is punctuated with utterances such as "Three cheers for the Red, White and Blue!" (260). Antin's version of Americanism not only seems tinged with religious fervor but skirts idolatry. Writing of her feelings about George Washington, she takes care to explain, "Never had I prayed, never had I chanted the songs of David, never had I called upon the Most Holy, in such utter reverence and worship as I repeated the simple sentences of my child's story of the patriot. . . . As I read about the noble boy who would not tell a lie to save himself from punishment, I was for the first time repentant of my sins. Formerly I had fasted and prayed and made sacrifice on the Day of Atonement, but it was no more than half play, in mimicry of my elders" (223).

What Orthodox Judaism could not effect, the religion of Americanism could. Antin does not integrate her past with her present as much as replace one set of beliefs with another. In fact, the death of her foreign self has been necessary for her to write the book: "I am just as much out of the way as if I were dead, for I am absolutely other than the person whose story I have to tell. . . . My life I have still to live; her life ended when mine began" (ix). Antin's performance asserted not a particular ethnicity but her ability to kill her ethnic self, or at the very least to replace it with another, more acceptably Americanized self.

However, as Keren McGinity has pointed out, the manuscript version of Antin's book, altered before publication, was far more equivocal about Antin's role as truth-telling model immigrant.[23] The manuscript of *The Promised Land* offers a vision of a more dimensional but less trustworthy self. "In my heart I cherish the pretense that it is all history," wrote Antin in the manuscript, "because I wish that it had been so."[24] The transparent self of the published autobiography—the eager, simple immigrant—is absent in the manuscript. "I confess that I have lied," she wrote there. "I further confess that I clearly love effect."[25] Most of all, in her unpublished manuscript Antin offered a definition of ethnicity that was indissoluble, and of a Jewish identity that had more to do with blood, with racial identity, than with mutability—something that clearly contradicted her published account of Jewish identity as a dissolving tincture. Writing of a convert to Judaism, she asks, "Could he *understand*? Like a born Jew? A Jew understood a great ever so many things without being taught."[26] This section, like the others cited above, did not appear in the published version. Whether imposed by Antin herself or by Sedgwick, these changes in the manuscript point to her need not only to present her stance toward her readers as unambiguous, but also to deracialize Jewish identity, to present it as something dissoluble rather than an essential quality, present at birth.

Antin's autobiography posited identity not as performative, but mutable. However, her autobiography was no less theatrical, in its way, than the staged performances of national identity. Although Antin played the eager, one-dimensional immigrant, she did not acknowledge her performance as such. Rather, she obviated any traces of calculated rehearsal from her autobiography. In the prewar period the performance of dissolving identity could still succeed. Native-born Americans were still willing to accept a fellow citizen who was reborn, if not born, on U.S. soil.

Special Sorrows: Ethnic Autobiography

Although Antin's autobiography is, as Werner Sollors has pointed out, only one of many transformation narratives, including Edward Steiner's *From Alien to Citizen* (1914) and Michael Pupin's *From Immigrant to Inventor* (1922), it does not necessarily reflect what Sollors describes as "affinities of ethnicity and heathendom."[27] In fact, these conversion narratives appear to have much more to do with class than with religion. They have their roots less in Cotton Mather than in Ben Franklin and Horatio Alger. They are literally moves not toward Christendom, but away from religious belief. The postwar narratives especially are about losing one's soul, not gaining spirituality.

Both Antin's autobiography and Zangwill's play were successfully produced in the less virulent atmosphere before World War I. By the end of the war, a wave of anti-Semitism and anti-immigrant sentiment had considerably complicated the climate in which immigrant autobiographies appeared. New immigration laws made deportation easier. Typical of this spirit of nativism was a remark made by the former president of the Native Sons of the Golden West, that every immigrant "must live for the United States, and grow an American soul inside him, or get out of the country."[28] Immigrant classics such as Anzia Yezierska's *Bread Givers* (1925), Abraham Cahan's *The Rise of David Levinsky* (1917), Samuel Ornitz's *Haunch, Paunch, and Jowl* (1923), and Michael Pupin's *From Immigrant to Inventor* were published in a time when the attitude toward immigrants was considerably uglier than it had been previously. Melting into Americanism was no longer an option for many eastern and southern Europeans. The autobiographies written in this period tended to be less conversion narratives (there were no missionaries of the American way eagerly awaiting notice that the newcomers had cast aside their heathen ways) than a literature much more ambivalent and ambiguous.

By the time Ornitz's work appeared, Jewish immigrant autobiography was an established part of the reading culture and could be used as the framework not only for novels—nearly indistinguishable from "straight" autobiography, and often read as such—but for self-parody. Immigrants writing in this hostile climate were able to use fictional forms nearly interchangeably with autobiography. In a sense, the success of an immigrant narrative rested not on its presentation of the immigrant self, but on its demonstration of the death of that self. Immigrants trying to show their adaptability had to prove not how authentically "other" they were from their native-born readers, but how able they were to dissolve their former identities into Americanism. It is also true that immigrant fiction was read and interpreted by critics as autobiography. Immigrants, after all, had but one story to tell.

This story was debated, rewritten, and parodied by the immigrant authors themselves during the 1920s. For instance, Abraham Cahan's *The Rise of David Levinsky* (1917) served as commentary on Mary Antin's *The Promised Land*. Cahan's work was in turn both echoed and deconstructed by Samuel Ornitz's *Haunch, Paunch, and Jowl*. Yet the very self-consciousness of immigrant autobiography at this point indicated how far it had come. While Mary Antin had to present herself as a cardboard character—one of the first public exemplars of the immigrant—later autobiographers had the freedom to work within an established genre.

Although earlier native-born writers such as Charlotte Perkins Gilman and Henry James had described how appalling it was for the "foreign mixture" to be spread over America, by the 1920s a wide readership had accepted the immigrant voice that was raised in debate with those who would "purify" America and halt the decline of the Anglo-Saxon race. Native American autobiographers could write from the perspective of a romantically lost race, but immigrants wrote as individuals who had, at least for the foreseeable future, no real chance of increasing their ranks. Thus eastern and southern European immigrant autobiographies, written during the height of KKK influence and after America's entrance in World War I, were freed to some extent from the earnestness of an Antin or from the melodramatic public-spiritedness of a Zangwill. It is fitting that the *New York Times* editorialist marking Zangwill's death in 1926 noted that "the country and Immigration law are far away from that pious belief, expressed in the play about which such a hullabaloo was made here some twenty years ago, that the melting pot is 'God's crucible.' "[29] Yet this very absence of "pious belief" also liberated immigrant autobiographers to critique the United States rather than plead for their inclusion in the nation.

As Alan Dawley writes, "Although the National Origins Act remained the law of the land, the assumption behind its passage, that the United States was a biological republic governed by Nordics, did not square with the character of American society. No amount of Anglo-Saxon ancestor worship or eugenics fantasy could erase the fact that America was a multiethnic society in which descendants of British Protestants were in a minority."[30] Into the contradictory world of 1920s America a new kind of ethnic autobiography and fiction was born: success stories steeped in a sense of loss and tinged with ambivalence. Although the official climate had become decreasingly friendly to eastern and southern European immigrants in the late 1910s, not until the 1920s and the passage of more restrictive immigration laws did the new literature find its audience.

The new autobiographers produced more sardonic commentaries than had earlier writers such as Antin. Michael Pupin, in recounting his arrival at Castle Garden in 1874, asked his readers, "What has a young and penniless immigrant to offer who has no training in any of the arts and crafts and does not know the language of the land?" From his position as professor of electro-mechanics at Columbia University, Pupin answered his own rhetorical question somewhat bitterly: "Apparently nothing, and if the present standards had prevailed forty-eight years ago I should have been deported."[31] Pupin, in insisting that "there are . . . certain things which a young immigrant may bring to this country that are far more precious than any of the things which the present immigration laws prescribe," refused to, like Antin, present himself as a blank slate—refused to erase his previous identity.

Abraham Cahan's novel in the form of an autobiography was published the same year that Congress passed the Literacy Act, excluding illiterate aliens, over President Wilson's veto. The opening words of *The Rise of David Levinsky* echo Antin's, but with an important difference. As David Levinsky introduces himself to the reader, "Sometimes, when I think of my past in a superficial, casual way, the metamorphosis I have gone through strikes me as nothing short of a miracle. I was born and reared in the lowest depths of poverty and I arrived in America—in

1885—with four cents in my pocket. I am now worth more than two million dollars and recognized as one of the two or three leading men in the cloak-and-suit trade in the United States."[32]

Until this point Cahan seemed to be echoing not only Antin but scores of American success stories. A mention of early poverty was standard, after all, for immigrant autobiographies. For example, Michael Pupin opened *From Immigrant to Inventor*, with these words: "When I landed at Castle Garden, forty-eight years ago, I had only five cents in my pocket."[33]

Yet the voice of David Levinsky continued with an important distinction: "And yet when I take a look at my inner identity it impresses me as being precisely the same as it was thirty or forty years ago. My present station, power, the amount of worldly happiness at my command, and the rest of it, seem to be devoid of significance."[34]

Absent was either an acknowledgment or even a desire for self-transformation. Levinsky's was no conversion narrative. In 1917, as Arthur Mann writes, "Absolute forgetfulness of ancestry was the price of becoming an American."[35] Levinsky and Cahan were unwilling to indulge in this amnesia. Cahan paid for his apostasy in sales, which numbered less than 8,000 in the book's first two years of publication. A cheap reprint edition issued in 1928 did somewhat better, but by that time the climate had changed again.

The appearance of Samuel Ornitz's *Haunch, Paunch, and Jowl* in 1923 signaled the birth of a best-seller and the death, in some respects, of the nonironic Jewish immigrant autobiography. *Haunch, Paunch, and Jowl* was a work of fiction masquerading as autobiography. Ornitz's narrator, a corrupt Jewish judge, seemed to be not only an anti-Semitic caricature, but one who attributed his success to his ability to manipulate public perceptions of his Jewishness. He blamed persecuted Jews themselves for their ill treatment at the hands of anti-Semites. *Haunch, Paunch, and Jowl* not only parodied the immigrant autobiographies, such as Antin's *The Promised Land*, that had provided an eloquent defense of immigrants as active and willing participants in American political and cultural life. It also, by thoroughly deconstructing the trope of the Jewish immigrant autobiography, offered a definition of ethnicity as performance, successful or unsuccessful, and laid the groundwork for the impersonator autobiography, Elizabeth Stern's *I Am a Woman—and a Jew* (1926).

Horace Liveright, the publisher of *Haunch, Paunch, and Jowl*, issued Samuel Ornitz's work not as his own but as the actual "anonymous autobiography" of a judge five years deceased. Press releases claimed that Ornitz had simply organized and prepared the manuscript. Many publishers had rejected the work on the grounds that it would prove offensive to Jewish readers, and it is possible that Liveright was protecting itself against anticipated accusations of anti-Semitism. In fact, the novel was a great commercial success.

Although denounced by some rabbis as "lecherous and degrading," the book was praised by many Jews and Jewish organizations and serialized in both the pro-Communist *Morning Freiheit* and, some years later, in Germany in the *Rote Fahne*. Moreover, it was later presented onstage by the workers' theater Artef, an acronym for Arbeiter Teater Verband, or the Workers Theatrical Alliance. Artef was a conglomeration of leftist fraternal organizations, women's councils, and labor unions that supported the Yiddish Art Theater but wanted to produce more revolutionary material.[36]

Haunch, Paunch, and Jowl played not only on American mythologies of success and on popular perceptions of ethnic neighborhoods as dangerous, crime-ridden zones, but also on conventions of autobiography itself. The work starts by questioning its own validity: "I begin my history. I want to tell everything. Everything: so that even if I tell pathological lies the truth will shine out like grains of gold in the upturned muck. . . . I shall grope for first definite memories" (13). Having thrown all that he will subsequently say in doubt, the narrator, Meyer Hirsch, tells the story of his spectacular rise in the world, which he effects through time-honored methods of business organization.

Hirsch learns early to behave as an assimilated immigrant—a model American boy—in order to further his criminal career: "My ways are modest, my talk quiet, respectful, aye, pious, and thus I beguile the shopkeeper whilst my accomplice lifts and loads. . . . Even in the beginning, when I started to play the game of life, I found it was better and safer to use my wits and let the other fellow do the manual or risky share of the job—the dirty work" (30). Here piety is a cover for criminality, and the management skills popularized by the business apostles of the 1920s are used for unsavory ends. When Hirsch tells us about the time "I first seized upon a plan that suggested to me the policy I followed throughout my career—to make every situation return a profit" (37), he is offering the kinds of lessons dear to Rotarians. Never mind that he is talking about collecting protection money from storekeepers. Hirsch takes an approach opposite that of the model student Antin when it comes to the lessons he learns in school: "It was a heart-breaking task for the teacher and a dull session for the pupil. It became tiresome to hear daylong the same spiritless voice droning away at dates, sums, platitudes and scolding preachments" (71). However, his street education continues without interruption.

Hirsch frames the entire political debate surrounding immigration in terms of corruption and criminality. The freedom that Antin celebrates is appreciated by Hirsch and his cohorts for very different reasons. As his uncle and mentor, Philip, says, "It's a good thing . . . this is a free country and I can exploit whom I like" (104).

As Alan Dawley suggests, one of the unintended side effects of immigration restriction was the development of a specifically ethnic identity: "Insofar as the stigma of exclusion rubbed off on immigrant groups already present, ethnic stereotyping actually encouraged Little Italies and Polinias to unify against assimilation. Instead of fostering the melting pot, nativist prejudice fostered the spirit of ethnic 'tribalism' that characterized the 1920s."[37] In *Haunch, Paunch, and Jowl*, Ornitz presented a disquieting view of ethnic tribalism.

Haunch, Paunch, and Jowl takes for granted the notion that ethnicity is a mask that can be put on and taken off at will. In a country where ethnic performances compete for attention, the winners are those who are best able to consciously manipulate the symbols of ethnic caricature. Sometimes the performance of ethnicity is quite literal, as when Hirsch is managing a nightclub and hires performers who will fulfill middle-class spectators' expectations of immigrant behavior.

> I hired three Chinamen with particularly yellow and malevolent faces to sit at a table smoking very fancy opium pipes. I instructed them to glower at the passing girls, who ordinarily would not be frightened by a thousand Chinamen, but, at my hint, they shrink back and cry out in alarm. . . . Millie joined our little play with gusto. As she passed the Chinamen's table, one of them leaped up and placed his taloned fingers around her neck. She drew back, of course to the center of the dance floor so the slummers would miss nothing, and apparently a Chinaman was choking to death a girl of twelve. Finally the Chinaman dropped Millie to the floor, where she lay in a convulsed heap. She cried out, "Don't kill me, Ly Chee, don't kill me. I'll bring you all the money next time." Ly Chee was an intelligent fellow and could speak a pretty fair English but for this occasion he spoke pidgin English. "Me killee lou, me killee lou, bling allee timee allee money, no floget, me killee lou" (152–53).

Outside the nightclub stage, Hirsch and his cohorts are what he terms Professional Jews, for whom Judaism is a way of getting ahead and ethnic performance is a way of squelching enemies. Others in the "Professional Jew game . . . call upon me, leading sheep-like committees, and ask me as the Leader of My Oppressed People in America to end this or that discrimination. . . . In short, their conduct assured them a steady political future in New York, and a rise from poverty to riches" (211). In this construct, the assertion of ethnic identity is a power move, a political performance devoid of content. In order to silence an Irish activist, "I have suggested to the temple that our congregation start a social settlement in the Ghetto to salvage the drifting spiritual life of the new generation, who are falling too much under the un-Jewish influence of persons like Finn" (259). The congressman elected by Hirsch and his cohorts has one speech only, which he presents during each term in Congress. "In time this speech became an East Side classic: our best heads had concocted it. It was a hair-raising recital of the horrors of Jewish persecution in Russia that splashed vitriolic denunciations upon the Tsar and his government as being officially responsible for the pogroms and ended with an hysterical plea to the American government to sever relations with the Tsar's government until the massacres were stopped" (212).

This notion of ethnicity as performance clearly has troubling implications, which are made explicit when one of Hirsch's childhood friends, who grows up to be what Hirsch describes as an honest politician, proposes his theory of the pogroms to counter the position of the one-speech congressman. "Avrum had said that Jewish ways made it easy for the Russian agents-provocateurs to inflame the peasants against the Jews. . . . He did not say that the Jews as a whole cheated the peasant and deserved his resentment, but accused the trader and money-lender classes. . . . Where is our fault, in what way do we help along the happening of pogroms!" (212). Avrum's solution, in order to stop pogroms or at the very least increase international outrage when they do occur, would be to change the behavior of Russian Jews: "How different it will be when the Jews come to the world with clean hands and clear consciences!" (213). In other words, Jews must change their ethnic performance; they must shed the gestures caricatured by anti-Semites and adopt a theatrics of invisibility. To avoid being targeted by anti-Semites, they must stop being identifiably Jewish.

This argument is never countenanced within the book; Avrum becomes a persecuted figure. Another speaker, who is given plenty of space to air his views, is an assimilated Jewish doctor who similarly says, "The Jews will create a Jewish Question in America as long as they cling to their bizarre Jewishness" (198). Dr. Crane begs his auditors to "get rid of the foul fungus of the Ghetto. If you do not become an integral, euphonious part of the American nation, you will again isolate yourself and stand out yellow-badged among the people of the New World . . . again . . . alien, wandering, strange figures . . . again . . . distrust, dislike, persecution" (201). Once again Dr. Crane asserts that Jews are in some way responsible for anti-Semitism. In his view, intermarriage and assimilation are the only solutions. "Racial vanity" (199) is the problem.

Put another way, the ethnic performance is one that, in Crane's view, can only win enmity. It is Crane who introduces the term "Professional Jew," saying that "in America the Professional Jews stir up rumpuses, alarms, furors over every fancied grievance, insult and reflection. They focus a spotlight upon the Jews" (198). Because Hirsch enacts the behavior Dr. Crane describes, and because he in fact uses it as a means of personal profit, *Haunch, Paunch, and Jowl* finally seems to endorse his notions and those of Avrum Toledo, who believes that Jews bring pogroms upon themselves. *Haunch, Paunch, and Jowl* represents ethnicity as performance, certainly, but it goes far beyond its satire of the myth of the self-made man, its parody of American autobiographical conventions, and its mockery of the genre of the immigrant autobiography. With its core of anti-Semitism it seems strange that *Haunch, Paunch, and Jowl* would be serialized in the Communist press and staged in the radical Yiddish theater. The book is clearly intended for a gentile audience. Yiddish terms are defined throughout the book, and Jewish customs are explained. Although the work is certainly a critique of the bourgeoisie, it is a critique tinged with anti-Semitism. While many proletarian novels of the period feature unsympathetic yet strong representations of the bourgeoisie, these are always engaged by other voices in dialogue, whether those voices belong to the narrator or to other characters. Yet within the world of *Haunch, Paunch, and Jowl*, no characters challenge this view; no voice is raised in opposition.

By the 1920s, immigrant autobiography was uniquely qualified to challenge the rags-to-riches success stories that were the conventional form of popular autobiography. Other forms of ethnic autobiography were popular, but Native American and African American autobiographers did not have the luxury of self-transformation. They could not, like Mary Antin, claim to shed their skin, since their skin, or their skin color, was the primary definer of their social status in America. Yet, since their presence was clearly not desired by lawmakers, Klansmen, popular authorities on racial matters such as Madison Grant, and the readers of books such as *The Passing of the Great Race*, Jewish immigrant authors also had an undeniable exoticism for readers. Immigrant autobiographers could and did document how they assimilated—through their self-conscious acquisition of new clothing, new language, and new manners—and how they had to leave their culture behind in order to succeed. In doing so, they were presenting a more theatrical form of the self-fashioning that native-born Americans had to effect in order to move up the class ladder.

From Ben Franklin through Horatio Alger through success writers of the first two decades of the twentieth century, such as Orison Swett Marden, editor of *Success* magazine and author of many success manuals, native-born American mythologies of the self-made man have depicted a vision of success in which what was left behind simply did not matter. Not only the past, but any notions of sensual pleasure could and should be left behind for the sake of success. These manuals, while they offered advice on how to abandon old habits and old traits, allowed little space for mourning what was lost.

Franklin's autobiography turns even the death (from smallpox) of the author's son into an opportunity for a lesson. "I long regretted bitterly & still regret that I had not given it to him by Inoculation; This I mention for the Sake of Parents, who omit that Operation on the Supposition that they should never forgive themselves if a child died under it; my Example showing that the Regret may be the same either way, and that therefore the safer may be chosen."[38] Although Franklin offered thirteen rules to follow to approach moral perfection, his list of virtues with their corollary precepts gave no sense that a life of moderation, silence, frugality, industry, resolution, and chastity might be anything but satisfying. He allowed no room for mourning the loss of venery, trifling conversation, drinking to elevation, or eating to dullness.

Ragged Dick, Alger's first and most widely read boys' novel, was used extensively in schools in the 1920s. The eponymous hero of the story takes his first steps up the class ladder when he advances from being a homeless shoe-shine boy and becomes a clerk. As Ragged Dick, he enjoys treating his friends to meals, attending the theater, and joking around with little respect for class barriers. Only when he learns to feel shame is Dick able to give up his pleasures, start saving money, curtail his social life, and begin learning to read and attending Sunday school—all for the sake of respectability. Richard Hunter, as he is known by the end of the novel, has become a class-conscious, somewhat joyless, yet highly respectable youth. Nowhere in the story is he given a chance to mourn the connections he lost in his relentless pursuit of success.

The Horatio Alger model of self-transformation was echoed in any number of inspirational texts. In the introduction to Marden's *Little Visits with Great Americans* (1905), published by the Success Company, the editors explained that they had been "for many years in quest of the elements of a grand, healthy, symmetrical, successful man—the ideal man." This ideal is possible for their readers, presumably, since "character, it has been wisely said, is the result of choices. It appears again and again in the reminiscences of those who have succeeded, that from time to time they have deliberately chosen a course of action which by force of habit has become a personal characteristic." It is possible to remake oneself, indeed, to ensure that "life habits [are] hardened into enduring character," that pure will becomes transformative.[39]

The 1910s and 1920s were a period when success manuals enjoyed their greatest popularity and when the idea of the self-made man reached its peak.[40] While the notion that developing one's will or personal magnetism could lead to success—the so-called New Thought—replaced older ideas about character-based paths to success, success ideologies of the period still stressed personal transformation as a means to getting ahead and discouraged readers from glancing backward. *The Success Course of Will: Culture and Concentration for Power and Success* (1918), for instance, urged students to develop their will as an all-powerful instrument. William W. Woodbridge's inspirational short story *"Bradford, You're Fired!": A Story of the Super-Self* (1917) even posited a character who split into two men and fired the pleasure-seeking, relaxed component of his personality in order to achieve greater worldly success.[41] Bradford's id, in this formulation, slunk away and was never missed by his Super-Self. In the world of success manuals, one could lose half of one's self and experience only relief.

While *Haunch, Paunch, and Jowl* may have provided the most savagely ironic version of success ideologies, by the mid-1920s the immigrant autobiography and the immigrant novel offered a poignant counterpoint to the traditional success story. Sara, the narrator of Anzia Yezierska's *Bread Givers*, describes a process of assimilation with a high price. For Sara, the American economy is an "economy of pain," to borrow William Dean Howells's memorable phrase. One person's gain is another's loss. When the book opens, one of Sara's sisters has waited in vain for a shirt factory job, where "there was such a crowd of us tearing the clothes from our bodies and scratching out each other's eyes in the mad pushings to get in first" that the police were called to keep order. "And after we waited for hours and hours, only two girls were taken" (2). For Ragged Dick, his first purchase of toiletries is an event to celebrate. Yet when Mashah, Sara's most Americanized sister, buys her own toothbrush and towel, it is a tragic occurrence in the family: "Mother tore her hair when she found that Mashah made a leak of thirty cents in wages where every cent had been counted out. But Mashah went on brushing her teeth with her new brush and wiping her face with her new towel. And from that day, the sight of her toothbrush on the shelf and her white, fancy towel by itself on the wall was a sign that Mashah had no heart, no feelings, that millionaire things willed themselves in her empty head, while the rest of us were wearing out our brains for only a bite in the mouth" (6).

Although Sara, who subtitles her book "A Struggle between a father of the Old World and a daughter of the New," struggles upward in approved Horatio Alger fashion, she records the price of her success at every turn. When the family moves from the overcrowded tenement to a New Jersey suburb, Sara feels out of place: "The loneliness of that little town! And the cold, stiff people there. It was like living among walking chunks of ice. The each-for-himself look froze me to the bone" (129). Sara welcomes the chance to break free of Old World constraints. "In America," as she tells her father, "women don't need men to boss them" (137). Yet she is never unconscious of loss. She relishes the chance to spend an hour alone for the first time in her life but finds herself lonely. When she looks at herself in the mirror, she sees "a set sadness about the lips like in old maids who'd given up all hope of happiness" (181). She feels her failure to be accepted by the native-born, middle-class Americans with whom she attends college. "Help me not to want their little happiness," she prays. "I have wanted their love more than my life. Help me be bigger than this hunger in me" (220).

She must, like the characters of *Haunch, Paunch, and Jowl*, become aware that in the New World, the claims of community can easily be false. Here, once again, ethnic performance is something to be distrusted. When Sara's father buys a grocery store whose owner had advertised in the *Ghetto Times* that he needed to sell quickly to return to Russia, the ethnic solidarity her father hopes to trade on proves to be just another American hard sell. He arrives when the store is bustling, and the owner pushes away another prospective buyer who has arrived first. "Because the other man was Italian, . . . the owner sold me the bargain only because I was a Jew" (116). However, the Italian was a former employee, hired by the owner to put on a charade, and the oatmeal boxes are empty, the sugar bin full of sawdust. It has been a mistake to trust ethnic solidarity.

Even in her moment of greatest triumph, when she returns from college with enough academic prize money to purchase a new, respectable suit, to rent a clean room, and to "enjoy the honeymoon of my career" (241) as a public school teacher, she is caught between Old World and New. At her mother's deathbed, when the undertaker rends her father's and her sisters' clothing, Sara refuses:

"'I don't believe in this. It's my only suit, and I need it for work. Tearing it wouldn't bring Mother back to life again.'

"A hundred eyes burned on me their condemnation.

"'Look at her, the *Americanerin!*'" (255).

By contrast, Ragged Dick wears his new, respectable clothes with smug satisfaction. He enjoys the fact that he is literally unrecognizable to his friends. For Dick, passing as a middle-class boy when he is still a bootblack has no emotional price. Although it may be clear to readers that it is sad to lose one's friends and one's identity and to become literally unrecognizable to former intimates, there is no room in the text for such an acknowledgment. Dick is relentlessly cheerful, as is the book's narrator; the reader's doubts are forced underground.

For Sara there is no happy ending, no leaving behind the former, ethnic self. Although she has embarked on her own, assimilated life, Sara agrees to take in her oppressively traditional father to live with her and new husband. The final words of the book speak to the futility of attempting to remake oneself: "I felt the shadow still there, over me. It wasn't just my father, but the generations who made my father whose weight was still upon me" (297). The popularity of Horatio Alger stories declined dramatically after World War I. Immigrant narratives from the postwar era substituted a recognition of the losses incurred while struggling upward for the relentless can-doism of Alger's heroes.[42]

Pushed to the margins by anti-immigrant sentiment and legislation, immigrant autobiographers of the 1920s were unable, like Antin, to dissolve their selves and be reborn into the center of American life. The birth of new selves seemed impossible in this context. Yet this very problem created space for a more theatricalized presentation of identity and a critique of American class mythology. By linking ethnicity and class, ethnic autobiographers were able to work from the margins to critique American self-fashioning. In doing so, they provided a model for an ironized and theatrical self-presentation. While some ethnic autobiographers used the model of ethnic autobiography to critique class mythologies, Ornitz went one step further and explicitly discussed how the performance of ethnicity could be used to play the class game and win. In doing so, he opened up possibilities for one autobiographer to use ethnicity as a metaphor.

Imaginary Jews: Elizabeth Stern's Autobiography As Amnesia

When ethnicity itself is a performance, the impersonator ethnic autobiography seems a natural development. Elizabeth Stern's *I Am a Woman—And a Jew* has all the hallmarks of a real autobiography of the 1920s. The 1991 Jewish Publication Society anthology, *Writing Our Lives: Autobiographies of American Jews, 1890–1990*, edited by Steven J. Rubin, contains standard works such as the memoirs of Mary Antin, Edna Ferber, and Isaac Bashevis Singer. In the preface to the excerpt from Stern's best-selling autobiography, Rubin traces details of Stern's life, including her 1890 birth in Skedel, Poland; her early immigration to the United States; her dual careers as social worker and writer; and her twenty-three years (1914–37) as a feature writer for the *New York Times* and as a columnist for the *Philadelphia Inquirer*. In addition, Rubin notes, Stern was the author of three novels, a biography of Gandhi's wife, and two autobiographies, the first of which, *My Mother and I* (1917), appeared, like Zangwill's *Melting-Pot*, with a preface by Theodore Roosevelt. Although Stern was an early feminist and assimilated American, Rubin continues, "she was also able to acknowledge proudly her own Jewish identity and her unbroken ties to her people."[43]

Indeed, Stern's best-known autobiographical work, *I Am a Woman—And a Jew*, published under the pseudonym Leah Morton, explores issues common to many Jewish immigrant autobiographies and autobiographical novels of the period: conflicts between old and new worlds, between Orthodox Judaism and assimilation, and between spiritual and worldly success. What makes Stern's work so appealing to contemporary audiences and ensures its inclusion on the syllabi for college courses on women and Judaism is her limning of feminist issues. As Magdalena J. Zaborowska points out, in comparison to Mary Antin, Stern described a greater rebelliousness against the strictures under which women in Orthodox families operated. In comparison with Yezierska, with whom she also shares many characteristics, Stern stressed the benefits of collective action and of active involvement in the political issues of the day, rather than individual achievement. While in *I Am a Woman—And a Jew*, Zaborowska writes, the "idea of the melting pot might seem attractive as a theory, . . . as Stern shows us, it meant virtual death to the immigrant's ethnicity in the process of his or her Americanization."[44]

Yet, wrote her son in his 1988 memoir, *Secret Family*, Stern was not who she claimed to be. In his first chapter, "Imaginary Jews," Thomas Stern begins to lay out the patterns of deception he claims characterized his mother's life. Rather than being, as she claimed, the Orthodox, East Prussian-born daughter of rabbi Aaron Levin and his wife, Sarah, she was the Pittsburgh-born, illegitimate child of a Welsh Baptist mother, Lillian Morgan, and a German Lutheran father, Chris Limburg. Placed with the Levins as a foster child when she was seven, she remained with them until she was seventeen, when she returned to the home of her natural mother. She eventually married another illegitimate child who, like her, had been raised in a Jewish foster family; both took on Jewish identities. As an adult, according to her son, she and her husband moved nearly effortlessly among various ethnic identities. When she enrolled in social work school, for example, "She said she was Elizabeth Levin, the daughter of a Jewish rabbi. But Elizabeth was far from constant in her tale. Frequently she boasted that she was the daughter of a prosperous German merchant, Chris Limburg. And often she boasted that she was a Morgan, the offspring of 'important people' in Pittsburgh, who were Welsh or English. Sometimes Elizabeth admitted that the Morgans were coal miners, even though that lowered her status."[45]

Thomas Stern records a childhood of "ethnic confusion." His parents were employed by a Jewish immigrants' resettlement organization, but they were fired when the director learned that they were "false Jews." Thomas spent years moving from the Lutheran world of his natural grandfather, a prosperous merchant, to the home of his Welsh grandmother, to the Orthodox Jewish world of his foster grandparents.

Eventually, from among the identities available to her, Elizabeth chose one. Her decision to pass as Jewish was motivated by more than her simple desire to hide her illegitimate origins. According to her son, during the years she lived with the Levins, Aaron sexually abused her. She became pregnant by him when she was fourteen, and after forcing her to have an abortion, he let her alone. When Elizabeth was grown, although Aaron wanted to forget she existed, she had a hold on him "because of the awful things he did to me, when I was a girl."[46] Given this version of events, it is possible to read the opening of Elizabeth Stern's book very differently than does Zaborowska. Citing the powerful opening paragraphs of the memoir, as Stern recounts gazing down at the face of her dead father, Zaborowska notes that "as a symbol of her Jewishness and Old World roots, the narrator's father in *I Am a Woman—And a Jew* also represents her ethnic language, and his death can thus be seen as its metaphorical obliteration."[47] However, once we know more of Stern's background (or her son's version of it), her description of this experience takes on a very different coloration: "I remember looking down at the face of my father, beautiful and still in death, and for a brief, terrible moment feeling my heart rise up—surely it was in a strange, suffocating relief?—as the realization came to me: 'Now I am free!' "[48] To gaze down upon the face of the man, now dead and powerless, who had sexually abused her could have left Stern feeling free indeed.

Autobiographical accounts in direct contradiction to one another only highlight the fragile nature of memory and the incredible strength of the human desire to create a past one can live with. It is possible that writing each autobiography was a cathartic experience. Thomas Stern, describing his childhood, writes that "we shifted identity even more violently than before. We were our true selves; and our false selves. We were superior and inferior to everyone. Our oscillations dizzied me." His writing of the autobiography is not only a way to make sense of a complex past, but a way of banishing the memories that haunted him: "I had dark Freudian dreams about black snakes. They were partly inspired by the stories that Elizabeth told about her rapes by Zadie Levin, and partly by Aunt Lillian's tales of her whippings with a black leather belt by Chris Limburg. I had those nightmares repeatedly for fifty years, until I began to write this book."[49] Elizabeth, by his account, had very different reasons for publishing *I Am a Woman—And a Jew*:

> In our living room, I told Elizabeth, "I think you shouldn't publish that book! It isn't true. It twists our family. It makes us what we are not."
> Elizabeth screamed, "I have to publish my book! It makes me what I want to be. It shows our family as I want people to see us."
> Although my nerve was fading I said, "When I read your book, Mother, I forget who we are. I don't like that. I want to remember myself, and our family."[50]

Ellen Umansky, who wrote the introduction to the 1986 reprint edition of *I Am a Woman—And a Jew*, did extensive genealogical research after Thomas Stern contacted her with his allegations about Elizabeth's background. Although many records were destroyed by Elizabeth Stern, making certainty about the true circumstances of her birth impossible, Umansky reports that "scattered pieces of information . . . do seem to substantiate Thomas Stern's assertions." According to Umansky, "If her eldest son's story of his family origins—a story that apparently took him thirteen years of research to unravel—is even half true, it sheds new light on Elizabeth Stern's representations of Jewish women."[51]

Just as the immigrant's account of assimilation into the hostile culture of success resonated with members of a native-born reading public mourning their own losses as they became successful, so Stern's account of sexual abuse found perfect metaphor in the preexisting genre of the female immigrant autobiography. Reading *I Am a Woman—And a Jew* through the filter of sexual abuse makes haunting the parallels between it and *Bread Givers*. Anzia Yezierska ends her narrative with the image of her father still casting a shadow over her; for her part, Elizabeth Stern writes, "I had thought that, by marrying a Christian, I, who was in my heart no longer a Jew, would be free. I was to find not only that on that day of my father's death, but twice again, how mistaken I had been" (2). The domineering father whose beliefs and behavior "would destroy everything in his life, the very happiness of his children" (1), still held sway over her.

Of course, a female reader need not have experienced incest to sympathize with a daughter attempting to escape the yoke of a tyrannical father. The feminist struggles of native-born women in the 1920s were presented in amplified form in the autobiographies of immigrant women. When Sara Smolinsky, in *Bread Givers*, writes of the division of goods within her house, it is a scene with which many native-born women could identify: "Since men were the only people who counted with God, Father had not only the best room for himself, for his study and prayers, but also the best eating of the house" (10). When she describes sitting down at the dinner table with her sisters, it seems a perfect metaphor for women struggling to achieve a more equitable division of wages and legal rights. "With watering mouths and glistening eyes we watched Mother skimming off every bit of fat from the top soup into Father's big plate, leaving for us only the thin, watery part" (10).

Like Yezierska, Elizabeth Stern makes clear what is lost through assimilation—for the father as well as for the daughter. Although she recounts a story of being permanently banished from her father's presence for marrying a Christian, she is alive to the pain suffered by her father: "I was to hear in my classrooms many lectures on the 'problem of the immigrant,' on 'Americanization'; but none were to speak for that which my father represented, the old immigrant whose dream it was, as it was the Quaker's and the Puritan's, to find a new home of religious freedom in the new land, and who was, instead, to lose his children to that new land" (41).

Although Stern recalls one instance after another of the anti-Semitism she suffers, she is clear about her desire to avoid iconicity. When a classmate speaks to her of "the spiritual sweetness of your people," she is irritated. "I did not wish her to see me carrying a pale golden torch for my people. I wanted to be myself, apart from every one, from every people" (61). She is eager to become as assimilated as possible, as soon as possible: "I was no Biblical Rebecca sorrowfully pleading for her race. I was an American, now" (64). Yet later, after her father's death, she regrets her assimilation: "I had gone out because of my ignorance, because of this land where the Jew was robbed of his most precious possession, his racial integrity, by the soft words of those who pretended to be his friends" (225). Like Meyer Hirsch of *Haunch, Paunch, and Jowl*, she insists that Jews are responsible for their social ostracism: "The truth is, it is the Jew who excludes himself. The pride of his race and in his faith builds a wall between himself and all mankind" (226).

While she insists on her individuality, Stern imputes racial characteristics to others. She writes of her maid, "It was only because of that innate kindliness of negroes that she did her work really well" (86). Of her polite future husband, she writes that "courtesy was part of his inheritance, for his father had been a Frenchman, his mother an Englishwoman of good family" (48).

Although Stern may want to avoid "carrying a pale golden torch" for her people, she is finally unable to avoid casting herself as a representative of her people. She feels trapped, as a writer, by her ethnic background and by her father's voice: "Whatever the Jew has given to the written art of America has been Jewish, a heritage and gift of the Jew who came to the new land, America. My father thought he had no part in this new land; he had cut himself off from me. But every word I wrote carried his feeling, his Jewish humor and, it might be, if one were sometimes blessed and happy,—a little even of his Jewish poetry" (124). By the end of the book, she feels she knows "what every Jew is and does, is something that must, indeed, belong to his people; that no other people living have our peculiar quality, which is not individual, but racial, and which gives to each of us who accomplishes with genius, the ability to express himself only through the accumulated genius of his race, so that every Jewish writer, statesman, actor, is not only himself, but the mirror of his people, the voice of his people" (359). She finally realizes that she cannot escape what she sees as her racial destiny: "We Jews are alike. We have the same intensities, the sensitiveness, poetry, bitterness, sorrow, the same humor, the same memories. The memories are not those we can bring forth from our minds: they are centuries old and are written in our features, in the cells of our brains." The individuality she grants members of every ethnic group, she denies for herself. "One is one's self. But not when one is a Jew" (360).

These last words are haunting. If Stern's memories are indeed written in the cells of her brain, can she not be talking about the memories of abuse at the hands of her foster father? In this formulation, her ethnicity is the result of a trauma; it is almost as though her foster father impregnated her with his Jewish identity when he sexually abused her. Jewishness becomes a metaphor for the memories she cannot escape and for the identity imposed upon her by her rabbi foster father when he began his abuse of her. If, as she writes of her father, "every word I wrote carried his feeling," then her "voluntary" ethnicity seems like less of a choice and more of a compulsion. The powerlessness she expresses, the inability to change this identity, even her loss of self—"One is one's self. But not when one is a Jew"—all seem metaphorical for the experience of surviving abuse. To be a Jew in this construct is to be forever linked with one's abuser. Assimilation into a new identity would be impossible. By her son's account, Stern insisted that "I have to publish my book! It makes me what I want to be. It shows our family as I want people to see us." Yet she apparently wanted to be seen as having a strong ethnic—and yes, familial—connection to the man who traumatized her. Perhaps for Elizabeth Stern, taking on her father's identity and writing about the impossibility of ever escaping that identity was an acceptable metaphor for her inability to escape her personal past.

The ethnic autobiography offered native-born Americans a site in which to experience the sorrows that could not be voiced in the culture of business success, but for Stern, if her son is to be believed, her Jewish identity bound her forever to the man who had sexually abused her. Although she opened her work with the image of herself standing above his prone corpse, a triumphant survivor, it ends with an affirmation that her embrace of his identity cannot leave her free to be herself.

chapter six

Passing As Poor

Class Imposture in Depression America

When Mary Antin and other immigrant autobiographers wrote about losing their ethnicity, it was in the service of American success. To be ethnic was to be poor, whereas there was nothing more American than upward mobility. During the 1910s and 1920s, when success manuals were at the height of their popularity, sociologists and folklorists began to study hoboes. They were, after all, a group that seemed to perversely turn its back on the success ideologies of the period. Surely hoboes had innate characteristics that prevented them from aspiring to American success. In this new formulation, to be poor was to be ethnic. The hobo jokes and comic "Weary Willie" stories that had begun to appear in the 1890s following the economic depression continued to have a place in American humor and literature throughout the 1920s, but they were augmented by academic studies of hoboes as well as by hobo auto-biographies and pseudo-autobiographies. Hoboes challenged mythol-ogies of American identity that posited movement from poverty to wealth, and from ethnicity to a "melted" identity. However, the crisis of the Depression shook—though by no means exploded—the notion that poverty was an essential identity.

The number of hoboes declined greatly in the 1920s, as agriculture was mechanized, refrigeration was widely used, and the need for automobiles increased.[1] Hoboes still held a powerful grip on the public imagination, however, as symbols of carefree defiance of social norms; as men who would not be domesticated (and who thus fulfilled American myths about "striking out for the territories"); and as exemplars of pure Anglo-American folk culture (a literature had arisen on Anglo-Saxon hoboes that emphasized their "one hundred percent American" background). However, the Great Depression and the huge increase in homelessness and in the numbers of transient workers changed this image. Suddenly, hobo jokes did not seem quite so funny to people whose belief in the idea of the self-made man and in the possibilities for their own upward mobility was shaken. If anyone could become a hobo, then where was the humor in it?

The crisis in American capitalism brought on by the Depression gave rise to a new kind of impersonation: passing as poor. As white men were stripped of many of the privileges they considered their due as Americans, such as the opportunity to work their way up the class ladder and to fashion their lives, some impersonators began to apply the logic of race to class. Hoboes, the most vivid exemplars of poverty, were represented in films and autobiographies as possessing an authentic ethnicity. A study of hobo autobiographies—and hobo impersonator autobiographies—inspires the question, What does it mean for poverty to behave as an ethnicity? Hoboes, beginning in the 1920s and continuing into the 1930s, were treated by sociologists and journalists as an exotic group and were ascribed "authentic" qualities that had little to do with economic realities and much to do with the projected fantasies and stereotypes of their examiners. Hoboes in the 1920s became the focus for an idealized American masculinity. In the 1930s they became symbols of a depoliticized poverty, as a group of working-class, native-born whites with no political valence. In a time when capitalism appeared to be failing spectacularly and when some government programs offered at least opportunities for minorities and women, hoboes were seen by sociologists as symbols of the tragedy of the lost opportunities facing white, male, native-born Americans. It was no longer clear that Anglo-Saxon heritage guaranteed participation in upward mobility; in fact, it was clear that it did not.

Early in the 1936 film *My Man Godfrey*, William Powell, the homeless

The 1936 class-impersonation film *My Man Godfrey* was only one of many Depression-era movies and autobiographies to pose the question, Are hoboes born or made? (Photo courtesy of MOMA Film Stills Collection.)

man captured as a prize in a socialites' scavenger hunt, is taken to the fancy hotel where the charity event is held and examined for his authenticity. His inspectors even make sure that his stubble is real and his rags are really ragged. Both the premise of this scene, that poverty is an essential identity, and the premise of the movie as a whole, that Powell is in fact a wealthy impostor merely passing as poor, form the basis for a Depression-era trope: class imposture. The genre, as *My Man Godfrey* suggests, revolved around the question, Are hoboes born or made?

The hobo, in fact, survived and was defined through impersonation—through an individual's ability to pass in any number of contexts and to assume an identity that will convince charities and individuals to support him or her. As Boxcar Bertha, the most famous (impersonator) hobo of her generation, wrote in her memoir, *Sister of the Road*,

Some of the girls made a specialty of all the words and attitudes that went with "being saved," and used them all successfully to get the watery soup and the coffee that were put out by rescue missions in the name of the Lord. Some of them made up circumstantial stories of their Jewish ancestry (being Irish) and got emergency help from Jewish agencies. Or they manufactured Roman Catholic backgrounds (being Jewish) and got help from Catholic missions. Others had acquired the language of various lodges and fraternal organizations and in the name of fathers and brothers and uncles who were Masons, Moose, Woodmen, Kiwanians, they were given food or clothes or money for transportation. (71)

To be a hobo, then, was to be an impostor, a shape-shifter, sometimes to the point of making limbs temporarily disappear (so as to seem an amputee). Yet paradoxically, a wide range of both hobo memoirs and sociologists' tracts posited the existence of an essential hobo identity. One could say that these studies conflated class and ethnicity—that hobodom became an ethnicity unto itself.

Although reformers in the early twentieth century had sometimes donned factory attire to expose conditions in sweatshops or packing plants, these journalistic efforts were instrumental rather than existential. They were done for the sake of bringing conditions to the attention of readers and legislators and effecting change. Starting in the late 1910s and 1920 and continuing in the 1930s, when poverty became a state feared by many middle-class people, a new kind of text about passing began to emerge, one that used temporary destitution as a means for an excursion into the soul.

This genre included more than texts that claimed to be something they were not, such as the female hobo's autobiography, *Boxcar Bertha*, authored by Ben L. Reitman, a Chicago reformer. It also encompassed works such as Lauren Gilfillan's *I Went to Pit College* (1934), narrated by a Smith College graduate who attempts to pass as a coal miner's daughter. In Hollywood a number of screwball comedies, including *It Happened One Night* (1934) and *Sullivan's Travels* (1941), introduced the idea of rich people pretending to be poor, or even homeless, Americans. These texts both challenged and confirmed the Horatio Alger myth of mutability by class. Paradoxically, however, the stress that the writers and critics of these texts placed on authenticity emphasized the social construction, rather than the material basis, of class as a category.

Although passing as poor is an American tradition going back to the Jacksonian era, the exaggerations tended to focus on the poverty of origins as a foil for present prosperity. Many successful adults have falsely claimed log cabin origins, or variations thereof; fewer have claimed present-day poverty. Rags-to-riches is part of the American mythology, but riches-to-rags is not. The rags-to-riches story glorified by Horatio Alger novels is one of mutability, of the erasure of origins.

Ragged Dick does not stay a homeless boy for long; his rise is relatively swift and triumphant.

Yet the romanticization of homelessness as the ultimate antidomestic gesture occurs simultaneously with the cult of success in America. Ragged Dick is much more appealing as a fun-loving, generous, homeless boy than as a respectable man. The Depression brought to the forefront these contradictions in American beliefs about poverty and, more specifically, hobodom. It was romantic and manly, the most and least American state.

After the Civil War, thousands of young men took to the road, riding the rails. The flood of immigrants into the United States starting in the mid-nineteenth century, and movement from town to town within the country, created a mobile class. The demands of late nineteenth-century capitalism ensured that the hobo class would be semipermanent. Although the crash of 1873 threw 3 million men into vagrancy, not until the appearance of the Bret Harte short story "My Friend the Tramp" (1877) did the hobo become a popular literary topic.[2] The depression of the 1890s further increased public awareness of tramps, especially through the popular works of Josiah Flynt and Owen Kildare, both of whom wrote from personal experience and presented a Weary Willie image of the tramp, which conformed to popular stereotypes. For when they were not seen as threatening criminals, tramps were seen as comic.

Yet as the twentieth century began, a new model of tramps began to appear in popular and academic discourse: hoboes as avatars of native-born American whiteness, and hoboes as men so manly that they needed no women.

The Ethnography of Hoboes

As eastern and southern European immigrants arrived in increasing numbers in the United States in the 1890s and began to assimilate, they used popular autobiographies to call attention to their Americanization. This expansive definition of Americanness was not welcomed in every quarter. In reaction, academics began to search for a "pure" American culture, untainted by foreign—or rather, non-Anglo-Saxon—influence. What they found, they publicized. And when they could not discover this authentic Anglo-American folk culture, they invented it.

The search for a pure, Anglo-Saxon folk culture brought folklorists to the Appalachian mountains to observe local customs. It also brought

New England settlement workers, who imputed to mountain folks a tradition that included morris dancing and the singing of English ballads. As David Whisnant has noted, "Over and over again the word went out from the settlement schools that mountain culture was 'Elizabethan.'" The 1910 newsletter of one such settlement school, Hindman, reported that "'our children come to us from pioneer homes, where the language of Shakespeare is spoken.'"[3] Settlement workers celebrated the "indigenous" folk culture of the mountain dwellers while ignoring the fact that British folklorists of the 1890s had traveled to Appalachia and taught mountain people their songs. Yet these same settlement workers, most of whom were New England Protestants, feared that the mountain people would be culturally contaminated: "More attention was given to ballads across the water than to Elizabethan speech, however. Hindman students were taken to perform ballads before 'outside' audiences in the 1920s, and as late as 1933—when the coal industry had been careening along at full tilt in eastern Kentucky for two decades—a newsletter announced that Hindman students were being encouraged to sing ballads 'so that these old folk songs will not be forgotten as the victrola and radio creep gradually into the hills.'"[4] It was clear that folk culture could not survive upward mobility and could exist only in conditions of desperate poverty. For as soon as mountain people had the income to buy radios or even to escape the region in which there were almost no job opportunities outside the mines, this culture would be "tainted." As Whisnant has pointed out, the folk culture sought by settlement workers and folklorists was one of depoliticized poverty. It was also, more or less explicitly, one of whiteness. The most pernicious examples of this view of Appalachian culture as pure white culture came from racists who encouraged poor white culture in contrast to the evils of race mixing. Composer John Powell, for example, champion of mountain music and cofounder in 1922 of the Anglo-Saxon Clubs of America, was instrumental in gaining the passage of strict antimiscegenation laws in his native Virginia.[5]

Although Appalachia remained a site for academics and folklorists to discover white folk culture throughout the 1930s, hoboes proved even more fascinating. After all, hobo folk culture was not geographically limited; it was more of an internal essence. When you took an Appalachian off the mountain and moved him to the city, he ceased to be folk and became something else. Hoboes, on the other hand, carried their culture with them wherever they went. The academic search for the truth about hoboes became tied up in the quest for the folk, for the primitive Anglo-American.

For instance, George Milburn's 1930 work *The Hobo's Hornbook: A Repertory for a Gutter Jongleur* celebrated the hobo song as Americana: "Tramps and hobos are the last of the ballad makers. Not in the Tennessee hills, or among the Sea Island Negroes, or in any other such arrested community is there a more vigorous balladry than that which has been flourishing for the past fifty years in America's peripatetic underworld" (xi). Just as settlement workers in Appalachia had created an ancient English tradition among the mountain people, so Milburn harked back to a folk tradition: "Denied the usual diversions of the modern world, both tramps and hobos have turned to devices that flourished centuries before. To relieve the tedium of dreary waits in jungle camps and long spells of incarceration in county jails, they have revived games that once flourished around the wassail bowl" (xii). Adopting an ethnographic posture, Milburn went on to observe that "extemporaneous rhyming was a favorite form of parlour entertainment in Georgian England" (xii). Drawing links as well to the Middle Ages, he noted that some tramp customs were "distinctly medieval in character" (xii) and that the relationship between a stronger and weaker hobo was "not dissimilar to that which once existed between the knight and his squire" (xiv). Like the settlement workers in Appalachia who were appalled by what they saw as the corruption of pure Anglo-Saxon culture, Milburn railed against hobo songs that had passed "over into popular circulation and become perverted. Many so-called bum songs, written for phonograph recording and vaudeville, have precisely the same relation to hobo balladry that 'Ole Man River' has to genuine Negro folk songs" (xv).

Milburn concluded his introduction with a confident, if tragically wrong-headed, prediction: "Both tramps and hoboes are anachronisms bound for extinction. It does not take a particularly astute observer to see the imminent doom of the hoboes, the migratory workers" (xviii).

Both the Hindman settlement workers and Milburn employed the model of an Anglo-American folk culture that existed outside capitalism. In his writings Milburn ignored the brutality of the market economy and its role in the creation of a hobo class. Instead, hoboes became a way of celebrating a pure American folk culture untainted by "alien" ethnicities. However, this essential American identity was economically circumscribed.

The Sociology of Hobodom

The rise of sociology as a discipline offered hoboes a new place in the American psyche: Anglo-Americans who defined the margins of whiteness. The most prominent hobo experts offered case studies in hobodom and impersonation. Nels Anderson was a former hobo who used his personal experiences as research material while passing them off as his results from countless interviews with hoboes. Ben Reitman, discussed later in this chapter, was a doctor who had achieved fame as the "King of the Hoboes" for his work among transients. Reitman became a public spokesman for the hobo, arguing for an authentic hobo identity while blurring "natural" class categories by throwing hobo banquets, publicity-garnering events that presented cocktail-drinking, steak-eating vagrants as media spectacle.

The first thorough sociological study of the homeless man was undertaken by Anderson in *The Hobo: The Sociology of the Homeless Man* (1923). Funded by Reitman, Anderson, a University of Chicago graduate student, documented life in Chicago's Hobohemia. The resulting work became a classic of "participant observation," the methodology for which the Chicago School of Sociology was famous.[6]

However, as Anderson explained in the introduction to the 1961 edition of *The Hobo*, his method was not what his colleagues had assumed it was. Anderson's classmate Pauline Young had written in her *Scientific Social Surveys and Research* (1951) that Anderson "identified himself with the life of a hobo for an extended period and gained insight into the inner life which would have been almost impossible had he not been able to eliminate social and mental distances through intimate participation." Anderson, however, begged to differ. Rather than passing as a hobo, he had instead passed as a middle-class graduate student: "I did not descend into the pit, assume a role there, and later ascend to brush off the dust. I was in the process of moving out of the hobo world. To use a hobo expression, preparing the book was a way of 'getting by,' earning a living while the exit was under way. The role was familiar before the research began. In the realm of sociology and university life I was moving into a new role" (*The Hobo*, xiii).

In his 1975 work *The American Hobo: An Autobiography*, Anderson expanded on this topic. His time at the University of Chicago had followed a lifetime of wandering (he rode the freights to get to Chicago to start school). Anderson reflected that although he could speak to his classmates, who were studying matters such as gangs and vice areas, about their work, "If I spoke of the hobo or other men in my sector of Chicago, their ways of life and work, it was all remote from their understanding. They would respond with some sort of weary willie humor, which reminded me over and over again of a sort of cultural gap between my colleagues and me. It seemed wise to talk as little as possible about my study among my middle-class fellows; their values and outlook were so different from mine" (*American Hobo*, 165).

Anderson had to pass, to assimilate into middle-class life in order to succeed as a graduate student. But to do so meant turning his back on his own history and reinventing himself. Anderson resolved this contradiction by publishing an autobiographical account of his life that was cloaked in the language of sociology and presented as a pure academic exercise. Using the credibility he had as a University of Chicago sociologist, Anderson was able to work against some of the most egregious clichés about hoboes. Writings about Weary Willie ignored the economic dimensions of hobodom and sentimentalized homelessness. By rendering hoboes as quaint folks rather than economic victims, this humor made hoboes palatable, even lovable, to a wide audience. In fact, *The Hobo* was a deeply personal work. After it appeared, Anderson was frequently asked to speak before clubs and classes: "I would come away each time dissatisfied with myself. Each time I had to evade personal questions. I would try to nurture the fiction that I was only a student with a curiosity about hobos and their ways" (*American Hobo*, 170).

Although *The Hobo* is written in sociological prose and lacks the structure of the typical autobiography, it fulfilled for Anderson one of the traditional functions of the ethnic autobiography: to correct stereotypes about an ethnic group. In his 1975 autobiography, Anderson remembered the time when he, as a college student at Brigham Young University, was assigned to report on the popular 1899 book *Tramps and Tramping*, by Josiah Flynt.

> [Professor Swenson] regarded [it] as good reporting. It probably was descriptive of the types in the eastern states with whom Flynt mingled, the weary-willie tramps. My report was negative. Flynt had not included the hobos, that large population of go-about workers found mostly in the Middle West and West. Even Swenson assumed that 'tramp' included all types over all the land. I felt that was wrong, but I made a poor showing at giving my views. Swenson was not convinced and the other students grinned, marking me a wise guy who thinks he knows more than the author of the book. The rebuke

smarted long after. . . . *The Hobo* was my answer to Flynt. (*American Hobo*, 128, 170)

A sociologist is probably a good candidate for writing an ethnic autobiography. In the title of his later work, Anderson indeed marks himself as iconic. He is a type, the American Hobo, and stresses this typicality rather than his individuality in the title.

As Anderson explained in the introduction to the 1961 edition of *The Hobo*, "Whatever his weaknesses, and I know them full well, I present him as one of the heroic figures of the frontier" (*The Hobo*, xxi). Instead of presenting hoboes as caricatures of comic poverty, Anderson posited hoboes as dignified figures who, rather than occupying a place on the margins, were central to American identity. Indeed, in the original text he stated unequivocally, "The tramp is an American product. The foreigners born in this group are chiefly of the older immigration" (ibid., 150). He continued the Americanization metaphor further when he described the informal social centers where hoboes congregate, although unlike many of his predecessors, Anderson offered an assimilationist, rather than a purely Anglo-Saxon, view of Americanness. "Absolute democracy reigns in the jungle. The color line has been drawn in some camps, but it is the general custom, and especially in the North, for Negroes, Mexicans, and whites to share the same jungle. The jungle is the melting pot of trampdom" (ibid., 19).

In 1931 Anderson published *The Milk and Honey Route*, a comic guide to hobodom that he wrote under the pseudonym "Dean Stiff." As he explained in the preface to his 1940 work *Men on the Move*, written when he was the director for the Works Progress Administration (WPA) Section on Labor Relations, *The Hobo* had become "that book which I have not been permitted to forget."

> It was a subject about which I had some personal knowledge then, and I thought to turn that knowledge to good account. To so many others, although it need not have been so, the hobo was a character of romance and perhaps of mystery. He was a stranger to my professors. For me, then, it was an ideal subject for a Master's thesis.
>
> I have never understood why *The Hobo* was never convincing to me. Perhaps it colored up too much the culture of the homeless in Chicago's Hobohemia. Perhaps I was too well aware of so much that was left unsaid. . . . Perhaps, too, I began to weary of being asked to speak before this group or that, always on the same subject.
>
> In time, unable to live down *The Hobo*, I began to be cynical about

the subject. In 1931 when it looked as though my feelings were crystallizing into a complex, I wrote another book on the subject. *The Milk and Honey Route* was a parody. I cleansed my soul by transferring all that emotion about *The Hobo* to one Dean Stiff, anonymous author of the parody. After that I began again to get interested in the subject of migrancy. (*Men on the Move*, 1–2)

Anderson had, in *The Hobo*, written an ethnic autobiography with the intent, common to so many ethnic autobiographers, of writing himself into Americanness. But because he did not feel at liberty to present the material as autobiography rather than sociology, he published a hidden autobiography, a memoir that concealed as much as it revealed. He was frequently confronted, thus, with the misconceptions of his examiners and the views of his audience that hoboes were romantic, mysterious folk figures. Because he did not feel free to present himself as a former hobo, he felt that he himself "colored up" too much the culture of hoboes; he "was too well aware of so much that was left unsaid." Paradoxically, in purging himself of his first hobo book, Anderson wrote another volume that angrily asserted the unknowability of hoboes by outsiders and posited hobodom as an essential, rather than an economic, identity.

In *The Milk and Honey Route*, Anderson presented the hobo as an essential identity. The prefatory note, identified as the work of Nels Anderson, begins with an attack on recent works on hoboes: "I have read most of them. I can approve of none. . . . Here and there in these many hobo books there is a grain of truth. The rest is chaff." He expounds on the impossibility of an outsider understanding the hobo: "No fictionist can explore the hobo's province by riding across it as Stevenson explored Europe on a donkey. Bumping over the terrain, like a stone rolling down hill, may be as good a way as any to go slumming or sightseeing; but Hobohemia does not yield to such inspection, except to distort the visions and shame the findings of these transient reporters" (*Milk and Honey Route*, vi).

The authenticity that Anderson was unwilling to claim in his previous works became a prerequisite for understanding. Anderson was thus caught in the trap of authenticity. Because his hobo self was invisible to the outside world as he passed as middle class, he could not be a "true" speaker. And in his formulation, authenticity is a prerequisite for understanding the hobo: "Assume that these reporters, these researchers, novelists, and spectacular artists are sincere—and that is being char-

As shown in this cartoon from a how-to book for hoboes, poverty was an essential identity.

The hobo is always born a hobo.

itable—sincerity is not enough. The hobo world yields its truth as grudgingly as a distant planet. . . . The true reporter must be of the blood, and they of the blood are few. He knows the truth because he lives it" (ibid., vii).

While Nels Anderson demanded that researchers not be tourists—that is, that only a hobo can write about a hobo—his alter ego, Dean Stiff, went further and asserted that it is impossible to become a hobo: "The hobo is always born a hobo. The American hobo is born to the caste and finds his niche in it as the actor born to the stage finds Broadway or as the naturally endowed plutocrat finds Wall Street." There is no connection between the hobo's "soul" and his environment: "Whatever the family background, unless you have in your veins the strain of gypsy blood, you will never go far in the labyrinth of hobo land" (ibid., 13). The hobo, by definition, is male, and is a man without a woman: "Where is the hobo who wants to be attached? To be matrimonially attached means to become domesticated, to be haltered. A domesticated hobo is a doomed hobo. He can no more endure captivity than his simian ancestor, the gorilla" (ibid., 149).

Nels Anderson assimilated into the middle class but built his career on research drawn from his own life. He deployed academic forms to write his autobiography because traditional autobiography would not be as effective for his purposes. A public accustomed, like his classmates and his professor at Brigham Young University, to comic tramps was not yet ready for the real voice of the hobo. Yet Anderson himself could not come to terms with the way he had colored up his descriptions of hobodom. Seesawing between worlds, between the desire to reveal and the need to conceal, Anderson settled, in the 1930s, for an angry, comic account that posited poverty as an essential identity. It was only in the 1970s that he could write his third and final autobiography, the only one in which he revealed his relationship to his earlier autobiographical works.

Homelessness As Masculinity:
The Übermensch on the Main Stem

The hobo as natural man, undomesticated by woman, became a powerful theme for writers of the 1920s. Nels Anderson's celebration of hoboes as frontiersmen striking out for the territories emphasized not only the Americanness of these men, but also their masculinity. They were males unfettered by female demands. They were unassimilated into the world of middle-class domesticity and retained their masculine essence. This theme was elaborated considerably in two popular hobo autobiographies of the time, Jack Black's *You Can't Win* (1926) and William Edge's *The Main Stem* (1927), both of which offered a homoerotic version of hobodom. Much as poverty was described as ethnicity in the folklorists' accounts of hobodom, these two works gendered and sexualized poverty. Written during a time of feminist gains that threatened to unsettle existing power relations between men and women, these autobiographies offered a vision of life in which women were no longer necessary.

As George Chauncey noted in his history of gay life in New York City between 1890 and 1940, homosexual relationships were, in fact, common among hoboes. A 1916 study of a hundred "vagrants" in New York City identified one-quarter as "perverts."[7] Hoboes often traveled in pairs, with the older man, or "wolf," protecting and requiring the services of a younger man, labeled a "punk" or "lamb." However, it is hard to find descriptions of hoboes as "sissies" or other derogatory terms for homosexuals. Hoboes, no matter what their sexual proclivities, presented themselves in their autobiographical narratives as epitomizing unfettered masculinity. Within this construct, working-class life—especially the life of a laborer—is masculine, and middle-class life is feminine.

Most hobo autobiographies of the 1920s depict a world without women and emphasize the manliness of their subjects. Jack Black's *You Can't Win* is a good example of the genre. As William Burroughs wrote in his introduction to the 1988 reprint edition, "I first read *You Can't Win* in 1926, in an edition bound in red cardboard. Stultified and confined by middle-class St. Louis mores, I was fascinated by this glimpse of an underworld of seedy rooming-houses, pool parlors, cat houses and opium dens, of bull pens and cat burglars and hobo jungles."

The autobiography proved influential on Burroughs's literary style. In fact, as his biographer Ted Morgan notes, *You Can't Win* served as a prototype for Burroughs's own first novel, *Junkie*. More than that, however, it offered a model for a homoerotic universe of tough men without any need for or contact with women. Reading Black's work, the reader once again learns that the true hobo is born, not made, and that even as a child, the true hobo will be masculine to an extreme, even at the expense of elementary hygienic practices. Writing of his mother, Black reminisces, "I can remember distinctly how angry I became when she brought me a nice, new toothbrush and showed me what to do with it.

"That was the greatest indignity of all—the last straw. I threw the thing down and refused to use it; told her up and down that I was 'no girl' and wouldn't have any 'girl things.' She did not get angry and scold; she just went on with her work, smiling. She may have been pleased with my manly outburst" (4).

Later, when he begins his descent into the criminal world, Black enters a society in which there are no women to speak of. As he writes toward the end of his narrative, which spans forty years of crime and homelessness, "My contact with women had been very limited" (324). In fact, one of the very few women with whom he spends time, a prostitute named Julia whom he met as a teenager, is more masculine than feminine. She has a "boyish face" (34), acts "more like a boy than a girl" (49), and seems a good companion. "What a partner she would have made for me if she were not a girl!" (52), Black writes with regret. Indeed, when he helps her escape from the tyrannical madam for whom she works and moves her into a room he has rented, he avoids physical contact with her, though they share a bed: "Once my body touched hers—it was hot and sticky. I pulled the sheets down between us and turned away" (62). The book had, writes Ted Morgan, "an enormous impact on the unfolding of [Burroughs's] life and work."[8]

Black's autobiography contains an extreme version of a theme popular in American discourse since the mid-nineteenth century that posited women as "angels of the household" and women's role as civilizing and taming men. Black presented himself as extremely masculine and, thus, as essentially untamable. Another work of the same period, William Edge's *The Main Stem*, had similar themes and concerns. However, Edge finally showed masculine authenticity as something that one needed to learn; like middle-class identity, it was another performance.

In 1927 Edge presented *The Main Stem* as his autobiographical account of life as a hobo. It was lauded by reviewers. Lisle Belle, writing in the *New York Herald Tribune*, noted, "If you are thinking of becoming a bum the book is most suggestive. And if you are not it is most entertaining."[9] Nels Anderson authenticated the text: "I sent a copy to a hobo serving time in San Quentin. I thought enough of the book to feel that he would enjoy it and I venture to say that it will pass from hand to hand till it is worn out. It is about the life of the outcasts written in the language they can understand. At the same time it is entertaining for the parlor folks."[10] There could hardly be higher praise than this anointment from the academic prince of hoboes.

In *The Main Stem* Edge recounts running away from home in 1918 to work in a factory, living in a boardinghouse, and being led into the hobo life by Slim, another factory worker who boards at the same establishment. Slim is, as Edge suspects, "not the ignorant laborer you pose to be" (4), but a Socialist lawyer who has escaped a confining marriage to a wealthy woman. Wealth is feminizing to Slim. "The marriage was duly solemnized," he tells Edge. "My education began. I wore everything from Harris tweeds to swallowtails. I lived in elegant Colorado camps and in sombre city houses. Try to visualize me. I couldn't say 'hey, flunkey' to hotel waiters. I couldn't swear. I couldn't tell people what I really thought of them. I had to drink wine instead of whiskey.

"I think I should have committed suicide had there been no alternative. Fortunately I had enough experience as a poverty-stricken wanderer to know that hoboing was open to me" (31).

In order to preserve his masculine identity, Slim needed to escape the middle class. His assimilation into married life—in other words, bourgeois existence—meant learning a new system of signs and performing at all times. The only way Slim could be his authentic self was through becoming a hobo. To be a hobo is to be truly masculine, a natural man unfettered by bourgeois (read feminine) conventions.

The Main Stem, although it is studded with Slim's socialist jargon and full of descriptions of factory work, is basically a gay love story. Edge worries, "Suppose Slim shouldn't want me? Perhaps he would think I was too green and soft to be a hobo. I was strong enough, but I lacked the hardness and toughness of Slim. I looked too sissified, too much like a dude disguised as a worker for the *Bal Boheme*" (8). Just as Slim rejected his performance as a middle-class married man, so the narrator is anxious that he himself lacks the hard core, the masculinity of an authentic hobo, that he is a sissy rather than a real man.

Soon, under Slim's tutelage, Edge is sending his dinner jacket, patent leather dancing pumps, and self-improvement books home to his parents. In rejecting the self-fashioning necessary to climb up the social ladder, he is refusing to assimilate into successful Americanness and is instead opting for a more authentic existence. He is becoming more masculine: "Neither Slim nor I was a ladies' man" (35). *The Main Stem* glamorizes male friendship, which Edge and Slim present as being most possible in the all-male environs of migratory laborers. Neither man has a good word to say about his relationships with women, but Slim rhapsodizes about a former intimacy with Jack, a handsome fellow hobo:

> It was funny to see him washing the greasy dishes, with his fine head cocked on one side to keep the cigarette smoke out of his eyes, and his large tattooed arms white with soap suds. He kept sober all this time, and our friendship grew rapidly. His hobby was reading aloud. He read well, and took pride in it. It was he who first introduced me to Veblen, whose circuitous language and irony delighted him. In that little room, with a second bed moved into it, and an extension to the electric fixture for better light, we supplemented each other's education, discussed many things, and lived clean, happy lives, full of companionship (73).

Unfortunately, this idyll is destroyed by a woman, Jack's sister, whom the two men visit together and who crushes Jack's spirit while Slim cools his heels sitting with her daughter, discussing "silly, indifferent schoolgirl things" (75). Slim has only contempt for females: "Bobbed-haired girls would be there, pretty lustful girls. But he would spurn them" (82). Edge, too, has little interest in women. Attending a dance, he thinks, "How I wished these girls were men. I could talk to the men" (127).

While the gay subtext of *The Main Stem* may be powerful, the text rejects it. Edge is repelled by his fellow workers "dancing in a disgustingly homosexual manner" (119). When he and Slim find their friendship cooling, he aligns himself with another cultivated young man, Frenchy, a Belgian teacher of gymnastics. This friendship ends, though, when he is warned by another worker that "Frenchy's a fairy (homosexualist). Steer clear of that frog if yer wants any respec' from de stiffs in dis camp" (125). Edge is not convinced, though, until his informant comes up to him "excitedly. 'If yer wants to see Frenchy in de act, foller me.' We went rapidly and silently to Frenchy's room. Through the keyhole one could see. There was a twelve-year-old boy in the room. The sight disgusted me. I felt sick" (126).

He soon replaces Frenchy with Charlie, whom he describes to Slim, from whom he has separated, as "a young Apollo—crisp, black hair, curly; fair complexion, straight as an arrow." Like Slim, he presents an idyllic relationship in which reading seems to stand in for sex: "We are reading lots of things together. He likes *Martin Eden*. But he has a convenient headache when I try to read him Kautsky" (134).

Although his narrative is class-conscious, it is apolitically so. Class is expressed in gendered, rather than political, terms. Edge does not see the homeless as economic victims but writes, "Migratory workers are forever waging a futile fight with respectability and a steady job" (20). In other words, these tramps are fighting to keep their essential masculine identities and resisting assimilation into the feminized world of middle-class existence. Edge, unlike other impersonators, never really immerses himself in the life of a hobo. He always maintains a supercilious distance from the men he tries to blend in with.

Slim, though he talks about the workers' revolution and complains about the "liberal bourgeois . . . with their diluted revolutionary theories" (54), is, in fact, something of a self-styled *übermensch*. As he tells Edge, "It's good to come into a new city with the feeling that you're the mental and physical superior to everybody in it" (39). At times, despite Slim's socialist rhetoric, his journey with Edge has the feeling of two dandies on a lark: "We saw a few gay Italians; and Slim, who knew a little of the language, captured their hearts by references to ravioli, Dante, and the papafighi of Dalmatian coasting vessels" (36). Aside from discussing ravioli with Italians, however, Slim and Edge tend to stay clear of immigrants and others whose heritage is not Nordic, for the superiority Slim expresses is racially and ethnically tinged. Slim's socialism certainly does not encompass solidarity of the working class, insofar as that class contains immigrants, blacks, and others who are not native-born whites. Edge is repelled by immigrants, by the "Polacks who smelled vilely and talked gibberish" (1) and the "traditional garlicky breath of the bohunks" (25). Slim shares Edge's racist contempt and expresses it while watching an African American woman curse a man who had wronged her: "'Shades of Schnitzler and the pithecanthropus! Vienna and the Neanderthal!' Slim exclaimed at this. 'Did you ever see such a paradox? Sophisticated love, and a frontal angle of forty-five degrees!'" (191). At times like this Slim sounds more like a scientific racist than like a Wobbly. *The Main Stem* never celebrates the melting pot. Rather, Edge frames his autobiography in the most Anglo-American tradition: "Like Benjamin Franklin, whose city we were bound for, I carried a loaf of bread under each arm" (71).

Finally, Edge loses faith even in the glamorous Slim: "Of course, it was pleasant to see Slim again. It was good to see that prize-fighter's mug he had, to hear his sharp, incisive witty words. But there was something lacking. An integrating philosophy one might call it. . . . He was brilliant. But why at his age, had he not done something more worthwhile than mere wandering?" (187). When they part, it is so that Slim can "take care of handsome Charlie. I'm afraid he won't get along by himself. Too damn' open and above-board in his actions. Reminds me of you when I first knew you. It is the irony of fate that, having made a respectable hobo out of you, I've got to train another gay-cat. But you are gratifying to the teacher, I'll say that, you long-legged, flop-eared, blond-headed, good-for-nothing, lousey bum" (195). Although hoboes are men in their natural state, they need to learn how to perform as hoboes.

Edge's adventure finally ends when he comes down with the flu during Armistice Day celebrations and returns home to his family. He is happy that illness has forced him out of his migratory life: "I had graduated into full-fledged hobodom. My hands, coarse and calloused, and with the dirt ground in, were evidences of hard living. My vocabulary and voice passed muster. My clothes were satisfactory; my general attitude, carriage, bearing, stamped me as a bum. . . . Will I ever be able to take my place again as a citizen in the world of the middle class?" (194). He adjusts easily to his old life, although, "of course, there were many disagreeable things. The petty moralities, the shibboleths of the middle class—these were intolerable. How I longed to hear blasphe-mous language roll trippingly from the tongue" (211). Charlie and Slim stay together for years, however.

Both Black's and Edge's autobiographies deal with the performance of masculine identity. Edge, especially, applied what writers of his time, like Samuel Ornitz, were describing in terms of ethnic performance to constructions of class and gender.

Expert Hoboes and Hobo Experts

The image and the reality of hoboes suffused American culture in the 1930s. Given the economic uncertainties of the time and the existence of a huge and visible population of hoboes, it would seem that "hobo" would become a slippery identity—that the line between hoboes and nonhoboes would start to blur. How, then, would the hobo autobiogra-phy be affected?

Statistics indicate but cannot fully express the horror of the Depres-sion. Following the stock market crash, the gross national product fell 29 percent from its high point in 1929 to its nadir in 1933. During the same period construction dropped by 78 percent; consumption expen-ditures, by 18 percent; and investment, by 98 percent. Unemployment rose from 3.2 to 24.9 percent.

The first hoboes to become famous were the Bonus Marchers. In June 1932 an event took place that became emblematic of the government's broken promises to the people: the Bonus March on Washington, D.C. The Bonus Marchers, a ragged army of 3,000 World War I veterans, began traveling from Portland, Oregon, to Washington, D.C., to demand the immediate payment of the World War I bonus Congress had prom-ised they would receive in 1945. The 20,000 men who eventually con-verged on the nation's capitol demanded, and got, the House to pass a bill calling for immediate payment of the bonus. Although the measure was defeated in the Senate, the Bonus Marchers stayed on in an encamp-ment in Anacostia Flats, a visible and much-reported-on presence. Act-ing on his own, General Douglas MacArthur ordered troops to disperse the marchers, a maneuver that was effected with the aid of tear gas and bayonets. The spectacle of soldiers setting fire to the encampments of the veterans and their families was shocking to people around the coun-try. These were the heroes of 1918, after all, who had become, as a popular 1933 film would have it, *Heroes for Sale*: men with no prospects and no hopes.[11] These men living in makeshift shacks and eating from soup lines were not carefree pioneers, ultra-masculine men without women, or Anglo-American folk with quaint traditions. They were men who, although they had fulfilled their commitment to the United States by fighting in World War I, were unable to survive in America.

President Herbert Hoover's optimistic declarations that "nobody is actually starving" rang hollow to men and women standing in charity soup lines and living in the makeshift shacks so sarcastically dubbed "Hoovervilles," or to those who benefited from the Princeton eating clubs' innovative scheme to send their table scraps to the poor. As bank failures swept the nation, the magnitude of the Depression reached its peak. The horror of the Dust Bowl, a natural disaster fueled by careless use of farmland, gave rise to the decade's sobriquet the Dirty Thirties. The drought that began in 1930 worsened the following year until the Dakotas and Montana became nearly as arid as the Sonoran Desert. Only Maine and Vermont escaped a drought in the years from 1930 to 1936; ultimately, 1 million Okies headed west for California.[12] It was difficult for observers to view these migrants as real men in retreat from the confinement of middle-class life or, following an earlier model, as criminals or comic characters. The face of homelessness had changed.

On the day that Franklin D. Roosevelt took office in January 1933, every bank in the nation was closed, 30 million families were without regular incomes, and private charity had reached its highest level in history. Although public spending on welfare was more than double what it had been in the 1920s, it was not nearly sufficient to stem the tide of misery.

It was all too easy for once middle-class Americans to imagine themselves becoming homeless. Perhaps most frightening was the development of a large class of homeless children. By August 1932 the Children's Bureau of the Department of Labor had discovered that two hundred thousand children were wandering across the country seeking food.

> The first report of this phenomenon came from Mr. Harry Ferguson of the United Press, who said that this "hungry horde" was "comparable only to the so-called 'wild children' of Russia." They were only the camp followers of a larger army, estimated in millions, of "white-collar bums" with whom railroads and cities chiefly in the South and Southwest were attempting to cope. Through El Paso forty-five thousand had passed in six months. Through Kansas City fifteen hundred were passing each day. The bureau quoted railroad men as saying that "'the policy is to remove the transients from the trains. But in

the last year we have been unable to do so because the numbers are so large.' "[13]

Thus, several years into the Depression, it was perhaps unsurprising that critics would laud the appearance of a new hobo autobiography, *Sister of the Road: The Autobiography of Boxcar Bertha*, written by a woman, for a change. *Sister of the Road* became the most famous hobo autobiography of its time. What was a little more surprising, though, was who Boxcar Bertha turned out to be. In her own way, she was as much a product of the University of Chicago sociology department as Nels Anderson.

The research Anderson did while at the University of Chicago was funded by Ben Reitman, who is perhaps best remembered today as the lover of Emma Goldman but who was famous in his day for funding events such as dinner parties for hoboes. His frequent lectures on the subject of hoboes as well as his directorship of Chicago's "Hobo College," a kind of adult education center for transients, made Reitman a celebrated gadfly. From the first hobo banquet that he held in Chicago in 1907, Reitman put himself squarely at the center of public debate about the role of the hobo in U.S. society.

However, it was his "as-told-to," or more accurately, "as-invented-by," autobiography of "Boxcar" Bertha Thompson, *Sister of the Road* (1937), that gave not only the 1930s but the post-1960s generations an enduring representation of the hobo as sexual free spirit. In 1972 Roger Corman produced *Boxcar Bertha*, a film directed by Martin Scorsese and starring Barbara Hershey and David Carradine.[14] As Reitman's biographer, Roger A. Bruns, writes, "Through the Hobo College, the debating forums, and his courtship of the press, Ben had remained one of the prominent figures in the world of hobohemia for more than three decades. In 1937, with the publication of his second book, *Sister of the Road: The Autobiography of Boxcar Bertha*, his stature was further enhanced."[15]

Reitman spent his life moving between categories, flirting, in his hobo banquets, with the quick transformation between rich and poor. Reitman was particularly anxious to shed his birth ethnicity and become assimilated into what he saw as Americanism. Born to Russian Jewish immigrant parents, Reitman had "a decided antipathy for Jews,"[16] carried a Bible with him often, and taught classes in Protestant Sunday school. Given his habit of shifting categories, it seems almost logical that he would write his autobiography as the narrative of a female hobo.

From the opening sentences of *Sister of the Road*, Boxcar Bertha defines her experience as iconic of the 1930s: "I am thirty years old as I write this, and have been a hobo for fifteen years, one of that strange and motley sorority which has increased its membership so greatly during the depression" (7). Just as Anderson presented the hobo as ur-American, Reitman depicted Bertha as a larger-than-life character who embodies the spirit of American rebellion. Her ancestry is Anglo-American, and her father is dedicated to genetic purity. She is the granddaughter of an abolitionist, one of John Brown's coworkers, and the daughter of "an active free-thought and eugenist propagandist." Bertha's parents refuse to marry on principle, for which they are punished by bourgeois society by being sent to jail: "All of them enjoyed their stay there. Grandfather wrote a series of articles which were published in the New York and London liberal papers. Father caught up on his back reading. Mother did the jail cooking and sewing, nursed me, and studied Esperanto and socialism" (12). Thus, even though Bertha is writing within the context of economic disaster, she presents her story as a tale of American rebellion against bourgeois existence, not as an economic critique.

As the description of infant Bertha's jail stay indicates, the entire autobiography has this dreamy, fairy-tale feeling. Bertha seems a vaguely left-wing male chauvinist's fantasy of the free woman. From a stint at a cooperative farm experiment she learns about "the dignity of labor and the necessity for preparing ourselves to live in a free cooperative society" (20). From her mother, who takes "care of the sex needs of some of the men" (22), "I learned the urge I now know so well, for serving men who work and talk" (13). Her first lover is an instructor in political economy and is also her mother's lover, a situation that continues for a year but is free, as is usual with Bertha, from "romantic pretensions" (47). At seventeen, Bertha is ready to hit the road on her own. On the rare occasions when she desires a less impersonal encounter with a lover, or even when she sees her father, who has no interest in her as his daughter, she tends to feel embarrassed by her clinginess: "I winced, and was ashamed of that stupid, hypocritical, typically feminine remark" (152).

The white abolitionist authors of ostensible slave narratives often evinced distaste for black bodies. Similarly, Bertha despises the feminine in herself. Although she has little respect for prostitutes who are in love with their pimp, at one point she finds herself becoming one of them: "How well Bill knows women, I thought" (164). But although she has "fallen in love with that bastard pimp of yours," she tells one of her co-prostitutes that she will embark on whoring as a sociological experiment: "I'm going to get something out of this experience. I'm going to learn why women let their feelings make slaves of them" (169).

On the road she encounters other women. A typical female hobo is "completely frank about her sexual promiscuity, frankly considered her body as her working capital" (39). Bertha stumbles across sociological statistics that tend to reinforce her impression that hoboes are Americans from the finest racial stock—that is, Anglo-Saxon. "One of the case-workers in an Alabama shelter which I visited later showed me a federal report about transients," runs one entry. "This said that eighty-six percent of the total number of transients on the road now (those that register at transient camps and shelters) are white and native-born, and that only eight percent are colored" (44). Bertha is not the only female hobo to have these sociological urges. One "Queen of the Hoboes" whom she meets in Chicago is not only, like Bertha, an ur-American—"from an enviable racial stock" (60)—but is equally interested in research: "If there were any new, perverted, vicious, crooked, anti-social terrible men in the community, Lizzie wanted them as lovers. Her love for the abnormal, the seared and the sordid, was only equaled by her admiration for good literature and scientific psychological research" (62). Bertha spends time with abortionists, heroin addicts, opium smokers, professional beggars, shoplifters, and grifters, all for the sake of research. On a train ride from Chicago to visit her mother, she happens to run into a consulting statistician who shows her statistics on prostitution that are so fascinating that "he let me use his portable typewriter and I made a copy of the tables he had compiled" (196). She includes these tables, of course, with her own statistics on her experiences as a prostitute (including topics such as how many men serviced each day and for how much money). She augments her work experience in social service bureaus by listening to relief agency head Harry Hopkins speak, and she records every statistic he drops.

Ultimately, though, like the plight of Nels Anderson's authentic hoboes, Boxcar Bertha's hoboing does not have much to do with the economic conditions she dutifully records in her statistics-gathering jobs or hobbies. Instead, she is a hobo because "I am truly married to the box cars. There's something constantly itching in my soul that only the road and the box cars can satisfy" (275).

Surprisingly, many reviews of the book were good. *Time* lauded the work's authenticity: "Her narrative is cauliflower-earmarked by the brutal truth, wears no wig."[17] Herbert Blumer, whom Boxcar Bertha describes in her autobiography as one of "the most noted professors and sociologists in America . . . a former college football star, large and dominating in body but with scholarly eyes and a quiet manner" (75), wrote that "the simplicity, naiveté, and humanness of the account permit the reader to form a satisfactory picture of the kind of world in which Box-Car Bertha moved. . . . Students of social pathology and those interested in the more undignified undercurrents of modern life should find this volume to be informative and provocative."[18]

The only subject she is squeamish about is homosexuality, which she regards as disgusting and pitiful. As one of her lovers, a former hobo who is a "brilliant teacher" and "inspiring speaker" (75), tells her in an explanation she passes on at great length and as received wisdom, "They are God's stepchildren. . . . My antipathy towards them is not because they are variants—God knows I do not demand that everyone be cut from the same pattern—but because they are typically anti-social, selfish and willing to exploit others. So few of them show a desire to earn an honest living" (149). Granted, this seems like a peculiar reason for resentment in the context of a veritable how-to manual for begging, prostitution, and petty theft, but this "expert" goes on for well over a page in the same vein, branding homosexuals as artificial, infantile, and constantly on the make.

Bertha's expressions of disgust for homosexuality appear in a text full of erotic descriptions of men, both sociologists (including Anderson, lauded for his "strong, rugged, purposeful face . . . a certain sweetness and tolerance that showed in his lips and in his voice" [74]) and Bertha's innumerable lovers. Considering that this book was authored by a man, *Sister of the Road* seems at times, like Edge's *The Main Stem*, to be a closeted gay narrative.

Nels Anderson could not gain authority by writing an autobiography of hobo life. After all, his experiences ran counter to the public's expectations of how hoboes should behave, and the public was accustomed to sentimentalized or comic hoboes. Thus, he had to write with academic detachment about his own life. On the other hand, Reitman, who as a doctor would appear to occupy a position of privilege, was able to express his antibourgeois feelings (as well as his misogyny) most effectively by speaking as a female hobo, for such a person would presumably know whereof she spoke.

Bertha clearly had a genuine hobo soul. She was as clearly to the rails born, by light of her authentically American and authentically rebellious heritage. But any discussion of hoboes as a legitimate ethnic group must return to the question posed at the beginning of the chapter: Are hoboes born or made? The best way to answer this question is to explore the possibilities for impersonating a hobo. Although Depression realities would seem to insist that hoboes were made by economic circumstances, cultural artifacts argue against this view.

Perhaps the most well known cinematic example of the journey into hobodom is *Sullivan's Travels*, Preston Sturges's 1941 comedy about a Hollywood director who becomes a hobo in order to learn more about America and American movie audiences. The film begins as Sullivan, director of such blockbuster hits as *Ants in Your Pants* and *Hey, Hey in the Hayloft*, has decided he wants to make real, gritty movies about the dilemma of the American worker. The studio bosses try to convince him of his inexperence and inadequacy to complete this task by regaling him with (invented) tales of their Horatio Alger-like backgrounds, which stand in stark contrast to his life of privilege. This is the first hint that within the world of the movie, class mobility is the exception rather than the rule. The bosses, however, cannot dissuade Sullivan from embarking on his trip across America. Sullivan's attempts to pass as a hobo are at first comically rendered. A handsomely outfitted tour bus, courtesy of the studio, follows him wherever he goes, ready to cater to his every whim. His bum's outfit is furnished by wardrobe, and his hitchhiking efforts land him back in Hollywood. Yet there is a sour tone beneath the comedy, one that grows stronger as the picture draws to a close, and Sullivan finds himself for the first time in serious trouble. Amnesiac, presumed dead by the studio, and dressed in a bum's wardrobe that is all too convincing, he is sentenced to six years of hard labor on a chain gang for slugging a cop who insulted him.

When Sullivan finally remembers who he is, it is as though he has reawakened into the plot of his own life. "Hollywood directors don't end up on chain gangs," he tells the warden, and in a matter of minutes he is released. Although he has been sentenced for a crime he did indeed commit, and although his punishment is not out of line with the penalties of the convicts whose fortunes he shares (who never, however, become more than shadowy background presences to us), the social order, as in any true comedy, has been restored. Rather than making

In the Preston Sturges comedy *Sullivan's Travels* (1941), a wealthy film director is assisted by his butler in transforming himself into a hobo. (Photo courtesy of MOMA Film Stills Collection.)

I Am a Fugitive from a Chain Gang of 1941, in order to expose the conditions still suffered by his former cellmates, Sullivan's next movie will be *Ants in Their Pants of 1939*, as the studio executives have suggested. In this rendering, it is impossible for a wealthy man to become a true hobo. Just as the studio bosses' upward mobility from poverty is a fantasy, so is downward mobility finally presented as a fiction. However, an autobiography from the same period presents a far grimmer picture of the voluntary descent into hobodom, one that contrasts the myths about hobodom to which its author subscribes at the beginning of his journey with the harsh realities he encounters along the way.

In his 1937 autobiography, *We Turned Hobo: A Narrative of Personal Experience*, Carl Schockman established his authenticity from the first pages. He presented himself as a rank amateur, writing only to transcend his miseries in the tuberculosis sanitarium and trying to forget the fiancée who jilted him. "I had been told and I had read that in the treatment of tuberculosis mental rest was as necessary as physical rest, so once again I decided to face the situation squarely," Schockman wrote. "But it's hard to forget when one is in bed and I found myself in a losing battle. Night after night I lay awake, and when several more months had passed and I saw time wasn't dimming my memories, I realized I must do something or I surely never would get well" (10).

His solution was to write the narrative of his adventures. "During the next few months I read many books of instruction on story writing and then I started writing" (11). His physical condition is a badge of his suffering on the road, and his naive stance as a writer ensures that the reader understands his production as authentic, untainted by literary concerns. As another badge of authenticity, the text is studded with photos of the author and his brother in their travels: hopping freights, getting ready to jump off, resting in the hobo jungle, and returning home. There is even a photograph of Schockman in bed in the sanitarium. The autobiographical "I," then, is familiar to readers of ethnic memoirs. It is a literary voice that presents itself as outside the purview of literature; it is a voice that claims to tell only the unvarnished truth, which disclaims the constructed nature of the memoir.

Schockman's is a story of an initially carefree descent into the abyss of hobodom, an adventure turned sour. A farmer's son and a business school graduate, Schockman found his and his brother Clarence's plans for adventure thwarted by economic circumstances: "At this time the depression was beginning to show its effect in the nearby towns, and try as we would we could not get jobs of any kind" (16). Although they resolve to stay home and help their father with farmwork, "finally the day came when it seemed as if we could endure it no longer. The lure of far places had entered our blood and we had to obey its call" (16). This, then, is a familiar story: the young American male's search for adventure, the desire to strike out for the territories and escape the confines of the homestead. The economic realities of the Depression and the mythology of the West make the prospect of hitchhiking cross-country seem appealing. As Clarence exclaims, "Why we could be picking oranges in California right now. I read an article in the paper the other day stating that the oranges were ripening. Boy, we'll have the time of our life!" (16). The boys "talked of nothing else; we made a thousand plans and pictured a thousand thrills and adventures" (17). Eventually, they wear down the resistance of their reluctant parents, who initially "did not take our plan seriously," but who finally give their consent "after several weeks had passed and more factories had shut down and everyone in our little community realized that the depression was just beginning" (17).

Schockman's memoir thus is unusual in that he connects his decision to turn hobo to economic hardship. However, soon he provides the reader with the true theme of his story: not economics but the tug between the domestic world (represented by his mother) and the anti-domestic realm ("the lure of far places had entered our blood and we had to obey its call"). The boys' leave-taking calls up the sign that is famously on the walls of each mission: When Is the Last Time You Wrote Your Mother? As Schockman notes, "We were as happy as could be until suddenly, while we were cheerfully wondering what town we would reach by night, all my pleasantry ended abruptly when mother raised her eyes to look at us. The tears were running down her cheeks. A shock went through me" (18).

At first the adventure goes well. Schockman regales his readers with details of "the blue sky all flecked with rosy clouds," of African-American farmworkers picking cotton ("and what a carefree lot they were" [36]), and of the kindness of strangers. "In fact, everyone with whom we had come into contact had treated us as if we were their own sons. Thoughts of mother, of father, crept into my mind but now they brought happiness, not sorrow. Yes, we would succeed. We would make mother and father proud of us. Other boys were sitting at home waiting for the depression to end. They had ridiculed our plan. They would talk differently when they heard we were working in California" (45).

Thus Schockman frames his hobodom not as an antidomestic gesture but as a means of being a responsible son—and not just his parents' son, but the child of everyone he meets on the road. However, when the boys arrive in the desert in Texas, their journey takes a wilder turn. Away from the familiar comforts of tilled land and friendly farmhouses—domesticated land—they must redefine themselves and discover their real identities. While Carl can maintain his familiar personality, he soon discovers that Clarence may have the soul of a hobo. He is no longer familiar to Carl.

The first hobo camp they enter is full of men who do not have the whole, white bodies of those surrogate parents they have hitherto en-countered: "Bending over the can was a big, tall black-headed man with a deep scar running the entire width of his forehead. As he turned I noticed that his left arm was off at the elbow. Besides him and the two boys the group consisted of two Mexicans, a big burly negro with a couple of front teeth missing, and two other white men who appeared to be about thirty years old" (71). Schockman, "trying to hide my igno-rance of hobo language," is reassured by the white hobo's declaration, "We'll treat you white" (73). His white identity has thus far not been threatened by his decision to "turn hobo"; rather, it has been reinforced. Prodded by his bolder brother, Carl assents to staying with the hoboes, though he does not feel it is right. He maintains his allegiance to the family and reflects, looking at a hobo his own age, "'What a pity,' I thought. A boy who should be at home under the guidance of his parents living with these hard bums" (76).

Yet when the brothers are separated for a day while riding the freights, they begin to take two very different paths. Carl finds the experience of riding the rails nearly unendurable: "When I entered the open country a terrible sense of loss assailed me. In the town people were together and I did not feel so lonesome. But now I was alone in a strange world" (98). Yet it does not take long for Clarence to become comfortable in the all-male, antidomestic world of the hobo. As soon as they reunite, Clarence teaches Carl the skills he has just learned from Tex, the one-armed hobo, such as begging meals, surviving sandstorms, and sleeping comfortably in boxcars.

However, both boys are entering a domain where survival seems uncertain and where the verities they have relied on all their lives—including their racial appearance—are thrown into doubt. After being fed by some kindly housewives, "we stopped at a service station and washed our hands and faces and then shaved. After that we looked more like white boys and we felt a lot better" (125). As long as the Schockman boys remain white in appearance, they can rely on the privileges that their white skin has always brought them. Their whiteness is more important than their poverty in determining their identity.

California proves to be freezing and gray, rather than the paradise they envisioned, and worst of all, Clarence seems unrecognizable:

"Gee, will I be happy when we find Tex! It'll be fun to bum with him even if it is cold." For a moment I thought he was joking but one glance at his face and I knew he was in dead earnest.

It's no use for me to try to explain the feeling of fear and regret that came over me. "It'll be fun to bum with him even if it is cold." It was some time before the stunning effects of those words let me think clearly. I turned over so that Clarence would not see the tears in my eyes. When we left home we had decided to go to California. Now upon our arrival we were both bitterly disappointed. We had dreamed of it as being a land of sunshine, of flowers, of orange groves, beautiful mountains and streams. But instead, here at Indio the empty miles of desert sand with the barren, snow-capped mountains looming in the distance surrounded us. (135)

Rather than reaching paradise, the boys seem to have arrived in hell.[19] Yet, like boys in sentimental stories before him, Carl discovers that he had left the real heaven of home to search for false happiness: "I was tired of this kind of life. I was ready to go home. Remorse and fear battled within me—remorse for not having listened to mother and father, and fear of what the future held. 'If you can't get any further by hitch-hiking, turn back for you'll always be welcome here.' The memory of these words seemed to be the single spear of silver in a sky that had so suddenly become ominous, lowering, and black." (136) Worst of all, Clarence seems to be turning his back on the promised land that home represents: "But could I persuade Clarence to go with me? I knew he had enjoyed the days he had spent with Tex. Now he wanted to find him and continue bumming with him" (136).

When they encounter Tex again, he has given up hoboing and enjoins them to return to their parents: "'Boys,' he continued, 'have you ever stopped to think of the things that could happen to you—things that would cause sorrow and grief to you and your family?'" (139). Tex warns them of the insidious nature of life on the bum: "'I'm tellin' you almost every hobo started out just like you two. They said they were hunting a job and that they would go back home if they didn't find one. But,' he added, raising his voice, 'most of 'em never found a job and they kept on the bum, and the few that did find work couldn't stick with it. They quit and went back to the freights'" (140). Tex explains how the hobo life can eliminate the desire for home: "'If you stay on the bum much longer you'll never go back home,' he went on earnestly. 'At least not to stay. You'll never be satisfied unless you're on the go. You'll just be a bum forever'" (140). The story he tells the boys of his own experiences, of his broken promise to his mother, and of his mother's death in his absence is enough to sober both boys into returning home. Even Clarence, who seems to be teetering on the edge of a commitment to a peripatetic life, is willing to go back to Ohio.

On their return trip the boys' identity is constantly mistaken by others; without displaying the signs of middle-class life, they are unrecognizable for who they once were. They are falsely accused of a robbery, arrested, and jailed. Even their whiteness cannot always be relied on. When they are refused service in a cafeteria, Carl sees himself in a mirror and realizes why: "I looked more like a Negro than a white boy" (154). When they approach a beautiful mansion to ask for food, they find that appearances lie. It is run by bootleggers who ply them with whiskey. While Carl objects to drinking and is ridiculed by the bootlegger ("ya claim to be on da bum and you're still mama's little boy" [157]), Clarence drains his glass and asks for more. It is clear that Clarence is still, beneath his middle-class facade, ever in danger of succumbing to his lawless impulses. Suspected by the bootleggers of being detectives, the brothers narrowly escape with their lives. Mistaken for army deserters, they are nearly arrested again. Since the signature on their emergency traveler's check is unrecognizable after weeks on the road, they must return home as bums and cannot effect a transformation into middle-class boys.

They encounter Tex, who has abandoned his job and gone back on the bum: "I suppose I've been on the road so long that I'll never be able to stick with any job. I'm just not satisfied unless I'm on the move" (169), he tells them. Tex's is a fate that Clarence seems to have narrowly escaped. As for Carl, he concludes his story wondering if his hoboing was the cause of his tuberculosis. He finishes the book with the words, in case he had not made his point strongly enough, HOME, SWEET HOME, BE IT EVER SO HUMBLE, THERE'S NO PLACE LIKE HOME (178).

His flirtation with antidomesticity has ended, if not ended well. It is fitting, at least in a literary sense, that Carl contracts tuberculosis, for he posits the wanderlust that led him to try life on the bum as something he felt in his blood. Hobodom is something one can catch, and once the condition settles in, it is difficult to dislodge it from one's body. However, Schockman differs in important ways from the hobo autobiographers who preceded him. He is explicit, finally, about how poverty erases racial differences and strips him of the visual signs—most notably, whiteness—that he had always relied on for privilege. Class, in this formulation, can erase race.

During the 1910s and 1920s, stories of hoboes and even hobo autobiographies were a means of exploring themes of ur-American whiteness and authentic American masculinity, posited against both immigrant culture and a feminized or feminist America. Sociologists and folklorists presented poverty, in this construction, as an ethnicity or even a gender. However, the realities of Depression life challenged these views. In a time of widely acknowledged slippage between classes, moviemakers and autobiographers insisted all the more forcefully on the essential nature of poverty. Applying thinking about race to class became, thus, a means of examining American success mythologies in a time of crisis.

chapter seven

Postwar Blackface

How Middle-Class White Americans
Became Authentic through Blackness

It is hard to pinpoint when blackface minstrelsy in its traditional form lost its acceptance in popular culture. For lifetime circus performer Mae Noell, who was born into a circus family in 1914 and later married a performer, that moment came in 1949:

> It was an easy switch-over for me to work with Bob when he did the blackface routines that were the same as I'd been doing with my father. We really had a lot of fun in those days and there was no evil intent when we did the blackface acts; in fact, our black audiences got as much fun out of them as anyone—maybe more. The last time he blacked up was in 1949. . . . For some years, we operated a different type of show, and by then (1949), the kids were big enough to help us. One day I said, "Bob, just for the heck of it, let's put on one of the old acts for the sake of the kids; they've never seen us do them." So we did.[1]

Given the history of blackface minstrelsy, it is no wonder that Mae and Bob Noell were so inclined. Blackface permeated American entertainment, whether in *Birth of a Nation* (1915), *The Jazz Singer* (1927), or *Swing Time* (1936), in which Fred Astaire, in tribute to Bill "Bojangles" Robinson, assumed blackface.[2] From the 1830s, when it first emerged, through the 1930s, blackface enjoyed a secure niche in American culture. However, by the end of the 1940s, traditional blackface entertainment was beginning to die out as an American institution.

"In the interim, a lot of things had been happening worldwide, and we didn't realize that we were doing anything that was going to hurt anyone's feelings," Mae Noell explained. "We were doing the act and the audience was laughing. . . . We laughed . . . then looked back at the audience, and with a most horrible, sinking feeling, we watched every black patron walk off the lot. . . . My husband . . . said, 'I'll never put the cork on again.' We felt terribly bad about it because we couldn't see how it would hurt anyone's feelings for him to do black when all our lives people had enjoyed so much laughter at the old routines we had done."[3]

The civil rights movement had gained enough force that large organizations, such as the National Association for the Advancement of Colored People (NAACP), as well as individual black spectators who voted with their feet were sending a clear message to the Noells that the old blackface routines were unacceptable. After all, by 1949 African Americans had seen their legal rights expand through a series of judicial decisions, including the 1946 U.S. Supreme Court decision prohibiting segregation in interstate bus travel, the Court's 1948 refusal to enforce restrictive housing covenants, and the decision of the supreme court of California that same year striking down a state law prohibiting interracial marriage. President Harry Truman's 1948 executive order calling for the integration of the armed forces was another milestone.[4]

Of course, the day that May Noell stopped blacking up was not the day that blackface ended, despite the protests of the NAACP and other segments of the black community. Witness the continued existence of *Amos 'n' Andy*, the blackvoice radio show starring Freeman Gosden and Charles Correll. *Amos 'n' Andy*, which premiered in 1926, was for decades the most established of all blackface acts. The radio show survived for another eight years, and the television offshoot, which premiered in 1951, lasted in syndication until the mid-1960s. However, CBS canceled the popular show after its second season, in large part because commercial sponsors, leery of the racial controversy surrounding the show, including a formal protest filed by the NAACP in 1951, were becoming more difficult to find.[5]

The old blackface may have been dying out during the late 1940s and 1950s, but it was being replaced by a new version that traditional black-face performers would not have recognized. No longer comic racial impersonations designed to entertain primarily white audiences, the new blackface was conceived as a political or spiritual journey into the heart of America. The new blackface performers shared the assumption that only African Americans could truly experience the complexities of the United States. Thus, the new blackface was deployed in search of a national identity. As the civil rights movement gained strength, black-face assumed a variety of new guises. In some instances, such as John Howard Griffin's *Black Like Me*, it changed from being a way of estab-lishing whiteness to an attempt to dissolve racial boundaries—an at-tempt, however misguided, at a radical gesture. In other cases, assuming cultural blackface—becoming, in Norman Mailer's phrase, a "white Negro"—meant escaping the responsibilities of whiteness as defined in the 1950s and avoiding a life of stultifying conformity. Later, as the 1950s turned into the 1960s and political unrest spread, cultural black-face also meant whites evading the feeling of responsibility for their racial crimes, memorialized in the television news images of southern sheriffs setting police dogs on black children. Paradoxically, as the 1970s and then the 1980s wore on, from the Symbionese Liberation Army (SLA) through the comic affirmative action film *Soul Man*, black-face became a way for whites to achieve authenticity of experience, or as one blackface impersonator of the late 1960s, Grace Halsell, put it in *Soul Sister*, "to get down to the essentials, to learn about soul" (115).

On November 16, 1952, two items of note appeared in the *New York Times*. One marked what would be a near-end point of the old black-face, and the other heralded the beginning of a new search for authen-ticity, often couched in racial terms. The first item, on the entertain-ment page, was a photograph of radio stars Freeman Gosden and Charles Correll, in commemoration of their ten thousandth broadcast of *Amos 'n' Andy*. The second was a commissioned article by Clellon Holmes titled "This Is the Beat Generation." As the twenty-six-year-old author of *Go*, the first beat novel, Holmes had ample authority for his pronouncements on the disillusioned youths who defined themselves as Beats. Holmes situated the new movement in the malaise of the postwar era: "Its members have an instinctive individuality, needing no bohe-mianism or imposed eccentricity to express it. Brought up during the collective bad circumstances of a dreary depression, weaned during the collective uprooting of a global war, they distrust collectivity." Contrast-ing the Beats favorably with members of the Lost Generation of the 1920s, Holmes wrote, "How to live seems to them much more crucial than why." The Beats had a conviction "that the valueless abyss of modern life is unbearable. . . . There have been few generations with as natural and profound a craving for convictions as this one, nor have there been many generations as ill-equipped to find them." The battle lines had been drawn between conformity and independence and between false values and authenticity. Throughout the 1950s these terms would remain in place, and conformity became a growing con-cern during the decade. As Barbara Ehrenreich notes, by 1957 confor-mity was the most popular topic for major speakers at college com-mencements.[6] Beat culture offered the most visible means of escape from the perceived dullness of life in corporate America. Holmes's arti-cle, thus, was the first mass-market harbinger of the new alternative to dreaded conformity. At least one prominent commentator, Norman Mailer, expressed the choice between authenticity and soullessness in racial terms. To be swallowed up by corporate culture was to be white, whereas to embrace black culture, both real and imagined, was to be hip. In the postwar era white, middle-class Americans, concerned about their lost identities, found their own authenticity in blackness. In the 1950s, when conformity was a thing to be discussed, dissected, feared, and lived, white, middle-class Americans looked to African Ameri-cans to provide them with the authenticity they felt they themselves lacked.

Previous generations of ethnic impersonator autobiographers had mimicked ethnic authenticity in order to find privilege. This new gener-ation of whites sought to escape stultifying privilege by becoming, at least temporarily, authentically other than what they were.[7]

The Escape from Conformity

In his 1950 study *The Lonely Crowd*, sociologist David Riesman, with Nathan Glazer and Reuell Denney, analyzed the anomie of Americans who had, he claimed, become "other-directed" conformists at the ex-pense of autonomy—had lost their authentic selves. The message found a receptive audience, and by the decade's end over a half-million copies had been sold. *The Lonely Crowd* became not only cocktail party short-hand but a cultural diagnosis.

The white, middle-class America depicted by Riesman was a nation of glad-handers, a place where "business is supposed to be fun" and individuality is to be feared, where "to outdistance these competitors, to shine alone, seems hopeless, and also dangerous." "The other-directed person tends to become merely his succession of roles and encounters and hence to doubt who he is or where he is going." Under these circumstances, the very notion of authenticity had become meaningless: "Unable to figure on a lifelong market for his personality as it is, he defends himself by amateurish market research, using his radar to adjust himself as a commodity."[8]

Discussions of conformity dominated the discourse of the 1950s. In *Must You Conform?* (1955) Robert Lindner attacked the conformist as "a slave in mind and body" and "a psychopath."[9] Yet in 1957 Norman Mailer clarified the terms of the debate: psychopathology was not a thing to fear, but to embrace.

In "The White Negro," published in *Dissent* magazine in 1957, Mailer offered the paradoxical solution to the problem of 1950s conformity. To be truly one's self, as a white person, one had to become a racial impersonator. This doctrine was embraced in one form or another by those who donned blackface for the next four decades, from John Howard Griffin to the soldiers in the SLA.

Although he, unlike many of his fellow essayists, laid the blame for widespread cultural malaise at the door of McCarthyism, Mailer began his essay in what was by this point a very familiar way: by deploring the texture of American life, as had so many before him. "These have been the years of conformity and depression," he wrote. "A stench of fear has come out of every pore in American life, and we suffer from a collective failure of nerve." Yet Mailer's solution was more drastic than those of the essayists who had preceded him: "to encourage the psychopath in oneself . . . exist in the enormous present." The hipster, "the American existentialist," was the focus of Mailer's admiration, and "the source of Hip is the Negro." To be Negro was to be psychopathic, criminal, and above all, authentic, for "the Negro (all exceptions admitted) could rarely afford the sophisticated inhibitions of civilization, and so he kept for his survival the art of the primitive, he lived in the enormous present, he subsisted for his Saturday night kicks, relinquishing the pleasures of the mind for the more obligatory pleasures of the body, and in his music he gave voice to the character and quality of his existence, to his rage and the infinite variations of joy, lust, languor, growl, cramp, pinch, scream and despair of his orgasm."[10]

Hipsters, wrote Mailer, were those who had embraced

> the black man's code. . . . The hipster had absorbed the existential synapses of the Negro, and for practical purposes could be considered a white Negro. . . . Hip is the sophistication of the wise primitive in a giant jungle, and so its appeal is still beyond the civilized man. . . . Psychopathy is most prevalent with the Negro. . . . The Negro chose . . . to move instead in that other direction where all situations are equally valid, and in the worst of perversion, promiscuity, pimpery, drug addiction, rape, razor-slash, bottle-break, what-have-you, the Negro discovered and elaborated a morality of the bottom, an ethical differentiation between the good and the bad in every human activity from the go-getter pimp (as opposed to the lazy one) to the relatively dependable pusher or prostitute.[11]

Despite Mailer's nod to the dangers posed by McCarthyism, his essay was deeply divorced from the politics of the moment. In 1957, 15,000 Americans, most of whom were black, led by Martin Luther King, Jr., gathered at the Lincoln Memorial to demonstrate support for a voting rights act. While Mailer described blacks as savage and psychotic, King and his followers presented themselves as the most civilized people in the United States, using good Christian values and following a doctrine of nonviolence to effect change. By that time a new era of racial upheaval had begun. The 1954 U.S. Supreme Court decision *Brown v. Board of Education* had rejected the doctrine of "separate but equal" and declared that the nation's public schools must be desegregated. In 1955 Rosa Parks had been arrested after refusing to give up her seat on a Montgomery, Alabama, bus, sparking a citywide bus boycott by blacks. The home of Martin Luther King, Jr., was bombed in 1956. The home of civil rights activist Fred L. Shuttlesworth was bombed in Birmingham the same year. In response to a six-month bus boycott by African Americans in Tallahassee, Florida, segregation was outlawed on buses there.[12] These were clearly not the Negroes with which Mailer was concerned; for him, blacks lived in the timeless world of fantasy. The "stench of fear" to which Mailer referred apparently was experienced by middle-class, white Americans, not the civil rights activists whose lives were actually in danger and whose organizations were targeted by the FBI and subject to COINTELPRO, or counterintelligence, extralegal harassment campaigns. Mailer, of course, could not have known that by 1957 the FBI was already monitoring the newly formed Southern Christian Leadership Conference, conducting a covert surveillance program in response to the organization's announced campaign to register eligible black voters throughout the South.[13] But one need not be a genius to realize that Joseph McCarthy and his allies had conducted smear campaigns against civil rights activists, and that political work on behalf of race relations could be the basis for blacklisting.

Mailer's critique of McCarthyism aside, this was the same old blackface in hipster clothes, what Eric Lott calls the "American tradition of class abdication through gendered cross-racial immersion."[14] In "The White Negro," Mailer depoliticized racial politics. During the height of the civil rights movement, he framed blackness as an existential, rather than a political, condition.[15]

Beyond the American/Un-American Binary: Becoming Black in the Postwar Era

Mailer's primitive, psychopathic, criminal version of blackface was not the only one to emerge after World War II. Mailer claimed to critique McCarthyism in his essay, but a similar assessment was made much more effectively by Sinclair Lewis in a novel that challenged essential notions of race in order to posit an internal blackface. The inner consciousness of blackness, according to *Kingsblood Royal* (1947), was not, as the passing novels and movies of the period would have it, a tragic condition; rather, it produced a revolutionary consciousness. In order to gain their political, emotional, and intellectual freedom, white Americans needed to break out of the prison of their whiteness.

Kingsblood Royal deals with a thoroughly conformist young banker on the rise who makes what is, to him, a shocking discovery. Lewis's protagonist, Neil Kingsblood, resides in a suburban subdivision in the midwestern town of Grand Republic. Kingsblood, "as free of scholarship as he was of malice" (7), and his wife, Vestal, constitute "a Happy Young American Couple" (8). In other words, Neil functions as a postwar Babbitt, a representative American. As part of this (white) American identity, he is also, at the beginning of the book, a thoroughgoing, if unconscious, racist. Neil and Vestal, in discussing their African American maid, trade what are, to them, truisms, such as "One thing is obvious: the whole biological and psychological make-up of the Negroes is different from that of white people, especially us Anglo-Saxons" (14). Neil asks his wife, concerning their four-year-old daughter, "How would you like it if your own daughter married a Negro?" As they continue to trade racist clichés, "the struggle of the honest and innocent Neil to express his racial ideas was complicated by the fact that he had no notion what these ideas were" (15).

Lewis loses no opportunity to make the Kingsbloods into icons of white Americanness. Nor does he miss a chance to draw attention to the disconnection between the old American symbols and the new, as exemplified by the Kingsbloods' "wondrous kitchen, with its white enamel electric stove and refrigerator and dishwasher and garbage-disposer, . . . crimson metal chairs at the deep-blue metal table—the Model Kitchen that had replaced the buffalo and the log cabin as a symbol of America" (12). On every level the Kingsbloods have lost touch with the imagined American past that has been central in their family mythology. In fact, the family's attachment to the idea of their pure and aristocratic Anglo-Saxon heritage prompts Neil's research into his past, which yields some unexpected results.

Neil's ideas of race come into sharper focus when his father asks him to do some genealogical investigating to confirm the rumor that "we have sure-enough royal blood in our veins" (38). Neil discovers, instead, that his great-great-grandfather was African American, making Neil, by his own calculations, $\frac{1}{32}$ black.[16] As he digests this fact, he is flooded with all of the "facts" he has accepted about race:

> To be a Negro was to be unable—biologically, fundamentally, un-changeably unable—to grasp any science beyond addition and plain cooking and the driving of a car, any philosophy beyond comic dream-books. It was to be mysteriously unable to take a bath, so that you were more offensive than the animals who clean themselves.
>
> It was to have such unpleasant manners, invariably, that you were never admitted to the dining-table of any decent house nor to the assemblies of most labor unions which, objectionable though they were to a conscientious banker like himself, still did have enough sense to see that all Negroes are scabs and spies and loafers.
>
> It was to be an animal physically. It was to be an animal culturally, deaf to Beethoven and St. Augustine. It was to be an animal eth-nically, unable to keep from stealing and violence, from lying and treachery. It was literally and altogether to be an animal, somewhere between human beings and the ape. (66–67)

As he contemplates the prospect of his blonde daughter, $\frac{1}{64}$ Negro, being "unmasked by jeering neighbors as a Negro—a nigger, a zigaboo, a disgusting imitation of a real human child, flat-headed and obscenely capering, something to be driven around to the back door," Neil Kingsblood has his first flash of awareness: "She's not like that. We're not like that. Negroes are not like that. Are we?" (67). As a white American, Neil is insulated from self-knowledge and understanding of his culture. Lewis depicts conformist culture not only as spiritually deadening, but as masking ugly political realities. To be (invisibly) black, in this formulation, is to have the opportunity to be educated about the real meaning of American culture, to become conscious of the racism lying just beneath the surface of life in Grand Republic.

Kingsblood Royal blends two models of postwar blackface: blackness as an escape from conformity (the more Neil learns about what it is like to be black in America, the more appallingly narrow-minded and dull he finds the suburban neighbors he once enjoyed), and blackness as spiritual odyssey (like John Howard Griffin in *Black Like Me*). As he contemplates his own body, which has become strange to him since his self-redefinition as a black man, Neil reflects, "I think God turned me black to save my soul, if I have any beyond ledgers and college yells" (74). Reflecting on his multiracial ancestry, Neil thinks of it as an opportunity for him to escape blandness: "It excited him to think that he had in him canoes and Kaffir knives as well as account-books and plowshares" (128). As he considers the stereotypes uttered so casually by friends, coworkers, and even his wife, Neil finds himself shocked. Attending a black church for the first time, surreptitiously, he listens to the hymns, and "Neil saw a turpentine camp and men molded in copper and ebony singing slow and stopping to laugh under the chains of the white men as they staggered, bound, into the swamps, into the sunrise.—This is my history, thought Neil; this is my people; I must come out" (100).

Of course, it is not as simple as that, and for a while Neil leads a double life. He becomes acquainted with the black citizens of Grand Republic, staying up all night for "race-talks," while lying to his wife as to his whereabouts. He almost has an affair with a beautiful African American nurse, but he realizes that "Sophie was his sister, his other self. . . . But Vestal, she was his love. Every thought that the brownskin Alabama girl might have was natural to him and familiar; every thought of the woman with whom he had gone to high school, played tennis, shared a bedroom for seven years, was exotic and amazing" (220).

However, the newly self-identified black man cannot maintain a double consciousness forever. At the annual lavish party given by the elite Federal Club, where the veteran millionaires of Grand Republic gather for an event that "resembled a bachelor-dinner given by J. P. Morgan the Elder to King Edwards VII" (222), Neil finally breaks down. As the city fathers discuss their plan to drive all two thousand African American residents of Grand Republic out of town, he stands up and reveals that he has $1/32$ Negro blood, saying, "I'm very cheerful about being a Negro, gentlemen, and about the future of our race" (229). His cheerfulness diminishes, however, as he is gradually shunned by neighbors and friends, is fired from his job and has difficulty getting another, and is forced to turn to menial labor.

"When he had warned himself, a month ago, that to be a penniless Negro in this Christian land would be difficult, that just to get through one day of the threat and actuality of snubs would be hard, he had not quite known that it would be hell in the cold, hell in the employers' insults, hell in the pocketbook so flat that you took coffee *or* soup at your grubby lunch, hell in the screaming tendons of the lame, jarring leg he had almost lost in defending the freedom of white Americans to refuse jobs to black Americans" (275).

In fact, World War II becomes the symbolic arena in which the battle over Neil's racial identity is played out. The bigots of Grand Republic focus many of their racial insults (and their anti-Semitism) on what they perceive as the cowardice of black (and Jewish) troops during the war. Neil must reevaluate what that war meant to him. As he and Vestal find themselves in a "social concentration camp" (290), they revert to the kind of Americanism more common during the Popular Front 1930s, which strove to be inclusive and identified Americanism with a revolutionary tradition, than the postwar 1940s. Vestal the Junior Leaguer defiantly refers to her unborn son as Booker T. When the mayor, chief of police, and a mob of neighbors try to drive them out of their all-white neighborhood, they assemble with their black friends and barricade themselves inside their home. Vestal, who had been initially horrified by Neil's revelation, announces to the officer trying to arrest her husband for starting a riot, "Then you'll have to take me. Didn't you know that I'm a Negro, too?" (348). After hitting the detective over the head with the butt of her automatic pistol, she too is herded into a paddy wagon, and there the novel ends.

Thus, to become a voluntary African American is to become a revolutionary, both to fight conformity and to challenge the basis for a bigoted, narrow definition of Americanism. Sinclair Lewis, who had written *Babbitt* (1922) and *Main Street* (1920), the definitive anti-business-culture, anticonformist novels of the 1920s, and had produced the important antifascist novel and Federal Theatre production *It Can't Happen Here* (1935), was now using blackness as a trope to rediscover a definition of Americanism that refused to fit the American/Un-American binary of the late 1940s and 1950s. Lewis seemed to be saying that whites could not be true Americans, but that only blacks, shut out of a limited definition of Americanism by virtue of race, could understand and question the nature of American life in the 1950s.

Blackness As Martyrdom: Black Like Me

"How else but by becoming a Negro could a white man hope to learn the truth?" (7), reflected John Howard Griffin in *Black Like Me* (1960). It was the same question Lewis had asked in his novel and, in some sense, the same issue Mailer had raised in his essay. Griffin, however, gained the authority of autobiography in answering his own question. While novels and essays are generally read as artifacts, as intellectual experiments, autobiography is read as undiluted experience. Thus Griffin's book had the imprimatur of authenticity in the eyes of its readers.

Black Like Me is the ur-text of the genre of postwar blackface, one which has spawned a number of descendants. *Black Like Me* sold over a million copies and won the Saturday Review Ansfield-Wolf Award. Many people still believe that John Howard Griffin died, years after he wrote *Black Like Me*, of skin cancer that was directly attributable to the melanin treatments he underwent in his attempt to transform himself into a black man.[17] In fact, he died of diabetes. Yet it is easy to understand why the rumors of Griffin's racial martyrdom might have started. John Howard Griffin was a man with a profoundly spiritual bent. His first novel, the best-selling *Devil Rides Outside* (1952), was a frankly autobiographical account of his spiritual experiences living in French monasteries. His later works included studies of Jacques Maritain and Thomas Merton. After he completed the Merton study, Griffin spent much of 1971 living in Gethsemani Abbey with Merton.

If Mailer echoed the traditions of antebellum minstrelsy, Griffin looked back to the sentimental traditions of *Uncle Tom's Cabin* to make his point. Although his journey may have had a specifically Catholic flavor, it also seemed very much like the course undertaken by Uncle Tom. Ironically enough, just as the authors of slave narratives shaped their writings after *Uncle Tom's Cabin* and made references to the work in order to gain credibility with readers, so Griffin harked back to Harriet Beecher Stowe's version of African American suffering. Griffin's description of his daily life in the South is akin to that of Tom on Legree's plantation. "But to live—to wear on, day after day, of mean, bitter, low, harassing servitude, every nerve dampened and depressed, every power of feeling gradually smothered,—this long and waiting heart—martyrdom, this slow, daily bleeding away of the inward life, drop by drop, hour after hour,—this is the true searching test of what there may be in man or woman," wrote Stowe (415). White-dominated culture "destroys the Negro's sense of personal value, degrades his human dignity, deadens the fibers of his being. Existence becomes a grinding effort," wrote Griffin (48).

Griffin's racial imposture had a political and spiritual urgency. In his preface he responded to anticipated criticisms from "some Whites" that "this is the white man's experience as a Negro in the South, not the Negro's." "This is picayunish, and we no longer have time for that," Griffin argued. "We no longer have time to atomize principles and beg the question. We fill too many gutters while we argue important points and confuse issues." Rather than highlighting the historical and geographical specificity of his imposture, Griffin points to the universal: "I could have been a Jew in Germany, a Mexican in a number of states, or a member of any 'inferior' group. Only the details would have varied. The story would have been the same."

The shape of the story, indeed, would be familiar to Christian readers; it is that of the spiritual autobiography. As he prepares to embark on his journey into blackness, Griffin reflects, "I felt the beginning loneliness, the terrible dread of what I had decided to do" (10). The process of knowing himself gets ever more complicated as he sees his new black self in the mirror for the first time: "I had expected to see myself disguised, but this was something else. I felt myself imprisoned in the flesh of an utter stranger, an unsympathetic one with whom I felt no kinship. All traces of the John Griffin I had been were wiped from existence" (15). Griffin, observing himself, feels literally split in two: "I became two men, the observing one and the one who panicked, who felt Negroid even in the depths of his entrails" (17). His racial imposture becomes the occasion for a spiritual crisis: "I had tampered with the mystery of existence and I had lost the sense of my own being" (17). Griffin's spiritual odyssey continues. When a white bully taunts him with racial slurs, he prays, " 'Blessed St. Jude,' I heard myself whisper, 'send the bastard away,' and I wondered from what source within myself the prayer had spontaneously sprung" (39). Griffin comforts himself by visiting the Catholic church, by reading from Catholic texts, and by thinking, in a moment of despair, of what Maritain or St. Augustine would have to say.

Yet just as Tom loses his bearings on Legree's plantation, where "the gloomiest problem of this mysterious life was constantly before his eyes,—souls crushed and ruined, evil triumphant, and God silent" (Stowe, 416), so Griffin finds himself adrift. One night, as he settles into his cheap hotel room in the black section of town, which he describes as "an infernal circus" (Griffin, 66), he looks at his reflection once more. "The bald Negro stared back at me from its mottled sheen. I knew I was in hell. Hell could be no more lonely or hopeless, no more agonizingly estranged from the world of order and harmony" (ibid., 67). When, finally, he is subjected to one more racial insult than he can take, "Suddenly, I could stomach no more of this degradation—not of myself but of all men who were black like me" (ibid., 127). For Tom, "Though the hand of faith still held to the eternal rock, it was with a numb, despairing grasp" (Stowe, 417). Yet in the deepest sense of despair, Tom manages to regain his faith and behave with moral courage. Similarly, Griffin has reached his breaking point, and it is here that the hair shirt of his blackness, which he has started to take off and reassume periodically, causes him enough pain that the ordinary becomes holy. Locking himself in a cubicle in the Negro rest room in the bus station where he has been insulted, he reflects, "In medieval times, men sought sanctuary in churches. Nowadays, for a nickel, I could find sanctuary in a colored rest room. Then, sanctuary had the smell of incense-permeated walls. Now it had the odor of disinfectant" (Griffin, 127). From here it is but a short journey to the Trappist monastery where he retreats to reflect and pray. Although he returns to his white identity, he concludes that "because I was a Negro for six weeks, I remained partly Negro or perhaps essentially Negro" (ibid., 156).

While Griffin's critique had the moral authority of individual experience, his story was essentially more about blackness as a spiritual condition—the condition, that is, of living in hell.

White Negroes in the 1960s and 1970s: The Quest for Revolutionary Authenticity

As a temporary African American, Griffin was able to speak with the twin authority of whiteness and blackness. In the postwar period many social scientists stressed not innate racial and ethnic differences between groups, but how it was indeed possible for one group to understand the experience of another. In view of Nazi ideologies, it seemed wrong to many intellectuals to posit inherent racial or ethnic differences. As Kenneth B. Stampp wrote in the preface to his important 1956 study *The Peculiar Institution: Slavery in the Ante-Bellum South,* "I have assumed that the slaves were merely human beings, that innately Negroes *are,* after all, only white men with black skins, nothing more, nothing less."[18] However, the Black Power movement (and the ethnic pride movements that sprang up in response to Black Power) challenged this view. It is fitting that Grace Halsell, the next person to attempt Griffin's experiment in racial impersonation, did not come out of her experiment with the feeling that Griffin had, that she was now able to understand the black experience and even "remain partly Negro" as a result. Halsell, by the end of her experiment, considered herself more authentically black than the African Americans she tried to impersonate.

By the late 1960s Griffin had distanced himself from *Black Like Me,* writing in the epilogue to the 1971 edition of his book, "The day was past when black people wanted any advice from white men" (196). As John Lewis of the Student Nonviolent Coordinating Committee (SNCC) declared in 1965, the civil rights movement, to be effective, must be "black-controlled, dominated, and led."[19] The Black Power slogans first shouted by Stokely Carmichael at a 1966 SNCC rally in Mississippi found a responsive audience. Carmichael declared, "The only way we gonna stop them white folks from whuppin' us is to take over. We been saying freedom for six hundred years and we ain't got nothin'. What we gonna start saying now is Black Power."[20] His audience agreed. Soon the slogan had spread, and revolutionary black nationalism was reborn.[21] The founding of the Black Panther Party in 1966 and its subsequent explosive growth, the widespread demands among African American students for black studies courses on college campuses, and the popularity of distinctively Afrocentric fashions and hairstyles were all manifestations of Black Power.

At the basis of the Black Power movement was a reconception of African American identity. Black Power advocates encouraged African Americans to undergo the "Negro-to-Black conversion process," as the psychological model was described, in order to "discover the blackness within themselves."[22] From accepting assimilation and integration as the only valid model for race relations (stage 1), to questioning received wisdom about the social order and considering alternative views of the black experience (stage 2), to becoming liberated from whiteness and embracing blackness (stage 3), former Negroes were said to move through pure anger at the white world to stage 4, the final stage, in which rage became leavened with reason and in which, as William Van Deburg writes, "their commitment to blackness came to be characterized by ideological flexibility, psychological openness, and a new self-confidence in personal relationships."[23] Some blacks undergoing this transformation, however, became struck at the third stage of this process and felt they were "blacker-than-thou": "Determined to 'out-black' their peers, such individuals took great pleasure in putting down others as Toms or mammies. Their oversimplified, either/or view of appropriate militant behavior was spurred by a desire to convince themselves that their blackness was pure and uncompromising. As a result, they tended to romanticize and exaggerate their grass roots origins—to talk loud and strike militant poses."[24]

This blacker-than-thou posture was reminiscent of the oversimplification and flattening of identity to which earlier ethnic autobiographers had often resorted in order to find their audience. It is striking that the racial impersonators of the late 1960s and early 1970s—Grace Halsell, the SLA, and to a lesser extent the White Panthers—all seem to have become stuck in their racial conversion process at the third stage of development.

If, for Griffin, blackface was a means of spiritual awakening, for Halsell, Griffin's first acolyte, it was, rather, a quest for authenticity through criminality and poverty. A White House correspondent during the John F. Kennedy administration and for three years a staff writer for Lyndon B. Johnson, Halsell was inspired by reading *Black Like Me* to embark upon her own odyssey, which she described in her best-selling memoir, *Soul Sister* (1969). Upon meeting Griffin, to whom she had written about her desire to try his experiment for herself, Halsell sensed that "we were intuitively close and understanding, like friends who have known each other in trust and affection all their lives" (15). Yet if Griffin had been inspired by Thomas Aquinas, Halsell seemed to have been initially inspired by a Hallmark card. Visiting Griffin's house and meeting a black dinner guest there, as well as his young daughter, she felt uplifted by the "wellspring of faith and love that radiated in the eyes of the *black* painter and Mandy, the glowing *blonde* child, a universal love that denies color and race, an innocence that surmounts the boundaries and the barriers of a caste-minded society" (18). In fact, Halsell's vision may have owed more to Harriet Beecher Stowe than to Hallmark, recalling as it did the ostentatiously blonde Eva St. Clair playing with Uncle Tom. However, unlike Griffin, Halsell seemed to have taken only the sentimentality of Stowe's vision and sought suffering without the Christian framework to give it meaning.

Throughout her memoir Halsell invokes images of slavery. However, her work exists in a curious relation to that institution. More than a hundred years before Halsell's writing, abolitionists had tried hard to break the link between race and class. In *Soul Sister* Halsell tries her hardest to forge that link ever tighter. It is not enough to say that Halsell blurs race and class. She contrasts the "fat, rich women in the Watergate Health Club who pay hundreds of dollars to lose one pound . . . with Rebecca, the black cleanup woman, who holds down two jobs, gets her exercise naturally, and probably has the best figure in the spa" (20). This is certainly a sentimental view of poverty and of the folk. Yet beyond this, what Halsell envisions as truly authentic blackness is something uncomfortably close to actual slavery.

At first Halsell is merely happy to renounce her worldly goods. Blackness, in this instance, is simply conflated with poverty, which she romanticizes. For this reason she is thrilled with the idea of giving up her material comforts, including her rides on Air Force One: "Since making the decision to live awhile as a black woman I have been happier" (23). Talking to Roscoe, the black maintenance man in her building, "I felt strangely, freely, unabashedly liberated from conventional ideas and notions of race and reality" (28). Indeed, she seems to see blackness as a path to self-knowledge: "I am beginning to see that many blacks truly know themselves because adversity has forced this self-knowledge upon them" (25).

Initially she uses the language of martyrdom, albeit without a Christian context, to describe her experience. To become black entails undergoing the torments of hell, both physically and psychologically. The black contact lenses she wears as part of her disguise "burn, itch, claw inside my head" (33). In Puerto Rico, where she has gone to finish her darkening process, she spends too much time on the beach, and after she arrives in Harlem, the terrible pain of her sunburnt feet forces her to fly to Washington to see her doctor. Her first trip to Harlem, however, is graphically envisioned as a descent. "So the bus moves towards Dante's inferno. No, not Dante's but Claude Brown's, James Baldwin's, Billie Holiday's. And through my roiling mind: *Abandon All Hope Ye Who Enter Here*" (51). While Griffin experienced his racial impersonation as a descent into hell, he imagined racism, not blackness, as hellish. Moreover, he did so within a specifically Christian tradition. For Halsell, the most hellish experience of all is to discover that the African Ameri-

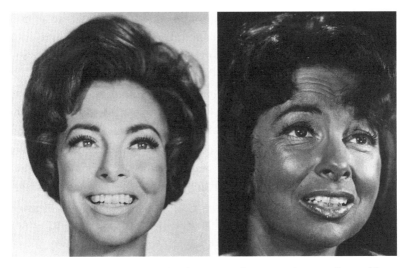

Grace Halsell's 1969 odyssey into blackness proved an agonizing experience. (Photo courtesy of Grace Halsell.)

cans she encounters do not share her vision of what blackness means, and that she herself may be more authentically black, in her terms, than they are.

Soon psychological terror is added to her physical pain. In Harlem Halsell rents a room in the guest house adjoining Adam Clayton Powell's Abyssinian Baptist Church, where she is made to live in the women's wing, "a female among females, a setting I have always found unnatural, depressing, alien" (78). She fears lesbian rape: "I think that the 'fate worse than death' would be assault by a female" (78). To Griffin's Christian vision, thus, is added, in a strange reversal, the threat of sexual martyrdom. The fear of sexual violation was a feature not only for Cassy of *Uncle Tom's Cabin*, but for the women who speak in many slave narratives, such as Elizabeth Keckley in *Behind the Scenes*, Harriet Jacobs in *Incidents in the Life of a Slave Girl*, or even Mattie Griffith in *Autobiography of a Female Slave*. However, in Halsell's case, the threat comes not from white men but from black women.

Desperate and alone, Halsell considers calling some of her black friends but rejects the idea: "They are 'white people' who happen to have black skins, and they cannot help me" (61). Presumably she means they are middle class and thus, in Halsell's terms, not poor enough to be truly black. In fact, she has nothing but scorn for "the middle-class Negro, who goes in for golf and identifies with the lost causes of thirty years ago and acts as master of ceremonies for programs whitey controls" (99). She is upset with a man who takes her on a date to a fancy restaurant: "Why wasn't he more natural, why hadn't he taken me to a soul food restaurant and spent five instead of thirty dollars for the meal?" The answer is obvious to her: "Why, I think, must he be *like so many white people I know?*" (104). To struggle upward, or even to succeed, is to become white. In Halsell's universe, African Americans who wish to stay authentically black must explicitly commit to an agenda of poverty. Yet Halsell does not let the inauthentic blackness of others stand in the way of her soul sisterhood. Before long she has completely merged her identity with those of the poorest African Americans in Harlem.

It is striking, however, that she envisions true blackness, even in 1969, as slavery: "For four hundred years we've smiled, licked boots, played prostitute, told the lies the white man wanted to hear. We put our best selves forward, giving the white man not only our physical energies as field and house slaves, but our best music and religious devotion. Now it's time for us to help ourselves, us niggers" (71). Halsell revels in her sense of degradation and constantly invokes images of bondage. When she goes out on a date, she notes that "he is still the master and I the slave" (103).

While Griffin is touched by the friendliness of the many black people who help him—inviting him home for dinner, asking him to spend the night when he needs a place to stay, or simply engaging in conversation—Halsell has a very different experience. Bluntly put, most people, black or white, just do not seem to like her much. The conflicts she engages in with African Americans have much to do with the fact that they do not share her perception of true blackness as involving degradation and even slavery. For instance, neither the men she dates nor her coworkers understand why she dresses like a domestic when she earns a decent salary at her clerical job. "Perhaps there is pretentiousness in my unpretentiousness, but I have flown the world of pretense, of fancy clothes, and I want to get down to the essentials, to learn about 'soul'" (115). When her supervisor insists that she wear stockings, she once again feels the weight of oppression on her shoulders; she is "cowed, beaten, feeling like a human being mistaken for a thing" (115). Halsell appropriates the language of slave narratives to describe a clash over an office dress code. Like the "Super Blacks" described by Van Deburg, Halsell upholds her own (imagined) blackness by questioning the authentic blackness of others. Speaking of her coworkers, she writes that "the black women were holding up the values of the white System"

(116). Yet she can find comfort in her own authentic blackness: "It is he, whitey, and the Uncle Toms, the black man or woman who apes whitey, who is alienated, lost, lost from himself" (116). She finally quits in protest. "I came to Harlem alone, with my white mind and white spirit, and I will leave now a darker shade of *soul*" (120).

Like Griffin, she experiences the fragmentation of herself: "The emotions I harbored belonged to two persons: a black woman and a white woman. I was cast in a twin, paradoxical role of oppressor and oppressed" (206). And like Griffin, she feels that her six-month odyssey has permanently changed her; as a result, "I am black as well as white" (207). Her ordeal has not only left her with greater empathy for the black experience, but with feelings of alienation all around: "So I passed unnatural days, not feeling black or white" (5). Things get so bad that she even feels alienated from her hairdresser. As she tells Roscoe the maintenance man, "That ole whitey expected me to be *smiling* at him. I'm not wasting my smiles on him!" (5). Halsell, finally, confuses her performance of race with reality.

The black nationalist slogans of the Black Panthers and the party's emphasis on armed self-defense offered white "revolutionaries" of the early 1970s a model for blackness that foregrounded criminality and poverty. White radicals were influenced by media images of rifle-wielding, beret-wearing Panthers but seemed ignorant of the party's grassroots efforts, such as the programs for free food, free busing to prisons, and even free plumbing.

Sometimes the commitment of their imitators to Panther ideology was fairly weak. As Wayne Kramer, lead singer of the late 1960s punk rock group the MC5 and member of the White Panther Party, explained, "So our political program became dope, rock & roll, and fucking in the streets. That was our original three-point political program, which later got expanded to our ten-point program when we started to pretend we were serious. Then we started the White Panther party, which was originally the MC5's fan club. Originally it was called The MC5's Social and Athletic Club. Then we started hearing about the Black Panthers and how the revolution was bubbling under, so it was, 'Oh, let's change it to the White Panthers. Yeah, we'll be the White Panthers.'"[25]

As Danny Fields, manager of the MC5, put it, "Of course they named themselves the White Panther Party because their role models, musically and politically, were black radical musicians and politicians. Bobby Seale and Huey Newton and Eldridge Cleaver were their political heroes. Albert Ayler, Sun Ra, and Pharaoh Sanders were their musical heroes." According to John Sinclair, head of the White Panthers, whose imprisonment for marijuana was later immortalized in a John Lennon song, "We were the voice of the lumpen hippie, just like the Black Panther party was the voice of the lumpen proletariat—which means working class without jobs." Although the Ann Arbor, Michigan, chapter of the Black Panthers hung out with the White Panthers and had shooting practice with them, the Oakland leadership of the Black Panthers ridiculed the White Panthers as "psychedelic clowns."[26] Like clowns, the MC5 mirrored back a distorted version of the Black Panther Party, a caricature of black revolution. They pretended to be serious and deployed race strategically for effect.

Revolutionary blackface as practiced by the Symbionese Liberation Army, kidnappers of Patricia Hearst, took on a more menacing form. As Hearst later wrote in her 1982 autobiography, *Every Secret Thing*, the members of the SLA, most of whom were white, "believed that *only* black and other oppressed people could lead the struggle for freedom. Only Third World people could know the *proper direction* which the struggle should take at any given time. White people were *incapable* of directing this struggle. Moreover, whites were not to be trusted in a leadership position because, *historically*, they had proven themselves to be traitors to the cause of oppressed peoples" (73–74). Ironically or not, the first public act of the SLA had been the 1973 assassination of Oakland's first black superintendent of schools, Marcus Foster, an action widely condemned by the radical left at the time. Like Halsell, SLA members adopted a blacker-than-thou posture. They despised the Black Panthers for "selling out," having "given up their guns and violence to embrace counterrevolutionary social activities, such as free breakfast programs for school children, education classes, and cooperative community programs in Oakland" (84).[27] While the White Panthers may have been ignorant of the Black Panther Party's grassroots programs, the SLA simply considered such efforts a betrayal of authentic revolutionary blackness. As Black Panther leader Elaine Brown later wrote, the SLA co-opted Black Panther Party rhetoric and "distorted the party line." The Black Panthers considered the cartoonish SLA to be an FBI invention.[28] What the SLA embraced as authentic blackness were the worst stereotypes of black poverty and criminality.

The white SLA members tried their best to assume a daily blackface of voice and manner. Thus the seven heads of the SLA cobra—their revolutionary insignia—had Swahili names, as did the SLA members themselves. "These were their 'reborn' Swahili African names, adopted for the revolution. They addressed one another only by these names. Their former 'slave' names had been renounced forever, or so they told me" (48). The SLA members seemed unaware of the irony of using Swahili as an alternative to slave names. As Elaine Brown wrote, in criticizing the "Blacker than black" US Organization, Swahili is "a bastard African tongue—bearing on the language's Arabic roots and utilization by Portuguese and other slave traders as a lingua franca."[29] Teko (William Harris), recalled Hearst, "cursed all the time and tried unsuccessfully to sound like a black man" (48). Fahizah (Nancy Ling Perry) "had such a close affinity to blacks that she could easily have been mistaken for one. While blindfolded, I had thought she was a black, and even with the blindfold off, her manner of speaking, walking, her posture led me to believe that at least one of her parents was black. But that was not even close to the truth. Her father was a successful white businessman in Santa Rosa, California, a Goldwater Republican" (143–44). However, Perry could not conceive of being white and revolutionary at the same time. Unlike the Communist Party during the 1930s, which adopted the slogan Communism Is Twentieth Century Americanism, and which sought to radicalize Americans of every ethnic and racial background, the SLA was a grotesque offshoot of new left identity politics. For the SLA, one's essential racial identity determined one's revolutionary abilities. It may have been unfortunate for most of the SLA members that they were white. However, that did not stop them from imitating what they saw as revolutionary blackness until they, like Grace Halsell, became blacker-than-thou.

When they moved to a new safehouse, all members of the SLA put on blackface: "Teko, in dark blackface and a medium-sized Afro wig, strutted about the room as happy as a minstrel singer, lowering the pitch of his voice as he spoke endlessly, mimicking the voice of a Negro of the Deep South. To me, he looked like a cheap imitation of Al Jolson in *The Jazz Singer*. But he was as joyful and as self-satisfied as I had ever seen him. He could not tear himself away from the bathroom mirror. In fact, he kept suggesting that he was so sure he could pass as a black that he wanted to go out and mingle with the local people" (181).

Teko, unable to tear himself away from the mirror, performs blackness for himself in a narcissistic moment. However, unlike blackface minstrel performers, he is most interested in performing blackness not for a white audience but for a black audience. Only when he is able to pass successfully as black among African Americans will he be able to qualify, in his own mind, as a revolutionary.

Not only the SLA members' whiteness interferes with their ability to be revolutionary. Their bourgeois backgrounds are also a hindrance. The members, in true Grace Halsell fashion, conflate blackness with poverty, and their notions about how poor people behave are bizarre. They inform Hearst that she must eat mung beans, because "that's what the poor people in America had to eat every night" (49). She absorbs a series of dictates about the life of the underclass: "Poor people don't paint their nails" (73). "Poor people always have bad teeth" (300). "Poor people, black people, hit back when they're mad" (208). Part of Hearst's revolutionary education is in "people's elocution," a *My Fair Lady* reversal in which Teko plays Professor Higgins to her Eliza Doolittle: "My prep school diction offended him. It would only alienate me from the people, according to Teko, so I had to consciously try to speak with double negatives, incorrect grammar, and, above all, I had to learn how to drop my final *g*'s" (299).

In the SLA racial mythology, African Americans are imbued not only with authenticity but with criminality. When Cinque (Donald DeFreeze), the only African American SLA member and, naturally, the leader, suggests that they rob not a liquor store but a bank, Teko is overcome with admiration: "Our whole background is so bourgeois that we're thinking too small. . . . We're too chickenshit and we're thinking all the time about small, chickenshit operations. . . . But blacks do this sort of thing for survival. That's why we need Third World leadership. We never would have thought of it ourselves" (109). Cinque's background as an ex-convict only adds to his revolutionary cachet.

In fact, blackness becomes a metaphor for everything the SLA members wish they could be. " 'We're so fucking white, bourgeois, chickenshit scared,' Teko stormed. 'Blacks go out all the time and snatch purses when they need money. They don't plan everything down to the last detail. They act. But we whites are so uptight we have to do surveillance and plan and all that crap' " (253). Cinque does not hesitate, for his part, to trade on his skin color. Avoiding the arduous calisthenics and strictures against alcohol faced by the rest of the group, he reminds the other SLA members that "I could be out leading black soldiers—I could have a whole army of black soldiers behind me—but I'm spending time with you whites because I want to teach you and help you. . . . I'm the black leadership of the SLA. Without me, you'd all be nothing. There'd be no revolution" (137). With this reasoning, Cinque can win any argument, because "their guilt over being white and not black was unanswerable" (189). No wonder that "Teko, listening to exploits described by Cin, would often pound the floor or beat one fist into his other hand, and mutter, 'Oh, I wish I were black!'" (145).

Although it seems unlikely that the SLA was an FBI invention—a theory that most of the Panthers abandoned following widely screened footage of Hearst's participation in an SLA bank robbery—it is certainly true that the SLA functioned as a parody of a black militant party. Like Halsell, the SLA members embodied stereotypes in their embrace of blackness and used their excursion into black identity to liberate themselves from the inhibitions they linked to their white selves. If John Howard Griffin became the Uncle Tom of Stowe's novel, then the SLA and Grace Halsell were cartoon versions of blacker-than-thou militant leaders. Their performance of race was a thoroughgoing, if unselfconscious, satire.

Blackface and Affirmative Action: Soul Man

If Griffin's 1959 journey into the brutal segregation of the Deep South reflected a church-based civil rights movement, and Halsell's 1969 odyssey into the twin "infernos" of Harlem and Mississippi reflected her desire for authenticity, what are we to make of C. Thomas Howell's 1986 voyage, as Mark Watson, a spoiled Southern Californian in blackface, into the hellish environs of Harvard Law School? Griffin and Halsell became black in search of knowledge they felt they could not gain as whites. They both approached their journeys into blackness with a great deal of trepidation. In the 1986 film *Soul Man*, though, Mark Watson "blacks up" in order to gain not wisdom or understanding but an affirmative action scholarship. Even loutish Mark will only accept a scholarship for black applicants to Harvard Law from the Los Angeles area because there are no eligible black applicants for it. He agrees with his appalled best friend, Gordon, played by Arye Gross, who tells him, "You can't just take a scholarship away from a black person."

As Mark tells Gordon, who wonders how Mark will survive three years as an African American, "It's gonna be great. It's the eighties. It's the Cosby decade. America loves black people." However, Mark soon finds out that this may not always be the case. *Soul Man* is a deconstruction of post–World War II blackface and, in larger terms, a satire on white fantasies about blackness. Set in what is commonly termed the post–civil rights era, the movie centers around its protagonist's discovery that the battles for civil rights are not, in fact, over. While *Soul Man* employs blackface, as did Halsell and Griffin, as a means of providing its

In the 1986 film *Soul Man* C. Thomas Howell gleefully dons blackface in order to gain an affirmative action scholarship. (Photo courtesy of MOMA Film Stills Collection.)

protagonist with an existential journey into the self as well as an education in American life, it is an education in which Mark learns lessons about class as much as about race. No matter how much Mark plays with the images of blackness of the preceding four decades, he is, at the end of the movie, left with the reality of class differences and with the role that racism plays in maintaining those differences. Mark starts his journey as a man completely ignorant of history, out of context. His journey is into context.

When the movie opens, Mark is the soul of insensitivity. He is in bed with a beautiful blonde woman whose name he cannot recall. He and Gordon gloatingly look forward to becoming corporate lawyers and making their first million by age thirty. Mark, thus, is an unlikely candidate for the kind of spiritual awakening felt by Griffin or Halsell. He becomes black for purely mercenary motives. Yet, as it turns out, Mark has a lot to learn. His privilege as well as his whiteness is entirely unselfconscious. He has the Reagan-era, post-1960s and -1970s sense that there is nothing wrong with avarice. Moreover, he sees racial politics as operating at the level of a joke. Since, as he reasons, all the civil rights battles have already been won—"America loves black people"— the symbols of what were, historically, deadly serious struggles in which lives were lost become easily exchangeable costumes for him.

Mark dresses as a Black Panther, in black beret, shades, camouflage pants, and a black turtleneck, for the first meeting of the Black Law Students Association. It is clear that he is clueless about civil rights history and has no idea of the often deadly shootouts between Panthers and police or of J. Edgar Hoover's war on black militant movements. For him, the Panther outfit is merely a fashion statement. In contrast to Halsell or Griffin, Mark approaches his African American experience in a blithely Southern Californian manner. He snickers at his racist landlord, takes criminal law because "the prof"—played by James Earl Jones—"is a brother," and answers "right on" when Jones calls the roll in his class.

His behavior does little to ingratiate him to either Jones or Rae Dawn Chong, who plays Sarah, his beautiful classmate. A divorced mom who lives in a small house with her grandparents and young son, Sarah works in the school cafeteria to pay her tuition. As Mark exults to Gordon after the first day of class, "I love the law, I love being black, I love this woman." While Mark's cartoonish blackness may not appeal to the movie's black characters, it works effectively on the movie's white characters. Mark's blackness proves a powerful lure for his landlord's daughter Whitney, a Radcliffe student who is writing her senior thesis on the civil rights movement. She tells him, in a postcoital moment, "I could really feel four hundred years of oppression and anger in each pelvic thrust." For Whitney, "there is no black and no white—only shades of gray."

Yet life as an African American soon becomes less fun for Mark. He is pulled over on a flimsy pretext by a racist Irish cop, thrown into jail overnight, and assaulted by a drunken Irish softball team that has just lost a game. The racist jokes he overhears from a pair of his classmates grate on him. The first time he overhears them, he says "no offense." The second time, they tell him "no offense," and he echoes "no offense." By the third incident, he can only level a hostile stare at them. James Earl Jones does not seem particularly beguiled by Mark's blackness. When Mark asks for a deadline extension following his jail ordeal, telling Jones that "I would think that you of all people would understand," Jones retorts, "You get no special treatment from me. If that means you have to work twice as hard as these little white shits, then you had damn well better work twice as hard." Mark sees white women clutch their purses when he steps into a crowded elevator. Worst of all, he learns that Sarah, who is finally warming up to him, is from San Diego and would have been awarded his scholarship had there been no applicants from Los Angeles. As Mark tells Gordon, who consoles him by telling him, "You didn't know," "I still had no right to take that scholarship. It's wrong. It's immoral." Mark's moment of reckoning comes when he arrives home to find a naked Whitney (still hot for an interracial experience) in his bed, Sarah on her way over to study, and his parents waiting on his doorstep for a surprise visit. Not only do the Watsons not recognize their son in blackface, but his dad wields a kitchen knife in self-defense. As all hell breaks loose, Mark has an epiphany of sorts. Trying to explain nude Whitney's presence to Sarah, he tells her, "She just likes me because I'm black. I mean, because she thinks I'm black. I mean, when I got involved with her I was really white—on the inside. Although I was black on the outside. But now a part of me is black on the inside—even though I'm white on the outside. I don't know, maybe I'm sort of gray on the outside—and the inside."

In fact, *Soul Man* demonstrates a much greater sense of the ironies of racial impersonation than its predecessors. After all, it is titled not for the Sam and Dave song of the same name, but for the 1980 Blues Brothers remake—the whiteface version of the soul hit. When Mark asks for a special meeting of the school's judiciary committee, headed by James Earl Jones, Gordon, in the role of his attorney, delivers an impassioned speech that is itself a blackface parody, 1980s style. In an attempt to excuse Mark from his still-unspecified crime, Gordon speaks of the "lack of understanding of my client's special needs that drove him to this crime." As a hostile white classmate whispers, "I'd say this whole thing is an argument against these affirmative action things," Gordon continues to try to exonerate his client, running through a litany of what sound like liberal clichés. He pleads with the court not to blame Mark, but to "blame those who made him what he is—weak, greedy, unable to support himself by honest labor. . . . Can we blame him for the environment in which he was raised—for the warped values which he learned from earliest childhood—for the people with whom he was surrounded—people who—as much as it pains me to say this—give daily evidence of underdeveloped intellect and deteriorating moral fiber." Of course we know, though his courtroom audience cannot, that the disadvantages Gordon refers to are those of class as much as of race, and that the real tragedy is that Mark's life of privilege has insulated him from the difficult experiences that would have made him self-sufficient, responsible, and empathetic—all the things that Sarah is and that he, at the beginning of the movie, was not. Like *Soul Sister*, *Soul Man* conflates race and class. As the camera cuts away to the stony expressions of

Sarah and another black student, Gordon ends his summation: "In short, can we blame him for the color of his skin? I think not." Which is, of course, the cue for Mark's entrance as a white man.

By the end of the movie, Mark is a changed man. He gives up his scholarship, pays Sarah the money by selling his fancy car and taking her job in the cafeteria, and agrees to devote one day a week to legal aid work and a percentage of his future salary to a scholarship fund. However, when James Earl Jones tells him, "You've learned something I can't teach them—you've learned what it's like to be black," Mark demurs. "I don't really know what it feels like, sir," he tells his professor. "If I didn't like it, I could always get out. It's not the same." Mark, who has always had material things handed to him, begins the movie feeling that it was possible to buy the experience of blackness as he would buy a Ferrari. Yet by the end of the movie he has become a wage-earner rather than continuing as a rich kid. He has a greater sense of earned experience. He does not believe, like Griffin or Halsell, that he remains partly Negro as the result of his experience. By 1986 the process of achieving true racial understanding looked a lot tougher and much more complicated than it had in the early postwar days. When Mark finally punches out his racist, joke-telling classmates, he does so as a white man.[30]

The performance of race in *Soul Man* starts as ironic and becomes de-ironized. Mark begins with the postmodern assumption that it is possible to manipulate the symbols of race and that race is, in fact, performance. However, faced with the difficulties of his life as a black man, Mark sees that his race, even when performed, has very real consequences. Earlier impersonators, such as Griffin and his clownish imitator Halsell, assumed that the very performance of African American identity would transmit to the performer some of the essential qualities of blackness. For them, the act of performance was enough to transform the actor. However, Mark in *Soul Man* takes a journey in which he rethinks the very notion of racial performance and of race itself. The costumes of blackness that he puts on and discards with such ease at the beginning of the movie—the Panther beret is the most obvious example—turn out, finally, to have historical weight and to weigh him down. Yet Mark is finally not so naive as to feel that performance is equivalent to reality, that he in any sense knows what it means to be black. The lessons he learns have as much to do with class as with race. Coming full circle from Mailer's white Negro, who escaped privilege and gained authenticity by becoming black, Mark loses many of his fantasies about race and class. He loses the sense of easy economic privilege he once had as a white man and that he sought to keep through remaking himself as a black man. White once more, he has rethought the relationship between race and class.

chapter eight

To Pass Is To Survive

Danny Santiago's *Famous All Over Town*

Danny Santiago's first novel, *Famous All Over Town*, appeared in 1983 to great critical acclaim. Reviewers praised it as a "flawless coming-of-age novel" and pointed to its "loving and knowledgeable irony," its humor, and its "complex language brew: murdered Spanish, murdered English, combine on the page to be intelligible, even eloquent."[1] John Kenneth Galbraith, in presenting the Richard and Hilda Rosenthal Foundation Award, given each year to one painter and one author of fiction, noted that "*Famous All Over Town* adds luster to the enlarging literary genre of immigrant experience."[2] In general, reviewers admired its verisimilitude, or what they imagined to be such. In praising the novel's "rich street Chicano English that pleases the ear like sly and cheerful Mejicana music," David Quammen confidently asserted in the *New York Times Book Review* that "I am totally ignorant of the Chicano urban experience but I have to believe this book is, on that subject, a minor classic."[3] Richard Price, in his effusive jacket blurb, went further to situate the book in a generic context: "Michael Gold's *Jews without*

Money, Betty Smith's *A Tree Grows in Brooklyn*, Mario Puzo's *The Fortunate Pilgrim*, Claude Brown's *Manchild in the Promised Land*, Edward Rivera's *Family Installments* . . . add to that list Danny Santiago's *Famous All Over Town* . . . a vital and artful addition to the literature of the Myth of the Melting Pot."

The myth of the melting pot indeed. Price's words took on an ironic significance when John Gregory Dunne, in "The Secret of Danny Santiago" in the August 16, 1984, edition of the *New York Review of Books*, let the cat out of the bag. *Famous All Over Town* was not what everyone had assumed it to be; instead it was "a Chicano *Bildungsroman* by a septuagenarian ex-Stalinist aristocrat from Kansas City" (26). Danny Santiago, whose photograph had never appeared on the book jacket, whose publisher and agent had never met him, and who had failed to pick up his prestigious Rosenthal Award, was actually Daniel James, WASP, a graduate of Andover, and the only member of the Yale class of 1933 to major in classical Greek. He had gone from working for his family's business peddling Limoges and Haviland china throughout Depression Oklahoma to working with Charlie Chaplin on the film *The Great Dictator*. A screenwriter who had joined and then left the Communist Party, James had been named by witnesses before congressional committees, closed and open, and had then refused to cooperate with HUAC. The writer's block that resulted from his experiences under blacklisting had been broken only by his adoption in 1968 of a new literary identity, Danny Santiago, and new material gleaned from his and his wife's informal social work in the barrios of East Los Angeles. The couple had begun this work when they visited an interracial camp in 1948 and subsequently received an invitation to re-create the traditional Mexican Christmas *posadas* in Lincoln Heights. For decades they continued forming and working with teenage clubs. By the time James began writing under his new pseudonym, he and his wife had baptized seven babies; had been *compadres de matrimonio* to three couples (which, as he pointed out, "gave us a special relation with some 20 families, to be asked to all celebrations from birth to death") (25); had shared death watches; and had attended countless weddings. When his novel was published, James told Dunne that "over the past 35 years we've known four generations in the best and worst of times" (25). As James explained to Dunne, an early and reluctant collaborator in the deception, Santiago "is so much freer than I am myself. He seems to know how he feels about everything and none of the ifs, and buts that I'm plagued with" (25).

Famous All Over Town and Daniel James's re-creation of himself as Danny Santiago indicate how ethnicity can be used to escape the strait-jacket of Americanism. While writers on ethnicity have discussed the loss of ethnic identity as the price for becoming American, James gained a new voice through his adoption of ethnicity after he was defined, by fiat of Congress, un-American. When James joined the Communist Party in 1938, the organization's slogan was "Communism Is Twentieth Century Americanism." In the 1950s HUAC narrowed the definition of what it meant to be American to the point where there was no room for political difference. James's authorship of *Famous All Over Town* was a triumph both personal and political: personal because it gave him back his writerly voice, long silenced, and political because it expanded the definition of Americanism one more time. The successful American, in the terms of James's novel, was not trapped by constrictive notions of identity but had the ethnic flexibility that was necessary to survive—a set of trickster skills that would prevent him or her from being trapped in muteness because of his or her heritage.

Daniel James was a product of the radical 1930s, a time when a national debate raged about what it meant to be American. While still at Yale, James joined the John Reed Club and marched in a hunger strike. After graduation he collaborated with his father on a play about a longshoremen's strike, then worked in the New York radical theater before signing on with Charlie Chaplin. The 1930s was really the last time in American history that radical writers felt themselves welcomed into a larger conversation about what it meant to be American. This conversation took place not only in radical journals and at meetings such as the American Writers Congress of 1935; it was also sponsored by the government itself. The decade was, as well, the last time in the history of the United States when the left focused to such a degree on reclaiming the nation's past and present, when it was possible to be both radical and patriotic. Perhaps most important for the fate of Daniel James, it was also the first and last time that the federal government not only tolerated widespread debate over the nature of Americanism but actually funded such debate. For while political debate certainly took place in conventional contexts such as presidential campaigns and the editorial pages of newspapers, during the 1930s arguments about the nature of American identity and revisionary views of American history were presented in song, dance, literature, theater, and film. Much of this work was produced with government funding, under the auspices of the Federal Arts Project. The official culture of the United States was both self-consciously multiethnic and tolerant of dissent. The government funded productions such as the Federal Dance Project's *How Long Brethren*, a dramatization of black protest songs. The WPA's Joint Committee on Folk Arts sponsored the fieldwork of John A. Lomax and his son Alan for the swiftly growing Archive of American Folk Music in the Library of Congress. Beginning with their tour of southern prison camps in the early 1930s, the Lomaxes made recordings in the South, New England, and the Midwest. By 1940 the Archive of American Folk Music had in its archives over four thousand recordings of folk music. Music project staffers went to Oklahoma to record and notate Native American music, to New Mexico for Spanish folk songs, and to Mississippi for African American work songs. The America represented by the Federal Arts Project thus included voices from across the political and ethnic spectrums. However, by the end of the 1930s, charges of un-Americanism were already starting to be heard from right-wing congressional committees.

The state guides of the Federal Writers' Project, the Living Newspapers of the Federal Theatre Project, the dances, the murals, and the Archive of American Folk Music portrayed a highly heterogeneous nation fraught with contradictions and populated by citizens of often competing interests. However, by the time the United States entered World War II, the debate on Americanism was narrowing. The left was in disarray, following the signing of the Soviet-Nazi pact in 1939. The government's focus shifted from tolerating and even encouraging a wider cultural debate on national identity to maintaining the war effort. The uneasy wartime alliances between the domestic left and right and between the Soviet Union and the United States were not stable enough to permit the kinds of debates that were possible during the 1930s, and charges of disloyalty held greater weight during wartime than they had previously. The national focus had shifted. Americans were no longer gazing inward and had largely stopped searching for a usable past. Rather, they were looking overseas. By the time the war was over, the cultural landscape of the 1930s had been radically altered.[4]

With the end of World War II and the beginning of the Cold War, the acceptable options for Americanism narrowed further. Just as there were fewer ways to be American, so there were many more ways to be un-American. HUAC, which began hearings shortly after the war, called writers, directors, and actors to the stand to defend their unpatriotic activities during the 1930s. Loyalty oaths became commonplace in business and government; by the 1950s it seemed almost inconceivable that less than twenty years previously an American president had strenuously insisted that government relief projects should hire workers regardless of their political affiliations.

When Daniel James left the Communist Party in 1948 it was not, he told Dunne many years later, "a purely intellectual decision. There was plenty of fear in there, really chilling fear and with some reason in view of what happened later. And shame because of that fear" (Dunne, 22). Indeed, James and other leftists had plenty to fear. In 1951 James was called in front of HUAC, refused to inform on his friends and acquaintances, and was subsequently blacklisted. The Americanism HUAC insisted on was suspicious of ethnic differences and condemned interracial alliances. Membership in groups such as the American Committee for the Protection of the Foreign-born or End Jim Crow in Baseball, which were on the attorney general's list of Communist-front organizations, could end a career. Congressman John Rankin, a HUAC powerhouse, was openly anti-Semitic and given to racist harangues. At one point in 1947 he read a list of stars' names into the congressional record—along with the Jewish names they had left behind. "There are others," he concluded, "too numerous to mention. They are attacking the Committee for doing its duty in trying to protect this country and save the American people from the horrible fate the Communists have meted out to the unfortunate Christian people of Europe."[5] In the vision of the United States shared by Rankin and other HUAC members, each American knew his or her place and stayed in it.

While James was eking out a living during the lean, post-blacklist years and working as a volunteer social worker in the barrios of East Los Angeles, he had an opportunity to observe firsthand the development of new left identity politics. With the resurgence of black nationalism in the late 1960s, what Stephen Steinberg has termed ethnic fever broke out in full force, first among Native Americans, Chicanos, Asians, and Puerto Ricans, and then among "white ethnics." Ethnic fever was manifested not only in the development of university courses in ethnic studies. In 1972 the federal government passed the Ethnic Studies Heritage Programs Act, which provided for funds to be set aside in order that Americans might explore their ethnic roots.[6] With the growth of self-conscious, "unmeltable" ethnicity (to borrow a term from Michael Novak's popular *The Rise of the Unmeltable Ethnics* [1972]), demands for ethnic authenticity arose from inside as well as outside ethnic communities. *Famous All Over Town* can thus be viewed as a rewriting of American identity by a member of the old left who survived narrowing definitions of Americanism and went on to experience the identity politics inspired by the new left.

Famous All Over Town is a novel that critiques the notion of ethnic essentialism and violates audience expectations of ethnic autobiography. It presents the ability to cross ethnic boundaries as not only possible but as necessary to successful survival in America. James, whose identity as a working screenwriter was effectively erased by fiat of congressional committee and who translated his name into Spanish and his identity into that of a young Chicano, gives us an ethnic autobiography that is a paean to the necessity—and the sometime joys—of imposture. James, as a B-movie screenwriter, had to be an expert in bending to the demands of the genre (as he would have to later, post-blacklist, while writing monster pictures under an assumed name). What he does so effectively in *Famous All Over Town* is offer us a narrative that is generically impeccable and yet undermines the very genre it mimics.

An autobiographical novel is not an autobiography. Nonetheless, the reception of *Famous All Over Town* indicates that it was taken by reviewers and, presumably, other readers as having not only autobiographical significance but as being emblematic of the Chicano experience as a whole. This slippage is evident from the reviewers' comments quoted at the beginning of this chapter. John Kenneth Galbraith, in his capacity as spokesman for the Rosenthal Foundation, included the work not in the genre of fiction or autobiography, but of immigrant experience. Even more to the point, Richard Price, in contextualizing the book, failed entirely to distinguish between the autobiographical novel, such as *Jews without Money*, and the autobiography that is clearly labeled as such, such as *Family Installments*. The sometime tendency of reviewers to blur fiction and autobiography became more pronounced because they were considering an ethnic autobiography. These reviewers did not take Danny Santiago's experience simply as his, but as that of the group he represented. Hence David Quammen's description of the novel as a "minor classic . . . of the Chicano urban experience." While G. Thomas Couser characterizes autobiography as having "special authority in America—prestige deriving from its apparent political warrant and its valorization of individualism,"[7] the opposite can be said of ethnic autobiography. Rather than what Couser describes as the Marxist view that "especially in America, where the ideology of the genre and of the mainstream culture seem so well matched, autobiography would seem to function as an opiate of the masses precisely because it denies their massiveness, their collectivity,"[8] ethnic autobiographers assume, in their readers' eyes, a metonymic relationship to the group they represent. Danny Santiago is Chicano; ergo his autobiography is a narrative of the Chicano experience. Santiago must, in this formulation, represent all Chicanos. He is, by virtue of taking on (or being draped with, by readers) the mantle of ethnicity, empowered to "tell it like it is."

Of course, in the autobiographical novel even more than in straight autobiography, there is a disjunction between the writer's experience and what is narrated. Just as Daniel James felt more freedom to express himself in the persona of Danny Santiago, so his first-person narrator must, as Santiago's authorial stand-in, be the "I" whose voice we consider in this discussion. This narrative encloses frames within frames: we hear the voice of Chato Medina at age fourteen as remembered and narrated by Medina at age twenty-eight and as written by Danny Santiago—who is, of course, the septuagenarian Daniel James. Just as the novel itself has multiple frames, so must a critical consideration of the work. It is necessary not only to consider the novel on its own terms—that is, as a critique of ethnic essentialism—but also to consider the author's role in this masked critique. A third frame is created in the barely articulated, unconscious collaboration between James and the reviewers who treat this autobiographical novel as autobiography, or who at the very least blur the generic distinctions. By writing to his agent and editor in the voice of Danny Santiago, the voice of his novel's narrator, James created a seamless persona. What makes the relationship between audience and text even more complicated is the fact that, as Dunne tells us, "Danny was the only persona in which Dan could write, even in his letters to my wife and me, who have shared his secret for sixteen years" (Dunne, 27). Thus impersonation was the only way Daniel James could regain the writer's voice he had lost decades before.

Even as we examine the core of the novel, the meaning that ethnic identity has within *Famous All Over Town*, it is important to keep in mind that it is not Richard Rodriguez, say, who is writing about the difficulties of choosing between remaining in working-class Chicano culture or assimilating into Anglo culture. Does the interrogation by James/Santiago of ethnic identity carry a different valence, then? Does it become an apologia for James's own act of impersonation?

When we first encounter the novel's narrator, Rudy M. Medina Jr., known also as Chato and, occasionally, as Rodolfo, he is on a drunken visit back to a neighborhood that no longer exists, with plans "to dig up various long-buried corpses." He is aware, even at this early stage, of the impediments that too great a reliance on ethnicity will cause him in this quest: "Not a truck, not a car, not a sound. My patriotic bumper was the loudest noise in sight.

" 'CHICANO POWER,' it yelled. 'BROWN IS BEAUTIFUL. FULANO FOR SHERIFF.'
" 'Shut up,' I told my bumper. 'Be quiet' " (7).

Identity politics will not avail him now. He has to silence his present insistence on ethnic affiliation in order to reexperience or fully understand the past. Indeed, much of the comedy of this very funny novel is predicated on the trouble people get themselves into when they invest too many of their assumptions on what it means for others, or for themselves, to belong to a particular racial or ethnic group. Extrapolations about an entire group based on an individual turn out, in every case, to be flawed. And of course the biggest joke is on the unwitting reader, who is doubtless approaching the novel with a host of assumptions—none of which proves to be true—about what it means to be Danny Santiago.

However, underneath the comedy is a serious discussion of the dangers of having too rigid a notion of what it means to belong to a particular group. The assumptions about their own ethnicity held by the novel's characters, particularly Chato's father, affect every area of their lives, including class and sexuality. A too-narrow idea of what it means to be Mexican, or Mexican American, becomes a straitjacket. In some sense the novel is about Chato's struggle to wriggle free of his father's constricting definitions of his identity.

It is easy to see, as the narrative of Chato at age fourteen begins, how reviewers could ignore the frames of which they had knowledge: that Danny Santiago, the writer, was offering us a first-person narrative of a fourteen year old, framed in its telling by a twenty-eight year old. Between the moment when twenty-eight-year-old Chato tells us that "I spread out old memories like hopscotch on the sidewalk, took a running jump and landed in the square of my fourteenth birthday" (8) and the moment when he starts talking to us as a fourteen year old, the reader enters what feels like an intimate pact with him. Chato's tone is confidential, chatty, and immediate. We are beguiled by Chato as he offers us details of the things a fourteen-year-old boy in a patriarchal culture would likely feel embarrassed about, such as his guilty awareness of his sister as a sexual being, his fooling around with a male friend, or his masturbating. Paradoxically, because these are details a fourteen year old probably would not feel comfortable confiding to a large audience, it is easy to feel as though he has taken the reader into his confidence. His comedy is disarming. Daniel James, in his correspondence with his editor and agent, also enabled them and, subsequently, reviewers to take the novel as autobiography. Because he stayed in the voice of Santiago—or, rather, of Chato—in correspondence as well as in the novel, there was little indication that what we were getting in the novel was not the undiluted voice of Chato Medina, alias Danny Santiago. The persona of Medina/Santiago spilled beyond the confines of *Famous All Over Town*, making it hard to remember that the two were distinct (let alone, of course, that there was a third element, Daniel James, controlling both narratives).

Our first glimpse of the struggle between Chato and his father comes on Chato's birthday. "Fourteen years makes a man," his father tells him as he slaps down his chicken-killer knife, "so prove yourself" (8). Chicken killing, for which his father is famous throughout the neighborhood, is given an ethnic or national valence: "The American Way of twisting necks off or chopping heads never pleased my father. It left the meat tough and angry, he claimed. So, Mexican style, he hung his chicken from her feet and slipped the blade into her neck so nice and easy she never felt it" (9). Here we see chicken killing as an art not unlike seduction, requiring grace and finesse. Chato's status as a man will depend, in his father's eyes, on his ability to carry out the task the right way—that is, what his father defines as the Mexican way.

Sexuality, like so much else, is a public matter. "You got a little window in your head," his father tells him as they sit with the neighborhood men prior to Chato's first attempt at killing a chicken, "and oh what I can see in there. You keep your hands in your pockets, here? or else we'll see hair growing on your palms" (11). Chato's sexuality has been suspect for three years, ever since "that bad day when my father caught [my friend Pelón and me] doing something" (12). The tone of Chato's disclosure is surprisingly intimate and unapologetic, given the painful nature of the material he is divulging. So against a backdrop of the neighborhood men waxing nostalgic for Mexican life, Chato prepares for his trial: "While my father's knife sang on the stone, his friends' Spanish words came rolling out like on rubber tires and they all turned patriotic Mejicanos" (13).

"My plan was to imitate my father exactly. I opened the gate and started clowning but those dumb kids never laughed even one time" (15). Chato is already failing in his attempts at replication. "Should I call your daddy, Junior?" the children next door taunt him (15). When he finally grabs the chicken, in a manner considerably less skilled than his father's, the sexual aspects of the scene are again emphasized: "With my left hand I stretched her neck out long for the knife, but it felt very funny to me, like something I had possibly felt before, only with feathers on it" (15). James here both reenacts and undermines the rite of passage into manhood that is a stock element in the adolescence of autobiographers. The tradition and the violence of that tradition are here, to be sure. What is different is not only that Chato is explicit about his failure to play the confident masculine role that his father plays, but that the rite of passage that is supposed to turn him into a man involves his own metaphoric castration.

Incapable of hacking off this uncomfortably familiar organ, unable to return to his father without having carried out his task, Chato decides to do things his own way: "Suddenly it came to me: What's so great about my father's crazy Mexican way of chicken killing? Why not try something new for a change, something more up-to-date?" (15). Unfortunately, Chato's inventive method, although successful, is not culturally acceptable: "It turned out to be the Shot Heard Around the World." It takes only minutes for Chato to be branded a chicken-shooter: "I heard that ugly word race up and down the block like a fire engine. But I ask you, 'What's the difference how you kill a chicken as long as that chicken gets dead?' Possibly I was the first in history to use a gun. But that's people for you, try anything new and different and they're sure to criticize, my father especially" (16).

Chato's dilemma, which forms the basis of the humor within this scene and which will be played out throughout the novel, is the war between his desire to identify strongly with his ethnic group and his desire for self-invention, for understanding himself as an original creation. This conundrum is not only at the core of impersonator autobiographies as a genre but is a central tension operating within American culture.

Daniel James's own desire to identify himself with the cultured WASPs of his background came to naught when he appeared before HUAC. As Dunne described the scene, "With his sense of the theatrical, Dan James carried in his pocket, from his father's library at Carmel, a first edition of *Candide*, which he hoped to introduce into testimony with the admonition that Voltaire had published it under a pseudonym—M. Le Docteur Ralph—and if the Committee worked its will, American writers as well would have to disguise their identities. The Committee would have none of this playlet and cut him off before he could begin" (Dunne, 22).

His cultured WASP background might have gotten him, as an inexperienced youth, a job working for Charlie Chaplin on *The Great Dictator* because, as James told Dunne, Chaplin "had a history of hiring tall, well-bred assistants who knew what fork to use" (18). But where he came from and who he was meant nothing to the congressmen in whose eyes James's identity hung on the question, Would he or would he not cooperate? Was he a patriot or a traitor? James could no longer define who he was. This was a job the congressmen would take over for him.

Chato's battle to carve out an identity for himself free of other's conceptions about what should be culturally determined plays out in many arenas. As he struggles to assert himself, we see the idea of ethnic essentialism interrogated through the book's non-Chicano characters. Although Dunne claims that "the Anglo characters are the book's weakest, flat and obvious" (26), I argue that it is these characters who hold the key to understanding not only the book but its genre. These outsiders offer Chato a new perspective on the idea of ethnicity (much as, perhaps, James, an outsider/insider himself, can effectively deconstruct the idea of ethnic autobiography). Most of these characters are men who come from dispossessed groups themselves—Jews, Japanese Americans, and African Americans—and have had to learn to translate who they are into languages not their own. The first non-Chicano character we encounter is an Anglo doctor dressed in Ivy League clothing. Dr. Penrose is well versed in the discourse of the dominant culture. He does not need translation skills in his life. However, because of his sexual preference he occupies a liminal role in the culture—and, perhaps, can translate himself into Chato's world.

When Chato's mother goes into labor, she and her husband are caught in the trap of his masculine ideals. "My mother should never be having this baby," Chato tells us, "but it shamed my father to have a two-kid family where on Shamrock six was usual, or five at least. And people used to tease him over it, those that dared" (20). By having another child he will assert his masculinity. By having it in the hospital he will assert his difference, not only from Anglos but from the Mexicans he feels are beneath him: "Was he some dumb Indian down there in the swamps of Yucatán to have his son born unscientific like the cucarachas?" (20). In this construct Mrs. Medina's only bargaining chip is her control over her own fertility. She gains the right to have her baby at home and save the hospital money for a trip back to Mexico, but only after threatening her husband, "You can just put that two hundred in my hand or I'll have that famous son of yours by knitting needle" (21).

Tested by his wife's threats and further stressed by his inability to contact the hospital when his wife goes into labor ("He was practicing that speech for days but now his words went Spanish on him and he shoved me the phone" [18]), Mr. Medina's sense of masculinity is further compromised.

His relationship with his son is further complicated when Dr. Penrose not only diagnoses Chato's appendicitis but provides him with an alternative model for masculine achievement. Chato's appendicitis, from which he suffers all day, is framed, significantly, as a feminine ailment, a pregnancy that competes with his mother's. The school nurse diagnoses his condition as "sympathetic nerves. Didn't I recall those movies in Life Science which showed how neatly kittens got born and puppies?" (19). His mother, too, remains unimpressed by Chato's pain and vomiting: "Who was supposed to be pregnant around here anyway, she asked, her or me?" (19). Chato himself considers this theory: "I touched my belly. It felt tight like my mother's. Could you catch a baby the way you catch the measles? Life Science said No, impossible. But what else could it be? God's punishment for shooting the chicken?" (22). Chato is reluctant to show pain: "What would my father say? Since Saturday his favorite name for me was Coward" (25).

During Mrs. Medina's medical crisis we see for the first time how the family members adopt disguises to deal with a racist world. When Lena, Chato's seventeen-year-old sister, is asked to hold the line while she is on the phone to the hospital, "Lena raved. If our name was O'Toole or Shitzenheim the damn doctor would be on his way already, she claimed. But Medina? End of the line, you dirty Mexican." Perhaps even more significant, in light of Santiago's (or James's) chosen genre, though, is Lena's triumphant remark after she finally gets the doctor to come by claiming to be twelve years old and fatherless: "They never believe you if you tell the truth" (20). Only through constructing a new (younger and helpless) identity does Lena get her message across effectively, just as James himself can only speak in the voice of another. A transgressive relationship to his audience is the only one he can maintain.

In fact, *Famous All Over Town* was not the first ethnic novel that James had written. As World War II drew to a close, and on the heels of a "terrible" (in his words) adaptation of a Howard Fast novel that he had written for Paul Robeson, James and his pregnant wife moved back to Kansas City, where he intended to research and write a novel of manners, "The Hockadays," about the upper middle-class life he had known. This novel, which would have been James's real ethnic novel, never found a publisher. Only when James transmuted himself into Santiago could he speak and be heard.

The doctor that his father sent Chato to years ago to cure his asthma fits well into Mr. Medina's construct of masculine professionalism. His name is Dr. Everhard, and he advertises on Mexican radio. He "was loud and bald and glad to see us. His treatment was the latest thing, all electric" (23). By contrast, the physician that shows up to help with the delivery is "very tiny. . . . His voice was cross and tired. His face looked dipped in flour except for black moons under his eyes. He had a long sharp nose and when he pointed it around the room everything got uglier" (25).

In the hospital, when Chato wakes up after his appendectomy, he wonders if his catheter is a punishment for his inadequacy as a male in his father's terms, for his sexual sins: "Or was it a lesson to me? For certain little sins I might have committed down there. Like that bad day with Pelón. 'Puto,' my father yelled at me, 'do you let him use you as a woman?' And wouldn't listen when I told him No, no, no" (28).

Dr. Penrose, whose gaze has made everything in Chato's home look shabby ("The cracks in our old plaster turned into gullies and the bare patch in our linoleum looked like a swamp" [25]), rescues him from the catheter and offers a different model for masculine success. Dr. Penrose, who "even combed me with his personal comb" (29), provides a suave contrast to Chato's father, whose masculine strength is untranslatable into this new context: "My poor father, he might be King of the Aztecs' club but here in County Hospital he looked uneasy and out of place for all his coat and tie. Every day he came to see me after work, but the high point of my hospital day was when Dr. Penrose visited the ward" (31).

Dr. Penrose teaches Chato medical terminology and "was very pleased how fast I learned that language. We could talk together like a couple of pros." Chato is able, for the first time, to imagine himself as a professional, and the doctor encourages his dreams. "Dr. Penrose brought me a Book of Bones to study. . . . I promised to learn two bones a day. After I got them all by heart I could start memorizing my muscles and my inside organs, and after that a Book of Germs, and then I would be in business" (33).

However, this knowledge may come at a sexual price. "He never once discriminated me," Chato tells us, but Dr. Penrose's "discrimination" may come in a different form. For him, Mexicans occupy, it would seem, the role of the alluring sexual other. "In fact, Mexicans seemed to be his most favorite class of people, and last year he flew down there to Acapulco with his friend Colin for vacation. He showed me their pictures on the beach, all tan and more muscley than you might guess. They had more or less adopted a shoeshine boy around my age, it seemed" (31).

Chato seems, if anything, a little jealous of the boy in the picture and expresses this by categorically distinguishing himself from, and raising himself above, the lowly shoeshine boy: "Personally, I didn't care too much for the guy's looks. He smiled too much. In every snapshot there was old Pepe with all his teeth on display. Dr. Penrose said they really had a ball in Acapulco except someone stole his gold wristwatch worth $400. I could guess who but naturally I didn't say anything. You can't trust those Mexicans down there. They aren't like us" (31).

In separating himself from "those Mexicans down there," Chato artlessly exhibits the prejudices that would make his father proud, as he later does when he makes nasty remarks about an African American boy his age who has had his hand amputated: "When I loaned him my Classic Comic about Dr. Jekyll and Mr. Hyde which Dr. Penrose gave me, the guy didn't even return it, which shows you how those people are" (33). (Of course, Chato does not apply the same standards to himself when he leaves the hospital with Dr. Penrose's Book of Bones but, instead, wishfully reinterprets the doctor's loan as a gift.)

When Chato has his existential crisis and must choose between life and death, Dr. Penrose rescues him, although his deliverance is not uncomplicated. Chato climbs out onto the fire escape at night and surveys all of Los Angeles: "So many millions of people and only one of me. How easy to get lost down there, one tiny ant chasing around with all those other ants. Was that all that God had spared me for? He had given me a second chance but what could I possibly do with it.

"'Why don't you jump?' came to me suddenly. 'Jump and all your worries will be over.' My knees shook so hard I had to hang on to the railing. And then the iron door swung open and there was Dr. Penrose" (35).

Dr. Penrose leads him to a private room and peels off his gown. "And let me tell you something. In all my nights in the hospital I never had a back rub like that one. . . . Mine wasn't the first back he ever rubbed, you could tell" (35). Dr. Penrose strips down the sheets, tells Chato his body is beautiful, asks him if he does not feel anything, and finally leaves him with a friendly slap on the butt. Chato himself does not dwell on the sexual implications of Dr. Penrose's attentions at this point. It will be up to his father to force Chato to choose clearly between his own version of masculine success and that offered by Dr. Penrose.

It is clear that Mr. Medina is threatened by his son's doctor. "He had very little to say till I possibly started bragging too much about Dr. Penrose and what a good friend he was to me" (49). Yet not until Mr. Medina's antipathy is fueled by ethnic rivalry do his true feelings emerge.

> He got up crossly from the table and went to the living room to turn on the fights.
>
> "Oh boy," Lena whispered, "pray the Coloreds don't win tonight."
>
> Because it was the policy of those wide-awake promoters at the Olympic Auditorium to match Coloreds and Mexicans when possible, which guaranteed a sell-out gallery full of browns and black plus a ringside of American sportsmen anxious to back the Mexican race in hopes it might give the Coloreds a good stomping. (49)

Ethnic pride is something that arises when actual power in the world is not forthcoming. The loss of the Mexican boxer in the ring fuels Mr. Medina's feelings of humiliation. His pride is so deeply tied up with his sense of ethnicity that every time his chosen representative Mexican fails to triumph, it reflects upon his sense of worth in the world. Thus he accuses the losing boxer of cowardice, as he has earlier accused his son when Chato failed to adequately represent him in the neighborhood arena. His sense of powerlessness makes the help of Dr. Penrose, who calls in the middle of the match to tell Chato that he has arranged for his hospital bill to be waived and to quiz him on the bones that he has memorized that day, more of an insult. Unfortunately for Chato, "the next bout at the Olympic was between two Coloreds. Heavyweights. My father didn't bother to watch. Let those niggers murder each other and who cares? was his point of view. So he gave me his full attention" (51). Mr. Medina's full attention is directed to pointing out the difference between himself and his rival, Dr. Penrose. After expressing doubts that an operation was even performed on Chato ("How do you know they cut it out? . . . How do we know it was yours? Did you ever see it before to recognize it? Did it have your name printed on the side, or initials even?" [51]), he tells stories about a man he knows who went into the hospital only to have the wrong leg amputated. When Chato makes the mistake of saying, "For your information, . . . I plan to study and go to college and be a doctor myself. And Dr. Penrose is gonna help me," Mr.

Medina launches full tilt into his real target. "'That desgraciado little puto?' my father shouted back. 'Help you what? Play stinky finger?'" (52). For Mr. Medina, the choice is clear: "'One certain night those doctors maybe saved your life,' he said. 'But who kept you alive all those other nights and days of your fourteen years? Who gave you to eat? Who put the roof over your head? Shoes on your feet? Some dumb Mexican, that's who. No white suit, no big words, no college education. No, he slaves for the S.P. railroad and every day they shit in his face. What's his name? I forget. Who cares anyway?'" (53).

Chato, offered this framework, feels nothing but shame. "Dr. Penrose saved my life. But he also touched my naked butt, was it in the wrong way? 'Puto,' my father called him, could Dr. Penrose be one of those? And what did that make me? . . . I lay there hating myself and hating him and his Book of Bones and his white suit from the Ivy League." It is interesting that Chato also sees him as a sort of impersonator, as having a double life. "Or was it like he couldn't help himself? Was that what he tried to tell me when he loaned me that 'Dr. Jekyll and Mr. Hyde' which my colored brother stole off me?" (53). His interactions with Dr. Penrose raise troubling questions for Chato about his own sexuality, and his father's framework places Chato in a double bind. The chance that Dr. Penrose has offered him to succeed in the Anglo world means becoming less of a man, relinquishing his heterosexuality.

Indeed, Chato's worries about his own sexuality, contrasted with his father's potent heterosexuality, are only reinforced when he musters all his courage to make a pass at the bewitching older woman in the neighborhood, Socorro Gutiérrez. He first encounters her when he goes to recover his father's car, which Mr. Medina had abandoned outside her house. Regretting his refusal of her offer of a soda, he cannot get her off his mind: "If only I'd said Yes, we could go upstairs together. It would be dark up there" (115). As the weeks go by, he reconsiders his lost opportunity: "All my life I heard good things about these older ladies and how they favor us young guys. . . . It was high time for me to become a Man" (143). Unfortunately for Chato, however, his return trip is a failure. Although he carries Soco's groceries up to her apartment, obtains the promised drink, washes her dishes, and even gets teased by her ("You're cute, Rudy Junior. I bet all the girls go crazy over you, huh?" [145]), his advances are most rudely rebuffed.

My drums began to beat. The hot water in the sink seemed running through my blood into my face. My eyes went misty. I could barely breathe, and finally, when she laughed and ran her fingers through my hair, I turned around and reached. I couldn't help myself. Her juicy chichis are what I touched and sank my fingers into.

"SHIT!"

Where did that yell come from? What hit me after? I was laying on the floor. The maddest female face I ever saw was glaring down at me. (145)

From here things can only go downhill, and they do, rapidly. It is bad enough when Soco asks him, "Think I want that ugly little worm of yours?" but her final blow is crushing: "Now, you go home and send me back your father. . . . Yes, your damn father, that's what I said. You heard me. He's been here plenty. Knocked me up, the son of a bitch and now won't even talk on the phone. Yes, you heard me right. Your fucking baby brother is what I got inside my belly where you wanted to go poking" (145).

Chato is deeply humiliated by this experience, needless to say. His anxieties about his own and his father's sexuality cannot help but be reinforced as he thinks about "her and my father on that brassy bed. My respected father, my father the preacher. 'Kiss the hand that feeds you. Do like I do and you won't go wrong' " (146). While he, as a protégé of Dr. Penrose, could be destined for asexuality or homosexuality, his father, the working-class ethnic, will be heterosexually virile where Chato fails.

However, Dr. Penrose is only the first of several characters who offer Chato a model for success either despite their impersonation, like Dr. Penrose, or because of it, like Bill Bozeman, his prison counselor, and Mr. Fujita, his parole officer. Chato's success will ultimately rest on his flexibility, his ability to translate himself from one culture to another, just as James's own success rested on the degree to which he convincingly translated himself into a new culture, and his voice into that of Santiago's. The successful characters in *Famous All Over Town* triumph through setting up expectations about their own ethnicity in the mind of their audience, and then defying those expectations.

It is Dr. Penrose, still, who writes a letter to Chato's junior high school and thereby introduces him to his next model for this act of translation. Chato's new guidance counselor, Max Pilger, is a crusty New York Jew. He is useful to Chato in that he is able to question and rage at the inequities that Chato takes for granted, and he offers him a way out. Ultimately, though, Mr. Pilger proves limited by his own ethnocentrism.

He is the first official presence in Chato's life, however, to wax indignant on his behalf. "Ai-yi-yí," he exclaims upon viewing Chato's transcript. "C-minus average with a D in Spanish? In *Spanish*, Rudy Medina?" (65). Chato, through long practice in dealing with school bureaucracy, fails to reveal the reason: "I didn't mention it but Miss Helstrom's Spanish was from Spain. If you talked Mexican, forget it. Only Anglos got A's with her" (65). Mr. Pilger is equally indignant with the teacher who claimed that Chato's 135 IQ was the result of cheating—until he discovers her name. "'Kaplan?' It seemed to take the heart out of him. 'God love you, son,' he finally said, 'teachers have their bad days like all the rest of us'" (66). Mr. Pilger, like Chato's father, needs to cling to a fixed version of his own ethnic group in order to continue. This strategy is not without its uses for Max Pilger. Chato claims that Pilger cannot see the tragic scenes Chato perceives in the Rorschach blots because "You're not a Mexican." "No, Rudy," the counselor replies, "I'm not a Mexican. I'm a Jew. Do you know what that means, son? You think you have it tough? We've been discriminated against for two thousand years. . . . Son, you think Audubon is bad? P.S. 153, New York City, was worse. Our teachers hated us. They made fun of our Jewboy haircuts and our oiyoi accents, but we fought those teachers, Rudy. We fought them for good grades. By being two times twice as smart as other kids. . . . Yes sir, Mr. Rudy Medina, we made it and I'm going to see you make it too" (68).

This profoundly American idea of self-fashioning, the notion that it is possible to reinvent oneself, appeals to Chato. It is, of course, what Daniel James did when he successfully assumed the identity of Danny Santiago. However, being able to rewrite oneself depends in large part on being a good reader, on having an intimate knowledge of one's chosen trope. Unfortunately, Chato's failure is one of literary interpretation. He cannot read the Rorschach blots as Mr. Pilger wishes he would. Instead of "happy dancing girls" in one picture, Chato sees "a giant man-eating butterfly. . . . It's got wings fifty feet across and look, there's blood dripping from its mouth. Bullets couldn't kill it, so it goes flying around the world eating everyone in sight" (67). Similarly, his ability to successfully turn over a new leaf, as he has promised Mr. Pilger, rests on his ability to read the texts offered him in a manner acceptable to his teachers. This reading rests on his not pointing out that these are, in fact, impersonator narratives he is being offered. Chato must vouch for the authenticity of the Chicano characters in the text in order to be seen himself as an authentically successful Chicano student.

This is not the easiest task for Chato. The story his class is reading "was supposed to be about a certain Mexican kid named Pancho which his father worked for the railroad and his sister María cleaned house for rich old ladies" (70). Thus, the characters in this text occupy the same position as Chato, whose father, like the fathers of most of his friend, works for the Southern Pacific Railroad. However, there are major differences between Chato's and Pancho's lives: "The story started out in New Mexico where this Pancho specialized mostly in killing rattlesnakes under the baby's crib. They seemed to follow the guy around like a dog" (70). The text offers, in effect, a heroic, sanitized version of Chato's existence in which racial and ethnic problems, although they may rear their ugly heads, can be solved within a paragraph. "As Pancho advanced to the 'mound,' a howl of disapproval arose from his teammates. 'Who ever heard of a Mexican pitcher?' the shortstop grumbled. 'I quit.' 'He doesn't even have a baseball mitt,' exclaimed the catcher. 'Then someone can lend him his,' Miss Brewster retorted. 'Thank you, Miss Brewster,' said Pancho, 'I'd rather do without'" (71).

Noble self-sacrifice, turning a blind eye to prejudice, and unfailing politeness are all hallmarks of the successful Pancho, who is also, most fortunately, athletically gifted. When he excels on the playing field, his teammates rally around him. "Pancho's 'strangeness' was now just a memory. Miss Brewster beamed. 'This should be a lesson to us all,' she remarked. But Pancho had no time to enjoy his triumph. He had promised his sister María to help clean house for rich Miss Murdock" (71). Add unceasing hard work to the list of Pancho's virtues. In some respects, in fact, Pancho's behavior is not entirely different from what Mr. Pilger recommends Chato's should be.

Chato's new tutor, Eddie Velasquez, may not be a social success on Shamrock Street, but he is an expert at fashioning a self that will ingratiate him to the powers that be in Audubon Junior High. Eddie, says Chato, "told me the Secrets of Success at School. First, look neat and well-combed and always sit up straight and don't stare out the window. . . . Put your hand up every chance you get and give your teacher a pleasant smile whenever convenient" (72). As important as constructing a physical self that is easily readable by Anglo teachers is the ability to correctly read literary texts. Given the question at the end of the textbook chapter, "What important lesson does this chapter teach us?" Eddie knows, as Chato does not, that the answer cannot be "Learn to catch barehanded."

"'Wrong,' he told me frankly. 'They expect something way bigger, like Attitude to Life.'

"Eddie studied the air.

"'Here you go,' he said. 'That chapter teaches us you can't keep a good man down irregardless of his race, how's that? So don't holler if they discriminate you, just be patient and your time will come. Can you remember that? Okay, tell it to Bontempo and there's an A for you every time'" (72).

However, Eddie can only read one way; he is culturally monolingual. He lacks a version of himself that will be acceptable within his own neighborhood. Chato, reflecting on Eddie's lesson, asks himself, "I could remember, but how could I recite it with Pelón in the classroom?" (72). Eddie is willing to sacrifice Shamrock Street approbation for his long-term goals: "'I know a lot of you guys call me a kiss-up,' Eddie went on, 'but give me ten years, then come up to my office and we'll see who's kissing whose? CPA, Rudy, Certified Public Accountant, that's where I'm heading'" (73). However, Chato is not prepared to cut himself off from neighborhood acceptance in the same fashion.

His first efforts at following Eddie's advice do not work quite the way he hopes they will: "When I caught Bontempo's eye, I flashed her a grade-A smile. It gave her such a scare she dropped the chalk" (75). Miss Bontempo explicitly guides students toward identification with their text: "A good book can whisk us off to India or deep into past ages, can it not? Reading takes us out of our little lives and opens whole worlds for us to roam in. Then, too, there is another kind of book which gives us insights into our own daily problems and helps us solve them. Our text for instance. Young Pancho and his sister María, are they so very different from the boys and girls seated in this room?" (75).

Miss Bontempo may be a caricature, but in some sense she is like all readers who wish to take the experience of an individual as a paradigm for all members of that ethnic group. Brushing off the students' objections, she explains, "'They're both Mexican-American young people like so many of us here. We can identify with them, can we not? And learn from their experience. For instance, from Pancho we can see how patience is rewarded when he proves himself. Isn't that the best way for us to deal with Discrimination? And far better than just sulking or shouting our heads off?'

"She had just killed Eddie's fine speech which I was all primed with" (75).

Although Chato is quickly able to recover with a question and wins the approbation he is looking for, "Pelón gave the back of his hand a fat juicy kiss" (75). Chato cannot please both constituencies at once. Unfortunately, while Chato is an expert reader in one sense—he is able to decode the formula of the text—he cannot read the teacher's expectations. When he is able successfully to predict the outcome of the story they are reading, he thinks he is "following Eddie to the letter." However, "Miss Bontempo's smile left her for far-off places." She cannot swallow the idea that the text is formulaic or that Chato has knowledge of the formula, and she challenges him. "I got quite hot. . . . 'Anybody can guess what happens in these dumb books, where on the television—' " (76).

Chato, although he might try, cannot conform to a script that requires his own stupefaction. His inability to perform in class echoes the experience of Daniel James when he was called in front of a congressional committee and asked not only to recant his past but to betray others and, by naming names, to destroy the careers of others in order to save his own. James brought with him an artifact, his treasured first edition of Voltaire, which signaled who he was and where he came from—a home, that is, where ideas were important, and a father who positioned himself in an American aristocracy of wealth and intellect. How quickly a treasured heirloom could be transformed into a useless prop. How quickly James's speech on the danger of writers being forced to conceal their identities could be silenced. Only the impersonator James can go unrecognized, can gain the psychic freedom to write freely.

Thus Chato, instead of being rewarded in class, is sent to the vice-principal's office. He has yet to learn the next important lesson in the value of disguise, which he will get from Bill Bozeman, a counselor for the juvenile justice system, and Mr. Fujita, his parole officer.

When Chato ends up in juvenile detention after he is apprehended during a joyride with Pelón, he is told by the police that "bloods . . . love that Mexican ass!" (168). This is, of course, his father's view of ethnicity as enmity. Thus he is terrified when a tall black man enters his cell: "I backed into a corner expecting you know what but it was my counselor, he said, and Bill Bozeman was his name" (170). Bozeman is, to all appearances, whom Chato has been raised to fear and to see as his enemy. A victory by an African American represents a defeat for the entire Mexican race, whether in a televised boxing match or a kids' marble competition. In fact, when Chato, as a twelve-year-old marble champion, lost the all-city competition to "a crippled colored kid from Watts," his Boys' Club leader, Ernie Zapata, "really had tears in his eyes for the Mexican race that day" (84). However, as the counselor attempts to establish solidarity with Chato across ethnic lines on the basis of class, he offers him another model for viewing the world. Actually, Bozeman has a wide repertory of rhetorical devices designed to make Chato talk and to make him reveal the identity he has concealed from the authorities.

"'Rudy M. Chato,' he sighed. 'Mr. AKA Nobody. Probably you got reasons to dummy up, hey baby? Couldn't blame you,' he said. 'Who wants to go out when they got a nice clean jail like this. Why go home when home's all busted up, unknown uncles kick your ass around the block for nothing. Welfare food, welfare clothes—.'" Bozeman is baiting Chato with the clichés of the underclass. Sure enough, Chato rises quickly to the bait:

> "Not my home," I interrupted. "My old man works steady."
> "Then why didn't you call him up?"
> I didn't say.
> "He have a heavy hand, your daddy?"
> "Pretty heavy," I admitted.
> "My daddy had the heaviest hand in Watts," he told me, "but you know what? When I had my little troubles, about your age too, police and all, that daddy of mine never laid a finger on me." (170)

The street-talking Bozeman presents to Chato a readily identifiable character. Yet even as he stays in this character, he begins to reveal to Chato that there might be a little more going on than meets the eye. "Mr. Bill Bozeman unfolded himself and rested his hands on the roof and looked at me. 'Well, Mr. Rudy Medina Junior Nobody, I won't waste no more of your time just now.'

"'Huh?'

"'Formerly of 114 Shamrock Street? And will be again if your 650 release goes through'" (170).

Bill Bozeman sounds as though he is having a casual conversation, but his interrogation of Chato is skillful. More skillful still are his translating abilities, as Chato finds out when, in his conference with his family, another counselor reads him Bozeman's assessment.

> "When interviewed, subject revealed that he comes from an economically viable household, in which, however, the father's role borders on tyranny. Far from being a stabilizing influence, it is per-

haps the major cause of this boy's antisocial behavior. If incarcerated the prognosis for rehabilitation is poor. Release in custody of the boy's parents will prove more productive but only under close supervision by the probation department. Signed, William P. Bozeman, Counselor."

I jumped. Was that black giant some kind of mind reader? And how could he write those high-class words when he talked like someone you might run into in a pool hall? (173)

Bozeman has the ability to read Chato effectively and to translate easily his own discourse from street talk to officialese. More importantly, this skill gives him power—in this case, the power to alter the dynamics in Chato's home. The flexible Bozeman, rather than Mr. Medina, trapped by his rigid ideas of ethnicity, will prevail here. Similarly, James has escaped the trap of his own ethnicity in writing this book. Of course, there is a difference between the positions inhabited by Bozeman, Fujita, and Medina and that of a wealthy WASP finding himself through an identity he can freely choose.

Even more to the point is the experience Chato has with his parole officer, Mr. Fujita. Based on his model of ethnicity, Chato is prepared to be wary: "Don't think I'm prejudiced against the Oriental class of people, but if this Mr. Fujita ever went to Audubon Junior High it would be only human for him to pay back the Mexicans for the rough times they gave him there" (193). Chato assumes that because he knows Mr. Fujita's ethnicity, he knows all the important information about him. As his mother, nervously anticipating Mr. Fujita's visit, asks Chato if she should make him a taco, Chato confidently informs her that "they eat only raw fish." Her reply is "Qué barbaridad!" (193). To both of them, Mr. Fujita is the barbarian other. Lena, secure in her belief that she is a mistress of deception, feels certain that she can present an easily readable, acceptable self to Mr. Fujita—a representation of the family not unlike that offered by Chato's English class textbook.

"Lena tried to hand me Dolores.

"'It'll look real good if he finds you holding the baby,' she argued. 'Is my hair okay?'" (193).

Indeed, Lena stage-manages every aspect of the meeting, including her father's choice of shirts. As her father's interpreter, she grants herself a great deal of latitude. Just as she tries to create a textbook family along the lines of Pancho and María, so Mr. Fujita, for his part, speaks a language that sounds directly lifted from a sociology book. "Regard me as a counselor, or family doctor," he tells the Medinas. "What we are dealing with here is a kind of illness, a social illness I shall call it, and we must understand its causes before we can expect a cure" (194). The play continues, yet with a great deal of direction on Lena's part. " 'Don't act so sullen,' Lena mumbled at me in that rapid-fire Spanish you use with English-speakers present. 'And smile once in a while,' she suggested, 'and tell him Sir.' My mother wondered if she might serve him coffee at least, but I shook my head. It might look like a bribe. A lot of very private Spanish got whispered into the cracks between Mr. Fujita's 1,000,000 questions."

The strategy seems to be working well, but when Mr. Medina "got quite excited in English[,] I bit my teeth and shut my ears." Mr. Fujita sounds more and more like Miss Bontempo as he speaks to Mr. Medina: " 'Telling' a boy is often not very productive. . . . Neither is threatening him or shouting at him. Mr. Medina, do you ever sit down for a straightforward man-to-man discussion with your son?" Chato is resentful of this approach and, characteristically, frames his feelings in ethnic terms: "My father might have his faults here and there but how could the Oriental type possibly understand them?" (195). Lena, even more resentful, escalates her fictionalizations: "Up to now she stuck fairly close to what you might call the truth but now Lena got carried away, she was like that. 'My father is a very good father,' she bragged. 'He takes us to the circus and the zoo and the ball games and to look at all those bones in the museum over there in Exposition Park' " (196).

The construction of a false self becomes a necessary response to Mr. Fujita's assumptions about how members of the family should behave. As Mr. Fujita flattens himself into a model social worker, so Lena responds by presenting him with an impostor family. Unfortunately, Lena's fictions must compete with the reality of her father's mistress screaming through the window.

"Oiga tú, pinchi cabrón! Tú sabes a quien hablo! Sálgase de aí, culón!"

She dared my father to come out. She called him everything. He sat frozen in his chair, but to Mr. Fujita it might have been just a passing train, and my sister didn't seem to hear. . . .

From outside came, "Sinverguenza, hipócrita, leave me pregnant with your brat, will you? Not Socorro Gutiérrez! You gonna pay up, entiendes?"

Thanks be to God she stood in Spanish.

"My father even helps my brother with his homework when he can understand it," Lena went on. "And if we need a few dollars for anything, all we have to do is ask. Yes, Mr. I-forget-your-name-excuse-me, we got a real warm and loving family here, no problems." (198)

Lena is not even willing to admit that Socorro could have any remote connection with her world. When she excuses herself to get rid of "that poor crazy woman outside," it is with the explanation that "she's a Metodista, you know the type and comes here once a week to preach at us Roman Catholics. If I give her fifty cents she'll go away" (197). Only an outsider could behave in such an inexplicable way, could be so rude and crazy. Although "in a minute Lena tripped in fresh like from the beauty parlor," after getting rid of Socorro, in the end Mr. Fujita has the last word:

And then, just as he started out the door he turned to Lena. Some question seemed to be on his mind.

"Dígame, qué dijiste a la borrochita?" Mr. Fujita asked in perfect barrio Spanish. "Cómo la corrió?" Meaning what did she say to that drunken lady to get rid of her.

Lena answered, "Huh?"

Others caught their breath.

We watched Mr. Fujita off the porch and down the steps.

"Mexican stepmother," he called back. "Five Mexican stepbrothers, for ten long years." (197–98)

The comedy of this scene boils down to a battle of wits, to who can be the better impersonator. Needless to say, Mr. Fujita wins hands down, and his reward is the information he needs and would have been unable to get had he not been able to slip in and out of his personae with such ease. Although Lena can laugh in admiration of a greater deceiver than she, "My father sat holding his head in both hands, squeezing it tight as if it might be a nut" (198). While Lena, who has been responsible for shaping the family identity, can learn from a master of deception, Mr. Medina remains trapped, not only by his ideas about ethnicity, but by his inability to adopt the trickster personality that seems necessary for survival in a hostile world.

While it might seem as though the simplest form of adaptation or impersonation—that is, the ability to assimilate—is all that is required for success, the example of Mrs. Medina's best friend shows the failure of this approach. Chato is pulled both ways throughout the text, both toward assimilation and the promised success in American terms that this would bring, and away from assimilation and toward a renewed attempt to come to terms with his own ethnic identity.

Virgie is the first person to take advantage of the Southern Pacific Railroad's offer to buy her house in preparation for the rezoning of the neighborhood. Virgie is a Horatio Alger immigrant, as eager as Ragged Dick to refashion herself and to make sacrifices. "To save money for her dream home, Virgie rented out the front house and lived in the little shack in back, one tiny bedroom with her four kids sleeping sideways on the mattress" (123). Like an Alger hero, she has no attachment to the past. She throws away most of her belongings in preparation for her move up in the world: "My father looked back in and sighed but you didn't notice Virgie spilling any tears" (123). Not only does she divest herself of most of the material reminders of the past, but her vigilance extends to poisoning what she does bring along, in an effort to get rid of the "cucarachas" that plague her: "Virgie was very scientific. Before anything could go into the trailer she sprayed it good, the chrome dinette set, the pots and pans and groceries and even the wet wash off the line. She sprayed the TV through those little holes in back and even the antenna off the roof. And how that Bug-go stank!" (123).

During the Mexican Revolution the term "cockroach" was first applied to the rebels, who were small, brown, and poor. Intended as a slur, the name was proudly adopted by those it was intended to insult: "La Cucaracha" became a popular revolutionary song. Not only did the tune retain its popularity, and not only did "La Cucaracha" become a movie classic, but as Oscar Zeta Acosta, the Brown Power leader of East Los Angeles, explains in his autobiography, *Revolt of the Cockroach People*, "the Chicano *knows* from birth he is a lowdown cockroach."[9] With this identification in mind, it is difficult not to see Virgie's actions, at least in part, as a form of self-loathing. Pointedly, Chato contrasts her assimilationist method of extermination with that of his father's friend Chuchu, who shows up with a box one night: "It was a demonstrator model, he announced, and fully guaranteed. . . . A young duckling it turned out to be, and when the light went on you should have seen the duck go for the cucarachas, slipping and slapping on the linoleum and quack-quacking with excitement while he fielded them right and left in his noisy bill. . . . It was a comical sight and for a week that duckling was our main event. It took the place of television until finally the poor thing died. Too much roach powder next door was my father's idea" (123–24).

The duckling is not only an effective roach-eater; it is a focal point of the community as well, replacing television. By contrast, Virgie even uses extermination powder on the TV, to make sure that it will be free from contamination. However, the duckling cannot survive in a world in which too many people use Bug-go rather than methods that will not harm them along with the roaches.

The odyssey that Virgie and her family undertake in their move to the suburbs involves much more than a geographical shift. When they arrive at the street of "all new homes which matched exactly except the doors" (126), Virgie's husband, Arturo, tells them, "'Call me Arthur if you please. I have been promoted. I am a very big man among the Eskimos.' And he pointed to his name spelled American on the mailbox. 'Nobody talks out here, compadre. They must be deaf and dumb.'" With assimilation comes isolation. Upon entering the new house Chato marvels, "In all my life I'd never been in a really high-class home like that one. I'd seen similar on the television but Americans always lived there" (127). The interior of the house has been designed with the assistance of the decorator from Sears, and the girls' bedroom matches the pom-poms of the drill team they are expected to join come high school. Not only is the appearance of the home American, but home ownership itself becomes, in Virgie's eyes, a form of social engineering. As she tells Mrs. Medina in advising her to follow Virgie out to the suburbs, "'A house like this is what my compadre needs to keep his nose to the grindstone instead of banging round the town and drinking beer and you know what all else. The payments, comadre, they'll make him save and be responsible. The payments will make a new man of him, like they have Arturo'" (129). In other words, the chaos that afflicts the Medina family, including the hysterical visits from Socorro, would end if only the Medinas would commit to upward mobility and assimilate into a bland form of Americanness.

Just as Virgie promises Mrs. Medina that assimilation will bring her husband's wayward sexuality under control, so Chato finds upward mobility desexualizing. On the car ride out to the suburbs, Chato has the good fortune to have one of Virgie's daughters sit on his lap. "When we turned onto the Freeway I fell in love. Debra's hair blew softly over my cheek, her little hand perched like a canary on my arm. My rocket busted and showers of sparks coasted slow and gentle through my blood while we cruised out east" (125). This encounter initially fuels Chato's fantasies of upward mobility: "Who knows? Virgie could be right for once. Back on Shamrock I might easily end up in jail or dead, where if my father bought that cute house with the red door I could well end up doctor. And Debra would be my nurse" (126). Yet when Chato and Debra finally get a chance to be alone, hanging up the family wash, the eroticism of the moment, fueled for Chato by his proximity to all that feminine underwear, is shattered. She takes the panties from him and begins talking about Little League. "How could she be sports-minded at a time like this?" Chato wonders.

"She turned into Virgie Junior. That dead fly had me cutting my hair in Paddy style, and Stand up straight and Look people in the eye when you talk to them. And no more speaking Spanish, plus two dozen ways to improve my personality. She had me mowing lawns to develop my muscles and my bank account, attending summer school to improve my grades. Then I could run for Class Vice-president and maybe have surgery on my nose to look more refined. Finally, in the middle of one of her sentences, I headed for the kitchen" (130).

Upward mobility becomes self-mutilation. Not only is it necessary that every moment of the day should be directed toward self-improvement (Little League, lawn-mowing, and student government), but one must relinquish one's language and even alter one's physical appearance in order to look "more refined"—that is, upper class. Hence even physical features become a text in which class and ethnicity can be read. There seems to be no room for sexual desire in this formulation. The body is to be used as a tool in service of class uplift—muscles strengthened through money-earning exercise, nose bobbed—rather than as an instrument of pleasure or a form unselfconsciously inhabited. All traces of ethnicity must be erased. Spanish must be forgotten, and hair must be cut in a style identifiably Irish (the group for whom Shamrock Street was named and the group that has succeeded in leaving poverty behind).

Not only does Debra's harangue kill Chato's desire, but upward mobility literally makes him sick: "After we unloaded the trailer, Virgie put out food for us but nobody seemed in the mood to eat. All I could taste and smell was Darwin's Bug-go. Suddenly my father of all people had to go to the toledo in a hurry, and I went running to the other one" (130). Virgie and her family are literally willing to poison themselves for the sake of leaving all traces of their past behind. As Chato is on his knees, heaving away, "I got a feeling someone was watching me. I quick looked around. Nobody. And the door was locked. And then I saw my audience. He was an old familiar friend from Shamrock Street, but not in the best of health. He could barely drag his six skinny little legs across the color-coordinated carpet, so I helped him along with my finger to where the rug ended and watched him scuttle down fine and safe and dark under the toledo.

"'Go with God, little cucaracha,' I told him in Spanish. 'Go find yourself a little wife'" (130–31). In the end, then, there is a possibility that the cucarachas will triumph after all, that the past cannot be entirely purged.

Although the time period in *Famous All Over Town* is not specified, Chato does tell us at the beginning that he has spent half his life— fourteen years—on Shamrock Street. When we first meet him, his car is plastered with the Brown Power stickers of the early 1970s. Thus it is not unlikely that he and his mother, avid fans of the Mexican cinema, would have seen the immensely popular film *La Cucaracha* in 1959. In any event, even before radical Chicanos proudly began calling themselves cockroaches, Mexican revolutionaries had used the humor of their popular song to lift the burden of the insulting term. By recontextualizing what was intended to brand them as inhuman, they managed to rise above the insult. Similarly, Chato helps the scourge of Shamrock Street ensure that the assimilationist efforts of Virgie's family will never be entirely successful.

Recontextualization, however, is a weapon that can be used against Chato as easily as it can be used in his favor, as he discovers during the city council hearings on rezoning the neighborhood. First, City Hall itself suddenly takes on a new aspect to him: "From Shamrock Street, City Hall was always a pretty sight. . . . But on that Thursday when we stood there in its teeth like a couple of ants I didn't care for its looks at all" (133). Chato and his father have a great deal of difficulty finding not only the hearing room but someone who will give them directions. "All I could see were the busy business type and their heels clicked and clacked on the marble floor. Ask them a question and they'll freeze your blood. I spotted some others that were more our kind but they looked lost too" (134). The world of government is hostile, impenetrable. "Finally my father noted someone more or less his own shade of brown who happened to be pushing a broom. They had quite some conversation. It seemed the man came from almost the same little town my father was born in, so he dropped his broom and escorted us to the right door and shook hands and introduced himself" (135). Only by reducing the world to a village can the Medinas make their way around.

Their dilemma only gets worse once they get inside the hearing room. "There were nine planners present, each one with his private sign, such as La Kretz, Torvaldsen, Kleinburger and other all-American names. You don't see much Gómez up there at City Hall, or García, at least not without a broom in hand" (135). The irony, of course, is that only a few years ago the names Chato reads were anything but all-American. Yet in Chato's context, these names are emblematic of the power he and his family can never possess. Beyond their, to him, non-ethnic names, the planners seem oddly unscarred and physically privileged: "Of all those 18 hands there was not a single missing finger which would be a world record for any 9 of our people" (135). The planners' intact bodies stand not only in contrast to that of Mr. Medina, who has lost a fingertip to the Southern Pacific Railroad, but also as a commentary on the physical mutilation that Virgie's daughter has suggested will be necessary for Chato's upward mobility. However, if Chato has felt the context of City Hall shift profoundly as his vantage point shifts from his neighborhood, where "it was a big part of all our sunsets and night skies too" (133), a familiar and attractive part of his landscape, how much more shocking his next sight will be. As a city planner pontificates, " 'What's he talking?' my father asked.

" 'All about a bunch of slums someplace,' I answered. 'They didn't get to Shamrock yet.'

"But I was wrong. Mr. Cockburn snapped his fingers and they splashed a very familiar picture on a big movie screen. My father gasped like shot. It was our own home, and how mean and ugly we looked up there between those marble columns" (135).

Out of context, Chato's life is literally unrecognizable to him. What to him is home is to the city planners a slum. Yet because Chato lacks the power to frame the issues in his way, the planners can continue to present what to him is a false narrative of his life and environment. "He showed us a parade of Shamrock houses from Main Street to the tracks, except he skipped Don Tiburcio's pretty garden, I noted. While the picture show was going on, he talked building codes and welfare families and dropouts from school. He preached Broken Homes and busted sewer pipes, trains passing day and night and no foundations to the houses. Too many kids to the bedroom caused TB and worse, he claimed. Mr. Cockburn had figures on everything, arrests, probations, sick and dead. And how he loved to add up all our troubles and all our little mistakes" (136).

Not only can Mr. Cockburn use his lens selectively to edit out the beauties of life on Shamrock Street; he can effectively present neighborhood life in terms of sociological clichés, the kind of clichés that ethnic autobiography has traditionally undermined. One of the traditional functions of minority autobiography in the United States, including slave narratives, has been to offer members of the dominant culture a recognizably human face to affix to the people whom they have perceived, and perhaps feared, only as a disadvantaged, unfamiliar group. Harriet Jacobs offered her white audience a portrait of a mother suffering as white women would when unwelcome sexual advances were forced upon them, and as white mothers would suffer when deprived of their children. In *Bread Givers*, Anzia Yezierska replaced the picture of a Lower East Side of New York unpleasantly teeming with alien masses presented by Henry James in *The American Scene*. She offered us instead a portrait of a young woman struggling to gain an education and help her community. Claude Brown showed white, middle-class readers the insides, the struggles, and the yearnings of those young men they crossed the street to avoid.

Now Chato is offered a representation of his life that seems as unreal to him as that embodied by cheerful Pancho and María in his school textbook, and he feels helpless to combat it. "But how could I keep up with all those ugly numbers? Was I deprived and disadvantaged like this man said, or destitúted? My father worked steady. I had never been sorry for myself before, except maybe two Christmases back. And here I was living in The Slums and never knew it, because by the time Mr. Cockburn added it all up, even a cucaracha would be ashamed to admit Shamrock Street was his home address" (136).

Not only Chato is powerless to refute this image. His father's friend Chuchu, who has organized the neighborhood petition drive to halt the rezoning, cannot offer his version of events. "There stood Chuchu in his overalls from work and cement dust in his hair, and he looked out over that sea of neckties. And then Chuchu that never lost a word before, ran out of gas" (137). When he finally does manage to begin speaking to defend the homes he has helped construct, "the planners started coughing and checking wristwatches." Mr. Cockburn's condescending speech, in which he tells Chuchu, "Rather than depriving you of your homes we're opening the door to a better and a richer life," is interrupted by the appearance of "a hunched-up monkey of a man on wheels" (138), the attorney for the Shamrock Street residents. Rather than expressing shame at his disability, he flaunts it, taunting the planners with his physical disadvantage.

" 'Must I stand before this distinguished body?' he asked and clattered out a pair of crutches.

" 'You may remain seated, Mr. O'Gara, as usual,' they sighed" (138).

Mr. O'Gara needs a cultural cliché as powerful as the dangerous ghetto in order to answer the planners, and he finds it in an appeal to patriotism. "'Tell me, Mr. Cockburn,'" he demands, "'just how many young men from Shamrock died on the bloody fields of Europe and Asia?'" (139). (In fact, the next installment of Pancho's story focuses on what happens when the sheriff who drives him and his sister home from their latest dramatic adventure recognizes their father: "'I'll be a monkey's uncle,' Sheriff Trotter cried, 'if it isn't my old buddy Charlie García from the Fighting 69th.'" This shared combat experience effectively erases all ethnic and class barriers, to the point where Sheriff Trotter offers Mr. García a job as deputy sheriff, a scenario so implausible to Chato that he cannot prevent himself from loudly saying BULLSHÍT [149–50].) Mr. O'Gara, who "went rolling on like the Sunset Limited" is as powerful, in Chato's and his father's eyes, as the railroad he is opposing. He offers the planners as well a history lesson. "'It was the S.P. railroad built that little street. Very convenient to have a pool of cheap labor so handy to the tracks. That labor was Irish first which is where the "Shamrock" came from. My own great-uncle lived there. Next it was Italians till they wanted better wages and now it's Mexicans'" (138). Rather than accepting the planners' vision of the residents as criminals and failures, he refers to them as "'honest workingmen'" (140). While he appears to Mr. Medina as "'San Patricio come again'" (139), he fulfills another function for the narrative. He casts Chato's story in the light of a more generalized form of ethnicity. Chato's story and that of the community are tied to those of the Irish and of the Italians and of the lives they built.

Unfortunately, this argument does not persuade Mrs. Medina, for whom ethnicity is still paramount and the basis of her distrust for Mr. O'Gara. Mr. Medina retaliates in kind. As Chato tells us, "I learned a lot of family history that day. My father recalled every Mexican that ever cheated him and my mother every gringo till finally she put her hands over her ears and slammed out back to tell it to her little birdies" (142).

However, the family arguments over ethnicity finally come to a head when all of the Medinas embark on a trip to Mexico to visit Mrs. Medina's family—the trip that Mrs. Medina had won for herself after threatening to abort her pregnancy.

Chato has high hopes for what a visit might do: "Was it possible my family could be born again down there?" (203). Initially he is reluctant because of his own linguistic insecurity: "I hate the way they talk Spanish down there, who can understand them?" (204). He also has a sense of ethnic superiority that his father has drilled into him: "And I'd be surrounded by a whole gang of Indians, as my father always called them" (204). However, he has considerations about his own identity: "And yet, on the other side, I had always wondered about Family" (204). The sexuality that Mexico embodies for him intrigues him: "And how about those little dark-skin girls, those morenitas that my father spoke of and his friends? Those plump and generous ones? Possibly they would find me quite thrilling coming down there from the city of L.A., California, to visit their dumpy little village" (204).

Predictably Mr. Pilger, who encourages ethnic pride, is very excited about Chato's plan to visit Mexico. Upset that Chato does not know who Dolores Hidalgo, Porfirio Díaz, and Benito Juárez are—that his education has been so inadequate—Mr. Pilger tells him, "Six whole months you wasted in that class! One day in Mexico will teach you more. . . . What an opportunity, Rudy. The temples of your ancestors, the land of your fathers, you'll see them with your own eyes." Through finding out about his forebears, Max Pilger feels, Chato can discover who he is: "Son, did I ever tell you I once followed in Moses' footsteps, by jeep of course. The Red Sea, Sinai, the Promised Land, yes, Max Pilger banged his head against the Wailing Wall and learned to be a Jew again. Go thou, Rudy and do likewise. Find your roots! Discover your identity!" (205). Mr. Pilger assumes, then, that identity is deeply rooted in ethnicity and that, in fact, there is some essential quality in one's nature that can be recaptured by a visit to a homeland, even if it is a homeland one has never seen before.

This belief in an overweening commonality based on ethnicity is shared by Mr. Medina, who shows no apprehensions as they head toward the Mexican border: "I'm still a Mexican citizen. They're our brothers" (210). Indeed he shouts, "Hermanos!" to the soldiers at the border. It does not even take him long to find an ideal Mexican boy, who offers to park their car at the customs station: "Right there my father fell in love with him.

" 'No lively ones like that in L.A.,' he said. 'No, señor, they're all too busy watching television.'

"I took no notice of his remark. The kid opened the door for us like kings. He reminded me of that famous Pepe that stole Dr. Penrose's $400 watch in Acapulco except this kid had three teeth missing where somebody had no doubt kicked them down his throat" (211).

Chato's jealousy is palpable. It is apparent that he believes that Parky Carro, as he dubs him, can be an ideal Mexican son to his father in a way that Chato himself never could—just as the shoeshine boy could capture Dr. Penrose's affections in a way that Chato had found threatening.

Mr. Medina continues to indulge his nationalistic feelings, ordering mariachis to sing "Méjico Lindo" because, as Chato tells us, "it always made him cry" (211). Chato, for his part, feels deeply alienated by this patriotic display, suspicious of Parky Carro, and irritated by his father's preference for Mexican beer: "To be honest I like our Lucky Lager better" (212). Mr. Medina is even, at this point, anxious to stay in Mexico for several months so he can get his mother-in-law's will rewritten to benefit his wife. "And then, muchacho," he tells his son, "after the old woman finally passes on, we'll live like kings, like emperors! No more slaving for the damn S.P. Down here we could be gente! Rich! I might raise horses like the Castillos" (212–13). Mr. Medina has, in his imagination, scripted a prodigal son narrative for himself, a scenario in which he will be elevated to the level of the Castilian nobility. When Chato shows his alarm at this idea, Mr. Medina tries to reassure him, saying, "It's the land of your blood, muchacho. It's your Patria and you're gonna love it here" (213).

This is a variation of Mr. Pilger's idea. Not only does ethnicity determine identity, but some mystical idea of blood is even more important than culture. A common Patria will be enough to erase distinctions of class, culture, and even, given that Chato was, after all, born on Shamrock Street, nationality. Considering what has transpired in the novel thus far, it ought to come as no surprise that this great faith in the power of ethnicity is destined to be rudely shattered.

His father's need to create a compelling narrative about the homeland is so great that he has a hard time acknowledging reality. When Chato objects to the big tip he gives Parky Carro, mumbling, "Anyone could be polite for money" (213), his father gets angry, contrasting his imaginary Mexican son to his real one: "'For hunger,' my father roared at me, 'which you don't even know the name of.' He made up a whole sad story about that kid, how the mother was a widow with twelve mouths to feed and if it wasn't for Parky Carro they would no doubt be dying of starvation. It was a very boring story.

"'Life's a wrestle down here,' my father went on. 'Work or starve and that's what builds men. You'll see, the next hundred years are gonna belong to the Mexicans and that kid's proof of it'" (213).

Once again, Mexicanness, as narrowly defined by Mr. Medina, is identified with masculine strength—the ability to feed women and children—and contrasted unfavorably with the effeteness, the weakness of one who has never known hunger, never had to struggle to survive in the way that Mr. Medina has and Chato (and Dr. Penrose) has not.

It is not long, however, before Mr. Medina's constructions of Mexican masculine superiority fall apart. When his wife gets nervous as they approach the Mexican customs station, he tells her, "You women don't know nothing. . . . I'll handle this my own way" (214). Worse still, the customs inspectors invert his idea of brotherhood. Mr. Medina gets angry at the easy passage through customs of a "brand-new Chrysler station wagon . . . full of blondies. Even their dog had yellow hair." When he asks the inspector, "Why not search *Them?*" the inspector answers, "Because they are honest tourists coming down to spend their dollars while you come to rob your brothers. Everything out! Hurry up now!" (215). Brotherhood thus becomes a two-edged sword. It is only, finally, Mrs. Medina's offer of her favorite earrings as a bribe that enables the Medinas to continue. "And after that," Chato tells us, "my father never saluted the Mexican flag again, and he talked more English than I had ever heard him speak in L.A., and louder too, in gas stations and other public places" (217).

Chato, for his part, experiences things Mexican as frighteningly primitive—including his mother's behavior as he watches her walk on her knees up the stone steps of her village church. "It was spooky to think my own mother had spent half her life in this foreign place" (219). His grandmother's home "was a round pointy hutch of sticks like made by cannibals" (220). Hoping to find the "plump little morenita" of his father's description among his myriad cousins, he is disappointed to discover that "they all wore those farmery braids and no-style skirts that hung around their ankles like gunnysacks" (223). Although Mr. Medina's narrative to Chato has been one of male supremacy, it is Mrs. Medina who begins dominating the situation. As he warns her, "Mexico's no place for a woman to start acting smart in" (223). While Mr. Medina wants to breed horses like a Castilian Spaniard, Mrs. Medina identifies herself as "one crazy Indian from Titatláln" (223). All of the class and gender relationships in which Mr. Medina has instructed Chato are inverted here.

Categories of ethnicity begin to dissolve and become increasingly muddled as the Medinas' stay continues. Chato fails to make an erotic connection with one of his "far cousins" as she stirs blood pudding ("I was sorry about that because our fingers might touch and we could even end up holding hands in that bowl of blood which could be quite exciting" [228]). However, he is soon busy mythologizing America and himself as American to his male cousins. He brags to them, "Take any average Sunday in L.A. . . . We start things off by drinking ourself a brew or two or possibly blowing some of that good Acapulco gold to get our horsepower up. And then if the weather's good we take us a carful of lively chicks to the beach and play Hide the Weenie" (229). Although his cousin the history teacher tries to impress on him the story of their ancestors, who were brutalized by the Aztecs and the Spaniards, Chato tell us that "to me they were a big disappointment. Who wants his grandpas to be losers every time?" (247). Chato may be, as he says, "their Man from Mars" (229), but his mother has become an alien to him as well. His father makes grandiose speeches to his in-laws: "He said he was a Mexican first, last and always, even if he lived in the U.S.A., because there were no boundaries high enough to divide La Raza Mejicana. And here with his beloved mamacita and in company with her family he felt himself among brothers ever united in pura confianza and amistad" (231).

However, he is simply trying to exploit his ethnic and familial connections to get money: "Did you believe all those pretty things I told you?" he asks his son. "I hope not. You don't know this people" (231).

It does not take long for the final disintegration to occur. Mr. Medina, it turns out, has slept with the same "far cousin" on whom Chato has his eye. When his mother-in-law confronts him with his adultery, he orders Chato to leave with him. For the first time, Chato refuses his father. When the entire family finally leaves, it is with only hasty goodbyes, and after the secret baptism of Chato's baby sister and an abortion that, unbeknownst to Mr. Medina, his mother-in-law has induced in his wife.

Rather than being the affirming experience that Mr. Pilger had promised him, the pilgrimage has been a fiasco. As Chato reflects, "This visit to Mexico that was supposed to unite the family had ended by tearing us apart, maybe for good" (255). However, ironically enough, the very failure of this exercise in finding roots may provide Chato with the independent identity that he has been searching for throughout the book. "When you're a kid, your father is like the sun in the sky. Your whole family circles him like a bunch of planets. He gives you your winters and your summers, your good days and your bad, and it's black night when his back is turned to you. But we had disobeyed him. We had shamed him in public and now our Gravity was all gone. The only thing that held us together was the Buick" (254–55).

Spinning freely on his own, it is up to Chato to discover who he is, apart from his father and his father's notions of ethnic identity. Yet when the family returns to find their house condemned, Chato does, in his imagination at least, place himself squarely in the context of Mexican history.

"Did you ever hear of Los Niños Héroes? They had their statue in that history book Mr. Pilger loaned me, guys around my age and they fought the whole U.S. Army down there at Chapultepec. Their elders all gave up but they stood on, and not one lived to tell the tale.

"Could we do the same for Shamrock Street?" (261).

Although Chato fantasizes a martyr's end, including heroic encounters with everyone from Mayor Sam Yorty to the president of Mexico (who sends him word to "stand firm for La Raza. All Mexico is behind you on the television" [262]), in the end there will be no heroics. His parents split up; his mother moves back to Mexico, taking her baby with her; and Lena elopes with her Mexican boyfriend. Even his gang disperses. Chato is left with nothing. Finally he addresses the reader directly for the first time: "How does a punching bag feel when you punch it in the face? Does a sidewalk hurt when you walk all over it? What does a nail think of hammers? Who knows if ants shed tears? How would you feel, man, if they came onto your street and tore it down. What would you do?" (276).

What he does do, finally, is become a writer. As he passes through the ruins of his neighborhood, "it came to me. Why not sign myself there and prove somebody's left alive at least? Or else why did I pick up that red Crayola?" (279). His identity now is neither that of his family nor that of his Brown Power allegiances some fourteen years later. He is CHATO de SHAMROCK. Nor does he write a narrative at this point: "I wondered should I write 'Down with the S.P. railroad'? or 'Chato will revenge you'? Things like that, news, but I decided No. Just write your name and keep them guessing" (279).

His signature alone, however, is enough to gain him ownership of what he has lost or never had: "I signed myself on Morrie's Liquor as new owner and on Flaco's Tacos and García's Short Change Department Store so I could drink and eat and dress in the latest style. . . . I kept my eyes open for cops of course, but they were all somewhere else and I cruised up Broadway getting rich. I took over Blackie's Barber Shop to get my haircuts free for life, and Cashen's Haberdash and the E.Z. Credit Furniture in case some day I might decide to get married and settle down" (279).

Not only does Chato write himself into ownership, he writes himself into literature: "I could have been the Invisible Man" (279). He has his final epiphany just as he finishes signing the Bank of America, a two-foot-high signature in four colors outlined in gold. He notices "one older man, very well-dressed, the All American type. When he saw my name it was like a gun aimed right at him" (283). Right before his capture by the police, "the Message finally came to me. The Message I'd been waiting all my life for. 'I don't need to be any fancy kind of Lawyer or Doctor or Big League ball player to make my mark in the world. All I need is plenty of chalk and some Crayolas, or better, paint cans which I'll mobilize tomorrow. L.A. may be a monster city but give me a month and I'll be famous all over town'" (284).

Although the cops sarcastically refer to him as "the Writer," he makes it clear in his final, paragraph-long chapter that this is indeed what he has become. Giving his readers hints about his new life with his sister and brother-in-law, he proclaims, "In case you're curious, you could possibly read all about it someday. When and if I ever get around to writing it down, that is" (285).

Just as Chato writes to get his revenge on those who have harmed him, so was Daniel James, through his translation into Danny Santiago, able to, trickster-style, escape from an identity that was imposed on him by the blacklist and gain his freedom. James's claim to citizenship was not threatened by his ethnicity; of Anglo-American background, his right to Americanism was unquestioned. However, his writerly identity was effectively voided, and he was redefined as un-American because of his politics. Perhaps this is why his protagonist is a boy caught up in battles over identity who survives by becoming a writer, even though he is carried away to jail the first time he picks up a pen.

As Daniel James he was subjected to the calculated humiliations imposed by a congressional committee, had his livelihood stripped from him, and was left with nothing but a name that rendered him unemployable and the memories of a trauma that would leave him unable to write for decades to come. As Danny Santiago he could exuberantly celebrate the triumph of disguise and the power of translation into another identity as a means of freeing himself from another's script. Literary impersonation is a risky business at best; for a privileged WASP to assume the identity of a working-class Chicano youth is fraught with difficulties. However, it is possible to view James's act, in writing *Famous All Over Town*, as one of courage and self-liberation as much as one of presumption. Far from being an exercise in literary facility, a tour de force, it is James's way of escaping the historical trap in which he found himself.[10] As he told Dunne, "I spent thirty-five years working on this book. Twenty years learning what it was all about, the last fifteen writing it. You don't spend thirty-five years on a tour de force" (Dunne, 27).

Ultimately, every autobiography is a narrative of survival. We read autobiographical texts in the comfortable knowledge that the narrator has gotten through whatever horrors he or she documents. We also read them not only to find out how other people succeed, but how we, too, can learn to prevail. The impersonator autobiography is a betrayal of this trust. Since the life documented did not really exist, there are, it seems, no lessons we can learn; there is no real knowledge of how we can get through difficult times as the autobiographer has. Paradoxically, *Famous All Over Town* is a narrative of a hidden survival; behind Chato's survival is concealed that of Daniel James. Yet the textual concealment is by no means complete. One character after another demonstrates the necessity of impersonation in order to escape a historical trap. That trap might be the very concrete dilemma of being born into the underclass and into a group that suffers from discrimination, or it might be, instead, the less clearly visible snare created by the blacklist. We too often read ethnic autobiography to find out the definitive truth of a group's experience. *Famous All Over Town* not only defies our expectations but teaches us their futility.

Rewriting the Ethnic Autobiography

The great commercial success of *The Education of Little Tree* in the early 1990s seems to indicate that the ethnic impersonator autobiography is alive and well. Yet Asa Carter's book may be part of a genre on the verge of extinction. Carter, as an old-fashioned racist, escaped into an Indian identity to avoid being trapped in a black/white binary. However, a new kind of memoir does more than offer a successful performance of ethnicity. Three recent autobiographies, Shirlee Taylor Haizlip's *The Sweeter the Juice: A Family Memoir in Black and White* (1994), Gregory Howard Williams's *Life on the Color Line: The True Story of a White Boy Who Discovered He Was Black* (1995), and James McBride's *The Color of Water: A Black Man's Tribute to His White Mother* (1996) are all testaments to and analyses of the consequences of choosing—or being assigned—a racial identity other than the one designated at birth. These books present not a successful performance of authentic racial or ethnic identity, but a deconstruction of racial categories.

The ethnic impersonator autobiography was born, I argue, in the

1830s as a strictly political tool, a means for white abolitionists to write what they saw as more effective and more reliable slave narratives. Paradoxically, the collaborative creation by abolitionists and former slaves of a fixed autobiographical genre, a story of an escape from slavery that had a recognizable form, led to the development of impostor fugitive slaves—and to abolitionist anxiety about being bilked by these impersonators. Although abolitionist newspapers may have trumpeted authenticity in slave narratives, they in fact eventually devoted far more critical attention to ersatz memoirs.

Autobiography provides the illusion of an unmediated relationship between author and audience, and of an authentic voice speaking to one reader at a time. As slave narratives, real and impersonated, became successful, other forms of ethnic impersonation developed as a powerful cultural force. In popular novels, staged performances, and fictions masquerading as biographies, readers and audiences were asked to ponder what it meant to be American in a context in which all persons were theoretically born equal and yet in which skin color and ethnic definition permanently defined class status.

Helen Hunt Jackson's *Ramona*, a novel focusing on American mistreatment of Indians and centering around its heroine's passage from one ethnic identity to another, became a national best-seller. Crucial to the creation of a mythical past for Californians, *Ramona* came to occupy, for generations of readers, a shadowy territory somewhere between fiction and history. In their hunger for a usable past, readers went to great lengths to turn fiction into history.

The many forms of theatrical ethnic performance deployed during the second half of the nineteenth century made it possible for autobiographers working in the first decades of the twentieth century to commodify their ethnicity and package themselves. Successful ethnic impersonators took what they had learned from popular entertainment and presented these elements as authentic, lived experience. Thus, in the 1920s Sylvester Long used his knowledge and experiences from a stint performing with a Wild West show to create a new self, bolstered by a best-selling ethnic impersonator autobiography. In turning himself into Chief Buffalo Child Long Lance, Long gradually modified his "Indian" costume to create a character that audiences would recognize from the Wild West shows.

However, ethnic impersonator autobiographers refashioned not just theatrical performances of ethnicity but popular ethnic autobiography. Samuel Ornitz modeled his parodic autobiography on the Jewish immigrant autobiographies that had played a major role in shaping the debate on immigration. Working with the contradiction between the seeming disingenuousness and the rigid structure of the immigrant autobiography, Ornitz called attention in his work to ethnicity as performance, and to that performance as a crucial ingredient in American success. He mocked the naive credulity of readers as well as the generic, stock nature of ethnic autobiographies.

As Ornitz noted, the ability to manipulate the performance of self was closely tied to the success ethic. Autobiography, after all, was an effective tool for marketing the self. However, during the Depression, the near-collapse of capitalism challenged American mythologies of upward mobility. The immigrant autobiographies of the first twenty years of the twentieth century had applied American mythologies about class to (the disappearance of) ethnicity. As immigrants became more successful, they lost their ethnicity. This was a political move, designed to show that, in fact, ethnicity was not an essential quality of selfhood but a characteristic that could be made to wither away as the immigrant became indoctrinated into the success ethic. However, the impersonator autobiographers of the 1930s applied an older kind of thinking about ethnicity to class. In doing so they posited American—that is, native-born, WASP—poverty as an essential state. The hobo autobiographies of this period labeled hobodom as a quality of the soul rather than an economic condition. Toward the end of the Depression, a work appeared that proved a harbinger of the ethnic impersonator autobiographies to come. Carl Schockman's memoir, *We Turned Hobo*, did not pretend to be something it was not. Rather, it was an autobiography in which the author shared his transformation with readers and invited them to watch his change in identity. Schockman's autobiography, unlike many that followed, did not presume to inform readers about what it was like to really, permanently, be a hobo.

The Depression challenged success mythologies and American notions of self-fashioning. This had a dampening effect on ethnic impersonator autobiographers of the old school, who applied the thinking of class to a construction of race. The successful ethnic impersonator autobiography depended on the performance of racial and ethnic stereotypes. Yet the end of World War II and the revelations about the character of Nazi Germany left many social scientists uneasy about publicly trumpeting essentialist ideas of race. However, these essentialist ideas still determined the treatment Americans received in their daily lives, according to their skin color. The disjuncture between what people were beginning to suspect—that racial essentialism was a dangerous and discredited philosophy—and what they experienced in their daily lives spurred the appearance of a new kind of ethnic impersonator autobiography in which white Americans temporarily became black and wrote memoirs reporting on their experiences. The idea that white and black were alike under the skin and that experience of racial discrimination was easily transferable led to the popular embrace of these narratives. However, the less sophisticated of these memoirs, exemplified by Grace Halsell's *Soul Sister*, pointed up the limitations of the genre. Halsell, once she mastered what she felt were the gestures that made up a successful performance of black identity, considered herself more authentically black than most African Americans. Like the white authors of slave narratives, Halsell could trust only herself, a white woman, to properly exemplify blackness. Even the more sophisticated John Howard Griffin, who did not share Halsell's presumptions, was chagrined to find himself viewed by some whites as a more reliable spokesman on black issues than African Americans.[1]

White Americans who could not hear the voices of black Americans would listen to authors with whom they could racially identify yet who had made the journey into blackness. Such works were more travelogue than autobiography. The autobiographer penetrated the terra incognita of a different racial identity and returned to tell readers what it was like in that strange country. These writers documented their successful performance of blackness but did not question the categories of black and white. Although autobiographies about passing were written in the 1980s, a striking trend emerged in the 1990s: autobiographies that described not temporary racial passage but racial redefinition. Haizlip's *The Sweeter the Juice*, Williams's *Life on the Color Line*, and McBride's *The Color of Water* all describe race as a more or less permanent choice. Haizlip contrasts the various fortunes of members of her family who chose to pass as white with those who remained black. Williams discusses his redefinition from white to black at age ten. McBride writes about his mother, a Jewish woman who decided, in her late teens, to live as a black woman, and who made that choice permanent. All three works, which describe race as a choice that can be made by some people of ambiguously light-skinned appearance, show racial classification as arbitrary, albeit with very real consequences.

These autobiographies refuse to posit racial identity as essential. Instead, they question the very idea of racial identity. In doing so, they invite readers to ask more questions about identity, rather than offering answers. They open up the national conversation about race. They cannot properly be called autobiographies of racial impersonation. Rather, they are autobiographies that, by questioning the existence of race as an essential category, resist the idea that impersonation is possible. Perhaps a more appropriate term would be "autobiographies of racial recategorization." Just as former slaves wrote themselves into Americanness through narrating their experience of slavery, so these new autobiographers write themselves out of the trap of racial identity by questioning the meaning of race itself.

The Color of Water tells a story of a woman whose experience was in some important ways similar to that of Elizabeth Stern, author of *I Am a Woman—And a Jew*. According to McBride, his mother, like Stern, left her birth identity completely behind her: "Mommy refused to acknowledge her whiteness" (2). McBride's mother, born in Poland and the daughter of an orthodox rabbi, had already experienced one transformation, from Ruchel Dwajra Zylska to Rachel Deborah Shilsky, her Americanized name. At age nineteen, she tells her son, she shed that identity: "Rachel Shilsky is dead as far as I'm concerned. She had to die in order for me, the rest of me, to live" (2).

Like Elizabeth Stern, Ruth McBride was molested by her rabbi father over a period of years when she was a child. But unlike Stern, who in her autobiography took on the identity of her victimizer, Rachel Shilsky, in becoming Ruth McBride, moved as far from her birth identity as possible. On Passover, she remembers, "I used to see the empty chair we left for Elijah at the table and wish I could be gone to wherever Elijah was, eating over someone's house where your father didn't crawl into bed with you at night" (43). Rather than assuming the identity of her abuser, as had Stern, Rachel Shilsky moved into a new identity where acceptance by her abuser would be impossible. While literally killing herself in the eyes of her abusive father, she created a life that would sustain her, her two husbands, and her twelve children. She fled to Harlem, married a black man, settled in the Red Hook housing project of Brooklyn, founded a Baptist church, and put all of her children through college.

As the daughter of a failed rabbi who became a grocer in a black area of Suffolk, Virginia, Ruth McBride was caught in a historical trap. Born in 1921, she remembered the Klan riding through town. She was isolated as a Jew living in the South, where housing covenants prevented her family from residing in the white, Anglo-Saxon Protestant sections of town. "The Jews in Suffolk did stick together, but even among Jews my family was low because we dealt with *schvartses*. So I didn't have a lot of Jewish friends either" (81). With her harsh home life, the teen-aged Ruth felt unloved until she got involved with a black boy in the neighborhood. "You know the thing was, I was supposed to be white and 'number one' too. That was the big thing in the South. You're white, and even if you're a Jew, since you're white you're better than a so-called colored. Well, I didn't feel number one with nobody but him, and I didn't give a hoot that he was black" (113). When she got pregnant, however, it became clear to her and her boyfriend that she must disap-pear, since to stay would mean risking his life. Although she returned from having an abortion in New York to find that her boyfriend had impregnated and was marrying a black girl, Ruth had begun the journey that took her far away into another life. When she left her past behind, she did so completely. Not only was she disavowed by her Orthodox family, who mourned her for dead, but there was a near-complete discontinuity between her past and present selves. And yet, rebirth is never that easy or that complete. In her son's words, "Her memory was like a minefield, each recollection a potential booby trap, a Bouncing Betty—the old land mines the Viet Cong used in the Vietnam War that never went off when you stepped on them but blew you to hell the minute you pulled your foot away" (254).

Ironically, her story echoes that of Mary Antin and other Jewish immigrants from eastern Europe who needed to eradicate their pasts in order to live as Americans. Considering the life of Ruchel Dwajra Zylska, who became Ruth McBride Jordan, recalls the words with which Mary Antin begins her autobiography: "I am just as much out of the way as if I were dead, for I am absolutely other than the person whose story I have to tell. . . . My life I have still to live; her life ended when mine began."[2] In Ruth McBride's story, the Jewish immigrant narrative comes full circle; it is in many ways the natural terminus of a peculiarly American story. Although she, like Antin, found happiness by leaving her immigrant identity far behind her, McBride's is a success story such as Mary Antin could never have imagined.

In striking contrast to *Secret Family*, the memoir written by Elizabeth Stern's son Thomas, *The Color of Water* is a celebration of McBride's choice to enter a new ethnic and racial identity. While Stern's memoir excoriated his mother for lying, McBride's book is a warm celebration of his mother's choice and of her creative path to survival. Thomas Stern confronted his mother when he found out that she was planning to publish *I Am a Woman—And a Jew*. The dizzying sense that the past could be lost, that there is no truth, and that identity is not fixed horrified Thomas Stern. McBride, on the other hand, saw his mother's choice as an achievement.

Robert Sayre has written of American autobiographers as "architects of American character."[3] In a culture that resists ideology, popular autobiography has the moral authority of authentic, individual experience. Thus, the power of individual testimony can help reshape public thinking and public discourse about race. While race may be a construction, it wields tremendous power in the lives of most people, for whom racial and ethnic categories are far from abstractions. Autobiography is a form uniquely suited to American mythologies. These new autobiographies of racial unmasking can help Americans rethink the meaning of racial and ethnic categories.

Notes

Introduction

1. "Big Sales for New Mexico's 'Little Tree,'" 49.

2. Peter Moulson, interview with Douglas Newman, October 22, 1993.

3. Dan T. Carter, "Transformation of a Klansman," A31.

4. Although I use the term "ethnic impersonator" throughout this work, it is not without wincing. Impersonation implies that there is an authentic identity that can be imitated. I thought for a while of employing the term "voluntary ethnicity" but rejected it because it seems to downplay the cultural leap that is taken by these impersonators.

5. The only other rash of ethnic impersonator works of which I am aware occurred in Australia, which in the past several years has seen a number of impersonators. Helen Demidenko, winner of the prestigious Miles Franklin literary prize for her autobiographical novel about the role of Ukrainians in atrocities against Jews during the Holocaust, turned out to be Helen Darville, of English background. As a *New York Times* article on the subject noted, "Miss Darville's hoax has revived allegations that the Australian literary establishment has blinded itself with 'political correctness,' taking more notice of the gender and ethnic background of authors than of their literary talent" (Philip Shenon, "For Fiction, and Fibbing, She Takes the Prize," *New York Times*, September 26, 1995). Two years later it turned out that Eddie Burrup, a young male Aboriginal artist considered one of the most promising in Australia, was in fact Elizabeth Durack, an eighty-two-year-old woman of Irish descent. Her exposure took some time, since few curators had met the artist, who

was said to live in a remote area and speak little English. Wayne Bergmann, the director of the Kimberley Aboriginal Law and Cultural Center, was quoted as calling this "the ultimate act of colonization" (Peter James Spielmann, "Acclaimed Aboriginal Artist Is a Fraud," *Richmond Times-Dispatch*, March 8, 1997). Just one week later the author of an autobiography of an Aboriginal woman was revealed to be a white male. Wanda Koolmatrie's memoir had received a national literary award as the best first work by an Australian woman writer. In the 1980s B. Wongar, the Aboriginal author of books including *Walg* and *Karan*, turned out to be Ukrainian immigrant Streten Bozik (Peter James Spielmann, "Aussie Icon No. 2 Bites the Dust," *Richmond Times-Dispatch*, March 14, 1997). It is tempting to speculate about the fact that Australia, like the United States, is a nation of immigrants with a substantial native population that was severely maltreated by the colonists. Many American ethnic impersonators act as Native Americans; Australians seem to take on Aboriginal identities.

6. Franklin, *Autobiography*, 73.

7. Abbott, *States of Perfect Freedom*, 5.

8. Leibowitz, *Fabricating Lives*, 49.

9. The first Native American autobiography, *Life of Ma-Ka-Tai-Me-She-Kia-Kiak*, or Black Hawk, appeared in 1833; its popularity was great enough to warrant the printing of four more editions the following year. See Krupat, *For Those Who Come After*, 53.

10. Benedict Anderson, *Imagined Communities*, 7; italics author's.

11. McFeely, *Frederick Douglass*, 95.

12. A good example of this is the Uncle Hoskins episode in *Black Boy*, in which the narrator is taken, as a child, out into the middle of the river by his uncle so the horse can drink. The incident altered forever Wright's feelings toward his generous uncle: "I did not answer; I could not speak. My fear was gone now and he loomed before me like a stranger, like a man I had never seen before, a man with whom I could never share a moment of intimate living" (61). This episode was, in fact, based on something that Ralph Ellison had told him about an occasion when Ellison's father had been teasing him, not realizing his son's terror, as he went into the river to get sand for a sandpile; it never happened to Wright. See Webb, *Richard Wright*, 409 n.

13. Sau-ling Cynthia Wong, "Kingston's *Woman Warrior*," 254.

14. Indian captives wrote autobiographies about their sufferings but also occasionally refused to be freed from captivity. John Demos's *Unredeemed Captive* gives the example of Eunice Williams, who in 1704 was captured by Abenaki and Caughnawaga Indians from her home in Deerfield. Though offered the opportunity, she refused to return and lived out her life with Indians, as an Indian. See also Namias, *White Captives*; Heard, *White into Red*.

15. Sollors, *Beyond Ethnicity*, 6.

16. See, for instance, Stephen Jay Gould, *Mismeasure of Man*, for a classic example. See also Lawrence Wright, "One Drop of Blood."

17. The two biggest growth areas in the study of racial formation have been whiteness studies and studies on black/white passing. As David Stowe's 1996 article "Uncolored People" pointed out, the 1991 publication of Roediger's *Wages of Whiteness* spurred the publication of a vast number of books on whiteness, including Morrison's *Playing in the Dark* (1992), Frankenberg's *White Women* (1993), Theodore Allen's *Invention of the White Race* (1994), Ware's *Beyond the Pale* (1994), Segrest's *Memoir of a Race Traitor* (1994), Ignatiev's *How the Irish Became White* (1995), and Haney-López's *White by Law* (1996). Since then, other works have

appeared, including Grace Elizabeth Hale's *Making Whiteness*, Rogin's *Blackface, White Noise*, and Gubar's *Racechanges*. For a helpful overview, see also Fishkin, "Interrogating 'Whiteness,'" which lists about five hundred articles and books that have recently appeared on the subject.

While the agreement among scholars that it was inadequate to treat whiteness simply as a neutral background against which the drama of race and ethnicity could be played out—what Sollors refers to sarcastically as "The Mysteries of Un-Region and Un-Ethnic Group" (*Beyond Ethnicity*, 176)—was firmly in place by the mid-1990s, the pendulum of scholarly thought was swinging in the other direction, toward a view that since race is a construction, we must treat it solely as such.

18. See Ignatiev, *How the Irish Became White*; Lott, *Love and Theft*; Roediger, *Wages of Whiteness*, on the assimilation of Irish immigrants. See also Sacks, "How Did Jews Become White Folks?"

19. Sanjek, "Enduring Inequalities of Race," 9.

20. Ibid., 10.

21. Sollors, *Beyond Ethnicity*, 36.

22. The danger of thinking of blackness as just another ethnicity is illustrated clearly by statements made by self-identified white ethnics. Many Americans, especially since the "ethnic fever" of the 1960s and 1970s, a period when ethnic studies courses burgeoned in universities and identity politics became a force in American public life, have exercised what Waters calls "ethnic options." That is, these white Americans of mixed ethnic heritage have chosen to identify themselves with the ethnicity of one of their four grandparents. Even as many recent writers have described the process by which European ethnics have assimilated into whiteness, there has been, since the 1960s, a countermovement by which assimilated whites have reasserted their ethnic identities in opposition to what they see as the ethnic identity of blackness. It is here, very clearly, that racial and ethnic identities can be seen as distinct, for as Waters writes of the subjects she interviewed—a group of white Catholics—about their ethnic identifications, "the reality is that white ethnics have a lot more choice and room for maneuver than they themselves think they do. The situation is very different for members of racial minorities, whose lives are strongly influenced by their race or national origin regardless of how much they might choose not to identify themselves in ethnic or racial terms. Yet my respondents did not make a distinction between their own experience of ethnicity as a personal choice and the experience of being a member of a racial minority" (*Ethnic Options*, 157–58).

23. In *Retreat from Race* Takagi writes about how binary thinking has affected the dialogue on Asian American admissions at elite universities: "Asians are perceived to be either like whites or not like whites; or, alternatively, like blacks or not like blacks. In a sense, Asian Americans have functioned as a wild card in the racial politics of higher education—their educational experiences could be and have been incorporated into arguments both for and against discrimination, diversity, and affirmative action" (11). In current debates about race, ethnicity is often deployed in such ways. As Shawn Wong writes, Asian Americans function as a model or loyal minority in contradistinction to disloyal minorities. During the 1960s Asian Americans were favorably portrayed in the media, in contrast to black militants ("Is Ethnicity Obsolete?," 230). That is, Asian Americans could be considered in terms of blacks—seen as the less-than-model minority—or whites. When discussions about caps on Asian American admissions were taking place on elite campuses across the nation during 1986, Berkeley professor Ling-chi Wang, in an interview with the *New York Times*, compared caps on Asian American enrollment to quotas imposed

against Jews in the 1920s. By aligning Asian Americans with a former racial minority—as Jews were considered in the 1920s—now deemed white, he brought the issue to the forefront of public debate (Takagi, *Retreat from Race*, 50).

24. Reed, "America's 'Black Only' Ethnicity," 227.

25. With the emergence of whiteness studies as an academic discipline came the founding of the journal *Race Traitor* in 1992 by Noel Ignatiev and John Garvey, whose credo is that "treason to whiteness is loyalty to humanity." As David Stowe notes, the journal's "operative principle is simple: to break the power of whiteness in this country by encouraging people to renounce the wages of whiteness" ("Uncolored People," 74). While this theory may have its attractions, it remains, of necessity, purely an abstraction. To renounce the privileges of skin color may be a wonderful gesture for the person doing the renouncing, but it is hard to imagine that renunciation being taken seriously by anyone else.

26. Diamond, *Performance and Cultural Politics*, 5.

27. Ginsberg, *Passing and the Fictions of Identity*, 16.

Chapter One

1. Sollors, *Beyond Ethnicity*, 38.

2. Walters, *American Reformers*, 78–88.

3. As Karcher has pointed out, Child used the insights gained from Jacobs to inform her own characterizations of the slaveholder featured in her 1867 novel, *A Romance of the Republic*. See Karcher, "Lydia Maria Child's *A Romance of the Republic*," 85.

4. Douglass, *Narrative of the Life of Frederick Douglass*, 293.

5. Edmund Wilson, *Patriotic Gore*, 3.

6. *Anti-Slavery Bugle*, November 3, 1849, 1, quoted in Davis and Gates, *Slave's Narrative*, 28.

7. Abbott, *States of Perfect Freedom*, 17.

8. *Anti-Slavery Bugle*, October 1, 1859.

9. *Christian Examiner*, July–September 1849, 61–63, quoted in Davis and Gates, *Slave's Narrative*, 19.

10. Quoted in Davis and Gates, *Slave's Narrative*, xxi.

11. Sekora, "Is the Slave Narrative a Species of Autobiography?"

12. Olney, "I Was Born."

13. *Liberator*, June 4, 1858, 91.

14. From "Miscellaneous Items," *Anti-Slavery Bugle*, September 4, 1858.

15. See Gossett, *Race*, 65. For a fuller discussion of the reception of the work, see Stanton, *Leopard's Spots*, 161–73. See also Stephen Jay Gould, *Mismeasure of Man*, chap. 2.

16. "The One Drop of African Blood," *Anti-Slavery Record*, December 1835, 150–51.

17. "A White Slave Manumitted," *Anti-Slavery Bugle*, March 27, 1858, 4.

18. "Selling White People As Slaves," *Anti-Slavery Bugle*, September 7, 1859, 1.

19. *Liberator*, March 9, 1838, 39, reprinted in Davis and Gates, *Slave's Narrative*, 9–11.

20. "Interesting Narrative," *Liberator*, February 2, 1838.

21. "Beware of Impostors," *Liberator*, March 7, 1856, 39.

22. "New Publications," *Liberator*, November 28, 1856, 190.

23. "A Remarkable Work," *Liberator*, January 23, 1857, 1.

24. "Literary Intelligence," *Christian Examiner*, January 1857.

25. Quoted in Michaels, *Gold Standard and the Logic of Naturalism*, 115.

26. *New York Christian Examiner* review reprinted in *Liberator*, January 23, 1857.

27. "A Great Anti-Slavery Book-Letter from a Lady," selections, *Liberator*, August 14, 1857.

28. Zafar, "Over-Exposed, Under-Exposed," 4.

29. William C. Nell, "Linda, the Slave Girl," *Liberator*, January 25, 1861.

30. Quoted in Davis and Gates, *Slave's Narrative*, xvi.

31. A. F. R., "Frederick Douglass in Boston," *Liberator*, December 13, 1861.

32. I have to take issue, thus, with the scolding Ellen M. Weinauer, in her essay "'A Most Respectable Looking Gentleman,'" seems to give William Craft. Weinauer notes that Craft assumes that his wife's gender is fixed, not fluid, and scolds him for his "efforts to contain Ellen's unruly *gender* identity with an insistence on her 'true' womanhood" (48). It does not seem to occur to Weinauer that Ellen herself might see gender identity as something that she would, in the general run of her life, wish to have fixed, and that, after all, slave women were denied the perks of white middle-class womanhood.

Chapter Two

1. Roediger, *Wages of Whiteness*, 117.

2. Woodham-Smith, *Great Hunger*, 243; Roediger, *Wages of Whiteness*, 141.

3. See Roediger, *Wages of Whiteness*; Lott, *Love and Theft*; Ignatiev, *How the Irish Became White*.

4. Lott, *Love and Theft*, 7.

5. Ibid., 97.

6. Cantwell, *Bluegrass Breakdown*, 262.

7. Roediger, *Wages of Whiteness*, 133.

8. See Cantwell, *Bluegrass Breakdown*.

9. Roediger, *Wages of Whiteness*, 127.

10. Ibid., 125.

11. Takaki, *Iron Cages*, 103.

12. Boatright, *Folk Laughter on the American Frontier*, 36.

13. *Sketches and Eccentricities of Colonel David Crockett*, 117.

14. Hauck, "Man in the Buckskin Hunting Shirt," 13–14.

15. Ibid., 11.

16. Schechter, *Satiric Impersonations*, 34.

17. Halttunen, *Confidence Men and Painted Women*, 35.

18. Ibid., 37, xv.

19. Quoted in Harris, *Humbug*, 40.

20. Ibid., 23.

21. Ibid., 36.

22. Adams, *E Pluribus Barnum*, 2–7.

23. Ibid., xii.

24. Bruce A. McConachie, "Museum Theatre and the Problem of Respectability," in Engle and Miller, *American Stage*, 66.

25. Adams, *E. Pluribus Barnum*, 161.

26. Werner, *Barnum*, 204. Barnum's stunt proved prophetic. In 1930 African American novelist George Schuyler wrote a hilarious satire titled *Black No More* about two black scientists who discover the formula for whiteness. Needless to say, chaos ensues.

27. Barnum, *Struggles and Triumphs*, 128.

28. September 24, 1843, letter, quoted in Harris, *Humbug*, 53.

29. Barnum, *Struggles and Triumphs*, 125, 126.

30. *New York Herald*, November 19, 1890, quoted in Blackstone, *Buckskins, Bullets, and Business*, 25.

31. Blackstone, *Buckskin, Bullets, and Business*, 86.

32. See Kasper, *Annie Oakley*, 36; Moses, "Wild West Shows, Reformers, and the Image of the American Indian" and *Wild West Shows and the Images of American Indians*, 21.

33. *The Critic: A Weekly Review of Literature, Fine Arts, and the Drama*, November 22, 1828, 1, quoted in Sally L. Jones, "The First but Not the Last of the 'Vanishing Indians.'"

34. Forrest, like Buffalo Bill after him, insisted on the authenticity of the performance he offered. According to William Rounseville Alger, author of the two-volume *Life of Edwin Forrest, the American Tragedian* (1877), Forrest left an 1825 theatrical engagement in New Orleans to visit the Choctaw chief Push-ma-ta-ha, with whom he stayed, eating, drinking, dressing, and living as a Choctaw and taking part in their hunts and dances. Jeffrey D. Mason, in *Melodrama and the Myth of America*, 56, disputes this claim of Forrest's. What seems important, however, is not the veracity of the actor's contention but the early introduction of authenticity into popular evaluations of Native American performance.

35. *New York Daily News*, June 27, 1886.

36. *St. Louis Globe Democrat*, October 4, 1885.

37. *Censor* (Rahway, N.J.), July 15, 1886.

38. *Inquirer*, June 8, 1886.

39. *Brooklyn Citizen*, April 14, 1897.

40. *Brick Pomeroy's Democrat*, July 10, 1886.

41. *Evening Bulletin*, June 14, 1886, among other places. The similarity or, rather, downright duplication of phrases in reviews appearing in papers all over the country suggests that the Wild West show itself supplied the boilerplate.

42. *Sunday Dispatch* (Philadelphia), June 6, 1886.

43. Quoted in Prucha, *Americanizing the American Indians*, 311.

44. *New York Herald*, November 19 1890, quoted in Blackstone, *Buckskins, Bullets, and Business*, 25.

45. Yellow Robe, "Menace of the Wild West Show," 224.

46. Moses, *Wild West Shows and the Images of American Indians*, 279.

47. *News* (Providence, R.I.), June 1, 1897.

48. Blackstone, *Buckskin, Bullets, and Business*, 58.

49. *Morning Union* (Bridgeport, Conn.), May 17, 1897.

50. "The Red Indian: A Premier Attraction at the Wild West Show," *Manchester Dispatch*, July 14, 1903.

51. Other Wild West shows that employed Indians from other tribes often required them to dress as Sioux and enact Sioux rituals. For instance, an encampment of Crees who visited Cincinnati in 1895 "wore pseudo-Plains clothing in untraditional ways and decorated themselves with feathers that fell from some of the birds at the zoo" (Meyn, "Mutual Infatuation," 34).

52. Deloria, *Playing Indian*, 5.

53. *St. Louis Globe Democrat*, May 9, 1886.

54. *Brick Pomeroy's Democrat*, 1886.

55. Letter from C. L. Daily, Neuilly, France, 22nd/89, Western Historical Collection, Denver Public Library, Denver, Colo.

56. Pawnee Bill's Historic Wild West and Great Far East, Grand Ethnological Congress, program, 1904, ibid.

57. "Pawnee Bill's Wild West and Great Far East," courier, Watertown, July 4, 1907, from the collection of the Circus World Museum, Baraboo, Wisc.

58. Obituary for Wenona, *Billboard*, February 15, 1930, 95.

59. Mike Smith, "It's Only Natural: Monk Boudreaux and the Golden Eagles" (unpublished manuscript in author's possession).

60. See McNamara, *Step Right Up*, chap. 3.

61. Quoted in ibid., 78.

Chapter Three

1. Starr, *Americans and the California Dream*, 12.

2. Rohrbrough, *Days of Gold*, 216.

3. Quoted in Quinn, *Rivals*, 17.

4. Marks, *Precious Dust*, 283.

5. Quoted in Rohrbrough, *Days of Gold*, 222.

6. Parins, *John Rollin Ridge*, 2.

7. Recall the *Christian Inquirer*'s review: "The tale is terribly sad and painful, and seems more so from the naked distinctness with which it is told, its harsh features wanting the softness which skill and grace of literary execution would give" ("A Remarkable Work," *Liberator*, January 23, 1857, 1).

8. Mathes, *Helen Hunt Jackson and Her Indian Reform Legacy*, 22.

9. Ibid., 77.

10. Ibid., 83.

11. Haas, *Conquests and Historical Identities in California*, 30.

12. Schurz, "Present Aspects of the Indian Problem," 16.

13. Whisnant, *All That Is Native and Fine*, 257.

14. *Ramona: A Story of Passion and Protest*.

Chapter Four

1. Bernard De Voto, introduction to Bonner, *Life and Adventures*, xix.

2. Parkman, *Oregon Trail*, 178.

3. Christy, "Personal Memoirs of Capt. Charles Christy," 16, quoted in Elinor Wilson, *Jim Beckwourth*, 7.

4. Bonner, *Life and Adventures of James P. Beckwourth*, 14. Unless otherwise noted, page numbers in the text refer to this edition.

5. It was not just Beckwourth's racial identity that was challenged by his contemporaries. Even the ownership of Beckwourth's memories of his Crow life was questioned. Upon publication of his biography, Beckwourth was angrily denounced by Robert Meldrum, a fellow trapper from Kentucky. Meldrum attacked him for the usual racial reasons, on the grounds that his mother had been a Negress and that he was therefore a mulatto. Stronger than a desire to debunk, however, was a competitor's jealousy. According to the journals of Lieutenant James H. Bradley,

Upon quitting his service, enamoured of the savage life he had tasted for three years, [Meldrum] remained upon the plains making his home among the Crow Indians. Adopting their dress, gluing long hair to his own to make it conform to the savage fashion, having his squaw and lodge, and living in all respects the life of an Indian, he was quickly enabled by a superior intelligence and courage to acquire great influence with his savage associates. . . . He was a man of many adventures, and was accustomed to complain bitterly that Beckwourth in the autobiography published by Harper Brothers, had arrogated to himself many of his own experiences. (Quoted in Elinor Wilson, *Jim Beckwourth*, 66.)

However, Meldrum refused to be mollified by Harper Brothers' offer to publish his authentic memories. As Bradley recalls, "He proudly rejected all overtures."

6. T. D. Bonner, *The Life and Adventures of James P. Beckwourth*, edited with a preface by Charles G. Leland (London: T. Fisher Unwin, 1892), 9; italics in original.

7. Richardson, *Beyond the Mississippi*, 299.

8. Katz, *Black Indians*, 121.

9. Brackett, *Follow the Free Wind*. Other juvenile biographies of Beckwourth include Olive Burt, *Jim Beckwourth: Crow Chief* (New York: Julian Messner, 1957); Harold W. Felton, *Jim Beckwourth: Negro Mountain Man* (New York: Dodd, Mead, 1966); Lawrence Cortesi, *Jim Beckwourth: Explorer-Patriot of the Rockies* (New York: Criterion, 1971); and Sean Nolan, *James Beckwourth* (New York: Chelsea House, 1992).

10. Samuel Thurston, quoted in McGlagan, *Peculiar Paradise*, 30–31.

11. Quoted in Katz, *Black Indians*, 115.

12. De Voto, *Year of Decision*, 63.

13. For a discussion of the "Friends of the Indian," see Prucha, *Americanizing the American Indians*.

14. Cobb, foreword to *Long Lance*, unpaginated.

15. See Donald B. Smith, *Long Lance*, chap. 10, also 100–101. For biographical information about Long Lance, I have relied extensively on Donald B. Smith's *Long Lance*, a work invaluable for its thoroughness.

16. Cobb, foreword to *Long Lance*.

17. Brumble, *American Indian Autobiography*, 152.

18. Feest, "Europe's Indians," 323.

19. This nostalgia extended to Buffalo Bill's Wild West Show, whose bandmaster, Karl H. King, dedicated an intermezzo, *Passing of the Red Man*, in the 1914 and 1915 shows. See Russell, *Wild West*, 88.

20. Long Lance, "My Trail Upward," 138.

21. Long Lance, *Long Lance*, 278.

22. Krupat, *For Those Who Come After*, 34.

23. Beverly Smith, "One Hundred Percent American."

24. Tugend, "*Silent Enemy*," 36.

25. Hertha Wong, *Sending My Heart Back across the Years*, 142.

26. In a slightly different context, see Gilroy, *Black Atlantic*, for a useful discussion of how persons caught between racial categories—for instance, black Europeans—undermine binary definitions of race.

27. Krupat, *For Those Who Come After*, 48.

28. Findahl, *Manhattan Babylon*, 45–48, my translation.

29. Although it is true that Native American tribes were often elastic rather than essentialist in their definition of who might be considered a member, this is clearly an area too vast for inclusion here. For more extensive discussion of this and related issues, see Halliburton, *Red over Black*; Littlefield, *Cherokee Freedmen*; May, *African Americans and Native Americans*; Katz, *Black Indians*.

30. Yellow Robe, "Menace of the Wild West Show."

31. Donald B. Smith, *Long Lance*, 95.

32. Ibid., 94.

33. Eastwood, who became a close friend of Carter's, wrote a letter to the *New York Times* after Asa Carter was exposed for the second time, defending his friend's capacity for—and right to—change: "If Forrest Carter was a racist and a hatemonger who later converted to being a sensitive, understanding human being, that would be most admirable" (quoted in the *Montgomery Advertiser*, October 26, 1991).

34. Nor in the consciousness, according to Greenhaw, of Dan Carter, who wrote a 1991 *Times* story without acknowledging Greenhaw's earlier exposé. See Greenhaw's letter in *Publishers Weekly*, November 15, 1991, 8.

35. McWhorter, "Little Tree, Big Lies."

36. Strickland, foreword to *Education of Little Tree*, vi. Although Strickland continued to defend Carter after his unmasking, other Cherokee historians were less charitable. Geneva Jackson, a member of the Cherokee Eastern Band in North Carolina, called the book "the closest thing to a farce that has been published in the Cherokee name." The position of "storyteller-in-council to the Cherokee Nation," as Carter was described in promotional copy, does not exist. And there was no evidence, according to tribal officials, that Carter ever made any of the donations to the tribe from his book royalties, as he had claimed (quoted in McWhorter, "Little Tree, Big Lies," 120).

37. As Sam Gill notes, Mother Earth, though of great importance among pantribal groups today, is a concept of relatively recent origin. Gill dates the introduction of the Mother Earth story as an essential ingredient of Native American mythography by European writers in 1885. "Examination of the history of this figure," Gill writes, "shows that she arose in the process of the formation of a pantribal identity among native Americans who, in this century, have increasingly forged a common identity in the face of a common experience of oppression and loss. As the Indian peoples lost the land base on which their various group identities depended, the Mother Earth figure grew in importance among them" (Gill, "Mother Earth: An American Myth," 142).

38. Hayman, "Grey Owl's Wild Goose Chase," 43.

39. Indians have not consistently been seen by Euro-Americans as having such mystical ties to the earth. In a 1905 speech to the Chicago Literary Club, for example, George E. Adams, a trustee of Chicago's Newberry Library and Field Columbian Museum, informed his audience that the beauty of the New Hampshire mountains dated from the arrival of European settlers and explorers. Before then, "there was no eye to see it, no soul to feel it. True, the Indians were there . . . but the red Indian, being a primitive man, did not have that delicate sense of beauty, of form and color, which has been developed in the modern man, the heir of centuries of civilization" (quoted in Levine, *Highbrow/Lowbrow*, 145–46).

40. The name that Sylvester Long chose for his new identity seems hardly random. In fact, while Long Lance was living at the Explorers Club, the Scottish chieftain in the room next door had a standard reply for the scores of women who called for his neighbor at all hours of the day and night: "No, this is not Long Lance. . . . I am chief Longer Lance" (see Donald B. Smith, *Long Lance*, 189).

41. By contrast, Long Lance opens his autobiography with the memory of his mother cutting off one of her fingers in mourning for a brother who had been slain in war. Long Lance's account of his upbringing stresses customs such as the whipping of children to toughen them, enforced daily plunges into icy water, and severe punishments for dishonesty. Long Lance's was a childhood designed for a more strenuous age. It is not surprising that many of the practices he described did not occur in Blackfoot culture but were borrowed by him from other tribes or invented entirely.

42. Dana Rubin, "Real Education of Little Tree," 80.

43. Douglas Newman, interview with Wayne Greenhaw, April 4, 1994.

Chapter Five

1. Archdeacon, *Becoming American*, 113, 124, 139.

2. Quoted in Gordon, *Woman's Body, Woman's Right*, 277; Dawley, *Struggles for Justice*, 108–10; Higham, *Strangers in the Land*, 151.

3. Takaki, *Different Mirror*, 305, 307.

4. Cook, *History of Narrative Film*, 78.

5. Rogin, "'Sword Became a Flashing Vision,'" 124.

6. Mays, *Born to Rebel*, 60.

7. Rogin, "'Sword Became a Flashing Vision,'" 180. Other important recent work on *The Birth of a Nation* includes Simmon, *Films of D. W. Griffith*; Gunning, *D. W. Griffith and the Origins of American Narrative Film*; and Staiger, "Birth of a Nation."

8. Roediger, *Wages of Whiteness*, 115.

9. See Rogin, *Blackface, White Noise*.

10. See Deloria, *Playing Indian*.

11. Carnes, *Secret Ritual and Manhood*, 97–107.

12. Blee, *Women of the Klan*, 125.

13. Quoted in Maclean, *Behind the Mask of Chivalry*, 133.

14. Blee, *Women of the Klan*, 163–65.

15. Prevots, *American Pageantry*, 14–15, 30.

16. Glassberg, *American Historical Pageantry*, 252.

17. Jacobson, *Special Sorrows*, 87.

18. Howe, *World of Our Fathers*, 466.

19. Zangwill, *Melting-Pot*.

20. Mann, *One and the Many*, 100–101.

21. Sollors, *Beyond Ethnicity*, 66.

22. Antin, *At School in the Promised Land*, iii, quoted in Holte, *Ethnic I*, 28.

23. McGinity. "Woman Divided."

24. Antin, "Promised Land," chap. 3, pp. a–e.

25. Ibid., chap. 4, pp. 113–20.

26. Ibid., chap. 1, p. 35.

27. Sollors, *Beyond Ethnicity*, 32.

28. Quoted in Higham, *Strangers in the Land*.

29. *New York Times*, August 3, 1926.

30. Dawley, *Struggles for Justice*, 290.

31. Pupin, *From Immigrant to Inventor*, 2.

32. Cahan, *Rise of David Levinsky*, 3.

33. Pupin, *From Immigrant to Inventor*, 1.

34. Cahan, *Rise of David Levinsky*, 3.

35. Mann, *One and the Many*, 131.

36. The 1936 Artef dramatization, begun by Ornitz and Donald Davis and finished by Proletpen writer Chaver Paver, was a failure. It was one of only two plays with American Jewish themes among the eighteen productions mounted by Artef in its first ten years of existence, and one of the theater's few flops. Although the *New York Times* reviewer had an "enjoyable if not exciting evening" (December 27, 1935), most other reviewers begged to differ, complaining about the flimsy plot and

lack of characterization. The reviewer for *Justice* found the fault for the production's failure in Artef's "curious and unaccountable ignorance of the America-Jewish scene" (January 15, 1936). Theatrical designer Mordecai Gorelik, one of the most influential set designers of the 1930s, found Artef's impressionistic production style for "*Haunch, Paunch, and Jowl,*" which he termed "*Chassidic* grotesque," to be problematic. See Lifson, *Yiddish Theatre in America*, 464–65. See also Sandrow, *Vagabond Stars*; Leah Shampanier Gould, "Artef Players Collective."

37. Dawley, *Struggles for Justice*, 291.
38. Franklin, *Autobiography*, 112.
39. Marden, *Little Visits with Great Americans*, 8, 12.
40. For example, see Decker, *Made in America*, 62.
41. Huber, *American Idea of Success*, 192–93.
42. Cawelti, *Apostles of the Self-Made Man*, 103.
43. Steven J. Rubin, *Writing Our Lives*, 40.
44. Zaborowska, *How We Found America*, 100.
45. Stern, *Secret Family*, 1.
46. Ibid., 3.
47. Zaborowska, *How We Found America*, 101.
48. Morton, *I Am a Woman*, 1.
49. Stern, *Secret Family*, 147.
50. Ibid., 186.
51. Umansky, "Representations of Jewish Women," 167.

Chapter Six

1. Chauncey, *Gay New York*, 78.
2. Alsop, *Hard Travellin'*, 105.
3. Whisnant, *All That Is Native and Fine*, 57.
4. Ibid.
5. See J. David Smith, *Eugenic Assault on America*, 16–20. Of course, not every form of poor white culture was seen by racists as benign. Eugenicist Henry Goddard, who in 1912 published *The Kallikak Family*, traced degeneracy through generations of a poor white family and successfully urged sterilization laws to control such a phenomenon.
6. See Bulmer, *Chicago School of Sociology*; Hammersley, *Dilemma of Qualitative Method.*
7. Chauncey, *Gay New York*, 90. Chauncey very properly adds that "any such estimates are to be regarded with suspicion"; however, most commentators assumed gay relationships to be prevalent among hoboes.
8. Ted Morgan, *Literary Outlaw*, 38.
9. Lisle Belle, "Flops and Feeds," *New York Herald Tribune*, September 25, 1927.
10. Nels Anderson, "On the Bum."
11. For general accounts of the Depression, see Leuchtenberg, *Roosevelt and the New Deal*; McElvaine, *Great Depression*. For a contemporary treatment of events, look to Frederick Lewis Allen, *Since Yesterday*. For a detailed account of the Bonus March, see Cowley, *Dream of the Golden Mountain*.
12. For the best account of this tragedy, see Worster, *Dust Bowl*. For a great account of traveling through the dust belt, see Asch, *The Road*, 99–104.
13. Seldes, *Years of the Locust*, 288.
14. In Christian Blackwood's 1978 documentary *Roger Corman: Hollywood's*

Wild Angel, Scorsese recalls that he was allowed to direct the film on the condition that he have at least one shot of Hershey's exposed breasts every ten minutes, a feature that made the film in many ways very true to its source.

15. Bruns, *Damnedest Radical*, 262.

16. Ibid., 5.

17. *Time*, July 12, 1937.

18. Herbert Blumer, review of *Sister of the Road*, *American Journal of Sociology* 43 (January 1938): 370.

19. Disenchantment with California as the symbolic "land of opportunity" became close to a literary trope during the Depression. John Steinbeck's *The Grapes of Wrath* (1939) is the best-known example; even more pointed is Rorty's bitter 1936 travelogue *Where Life Is Better*. Rorty took the title of his book, now used with the most cutting irony, from a "boost" pamphlet he himself had written ten years previously for an organization called Californians, Inc., and of which over a million copies were distributed.

Chapter Seven

1. Noell, "Recollections of Medicine Show Life," 216.

2. See Rogin, *Blackface, White Noise*.

3. Noell, "Recollections of Medicine Show Life," 216.

4. Hornsby, *Milestones in Twentieth-Century African-American History*, 46–47.

5. Initially Alvin Childress, the African American actor who played Amos, was "blacked up" so that he would look more authentically Negro to television audiences. He successfully protested this treatment. Freeman Gosden and Charles Correll appeared on the set during the early days of filming the show, and Gosden did not hesitate to offer his advice to the television performers. Childress recalls the resentment that he and other experienced black actors felt at the idea of "a white man teaching a Negro how to act like a white man acting like a Negro." See Ely, *Adventures of Amos 'n' Andy*, 206.

6. Ehrenreich, *Hearts of Men*, 30.

7. Of course, the post–World War II blackface impersonators were not the first to try to find authenticity through blackness. Mezz Mezzrow, a jazz clarinetist who began working in the 1920s, decided in his teens that despite the fact that he had been born into a Russian Jewish immigrant family, he was going to become a musician—a black musician. However, rather than temporarily becoming black, Mezzrow made a lifetime commitment to his choice, eventually getting the U.S. government to reclassify him racially. See Wolfe, *Really the Blues*.

8. Riesman, *Lonely Crowd*, 142, 146, 147.

9. Lindner, *Must You Conform?*, 23.

10. Mailer, "White Negro," 338, 339, 340, 341.

11. Ibid., 341, 343, 348.

12. Hornsby, *Milestones in Twentieth-Century African American History*, 55–60.

13. See Gentry, *J. Edgar Hoover*, 442, 501–9. See also Branch, *Parting the Waters*, esp. 121–22.

14. Lott, *Love and Theft*, 51.

15. Of course, it is all too easy to take potshots at "The White Negro," as evidenced by the number of essays doing just that. See, for example, Podhoretz, "Know-Nothing Bohemians"; Lott, "White Like Me"; Gubar, *Racechanges*, esp. 179–81.

16. *Kingsblood Royal* harks back in many ways to George Schuyler's 1930 satire *Black No More*, the plot of which revolves around two black scientists' discovery of

the formula for whiteness. Schuyler dedicated his book "to all Caucasians in the great republic who can trace their ancestry back ten generations and confidently assert that there are no black leaves, twigs, limbs, or branches on their family tree."

17. I find it hard to agree with Gubar's speculation that "perhaps rumors of Griffin's death-due-to-passing reflect a widespread belief that, as Isaac Julien has put it, 'crossing racial lines usually results in punishment' (263) or, indeed, that it should result in punishment" (Gubar, *Racechanges*, 30). Rather, I suggest that the myths surrounding Griffin's death reflect his own positioning of himself as a racial martyr—one who, in this construct, died so that the rest of white America might become more enlightened.

18. Stampp, *Peculiar Institution*, vii–viii.

19. Quoted in Van Deburg, *New Day in Babylon*, 49.

20. Ibid., 33.

21. As Van Deburg points out, revolutionary black nationalist movements predated the Civil War.

22. Ibid., 53.

23. Ibid., 54.

24. Ibid.

25. McNeil and McCain, *Please Kill Me*, 46.

26. Ibid., 45, 49.

27. In their criticism of the Black Panthers, SLA members were actually closely allied to the position of Panther dissident (and future visitor to the Ronald Reagan White House) Eldridge Cleaver, who claimed that "the vanguard party has become a breakfast-for-children club" (quoted in Elaine Brown, *Taste of Power*, 220).

28. Ibid., 342.

29. Ibid., 143.

30. For a powerfully funny commentary on the genre of whites passing as black, see the 1970 production *Watermelon Man*, directed by Melvin Van Peebles. In it Godfrey Cambridge, initially in whiteface, plays an uptight businessman who wakes up one morning to discover that he has turned black. Havoc ensues, naturally.

Chapter Eight

1. Clancy, review of *Famous All Over Town*; Wimsatt, review of *Famous All Over Town*.

2. Quoted in Dunne, "Secret of Danny Santiago," 17.

3. *New York Times Book Review*, April 24, 1983, 12.

4. See Browder, *Rousing the Nation*, for a fuller version of this argument.

5. Quoted in Navasky, *Naming Names*, 369.

6. Stein and Hill, *Ethnic Imperative*, 195.

7. Couser, *Altered Egos*, 14.

8. Ibid., 24.

9. Acosta, *Revolt of the Cockroach People*, 67.

10. In his fascinating essay "Abbie Hoffman's Other Life," Joel Schechter points out that only when Hoffman went undercover for two years in the late 1970s, undergoing plastic surgery and dying his hair and assuming the identity Barry Freed, was he able to become a truly effective political activist. The Save the River campaign begun by the soft-spoken, shy environmentalist Freed and his companion, Johanna Lawrenson, effectively halted an Army Corps of Engineers "plan to dredge the St. Lawrence River, dynamite several islands in the area, drain the water, and open a winter shipping channel" (Schechter, *Satiric Impersonations*, 125). As

Schechter astutely notes, this "underground theater performance" of Hoffman's enabled him to act without the clownish gestures, such as dropping dollars from the visitors' gallery of the New York Stock Exchange in 1967, that had gained him renown as a political performer but had perhaps prevented him from being an effective political agent. Only by exchanging his clown mask for a star turn as a modest, serious man could Hoffman effect meaningful political change within the mainstream arena. Moreover, he had admirably fulfilled his purpose in going underground. "He became a respectable community leader, and for that reason, among others, he was unrecognizable. He had found," writes Schechter, "an almost perfect disguise; no one expected Abbie Hoffman to become a self-effacing environmentalist" (ibid.).

Conclusion

1. Wald, "White Identity."
2. Antin, *Promised Land*, ix.
3. Sayre, "Autobiography and America," 168.

Bibliography

Abbott, Philip. *States of Perfect Freedom: Autobiography and American Political Thought.* Amherst: University of Massachusetts Press, 1987.

Acosta, Oscar Zeta. *Revolt of the Cockroach People.* 1973. Reprint, New York: Vintage, 1989.

Adams, Bluford. *E Pluribus Barnum: The Great Showman and the Making of U.S. Popular Culture.* Minneapolis: University of Minnesota Press, 1997.

Alcott, Louisa May. *Little Women and Good Wives.* 1871. Reprint, New York: Dutton, 1979.

Alger, Horatio. *Ragged Dick.* 1868. Reprint, New York: Penguin, 1985.

Allen, Frederick Lewis. *Since Yesterday: The Nineteen-Thirties in America.* New York: Harper & Brothers, 1939.

Allen, Theodore. *The Invention of the White Race.* London: Verso, 1994.

Alsop, Kenneth. *Hard Travellin': The Hobo and His History.* New York: New American Library, 1967.

Anderson, Benedict. *Imagined Communities: Reflections on the Origin and Spread of Nationalism.* Rev. ed. London: Verso, 1991.

Anderson, Nels. *The American Hobo: An Autobiography.* Leiden: E. J. Brill, 1975.

———. *The Hobo: The Sociology of the Homeless Man.* 1923. Reprint, Chicago: University of Chicago Press, 1961.

———. *Men on the Move.* Chicago: University of Chicago Press, 1940.

———. "On the Bum." *Survey,* November 1, 1927, 171.

——— [Dean Stiff, pseud.]. *The Milk and Honey Route.* New York: Vanguard, 1931.

Antin, Mary. *At School in the Promised Land*. Boston: Houghton Mifflin, 1912.

———. *The Promised Land*. 1912. Reprint, Princeton: Princeton University Press, 1985.

———. "The Promised Land." Ms.H.6.3, Boston Public Library.

Archdeacon, Thomas. *Becoming American*. New York: Free Press, 1983.

Aresty, Esther B. *The Best Behavior*. New York: Simon & Schuster, 1970.

Armstrong, M. F. *On Habits and Manners*. Hampton, Va.: Normal School Press, 1888.

Asch, Nathan. *The Road: In Search of America*. New York: Norton, 1937.

Barnum, P. T. *Struggles and Triumphs*. 1869. Reprint, New York: Penguin, 1981.

Beadle's Dime Book of Etiquette: A Practical Guide to Good Behavior. New York: Beadle, 1864.

Benn, Alvin. "Asa, Forrest Carter Same, Widow and Agent Reveal." *Montgomery Advertiser*, October 26, 1991.

"Big Sales for New Mexico's 'Little Tree.'" *Publishers Weekly*, May 10, 1989.

Bird, Elizabeth S., ed. *Dressing in Feathers: The Construction of the Indian in American Popular Culture*. Boulder, Colo.: Westview, 1996.

Black, Jack. *You Can't Win*. 1926. Reprint, New York: Amok Press, 1988.

Blackstone, Sarah J. *Buckskins, Bullets, and Business: A History of Buffalo Bill's Wild West*. Westport, Conn.: Greenwood, 1986.

Blee, Kathleen. *Women of the Klan*. Berkeley: University of California Press, 1991.

Boatright, Mody C. *Folk Laughter on the American Frontier*. 1942. Reprint, Gloucester, Mass.: Collier, 1961.

Bonner, T. D., ed. *The Life and Adventures of James P. Beckwourth, Mountaineer, Scout and Pioneer, and Chief of the Crow Nation of Indians*. 1856. Reprint, New York: Knopf, 1931.

Bontemps, Arna, ed. *Great Slave Narratives*. Boston: Beacon, 1969.

Boskin, Joseph. *Sambo: The Rise and Demise of an American Jester*. New York: Oxford University Press, 1988.

Brackett, Leigh. *Follow the Free Wind*. Garden City, N.Y.: Doubleday, 1963.

Branch, Taylor. *Parting the Waters: America in the King Years, 1954–63*. New York: Simon & Schuster, 1988.

Browder, Laura. *Rousing the Nation: Radical Culture in Depression America*. Amherst: University of Massachusetts Press, 1998.

Brown, Dee. *Bury My Heart at Wounded Knee*. New York: Holt, Rhinehart and Winston, 1973.

Brown, Elaine. *A Taste of Power: A Black Woman's Story*. New York: Pantheon, 1992.

Brumble, H. David, III. *American Indian Autobiography*. Berkeley: University of California Press, 1988.

Bruns, Roger A. *The Damnedest Radical: The Life and World of Ben Reitman, Chicago's Celebrated Social Reformer, Hobo King, and Whorehouse Physician*. Urbana: University of Illinois Press, 1987.

Bulmer, Martin. *The Chicago School of Sociology: Institutionalization, Diversity, and the Rise of Sociological Research*. Chicago: University of Chicago Press, 1984.

Cahan, Abraham. *The Rise of David Levinsky*. 1917. Reprint, New York: Harper & Row, 1966.

Cantwell, Robert. *Bluegrass Breakdown: The Making of the Old Southern Sound*. Urbana: University of Illinois Press, 1984.

Carnes, Mark C. *Secret Ritual and Manhood in Victorian America*. New Haven: Yale University Press, 1989.

——, with Clyde Griffen, eds. *Meanings for Manhood: Constructions of Masculinity in Victorian America*. Chicago: University of Chicago Press, 1990.

Carter. Dan T. "The Transformation of a Klansman." *New York Times*, October 4, 1991.

Carter, Forrest. *The Education of Little Tree*. 1976. 15th ed. Reprint, Albuquerque: University of New Mexico Press, 1993.

——. *The Rebel Outlaw, Josey Wales*. Gantt, Ala.: Whipporwill, 1973.

Cawelti, John G. *Apostles of the Self-Made Man*. Chicago: University of Chicago Press, 1965.

Chauncey, George. *Gay New York: Gender, Urban Culture, and the Making of the Gay Male World, 1890–1940*. New York: Basic Books, 1994.

Christy, Charles. "The Personal Memoirs of Capt. Charles Christy." *The Trail*, October 1908.

Clancy, Cathy. Review of *Famous All Over Town. School Library Journal* 30 (October 1983): 180.

Clifton, James A., ed. *The Invented Indian: Cultural Fictions and Government Policies*. New Brunswick, N.J.: Transaction, 1990.

Cobb, Irvin S. Foreword to *Long Lance*, by Chief Buffalo Child Long Lance. New York: Cosmopolitan, 1928.

Conover, Ted. *Rolling Nowhere*. New York: Viking, 1984.

Cook, David A. *A History of Narrative Film*. New York: Norton, 1996.

Couser, G. Thomas. *Altered Egos*. New York: Oxford University Press, 1989.

Cowley, Malcolm. *The Dream of the Golden Mountain*. 1964. Reprint, New York: Penguin, 1981.

Cox, James M. *Recovering Literature's Lost Ground: Essays in American Autobiography*. Baton Rouge: Louisiana State University Press, 1989.

Craft, William. *Running a Thousand Miles for Freedom; or, the Escape of William and Ellen Craft from Slavery* (1860). In *Great Slave Narratives*, edited by Arna Bontemps, 269–331. Boston: Beacon, 1969.

Davis, Carlyle Channing, and William A. Alderson. *The True Story of "Ramona": Its Facts and Fictions, Inspiration and Purpose*. New York: Dodge, 1914.

Davis, Charles T., and Henry Louis Gates, eds. *The Slave's Narrative*. New York: Oxford University Press, 1985.

Dawley, Alan. *Struggles for Justice: Social Responsibility and the Liberal State*. Cambridge: Harvard University Press, 1991.

Decker, Jeffrey Louis. *Made in America: Self-Styled Success from Horatio Alger to Oprah Winfrey*. Minneapolis: University of Minnesota Press, 1997.

Deloria, Philip. *Playing Indian*. New Haven: Yale University Press, 1998.

Demos, John. *The Unredeemed Captive: A Family Story from Early America*. New York: Vintage, 1995.

De Voto, Bernard. *The Year of Decision, 1846*. Boston: Houghton Mifflin, 1943.

Diamond, Elin, ed. *Performance and Cultural Politics*. London: Routledge, 1996.

Douglas, Ann. *Terrible Honesty: Mongrel Manhattan in the 1920s*. New York: Farrar, Straus and Giroux, 1995.

Douglass, Frederick. *Narrative of the Life of Frederick Douglass*. 1845. In *The Classic Slave Narratives*, edited by Henry Louis Gates Jr., 243–331. New York: Signet, 1987.

Dunne, John Gregory. "The Secret of Danny Santiago." *New York Review of Books*, August 16, 1984, 17–27.

Eastman, Charles A. *From the Deep Woods to Civilization*. Boston: Little, Brown, 1916.

Edge, William. *The Main Stem*. New York: Vanguard, 1927.

Ehrenreich, Barbara. *The Hearts of Men*. New York: Doubleday, 1983.

Eighner, Lars. *Travels with Lizbeth*. New York: Ballantine, 1993.

Ely, Melvin Patrick. *The Adventures of Amos 'n' Andy: A Social History of an American Phenomenon*. New York: Free Press, 1991.

Engle, Ron, and Tice L. Miller, eds. *The American Stage*. Cambridge: Cambridge University Press, 1993.

Feest, Christian F. "Europe's Indians." In *The Invented Indian: Cultural Fictions and Government Policies*, edited by James A. Clifton, 313–32. New Brunswick, N.J.: Transaction, 1990.

Findahl, Theodor. *Manhattan Babylon: En Bok om New York Idag* [Manhattan Babylon: A book about New York today]. Oslo: Gyldendal Norsk Forlag, 1928.

Fishkin, Shelley Fisher. "Interrogating 'Whiteness,' Complicating 'Blackness': Remapping American Culture." *American Quarterly* 47 (September 1995): 428–66.

Fitzgerald, F. Scott. *The Great Gatsby*. New York: Scribner's, 1925.

Frankenberg, Ruth. *White Women, Race Matters: The Social Construction of Whiteness*. London: Routledge, 1993.

Franklin, Benjamin. *The Autobiography of Benjamin Franklin*. New York: Penguin, 1986.

Friede, Eleanor. Memo to readers of *The Education of Little Tree*, October 31, 1991.

Garfield, Deborah M., and Rafia Zafar, eds. *Harriet Jacobs and Incidents in the Life of a Slave Girl*. 1861. Reprint, Cambridge: Cambridge University Press, 1996.

Gentry, Curt. *J. Edgar Hoover: The Man and the Secrets*. New York: Norton, 1991.

Gill, Sam. "Mother Earth: An American Myth." In *The Invented Indian*, edited by James A. Clifton, 129–43. New Brunswick, N.J.: Transaction Publishers, 1990.

Gilroy, Paul. *The Black Atlantic: Modernity and Double Consciousness*. Cambridge: Harvard University Press, 1993.

Ginsberg, Elaine K., ed. *Passing and the Fictions of Identity*. Durham: Duke University Press, 1996.

Glassberg, David. *American Historical Pageantry: The Uses of Tradition in the Early Twentieth Century*. Chapel Hill: University of North Carolina Press, 1990.

Goddard, Henry Herbert. *The Kallikak Family: A Study in the Heredity of Feeblemindedness*. Garden City, N.Y.: Doubleday, 1923.

Gordon, Linda. *Woman's Body, Woman's Right: A Social History of Birth Control in America*. New York: Grossman, 1976.

Gossett, Thomas F. *Race: The History of an Idea in America*. 1963. Reprint, New York: Schocken Books, 1969.

Gould, Leah Shampanier. "Artef Players Collective: A History." M.A. thesis, Cornell University, 1953.

Gould, Stephen Jay. *The Mismeasure of Man*. New York: Norton, 1981.

Grant, Madison. *The Conquest of a Continent*. New York: Scribner's, 1933.

———. *The Passing of the Great Race*. New York: Scribner's, 1916.

Greenhaw, Wayne. "Is Forrest Carter Really Asa Carter? Only Josey Wales May Know for Sure." *New York Times*, August 26, 1976.

Griffin, John Howard. *Black Like Me*. Boston: Houghton Mifflin, 1961.

Griffith, Mattie. *The Autobiography of a Female Slave*. New York: Redfield, 1857.

Gubar, Susan. *Racechanges: White Skin, Black Face in American Culture*. New York: Oxford University Press, 1997.

Gunning, Tom. *D. W. Griffith and the Origins of American Narrative Film*. Urbana: University of Illinois Press, 1991.

Haas, Lisbeth. *Conquests and Historical Identities in California, 1769–1936*. Berkeley: University of California Press, 1995.

Haizlip, Shirlee Taylor. *The Sweeter the Juice: A Family Memoir in Black and White*. New York: Simon & Schuster, 1994.

Hale, Grace Elizabeth. *Making Whiteness: The Culture of Segregation in the South*. New York: Pantheon, 1998.

Hale, Sarah J. *Manners; or, Happy Homes and Good Society All the Year 'Round*. 1868. Reprint, New York: Arno Press, 1972.

Halliburton, R., Jr., *Red over Black: Black Slavery among the Cherokee Indians*. Westport, Conn.: Greenwood, 1977.

Halsell, Grace. *Soul Sister*. New York: World, 1969.

Halttunen, Karen. *Confidence Men and Painted Women: A Study of Middle-Class Culture in America, 1830–1870*. New Haven: Yale University Press, 1982.

Hammersley, Martyn. *The Dilemma of Qualitative Method: Herbert Blumer and the Chicago Tradition*. London: Routledge, 1989.

Haney-López, Ian F. *White by Law: The Legal Construction of Race*. New York: New York University Press, 1996.

Harris, Neil. *Humbug: The Art of P. T. Barnum*. Chicago: University of Chicago Press, 1973.

Hauck, Richard Boyd. "The Man in the Buckskin Hunting Shirt: Fact and Fiction in the Crockett Story." In *Davy Crockett: The Man, the Legend, the Legacy, 1786–1986*, edited by Michael A. Lofaro, 3–20. Knoxville: University of Tennessee Press, 1985.

Haygood, Wil. *King of the Cats: The Life and Times of Adam Clayton Powell Jr.* New York: Houghton Mifflin, 1993.

Hayman, John. "Grey Owl's Wild Goose Chase." *History Today*, January 1994, 42–48.

Heard, J. Norman. *White into Red*. Metuchen, N.J.: Scarecrow Press, 1973.

Hearst, Patricia Campbell, with Alvin Moscow. *Every Secret Thing*. Garden City, N.Y.: Doubleday, 1982.

Higham, John. *Strangers in the Land: Patterns of American Nativism, 1860–1925*. New York: Atheneum, 1981.

Hildreth, Richard. *Archy Moore, the White Slave; or, Memoirs of a Fugitive*. 1856. Reprint, New York: Negro Universities Press, 1969.

Holmes, Clellon. "This Is the Beat Generation." *New York Times*, November 16, 1952.

Holte, James Craig. *The Ethnic I*. New York: Greenwood, 1988.

Hongo, Garrett. *Volcano*. New York: Vintage, 1995.

Hornsby, Alton, Jr. *Milestones in Twentieth-Century African-American History*. Detroit: Visible Ink Press, 1993.

Howe, Irving. *World of Our Fathers*. 1976. Reprint, New York: Simon & Schuster, 1983.

How to Behave: A Pocket Manual of Republican Etiquette. New York: Fowler & Wells, 1856.

Huber, Richard M. *The American Idea of Success*. New York: McGraw Hill, 1971.

Ignatiev, Noel. *How the Irish Became White*. New York: Routledge, 1995.

Indian Removal Act of 1830. 4 Stat. 412 (May 28, 1830).

Jackson, Donald, ed. *Black Hawk: An Autobiography*. Urbana: University of Illinois Press, 1964.

Jackson, Helen Hunt. *Ramona*. 1884. Reprint, Boston: Little, Brown, 1939.

Jacobson, Matthew Frye. *Special Sorrows*. Cambridge: Harvard University Press, 1995.

James, George Wharton. *Through Ramona's Country*. Boston: Little, Brown, 1908.

Jones, Jacqueline. *The Dispossessed: America's Underclass from the Civil War to the Present*. New York: Basic Books, 1992.

Jones, Sally L. "The First but Not the Last of the 'Vanishing Indians': Edwin Forrest and Mythic Re-creations of the Native Population." In *Dressing in Feathers: The Construction of the Indian in American Popular Culture*, edited by S. Elizabeth Bird, 13–27. Boulder, Colo.: Westview, 1996.

Karcher, Carolyn L. "Lydia Maria Child's *A Romance of the Republic*: An Abolitionist Vision of America's Racial Destiny." In *Slavery and the Literary Imagination*, edited by Deborah E. McDowell and Arnold Rampersad, 81–103. Baltimore: Johns Hopkins University Press, 1989.

Kasper, Shirl. *Annie Oakley*. Norman: University of Oklahoma Press, 1992.

Kasson, John. *Rudeness and Civility*. New York: Hill & Wang, 1990.

Katz, William Loren. *Black Indians: A Hidden Heritage*. New York: Atheneum, 1986.

Keckley, Elizabeth. *Behind the Scenes; or, Thirty Years a Slave, and Four Years in the White House*. 1868. Reprint, New York: Oxford University Press, 1988.

Kingston, Maxine Hong. *Woman Warrior*. New York: Knopf, 1976.

Krupat, Arnold. *For Those Who Come After: A Study of Native American Autobiography*. Berkeley: University of California Press, 1985.

Leibowitz, Herbert. *Fabricating Lives*. New York: Knopf, 1989.

Leland, J. "New Age Fable from an Old School Bigot?" *Newsweek*, October 14, 1991, 62.

Lemay, J. A. Leo, ed. *Reappraising Benjamin Franklin: A Bicentennial Perspective*. Newark: University of Delaware Press, 1993.

Leuchtenberg, William. *Franklin D. Roosevelt and the New Deal, 1932–1940*. New York: Harper & Row, 1963.

Levine, Lawrence W. *Highbrow/Lowbrow: The Emergence of Cultural Hierarchy in America*. Cambridge: Harvard University Press, 1988.

Lewis, Sinclair. *Kingsblood Royal*. New York: Random House, 1947.

Lifson, David S. *The Yiddish Theatre in America*. New York: Thomas Yoseloff, 1965.

Lindner, Robert. *Must You Conform?* New York: Rinehart, 1955.

Littlefield, Daniel. *The Cherokee Freedmen: From Emancipation to American Citizenship*. Westport, Conn.: Greenwood, 1978.

"Little Tree, Big Lies?" *Time*, October 14, 1991, 62.

Lofaro, Michael A., ed. *Davy Crockett: The Man, the Legend, the Legacy, 1786–1986*. Knoxville: University of Tennessee Press, 1985.

Long Lance, Chief Buffalo Child. *Long Lance*. New York: Cosmopolitan, 1928.

——. "My Trail Upward." *Cosmopolitan*, June 1926.

Lott, Eric. *Love and Theft*. New York: Oxford University Press, 1993.

——. "White Like Me." In *Cultures of United States Imperialism*, edited by Amy Kaplan and Donald E. Pease, 474–95. Durham: Duke University Press, 1993.

McBride, James. *The Color of Water: A Black Man's Tribute to His White Mother*. New York: Riverhead, 1996.

McConachie, Bruce A. "Museum Theatre and the Problem of Respectability for Mid-century Urban Americans." In *The American Stage*, edited by Ron Engle and Tice L. Miller, 65–81. Cambridge: Cambridge University Press, 1993.

McDowell, Deborah E., and Arnold Rampersad, eds. *Slavery and the Literary Imagination*. Baltimore: Johns Hopkins University Press, 1989.

McElvaine, Robert. *The Great Depression*. New York: Times Books, 1984.

McFeely, William. *Frederick Douglass*. New York: Norton, 1991.

McGinity, Keren R. "A Woman Divided: Mary Antin's Original Promised Land." Paper presented at the Scholars' Conference of American Jewish History, Cincinnati, Ohio, June 1998.

McGlagan, Elizabeth. *A Peculiar Paradise: A History of Blacks in Oregon, 1788–1940*. Portland, Ore.: Gregorian Press, 1980.

Maclean, Nancy. *Behind the Mask of Chivalry*. New York: Oxford University Press, 1994.

McNamara, Brooks. *Step Right Up*. Rev. ed. Jackson: University Press of Mississippi, 1995.

McNeal, Violet. *Four White Horses and a Brass Band*. Garden City, N.Y.: Doubleday, 1947.

McNeil, Legs, and Gillian McCain. *Please Kill Me: The Uncensored Oral History of Punk*. New York: Grove Press, 1996.

McWhorter, Diane. "Little Tree, Big Lies." *People*, October 28, 1991, 119.

Mailer, Norman. "The White Negro." In *Advertisements for Myself*. New York: G. P. Putnam's Sons, 1959.

Mann, Arthur. *The One and the Many*. Chicago: University of Chicago Press, 1979.

Marden, Orison Swett. *Little Visits with Great Americans*. New York: Success Co., 1905.

Marks, Paula Mitchell. *Precious Dust: The Saga of the Western Gold Rushes*. New York: HarperCollins West, 1995.

Mason, Jeffrey D. *Melodrama and the Myth of America*. Bloomington: Indiana University Press, 1993.

Mathes, Valerie Sherer. *Helen Hunt Jackson and Her Indian Reform Legacy*. Austin: University of Texas Press, 1990.

Matlaw, Myron, ed. *American Popular Entertainment*. Westport, Conn.: Greenwood, 1979.

Mattison, H., ed. *Louisa Picquet, the Octoroon; or, Inside Views of Southern Domestic Life* (1861). In *Collected Black Women's Narratives*, edited by Henry Louis Gates. New York: Oxford University Press, 1988.

May, Katja. *African Americans and Native Americans in the Creek and Cherokee Nations, 1830s to 1920s*. New York: Garland, 1996.

Mays, Benjamin E. *Born to Rebel*. New York: Scribner's, 1971.

Meyn, Susan Labry. "Mutual Infatuation: Rosebud Sioux and Cincinnatians." *Queen City Heritage* 52, no. 1–2 (1994): 30–48.

Michaels, Walter Benn. *The Gold Standard and the Logic of Naturalism*. Berkeley: University of California Press, 1987.

——. *Our America*. Durham: Duke University Press, 1995.

Milburn, George. *The Hobo's Hornbook: A Repertory for a Gutter Jongleur*. New York: Ives Washburn, 1930.

Minehan, Thomas. *Boy and Girl Tramps of America*. 1934. Reprint, Seattle: University of Washington Press, 1976.

Moody, Anne. *Coming of Age in Mississippi*. New York: Dial, 1968.

Morgan, Ted. *Literary Outlaw: The Life and Times of William S. Burroughs*. New York: Henry Holt, 1988.

Morgan, Thomas J. "Wild West Shows and Similar Exhibitions." In *Americanizing the American Indians: Writings by the "Friends of the Indian," 1880–1900*, edited by Francis Paul Prucha, 309–316. 1973. Reprint, Lincoln: University of Nebraska Press, 1978.

Morrison, Toni. *Playing in the Dark: Whiteness and the Literary Imagination.* Cambridge: Harvard University Press, 1992.

Morton, Leah [Elizabeth Stern]. *I Am a Woman—and a Jew.* New York: J. H. Sears, 1926.

Moses, L. G. "Indians on the Midway: Wild West Shows and the Indian Bureau at the World's Fairs, 1893–1904." *South Dakota History* 21, no. 3 (1991): 205–29.

———. *Wild West Shows and the Images of American Indians, 1883–1933.* Albuquerque: University of New Mexico Press, 1996.

———. "Wild West Shows, Reformers, and the Image of the American Indian, 1887–1914." *South Dakota History* 14, no. 3 (1984): 193–221.

Namias, June. *White Captives: Gender and Ethnicity on the American Frontier.* Chapel Hill: University of North Carolina Press, 1993.

Navasky, Victor S. *Naming Names.* New York: Viking, 1980.

Noell, Mae. "Recollections of Medicine Show Life." In *American Popular Entertainment*, edited by Myron Matlaw, 215–26. Westport, Conn.: Greenwood, 1979.

Olney, James. "I Was Born." In *Studies in Autobiography*, edited by James Olney, 148–75. New York: Oxford University Press, 1988.

———, ed. *Autobiography: Essays Theoretical and Critical.* Princeton: Princeton University Press, 1980.

———. *Studies in Autobiography.* New York: Oxford University Press, 1988.

Ornitz, Samuel. *Allrightniks Row "Haunch, Paunch, and Jowl": The Making of a Professional Jew.* 1923. Reprint, New York: Markus Wiener, 1986.

The Outlaw Josey Wales. Directed by Clint Eastwood. Warner Bros., 1976.

Parins, James W. *John Rollin Ridge: His Life and Works.* Lincoln: University of Nebraska Press, 1991.

Parkman, Francis. *The Oregon Trail.* 1877. Reprint, New York: Penguin, 1982.

Payne, James Robert, ed. *Multi-Cultural Autobiography: American Lives.* Knoxville: University of Tennessee Press, 1992.

Podhoretz, Norman. "The Know-Nothing Bohemians." *Partisan Review* 25 (Spring 1958): 311.

Prevots, Naima. *American Pageantry.* Ann Arbor: University of Michigan Research Press, 1990.

Prucha, Francis Paul, ed. *Americanizing the American Indians: Writings by the "Friends of the Indian," 1880–1900.* Cambridge: Harvard University Press, 1973.

Pupin, Michael. *From Immigrant to Inventor.* 9th ed. New York: Scribner's, 1925.

Quinn, Arthur. *The Rivals: William Gwin, David Broderick, and the Birth of California.* New York: Crown, 1994.

Ramona: A Story of Passion and Protest. Produced by Teya Ryan. Written by Nancy Wilkman. Princeton, N.J.: Films for the Humanities, 1988.

Reed, Ishmael. "America's 'Black Only' Ethnicity." In *The Invention of Ethnicity*, edited by Werner Sollors, 226–29. New York: Oxford University Press, 1989.

Reid, Calvin. "Widow of 'Little Tree' Author Admits He Changed Identity." *Publishers Weekly*, October 22, 1991.

Richardson, Albert Deane. *Beyond the Mississippi: From the Great River to the Great Ocean.* Hartford, Conn.: American Publishing, 1867.

Ridge, John Rollin [Yellow Bird]. *The Life and Adventures of Joaquin Murieta.* 1854. Reprint, Norman: University of Oklahoma Press, 1955.

Riesman, David. *The Lonely Crowd: A Study of the Changing American Character.* 1950. Reprint, New Haven: Yale University Press, 1967.

Roediger, David R. *The Wages of Whiteness: Race and the Making of the American Working Class*. London: Verso, 1991.

Rogin, Michael. *Blackface, White Noise: Jewish Immigrants in the Hollywood Melting Pot*. Berkeley: University of California Press, 1996.

——. "'The Sword Became a Flashing Vision': D. W. Griffith's *The Birth of a Nation*." *Representations* 9 (Winter 1985): 151–95.

Rohrbrough, Malcolm J. *Days of Gold: The California Gold Rush and the American Nation*. Berkeley: University of California Press, 1997.

Rorty, James. *Where Life Is Better: An Unsentimental American Journey*. New York: Reynal & Hitchcock, 1936.

Royot, Daniel. "Franklin As Founding Father of American Humor." In *Reappraising Benjamin Franklin: A Bicentennial Perspective*, edited by J. A. Leo Lemay, 388–95. Newark: University of Delaware Press, 1993.

Rubin, Dana. "The Real Education of Little Tree." *Texas Monthly*, February 1992.

Rubin, Steven J. *Writing Our Lives: Autobiographies of American Jews, 1890–1990*. New York: Jewish Publication Society, 1991.

Russell, Don. *The Wild West*. Fort Worth: Amon Carter Museum of Western Art, 1970.

Sacks, Karen Brodkin. "How Did Jews Become White Folks?" In *Race*, edited by Steven Gregory and Roger Sanjek, 78–102. New Brunswick, N.J.: Rutgers University Press, 1994.

Sandrow, Nahma. *Vagabond Stars: A World History of Yiddish Theater*. New York: Harper & Row, 1977.

Sanjek, Roger. "The Enduring Inequalities of Race." In *Race*, edited by Steven Gregory and Roger Sanjek, 1–17. New Brunswick, N.J.: Rutgers University Press, 1994.

Santiago, Danny [Daniel James]. *Famous All Over Town*. New York: Simon & Schuster, 1983.

Sayre, Robert F. "Autobiography and America." In *Autobiography: Essays Theoretical and Critical*, edited by James Olney, 146–68. Princeton: Princeton University Press, 1980.

Schechter, Joel. *Satiric Impersonations from Aristophanes to the Guerilla Girls*. Carbondale: Southern Illinois University Press, 1994.

Schockman, Carl S. *We Turned Hobo: A Narrative of Personal Experience*. Columbus, Ohio: F. J. Heer, 1937.

Schurz, Carl. "Present Aspects of the Indian Problem." In *Americanizing the American Indians: Writings by the "Friends of the Indian," 1880–1900*, edited by Francis Paul Prucha, 13–27. Cambridge: Harvard University Press, 1973.

Schuyler, George. *Black No More*. 1931. Reprint, New York: Negro Universities Press, 1969.

Segrest, Mab. *Memoir of a Race Traitor*. Boston: South End Press, 1994.

Sekora, John. "Is the Slave Narrative a Species of Autobiography?" In *Studies in Autobiography*, edited by James Olney, 99–111. New York: Oxford University Press, 1988.

Seldes, Gilbert. *The Years of the Locust: America, 1929–1932*. Boston: Little, Brown, 1933.

Sherwood, M. E. *Manners and Social Usages*. 1897. Reprint, New York: Arno Press, 1975.

Simmon, Scott. *The Films of D. W. Griffith*. Cambridge: Cambridge University Press, 1993.

Sketches and Eccentricities of Colonel David Crockett. 1833. Reprint, New York: Arno Press, 1974.

Smith, Beverly. "One Hundred Percent American." *New York Herald Tribune,* January 19, 1930.

Smith, Donald B. *Long Lance: The True Story of an Impostor.* Lincoln: University of Nebraska Press, 1982.

Smith, J. David. *The Eugenic Assault on America: Scenes in Red, White, and Black.* Fairfax, Va.: George Mason University Press, 1993.

Sollors, Werner. *Beyond Ethnicity.* New York: Oxford University Press, 1986.

———, ed. *The Invention of Ethnicity.* New York: Oxford University Press, 1989.

Soul Man. Directed by Steve Miner. Paramount, 1986.

Staiger, Janet. "The Birth of a Nation: Reconsidering Its Reception." In *Interpreting Films,* edited by Janet Staiger. Princeton: Princeton University Press, 1992.

Stampp, Kenneth B. *The Peculiar Institution: Slavery in the Ante-Bellum South.* New York: Vintage, 1956.

Stanton, William. *The Leopard's Spots: Scientific Attitudes towards Race in America, 1815–1859.* 1960. Reprint, Chicago: University of Chicago Press, 1966.

Starr, Kevin. *Americans and the California Dream.* New York: Oxford University Press, 1973.

Stearns, Charles. *Narrative of Henry Box Brown, Who Escaped from Slavery Enclosed in a Box 3 Feet Long and 2 Wide.* Boston: Brown & Stearns, 1849.

Stein, Howard F., and Robert F. Hill. *The Ethnic Imperative.* University Park: Pennsylvania State University Press, 1977.

Stern, T. Noel. *Secret Family.* South Dartmouth, Mass.: T. Noel Stern, 1988.

Stowe, David. "Uncolored People: The Rise of Whiteness Studies." *Lingua Franca,* September/October 1996, 68–77.

Stowe, Harriet Beecher. *Uncle Tom's Cabin.* New York: New American Library, 1966.

Strickland, Rennard. Foreword to *The Education of Little Tree,* by Forrest Carter. 1976. 15th ed. Reprint, Albuquerque: University of New Mexico Press, 1993.

Swineford, H. B. *Our Manners at Home and Abroad.* Harrisburg: Pennsylvania Publishing Co., 1888.

Takagi, Dana Y. *The Retreat from Race: Asian-American Admissions and Racial Politics.* New Brunswick, N.J.: Rutgers University Press, 1992.

Takaki, Ronald. *A Different Mirror: A History of Multicultural America.* Boston: Little, Brown, 1993.

———. *Iron Cages: Race and Culture in Nineteenth-Century America.* New York: Knopf, 1979.

Thompson, Bertha, as told to B. L. Reitman. *Sister of the Road: The Autobiography of Boxcar Bertha.* 1937. Reprinted as *Boxcar Bertha.* New York: Amok Press, 1988.

Trennert, Robert A., Jr. "Selling Indian Education at World's Fairs and Expositions, 1893–1904." *American Indian Quarterly* 11, no. 3 (1987): 203–20.

Tugend, Harry. "*The Silent Enemy*: The Indian's Unhappy Hunting Grounds." *Exhibitors Herald-World,* May 24, 1930.

Turner, Patricia. *I Heard It through the Grapevine.* Berkeley: University of California Press, 1993.

Umansky, Ellen M. "Representations of Jewish Women in the Works and Life of Elizabeth Stern." *Modern Judaism* 13 (1993): 165–76.

Van Deburg, William L. *New Day in Babylon: The Black Power Movement and American Culture, 1965–1975*. Chicago: University of Chicago Press, 1992.

Wald, Gayle. "White Identity in *Black Like Me*." In *Passing and the Fictions of Identity*, edited by Elaine K. Ginsberg, 151–77. Durham: Duke University Press, 1996.

Wallace, George C. "The Inaugural Address of Governor George C. Wallace." Montgomery, Ala., January 14, 1963.

Walters, Ronald G. *American Reformers, 1815–1860*. Rev. ed. New York: Hill & Wang, 1997.

Ware, Vron. *Beyond the Pale: White Women, Racism, and History*. London: Verso, 1994.

Watermelon Man. Directed by Melvin Van Peebles. Columbia Pictures, 1970.

Waters, Mary C. *Ethnic Options: Choosing Identities in America*. Berkeley: University of California Press, 1990.

Webb, Constance. *Richard Wright: A Biography*. New York: G. P. Putnam & Sons, 1968.

Weinauer, Ellen M. "'A Most Respectable Looking Gentleman': Passing, Possession, and Transgression in *Running a Thousand Miles for Freedom*." In *Passing and the Fictions of Identity*, edited by Elaine K. Ginsberg, 37–56. Durham: Duke University Press, 1996.

Werner, Robert. *Barnum*. Garden City, N.Y.: Doubleday, 1923.

Whisnant, David. *All That Is Native and Fine: The Politics of Culture in an American Region*. Chapel Hill: University of North Carolina Press, 1983.

White Horse Eagle. *We Indians: The Passing of a Great Race*. New York: Dutton, 1931.

Williams, Gregory Howard. *Life on the Color Line: The True Story of a White Boy Who Discovered He Was Black*. New York: Dutton, 1995.

Williams, James. *Narrative of James Williams, an American Slave*. New York: American Anti-Slavery Society, 1838.

Wilson, Edmund. *Patriotic Gore*. New York: Oxford University Press, 1962.

Wilson, Elinor. *Jim Beckwourth: Black Mountain Man and War Chief of the Crows*. Norman: University of Oklahoma Press, 1972.

Wimsatt, Margaret. Review of *Famous All Over Town*. *Commonweal*, May 20 1983, 309.

Wolfe, Bernard. *Really the Blues*. New York: Random House, 1946.

Wong, Hertha. *Sending My Heart Back across the Years: Tradition and Innovation in Native American Autobiography*. New York: Oxford University Press, 1992.

Wong, Sau-ling Cynthia. "Kingston's *Woman Warrior* and Chinese-American Autobiography." In *Multi-Cultural Autobiography: American Lives*, edited by James Robert Payne, 248–79. Knoxville: University of Tennessee Press, 1992.

Wong, Shawn. "Is Ethnicity Obsolete?" In *The Invention of Ethnicity*, edited by Werner Sollors, 230–31. New York: Oxford University Press, 1989.

Woodham-Smith, Cecil. *The Great Hunger*. 1962. Reprint, New York: Signet, 1964.

Woods, E. M. *The Negro in Etiquette: A Novelty*. St. Louis: Buxton & Skinner, 1899.

World Columbian Exposition Illustrated. Chicago, 1893.

Worster, Donald. *Dust Bowl*. New York: Oxford University Press, 1979.

Wright, Lawrence. "One Drop of Blood." *New Yorker*, July 25, 1994, 46–55.

Wright, Richard. *Black Boy: A Record of Childhood and Youth*. 1937. Reprint, New York: Harper & Row, 1966.

Yellow Robe, Chauncey. "The Menace of the Wild West Show." *Quarterly Journal of the Society of American Indians*, July–Sept. 1914, 224–25.

Yezierska, Anzia. *Bread Givers*. 1925. Reprint, New York: Persea Books, 1975.

Zaborowska, Magdalena J. *How We Found America: Reading Gender through East European Immigrant Narratives*. Chapel Hill: University of North Carolina Press, 1995.

Zafar, Rafia. "Introduction. Over-Exposed, Under-Exposed: Harriet Jacobs and *Incidents in the Life of a Slave Girl*." In *Harriet Jacobs and "Incidents in the Life of a Slave Girl*,*"* edited by Deborah M. Garfield and Rafia Zafar, 1–10. Cambridge: Cambridge University Press, 1996.

Zangwill, Israel. *The Melting-Pot*. Rev. ed. New York: Macmillan, 1932.

Index